MODELS OF POLITICAL CHANGE
IN LATIN AMERICA

Models of Political Change in Latin America

EDITED BY PAUL E. SIGMUND

PRAEGER PUBLISHERS
New York · Washington · London

PRAEGER PUBLISHERS
111 Fourth Avenue, New York, N.Y. 10003, U.S.A.
5, Cromwell Place, London S.W.7, England

Published in the United States of America in 1970
by Praeger Publishers, Inc.

© 1970 by Praeger Publishers, Inc.

Library of Congress Catalog Card Number: 71-95692

Printed in the United States of America

Introduction

Teachers and students of contemporary Latin American affairs, in the United States and elsewhere, have been aware of a lack of basic Latin American source materials. This is true both because of the language barrier and because much of the most interesting current writing is difficult to secure outside the country of origin. This collection of documents, speeches, articles, and excerpts from longer works, composed in the main of translations from Latin American sources, aims to remedy this defect.

The present volume focuses on the problem of political change in Latin America. In recent years, economic development, the growth of communications, and rising popular expectations have stimulated demands for expanded opportunity, political participation, and social justice. These demands have produced a general climate of political instability. In some cases, the result has been revolutionary upheavals that have fundamentally altered the existing social and economic systems. In other cases, democratic governments have attempted to respond to the demands for change within the framework of constitutional government, majority rule, and minority rights. In still others, the military have intervened, sometimes to impede change but more often to control its direction or even accelerate its pace.

In this collection, political change is therefore considered under three principal headings: revolution, military rule, and constitutional democracy. The usual dichotomy of "reform or revolution" has been amended to include government by the military as a third alternative. It is the editor's opinion that political intervention by the military must be viewed as a permanent feature of the Latin American political scene rather than as a temporary phenomenon that will diminish in importance as Latin America attains higher levels of political development. As the selections below indicate, pressures for military intervention and the desire of military men to influence or control the course of national politics have tended to increase in periods of social and economic change. There is nothing inevitable about the triumph of civilians over the military in the immediate future, however desirable that may be from the point of view of constitutionalists in Latin America or the United States.

Three countries have been selected to serve as models of each of the three approaches to political development in Latin America. Each of these countries, whether because of its size or the particular problems it represents, has been influential outside its borders and is cited in other parts of the continent in the current debate over models of political change. Mexico, Bolivia, and Cuba have been chosen as regimes that derive their special character from revolution; Brazil, Argentina, and Peru as examples of countries currently under military rule; and Colombia, Venezuela, and Chile as leading constitutional democracies. It will be observed that the three countries that have built their regimes on a revolutionary ideology have differing political institutions today. Mexico is a constitutional democracy dominated by a single party; Bolivia is currently ruled by a military regime that claims to be continuing the goals of the 1952 revolution; Cuba has established a system based on the principles of Marxism-Leninism. Similarly, military rule can take a conservative, moderate, or radical direction; the present Peruvian junta, for example, has so far adopted more radical policies than have the Brazilian and Argentine military governments. There are also important differences between the traditionalist two-party system of Colombia, the social democratic orientation of the government established in Venezuela after 1958 by the Acción Democrática party, and the efforts of the Christian Democrats in Chile to carry out a democratic reform program on the basis of an ideology of Christian inspiration.

Each chapter begins with documents that illustrate the country's particular institutions and its approach to economic and social development and political change. These are followed by criticisms of the model of change by domestic and foreign observers, and by statements of national leaders supporting the model. In some cases, documents on relevant aspects of United States policy toward Latin America have also been included.

Particular attention has been paid to the agrarian reform programs of revolutionary, military, and democratic regimes; the student will find substantial excerpts from the agrarian reform laws of Bolivia, Peru, Venezuela, Colombia, and Chile. Among other themes receiving special emphasis are the increasing friction between the Castroite left and orthodox Marxists in Latin America; the frequent alliance between military regimes and orthodox economists; and, paradoxically, a declining faith in the possibility of democratic solutions to Latin America's problems combined with the increasing success and stability of Latin America's constitutional democracies.

Predictions as to the future course of Latin American politics are always hazardous. In the last decade, Latin American society was viewed by some political observers as being potentially revolutionary, while others emphasized its essentially conservative nature.* As the present collection indicates, both generalizations may be said to be correct. The forces of stability and of change are likely to be in contention in Latin America for the foreseeable future.

My thanks in the preparation of this volume go to the many individuals who responded to my requests for documentation, especially to Gil Calloway in Venezuela, Fernando Cepéda in Colombia, Shane Hunt in Peru, Chuck Grover in Bolivia, Sergio Undurraga in Chile. Tomás Donovan in Argentina, and Lois Wasserspring in Mexico. Gregory Treverton and Thomas Peters helped to collect materials and assisted in the preparation of the translations.

PAUL E. SIGMUND

Princeton, N.J.
January, 1970

* See, for example, Gerald Clark, *The Coming Explosion in Latin America* (New York: David McKay, 1963); Claudio Véliz (ed.), *Obstacles to Change in Latin America* (London and New York: Oxford University Press, 1965); Claudio Véliz (ed.), *The Politics of Conformity in Latin America* (London and New York: Oxford University Press, 1967); John Mander, *The Unrevolutionary Society: The Power of Latin American Conservatism* (New York: Alfred A. Knopf, 1969).

Contents

PART TWO: Military Rule

PART THREE: Constitutional Democracy

Contents

MODELS OF POLITICAL CHANGE
IN LATIN AMERICA

I. Mexico: The Institutionalization of the Revolution

There have been many irregular changes of government in Latin America that have been called revolutions. But for Latin Americans, the Mexican Revolution of 1910 symbolizes a genuine social and nationalist revolution that involved much more than the mere substitution of one elite group for another in power. The revolution began in Mexico with a simple appeal to the principle "Effective Suffrage and No Re-Election," a response to the decision of the eighty-year-old strong man Porfirio Díaz to stage another fraudulent election in 1910 and imprison his principal opponent, Francisco I. Madero. Madero escaped from prison and went to the United States, where he issued his Plan of San Luis Potosí (*Selection 1*). In addition to calling for the overthrow of Díaz, the plan also included a promise to return communally owned lands that had been taken away from the peasants by the large landowners, with the official support of the Díaz government. In the ensuing rebellion, the peasant leader Emiliano Zapata led the villagers of the state of Morelos in demands for the restoration of their lands. Díaz resigned, and Madero was elected president in 1911. But when the agrarian question was not resolved, and federal troops were sent against him, Zapata attacked Madero and called for a more drastic land redistribution, in his Plan of Ayala

3

(*Selection 2*). The *Zapatista* demands for land reform were reflected in the Constitution of 1917 (*Selection 3*), which also asserted control over Mexico's national resources, sharply reduced the power of the Church, and committed the revolution to an ambitious program of social welfare.

After a lengthy period of upheaval, characterized by violence, assassination, and power struggles among rival military leaders, Mexico attained stability in the late 1920's with the formation of a government political party, which has dominated Mexican public life ever since. President Lázaro Cárdenas (1934–40) also played a major role in institutionalizing the revolution by promoting agrarian reform, accelerating the unionization of workers and peasants, and nationalizing the Mexican oil industry, in 1938. As Cárdenas' 1939 speech on the expropriation of the oil industry (*Selection 4*) indicates, this action had the overwhelming support of the Mexican people. It also had repercussions throughout Latin America, for it demonstrated that a Latin American country could take control of foreign-owned mineral resources. The reaction of the Franklin Roosevelt administration, which put pressure on the British- and American-owned oil companies to settle with the Mexican government, is still recalled with favor in Latin America.

Under Cárdenas, the supremacy of the government political party over the military leaders who had been dominant since the revolution was finally established. Cárdenas organized the party—the Revolutionary Institutional Party (PRI), as it has been known since 1946—on a sectoral basis, giving formal recognition to the labor and peasant organizations, which had been strengthened during his term. The structure of the PRI is federal in theory but strongly centralized in practice (see *Selection 5*); the party continues to win overwhelming majorities in Mexican elections. Cárdenas also accelerated agrarian reform, and he and subsequent Mexican presidents placed particular emphasis on the organization of *ejidos*, agricultural cooperatives in which the land is owned communally but farmed individually. A description and evaluation of the Mexican land reform experience is included as *Selection 6*.

The Mexican government today bases its legitimacy on the continuation of the ideals of the 1910 revolution. Those who view the regime favorably stress its accomplishments in the fields of economic development, education, and health (*Selection 7*), as well as its responsiveness to new social groups and its adherence to democratic methods, in principle if not always in practice (*Selection 8*). The regime has been criticized, however, for the quasi-dictatorial power that it gives to the president (*Selection 9*) and for not extending the benefits of the revolution to the Indians and the rural poor (*Selection 10*). In 1968, student protests against the regime in Mexico City were brutally suppressed, and a number of protestors were killed. The student demands are included as *Selection 11*. The response to the student demands by President Díaz Ordaz in his state of the union message (*Selection 12*) illustrates the strength of the revolutionary myth in Mexican politics. Whether or not the party's skillful exploitation of its revolutionary antecedents will enable it to perpetuate its domination of the Mexican regime in the future, its past successes have made Mexico an influential model of political change in Latin America.

1. THE PLAN OF SAN LUIS POTOSÍ (1910)

FRANCISCO I. MADERO

1. The elections for President, Vice-President, justices of the Supreme Court, deputies, and senators held in June and July of this year are declared null and void.

2. Recognition is withdrawn from the present government of General Díaz as well as from all authorities whose power is supposed to be derived from the popular vote, since, in addition to the fact that they were not elected by the people, they have lost all claim that they could have had to legality by using the resources that the people put at their disposition for the defense of the popular interest in order to perpetrate the most scandalous electoral fraud in the history of Mexico.

3. To avoid wherever possible the disturbances involved in any revolutionary movement, we declare still in effect, subject to change by constitutional means when such change is required, all the laws and regulations adopted by the current administration, with the exception of those that are manifestly in conflict with the principles proclaimed in this plan. Also excepted are the laws, court decisions, and decrees that sanctioned the financial maneuvers of all the functionaries of the Porfirist administration in all its branches. As soon as the revolution has triumphed, investigating commissions will be established to determine the responsibilities of national, state, and municipal public employees. In any case, the agreements made by the Porfirist administration with foreign governments or corporations before the 20th of this month [October] will be respected.

In violation of the Law of Untitled Lands, many proprietors of small holdings, the majority of them Indians, have been dispossessed of their land with the agreement of the Minister of Public Works or by decisions of courts of the republic. It being entirely just to restore to their former owners the lands of which they have been so arbitrarily dispossessed, all such resolutions and decisions will be reviewed, and it shall be required of those who acquired them in this immoral fashion, or of their

Translated by the editor from Federico Gonzalez Garza, *La Revolución Mexicana—Mi Contribución político literaria* (Mexico City, 1936), pp. 207–9.

heirs, that they return them to their original owners and pay an indemnity for the losses incurred. In cases in which those lands have been sold to a third person before the promulgation of this plan, the former owners will receive indemnification from those to whose benefit the dispossession accrued.

4. In addition to the Constitution and existing laws, the principle of the non-re-election of the President, the Vice-President, the state governors, and the mayors of municipalities is declared part of the supreme law of the land, pending the necessary constitutional reforms.

5. I assume the office of Provisional President of the United States of Mexico with the necessary powers to make war on the usurping government of Porfirio Díaz. As soon as the capital and more than half of the states of the Mexican Federation are under the control of the popular forces, the Provisional President will call extraordinary elections for one month thereafter and will hand over power to the elected President when the election results are known.

6. Before he hands over his power, the Provisional President will render an account to the Congress of the use that he has made of the powers conferred on him by the present plan.

7. At 6:00 P.M. on November 20th all the citizens of the republic shall take up arms to wrest power from the authorities presently governing them. (Those who are situated away from the means of communication shall do so at sundown.)

8. When the authorities present armed resistance, they will be obliged by force of arms to respect the popular will. In this case, the laws of war will be rigorously observed, especially the prohibitions against dumdum bullets and the shooting of prisoners. Attention is also called to the obligation to respect the persons and interests of foreigners.

9. The authorities who oppose this plan will be imprisoned and judged by official courts when the revolution has ended. As soon as each city or village has recovered its liberty, it shall recognize as the provisional authority the principal military leader, who will have the power to delegate his functions to any other citizen, who in turn will be confirmed or removed from his office by the provisional governor. One of the first measures of the provisional government will be to liberate all political prisoners.

2. THE PLAN OF AYALA (1911)

EMILIANO ZAPATA

We the undersigned constituted as a Revolutionary Junta, in support and fulfillment of the promises of the revolution of November 20, 1910, now solemnly declare to the civilized world that judges us and to the nation to which we belong and which we love, the principles we have formulated to end the tyranny that oppresses us and to redeem the nation from the dictatorship that is imposed upon it. These aims are set forth in the following plan:

1. *Considering* that the Mexican people, led by Francisco I. Madero, shed their blood in order to regain their liberties and recover their rights which had been trampled upon, and not so that one man might take power in violation of the sacred principles that he took an oath to defend, under the slogan "Effective Suffrage, No Re-election," scorning the faith, the cause, justice, and the liberties of the people;

Considering that the man to whom we refer is Francisco I. Madero, the same man who initiated the aforementioned revolution and imposed his will and influence on the provisional government of the former President of the Republic, Francisco L. de la Barra, so as to have himself acclaimed liberator of the people. This act caused more bloodshed and repeated misfortunes for the nation because of the underhanded and ridiculous manner in which it was carried out. He [Madero] has no other goal than the satisfaction of his personal ambitions, his unbounded instincts as a tyrant, and his profound disrespect for the earlier laws emanating from the immortal code of '57, written with the blood of the revolutionaries of Ayutla; *

Considering that the aforesaid leader of the revolution of liberation of Mexico, Francisco I. Madero, because of his weakness and lack of integrity, did not bring to a happy conclusion the revolution that he began so gloriously with the support of God and of the people. Instead, he left in place most of the corrupt governing elements of the oppressive dictatorial government of Porfirio Díaz,

* A reference to the Liberal Constitution of 1857, which was adopted after a revolution that began at Ayutla in 1854.—ED.

Translated by the editor from Alfonso Reyes, *Emiliano Zapata, Su Vida y Su Obra* (Mexico City, 1963).

elements that are not and cannot in any way be legitimate representatives of national sovereignty. They are our bitter enemies and the enemies of the principles that we have defended to this day. They are provoking the destruction of the nation and are opening new wounds in the bosom of the people;

Considering that the aforementioned Francisco I. Madero is attempting to avoid fulfilling the promises that he made to the nation in the Plan of San Luis Potosí, restricting the above-mentioned promises to the agreements of Ciudad Juárez,* and that with intrigue and false promises he is nullifying, persecuting, jailing or killing the revolutionary elements that helped him to occupy the high post of President of the Republic;

Considering that many times Francisco I. Madero has tried to silence with the brute force of bayonets and to drown in blood all those who ask, solicit, or request the fulfillment of the promises of the revolution, calling them bandits and rebels, condemning them to a war of extermination without conceding or granting them a single one of the guarantees that are prescribed by reason, justice, or law . . . :

2. We cease to recognize Francisco I. Madero as leader of the revolution and President of the Republic for the aforementioned reasons. We demand the ouster of this official.

3. We recognize the illustrious General Pascual Orozco, aide to Francisco I. Madero, as leader of the revolution. In the event that he does not accept this post, General Emiliano Zapata shall be recognized. . . .

6. As an additional part of this plan, we declare that the lands, timber, and waters that have been usurped by landlords, *científicos,*† or political leaders under cover of tyranny and venal justice shall be returned immediately to the towns or citizens that have title to them. They have been dispossessed through the bad faith of our oppressors, who used arms to maintain themselves in possession at any cost. Usurpers who consider that they have a right to these properties shall be judged by special tribunals to be established after the triumph of the revolution.

7. In view of the fact that the overwhelming majority of Mexican people and citizens are not the owners of the land that they occupy, and that they suffer the horrors of poverty without being able to better their social condition in any way or to devote them-

---

* The treaty signed at Ciudad Juárez in May, 1911, ended the civil war with a victory for Madero, but retained many of Díaz' henchmen and ignored the sections of the San Luis plan that dealt with land reform.—ED.

† Literally, "scientists," the sarcastic Mexican term for the adherents of positivism, who were the ideological and political supporters of Porfirio Díaz in the last twenty years of his rule.—ED.

selves to industry or agriculture because land, timber, and water are monopolized by a few men, one-third of these properties shall be expropriated, with prior indemnification to the legal owners. This will be done so that the people and citizens of Mexico may establish cooperatives [*ejidos*], colonies, and legal properties for rural inhabitants to sow and to work so that the lack of prosperity and well-being of Mexicans may be ended once and for all.

8. The landlords, *científicos*, and political leaders who oppose this plan directly or indirectly will have their goods nationalized, and the two-thirds that would ordinarily be left to them will be used for war indemnification and pensions for the widows and orphans of victims who fall in the struggle for this plan.

9. To carry out [legal] proceedings with respect to the afore-mentioned goods, laws of disentail and nationalization shall be applied where appropriate. The laws issued by the immortal Juárez regarding the property of the Church shall serve as a norm and a model.* They shall serve as a warning to the despots and conservatives who in every era have tried to impose the ignominious yoke of oppression and reaction upon us. . . .

14. If President Madero and the rest of the dictatorial elements of the present and former regime wish to end the immense mis-fortunes that afflict the nation, let them resign immediately the posts that they occupy. In so doing, they may help to heal the grave wounds that they have opened in the bosom of the nation. If they do not resign, the blood and anathema of our brothers will fall on their heads.

15. Mexicans: Consider that the cunning, bad faith, and mis-government of one man is responsible for this scandalous blood-shed. Consider that his system of government is choking the nation and destroying our institutions with the brute force of bayonets; and thus, as our arms raised him to power, now let us turn them against him for forgetting his promises to the Mexi-can people and betraying the revolution that he began. We are not personalists. We believe in principles, not in men.

People of Mexico: Support this plan with arms in hand and you will establish the prosperity and well-being of the nation.

---

* The so-called Reform Laws of 1859, enacted by Liberal president Benito Juárez. The laws called, among other things, for the confiscation of all Church property (excepting houses of worship), without compensation.—ED.

3. THE CONSTITUTION OF MEXICO (1917)

(EXCERPTS)

Article 3. The education that the state imparts on the federal, state, and municipal levels shall harmoniously develop all the faculties of the human being and at the same time foster in him a love of country and a consciousness of international solidarity in independence and justice.

I. Since freedom of religion is guaranteed by Article 24, the standard that shall guide such education shall remain entirely free of any religious doctrine, and, based on the results of scientific progress, it shall fight ignorance and its effects—servitude, fanaticism, and prejudice.

A. It shall be democratic, considering democracy not only as a juridical structure and a political regime but as a way of life founded on the constant economic, social, and cultural betterment of the people.

B. It shall be national, insofar as, without hostility or exclusivity, it concerns itself with the comprehension of our problems, the use of our resources, the defense of our political independence, the assurance of our economic independence, and the continuity and growth of our culture.

C. It shall contribute to better human relationships, using all possible educational means to foster an appreciation both of the dignity of the individual and integrity of the family and of the general interests of society, while supporting the ideals of fraternity and equality of rights of all men and opposing all privileges of race, sect, group, sex, and individuals . . . .

IV. Religious bodies, ministers of religion, or corporations that, exclusively or predominantly, carry out educational activities, and associations or societies devoted to the propagation of any religious creed shall not participate in any way in institutions in which education is imparted . . . .

Article 5. The state cannot permit the execution of any contract, convenant, or agreement that has for its object the restriction, loss, or irrevocable sacrifice of the freedom of man, whether for work, education, or religious vows. The law thus does not permit the establishment of monastic orders, whatever their denomination or purpose. . . .

Translated by the editor from *Constitución política de los Estados Unidos Mexicanos* (México City, 1963).

Article 10. . . . The inhabitants of the United States of Mexico have the right to possess arms of any type for their protection and legitimate defense, with the exception of those expressly prohibited by law and those that the nation may reserve for the exclusive use of the Army, Navy, and National Guard; however, citizens may not carry arms in population centers without complying with police regulations. . . .

Article 27. The ownership of land and water within the national territory is vested originally in the nation, which has had, and now has, the right to transfer title to them to private individuals, thereby constituting private property. Expropriations may only be made for reasons of public utility and subject to indemnification. The nation shall at all times have the right to establish regulations for private property which the public interest may dictate, such as those regulating the use of natural resources for conservation purposes or ensuring a more equitable distribution of public wealth. With this end in view, the necessary measures shall be taken to break up the large estates [*latifundios*]; as well as to develop small agricultural property in cultivation; to create new agricultural centers with the necessary land and water; to encourage agriculture in general; and to prevent the destruction of natural resources and protect property from damage to the detriment of society. Population centers that lack land and water or do not have them in quantities sufficient for the needs of their people shall have the right to grants of these. They shall be made from adjacent large properties, always respecting the rights of small landholdings in cultivation.

The nation will retain ownership of all natural resources of the continental shelf and the underwater regions around islands; of all the minerals and substances that . . . constitute deposits that are of a nature distinct from the components of the land itself, such as the minerals from which are extracted metals and metalloids used in industry, discoveries of precious stones, of salt and salt pits formed directly by ocean waters; products derived from the decomposition of rocks, when their use necessitates underground work; discoveries of mineral or organic matter capable of being used for fertilizer; solid mineral combustibles; petroleum and all hydrocarbons, solid, liquid, or gaseous; and the space above national territory, to the extent and within the terms fixed by international law. . . .

In the cases referred to in the preceding paragraphs, ownership by the nation is inalienable and imprescriptible, and the exploitation, use, or appropriation of resources by private persons or by corporations formed in accordance with Mexican law may not be undertaken except through concessions granted by the federal executive, under the conditions and rules established by law. . . . With respect to petroleum and solid, liquid, or gaseous hydrocarbons, concessions and contracts shall not be granted; those already granted shall not be continued; and the nation shall carry out the mining of these products, under the terms of the respective regulatory law. It shall also be the exclusive right of the nation to generate, conduct, transform, distribute, and supply all electric energy in the public service. In this field [electricity], no concessions shall be granted to private individuals, and the nation shall make use of the goods and natural resources necessary for such ends.

The capacity to acquire property rights over the land and water of the nation shall be subject to the following regulations:

I. Only Mexicans by birth or naturalization, and Mexican companies, have the right to acquire ownership of lands, waters, and their appurtenances or to obtain concessions for the exploitation of mines or waters. The state may grant the same right to foreigners, but they must declare to the Secretary for Foreign Relations that they agree to consider themselves as nationals with respect to said goods and not to invoke the protection of their governments in matters relating to them, under penalty of forfeiting them to the state.

Within a zone running one hundred kilometers inside all frontiers and fifty kilometers from all coasts, no foreigner may acquire direct ownership of lands or waters. . . .

II. Religious institutions known as churches, regardless of creed, may not in any case acquire, possess, or administer real property or mortgages thereon; those they presently possess, directly or through an intermediary, shall become the property of the state, any person whatever being authorized to report any property so held. Presumptive evidence shall be enough to prove such claims. Places of public worship are the property of the state, represented by the federal government, which shall determine which of them shall continue in their present purposes. Bishoprics, rectories, seminaries, asylums, or schools belonging to religious associations, and convents or any other building built or intended for the administration, propagation, or teaching of a religious creed shall become the full property of the nation, to be used solely for the public service of the nation or the states, in their respective jurisdictions. Places of worship that may be erected in the future shall be the property of the nation. . . .

Article 59. Senators and deputies may not be re-elected for the immediately following term. . . .

Article 83. The President shall take office on the first day of

December for a period of six years. A citizen who has held the office of President, by popular election or by appointment as interim, provisional, or substitute President, may in no case and for no reason hold that office again. . . .

Article 123. The Congress . . . shall formulate labor laws that shall apply to workers, day laborers, domestic servants, artisans, and all labor contracts. The maximum work day shall be eight hours. . . . The minimum wage for workers shall be sufficient to satisfy the normal material, social, and cultural needs of a head of family and provide for the compulsory education of the children. In every agricultural, commercial, manufacturing, and mining enterprise the workers have the right to a share in the profits. . . . A social security law is considered of public utility and shall include disability insurance, life insurance, insurance against unemployment, sickness, accidents, and the like. . . .

Article 130. The federal authorities shall exercise the supervision required by law in matters relating to religious worship and outward ecclesiastical forms. . . . Marriage is a civil contract. This and other acts concerning the civil status of persons are within the exclusive jurisdiction of civil officials and authorities in the terms prescribed by law. . . .

The law does not recognize any [legal] personality in religious groups called churches. Ministers of denominations shall be considered as persons who practice a profession and shall be directly subject to the laws enacted on such matters. Only the legislatures of the states shall have the power to determine the maximum number of denominational ministers necessary for local needs.

To practice the ministry of any denomination in the United States of Mexico, it is necessary to be a Mexican by birth. Ministers of denominations may never, in a public or private meeting constituting an assembly, or in acts of worship or religious propaganda, criticize the fundamental laws of the country or the government authorities, specifically or in general. They shall not have the right to vote or to form associations for political purposes.

Permission to dedicate new places of worship open to the public must be obtained from the Secretary of the Interior after previous consent by the state government. In every church building there must be a representative who is responsible to the authorities for compliance with the laws on religious worship in that building and for the objects pertaining to worship. . . .

For no reason may validation, dispensation, or other action be taken to grant recognition for official purposes to studies undertaken in institutions whose purpose is the professional education of ministers of religion. . . .

Periodicals of a confessional character may not comment on national political affairs or report information about actions of the national authorities or of private individuals in relation to the functioning of public institutions. . . . Trials for violation of the previous provisions may never be held before a jury. . . .

4. THE EXPROPRIATION OF THE OIL INDUSTRY

LÁZARO CÁRDENAS

Our land, with valuable riches in its depths, was the object of penetration by companies that had been accustomed to regard the countries of Latin America as nothing more than colonies to be exploited, considering themselves as economic powers superior to the sovereign power of the state.

In the face of this problem the revolutionary government resorted to applying the provision [Article 27] of the 1917 Constitution that claimed the direct ownership of the subsoil as an inalienable right of the republic. Thus it was delivered from the tutelage of elements that were determined to make the rights of the nation a dead letter and to prevent the application of our fundamental laws through diplomatic pressure and mercenary revolts.

This administration took it upon itself to apply the law to the oil companies after they rebelled against the express commands of the highest tribunal of justice. Faced with the attitude of the people, who gave solid support to the defense of our institutions by the expropriation decree, the companies resorted to violent attacks in the foreign press and tried to upset our domestic economy. Fortunately, the government prevented economic collapse and consolidated its position, with the result that the principles of the revolution became rooted still more firmly in the heart of the nation, establishing an important precedent that was finally recognized as legitimate by foreign tribunals.

Translated by the editor from *Discurso pronunciado por el Señor Presidente de la República con Motivo del Aniversario de la Expropiación Petrolera* (Mexico City, 1939).

The attitude of Mexico could not be interpreted as an attack on industrial capital; rather it was an unavoidable measure of legitimate defense against the rebellious actions of businessmen who disregarded the welfare of society in the interests of their own vast profits. Among the salutary effects of this situation, I should note that many investors have adopted an attitude that is more understanding of the needs of the workers and of our country, without endangering reasonable profits on their part.

The reincorporation of the rights over subsoil petroleum under national control is a contribution to the integration of the national patrimony that all Mexicans must cherish, particularly those who, since 1917, have devoted themselves loyally to the fulfillment of the principles and goals of the revolution, and especially all the young people of the country who now receive into their custody this national patrimony which has stirred up so many disturbances, domestic struggles, and insatiable appetites. . . .

A conscientious and disciplined attitude on the part of the oil workers and frank collaboration by the directors and technicians in the operation of the industry have followed the nationalization carried out by the government of the republic. For its part, the Ministry of Economics is concluding an evaluation of the expropriated property, which will be published in a few days. The conflict that arose with the oil companies over the expropriation of their interests is in the process of being resolved through a plan of cooperation that the companies themselves are offering to the government. The plan involves the expansion of the industry through the investment of the indemnity for the property expropriated as well as new investments offered by the companies under a plan of cooperation by which the government will maintain its control over the administration of the oil industry.

5. STATUTES OF THE REVOLUTIONARY INSTITUTIONAL PARTY (PRI)

(EXCERPTS)

Article 1. The Revolutionary Institutional Party is a national association established by the progressive majority of the country to support and develop democratic and revolutionary institutions through the electoral activity of the citizenry and the political, social, and economic orientation of the Mexican people. The slogan of the party is "Democracy and Social Justice."

Article 2. The party is made up of organized labor and peasants, independent workers, public and private employees, members of cooperatives, artisans, students, professionals, small industrialists, businessmen, and farmers, and other elements with similar beliefs and interests who accept the principles of the Mexican Revolution and comply with the present statutes.

Article 3. The members of the party shall be grouped into sectors, which shall be: the Agrarian Sector, the Labor Sector, and the Popular Sector, depending on the organizations or groups to which they belong or their personal characteristics as factors in the economy of the country.

Article 4. The sector organizations to which Article 3 refers shall maintain their autonomy and the direction and discipline of their members in whatever concerns their specific purposes. Members of the party who belong to any of the sector organizations shall carry out their political activities through the organs of the party and subject to these statutes. . . .

Article 16. The National Assembly is the supreme organ of the party. It shall assemble with delegations from the party membership at the request of the National. Executive Committee, with the agreement of the National Council.

Article 17. The National Assembly shall meet at least once every six years, or when the National Council deems it convenient. . . .

Article 19. The National Council shall be made up of (1) the Chairman and General Secretary of the National Executive Committee; (2) the chairmen of the state directing committees; (3) fifteen representatives each of the Agrarian and Popular sectors, which will name and dismiss them freely; and a number of representatives from the Labor Sector, which the National Executive Committee shall fix in accordance with the following paragraph.

The labor representation in the National Council shall be made up of the number of councillors designated by the autonomous national trade unions and central federations in proportion to their membership, as determined by the National Executive Committee. . . .

Article 24. The National Executive Committee shall represent the party nationally and shall be made up of the following members: Chairman, General Secretary, Chief Official [*Oficial*

Translated by the editor from *Declaración de Principios, Programa de Acción, Estatutos,* published by the Partido Revolucionario Institucional (Mexico City, 1968).

Mayor], Secretary of Agrarian Action, Secretary of Labor Action, a senator as Secretary for Political Action, a federal deputy as Secretary for Political Action, Secretary for Organization, Secretary for Press and Propaganda, and Secretary for Finance.

Article 25. The Chairman and General Secretary shall be elected by the National Assembly. The Secretaries of Agrarian, Labor, and Popular Action shall be named and dismissed by their sectors. The Secretaries for Political Action from the Senate and the Chamber of Deputies shall be appointed and removed by the respective senators and deputies of the national Congress who are members of the Revolutionary Institutional Party. The Chief Official and the Secretaries of Organization, Press and Propaganda, and Finance shall be appointed and removed by the National Executive Committee. . . .

Article 114. To elect candidates for municipal offices . . . the party shall adopt the system of direct primaries by individual secret ballot of the party activists who live in the election districts that make up the municipality. The elections shall be carried out in conformity with the applicable regulations in these statutes and in the form and terms fixed by the election call.

Article 115. To approve party programs and to elect candidates for the offices of President of the Republic, state Governor, Senator, federal and local Deputy, and other relevant functionaries, the party shall adopt the convention system. . . .

Article 116. The conventions to which Article 115 refers shall be:

1. District conventions to choose candidates for the national Congress, the state legislatures, and the appropriate judicial offices. They shall take place in the headquarters of the respective election districts.

2. State conventions to choose candidates for state Governor, Senator, and appropriate judicial offices. They shall take place in the respective state capitals. The National Executive Committee shall decide the place in the federal district at which the convention to choose the candidates for Senator from the federal district will be held.

3. National conventions to choose the candidates for President of the Republic, which shall take place at the location fixed in the convention call. . . .

Article 141. The National Convention shall be made up of delegates from the Agrarian, Labor, and Popular sectors and from the assemblies of the various states.

Article 142. The voting of the delegates in the conventions shall be by sector. The delegates in the respective assemblies shall be seated for purposes of voting in the sector that corresponds to their characteristics as contributors to the national economy. . . .

Article 144. The State Committee shall review the proceedings of the district and state conventions that choose the candidates for Deputy, Senator, and Governor, and after passing judgment on them shall forward the documentation to the National Executive Committee, which shall authorize the registration of the candidates who have been legally chosen.

State conventions to elect candidates for Governor, shall forward not only the results of the nominating process, as indicated in the preceding paragraph, but also the electoral program adopted by the convention.

If the National Executive Committee finds irregularities in the procedure, it shall issue a call for a new convention or do what is appropriate in the circumstances. . . .

DECLARATION OF PRINCIPLES

. . . The best system for the election of the chief executive of the nation and the members of the Senate is by majority vote. For the Chamber of Deputies, we support a mixed system that includes the principle of majority vote balanced by one that works automatically and gives recognition to the voting strength of minority political parties, assuring them an adequate number of deputies with the same constitutional rights as those elected by the majority.*

Our electoral system assures the existence of genuine national political parties and avoids a proliferation of parties that cannot represent authentic currents of citizen opinion;† limits anti-democratic tendencies and processes that could develop because of the structure of political parties; stimulates a diversity of viewpoints and the functioning of an organic and responsible opposition; and increases the responsibility and perfects the organization and proceedings of the Chamber of Deputies. . . .

We defend the principle of no re-election, since it satisfies a popular demand that has a historical basis, contributes to both institutional stability and the flexibility of the political regime, and promotes the social mobility that is one of the basic democratic features of the Mexican community.

---

* A registered national party receives five seats in the Chamber of Deputies if it secures 2.5 per cent of the total vote and one seat for each additional 0.5 per cent of the vote up to a maximum of twenty seats.—ED.

† To be legally recognized, a party must have 75,000 members with at least 2,500 members in each of two-thirds of the states.—ED.

6. THE EJIDO AND MEXICAN LAND REFORM

WILLIAM C. THIESENHUSEN AND MARION R. BROWN

Mexico's land redistribution began in 1926, and enough time has elapsed to afford some tentative conclusions about the experience. The striking progress of the Mexican economy has led many to conclude that the revolution and accompanying land reform paved the way for development. Whether or not the reform was in fact responsible in important measure for this progress will likely be debated for a long time.

No other country in Latin America has made comparable strides in agricultural production over the past several decades. And among the Alliance [for Progress] countries, Mexico's only rival for improvement of income distribution is Bolivia.

Between 1941 and 1960 Mexico's per capita agricultural production increased by 46 per cent compared to a world average increase of 12 per cent, and a decline in Latin America as a whole. By one calculation, net agricultural output in Mexico trebled between 1934/38 and 1964/65. Between 1949/51 and 1960/62 the value of agricultural production grew by an average annual rate of 4.1 per cent.

Prior to the revolution [of 1917], land concentration in Mexico was among the highest in Latin America. Likewise, the social situation of *campesinos* [peasants] was probably more onerous than elsewhere in the region. An estimated 95 per cent of the rural population owned no land. Productivity in the agricultural sector was meager, and absentee landlordism was the rule. Wages were low and because peasants were tied to the farm by debts, money seldom changed hands between landlord and worker.

Now, a little more than forty years after the initiation of the land distribution in Mexico, more than 137 million acres have been given out in *ejidos*. These are properties owned jointly by communities, but on all but 3 to 4 per cent of them farming operations are carried on by individual families. In 1960 there

Excerpts from William C. Thiesenhusen and Marion R. Brown, *Problems of Agriculture*, published by the Subcommittee on Latin American Affairs of the Senate Foreign Relations Committee (Washington, D.C., 1967), pp. 19–22.

were about 1.6 million *ejido* members living on about 22,000 *ejidos*, which accounted for 45 per cent of the crop land, 54 per cent of all landholders, and 35 per cent of the value of all farm production in the country.

A third of the land now in *ejidos* was distributed between 1935 and 1940. Between 1941 and 1958 very little land was given out, but the rate increased again during the regime of President López Mateos (1958–64). The man-land ratio varies a great deal, but on the average there are about 67.5 acres of land per *ejido* member, of which almost 17.5 acres are crop land.

Ownership is circumscribed. A member of an *ejido* (*ejiditario*) may legally will the land to only one of his children; he may not sell or rent it (although infractions of this regulation are common); he may not mortgage it to secure a loan (which is responsible for a dual credit structure in Mexican agriculture). Furthermore, if an *ejiditario* fails to cultivate his land for two successive years, it may by law revert to the *ejido* to be reassigned. If he rents it out, a similar reversion is legally possible.

Ejidos are organized to provide for maximum local control. The general assembly elects an executive committee and a vigilance committee. Every member of an *ejido* gets a certificate of agrarian rights, and, ultimately, each is supposed to receive a title. (Only about 15 per cent of the *ejido* members actually have this title as yet.)

The *ejiditarios* did not pay for their lands. The government reimbursed the original owners a fraction of commercial value up until 1931, when it suspended the practice. Even when compensated, the owners gained little, since they were remunerated on the basis of their own personal declaration of value for tax purposes, a very low amount.

The revolution and land reform resulted in a dual system of agriculture, the *ejido* on one hand and the private farm on the other. Many commercial or potentially commercial farms remained in private hands throughout the revolutionary period. In some cases these were unexpropriated remnants of traditional large units. Production on these farms began to increase rapidly after 1940, when the private sector began to recover from the initial shock of the land reform. Frontier areas were left open for private development (*ejidos* were given out in the most densely populated regions) and there were large public investments in irrigation works which vastly improved production on these privately owned dry farms.

In contrast, little public money was used to support the *ejido* or to provide *ejido* farmers with modern inputs, extension, or markets. This is not to say that *ejidos* have remained completely outside any benefits of governmental investment in the agricultural sector. But they are, as one commentator has claimed, "underfinanced, underdeveloped, underirrigated, and overcrowded." [1]

Heretofore, most commentators have concluded that it took until 1940 before the production of corn, wheat, beans, and rice in Mexico regained 1920 levels. This is now being seriously questioned. One problem is that while statistics can be fairly accurate for most marketed surplus (which certainly did drop for the products mentioned), they cannot account well for the home consumption of produce grown by *campesinos*. It is quite possible that production remained the same after land reform or even increased, but that more was consumed by peasants. . . .

Thus, while the productivity picture is mixed, it is far from bleak. And Mexican *campesinos* are immeasurably better off in terms of employment, income, freedom, and possibilities for advancement than they were before the reform. As the peasant's buying power has risen, he has helped stimulate the industrial sector. And as the industrial sector grows, more and more *campesinos* are gradually finding their way into the city labor force. Reform has brought economic incentives that were absent under the old system. There is evidence that literacy in the countryside is increasing. Thousands of peasants who formerly had no claim on education and no participation in local government can now petition for schools or tax themselves to build their own.

Many former owners of haciendas who lost much of their land began to take better care of what they had left in order to avoid a ruinous drop in income. Capital accumulation and investment thus followed on the heels of reform. Reform (except possibly in the very short run) did not drive capital out of the agricultural sector but required it to be used more effectively. In transforming the political, social, and economic balance of the country, it is possible that land reform had its major impact outside of the *ejido* sector—maybe even outside of agriculture.

There are doubtless many improvements which could be made in the *ejido* sector. There is wide variability in performance which does not show through in gross data. The structure of the *ejido* itself merits serious rethinking. For example, *ejido* farmers should perhaps be allowed to sell their property to others within the community in order to get some return on their investment as they leave to take jobs in other parts of the economy. Then, too, there

---

[1] Wolf Ladejinsky, "Traditional Agriculture and the Ejido" (unpublished manuscript, October 26, 1966), p. 41.

is ample evidence that a large proportion of the sector suffers from lack of services. Public investments in market, extension, and credit would likely increase production. A more intensive focus on the *ejido* will become necessary as the frontier shrinks and expansion of agriculture at the "extensive margin" becomes more difficult.

In sum, the Mexican precedent generates optimism about land reform. Hopefully, reforms in other countries would need to be neither as violent nor as disruptive as was Mexico's. And it should be possible to shorten the time required to bring marketed supplies back to and above pre-reform levels.

7. THE ACCOMPLISHMENTS OF THE MEXICAN REGIME

CHARLES C. CUMBERLAND

For the first time in the history of Mexico, after 1940 a sustained and healthy economic growth outran population increase. Between 1940 and 1965 the population doubled, while the total of goods and services more than quintupled and agriculture quadrupled; the economic growth was somewhat tempered by inflation, but in general wages and salaries increased more rapidly than the cost of living, particularly after 1960. At prevailing average monthly income and yearly average retail prices in Mexico City in 1964, any skilled or semi-skilled worker could support a family of five through his own labor. A skilled cigarette-worker could give his family a balanced diet including meat or fish, fresh vegetables, fresh fruits, sweets, and cereal grains on less than a quarter of his income; including rent, one movie a week for each member of the family, cigarettes and beer for himself, and sufficient inexpensive clothing to meet the minimal needs of his family, his weekly essential expenditures ate up only three-fifths or two-thirds of his income. The remainder he could use to purchase luxuries or to put in savings. The steel or iron worker fared less well, but his income did meet the minimal requirement of article 123 of the Constitution of 1917 with its demand that income should "satisfy the

Excerpts from Charles C. Cumberland, *Mexico, The Struggle for Modernity* (New York: Oxford University Press, 1968), pp. 321–23; reprinted by permission.

normal needs of life," including "lawful pleasures." Those workers in the Federal District who received the minimum wages found it necessary to scrimp and scrounge in order to furnish the minimal needs for their families, but for the first time in the history of the country an unskilled worker could earn sufficient income to support a family and thus leave the children free to attend school.

Many pockets of real poverty—grinding poverty—still remained in 1960. Nearly a million peasants, outside of the *ejidal* system, worked plots of land too small to give sustenance to a family; the majority of them lived at a bare subsistence level and enjoyed few of the advantages accruing from the burgeoning economy. But even many of those who earned an income above the subsistence level lived in conditions far from ideal, reflecting none of the prosperity which the economic data indicate. One-half the population lived in housing averaging five persons to the room. Only one of every three Mexicans had access to running water within the building in which he lived, and only one of four dwelling places included a bathroom with running water. Two of every three families depended upon wood or charcoal for cooking and heating but, curiously enough, one of every three families owned a radio or television or both. These data give statistical support to a frequently observed phenomenon—Mexican economic gains have been funneled into a small segment of the population, with the vast majority benefiting only slightly from the impressive gains registered after 1950.

But one facet of social change after the Revolution clearly benefited the total population, regardless of class or income level— the nation's health improved enormously. In 1910 more than 300 of every thousand live-born children died before reaching the age of one; by 1940 that incredible figure had fallen to 125, by 1950 to 96, and by 1964 to 66. In 1964 infant mortality still compared unfavorably with the rate of approximately 24 in the United States, but it compared favorably with the rates in other countries in Latin America. The general mortality rate, which at slightly above 33 in 1910 was well over twice that of the United States, declined to 23 by 1940, to about 17 in 1950, and to a respectable 10.3 in 1964 compared to the 9.4 in the United States. This vast decline in death rates, coupled with a marked increase in marriage and birth rates, was responsible for an annual population increase of 3 to 4 per cent in the decade after 1950.

Viewed from any angle, the social and economic change evident in Mexico during the quarter century after 1940 was remarkable. During that twenty-five year span the population more than doubled, but productivity increased more rapidly than the population and demonstrated an accelerating rate in the last lustrum. Only Costa Rica among the Latin American republics, at the end of the period, spent a larger share of its national budget on education, and only three countries of Latin America maintained a better ratio of doctors to the population. In 1964, Mexican universities graduated as many medical doctors, proportionately, as the U.S. Only Argentina, Chile, and Uruguay—all traditionally literate and prosperous—circulated more newspapers on a per capita base, and no Latin American nation printed more papers daily. The number of movie houses and the admission prices allowed the Mexicans to attend more cinema productions than the nationals of any other Western Hemisphere country, save the United States. Only El Salvador and Costa Rica maintained proportionately fewer men in their armed service; Argentina's army was nearly four times the size of Mexico's proportionately, Brazil's was nearly two times, and Chile's more than two times. In most agricultural crops production after 1950 increased much more rapidly than in the world in general, and outstripped all other Western Hemisphere nations; the rate of increase in all grains nearly doubled the world rate and was half again as great as Latin America in general; the rate of beans more than doubled the hemisphere rate, as did sugar. Mexico became the third largest coffee producer in Latin America, the second in tobacco, and the third in raw milk. Among the Latin American nations, only Brazil increased manufacturing at a faster rate; the Mexican rate was twice that of Argentina, and greater than that of either the United States or Canada.

Despite these impressive data, Mexico by the mid-1960's had not yet arrived in the Promised Land. The nation still suffered from millions of illiterates, inadequate housing, and a mean real income which most Western Europeans would perceive to be near destitution. Whether the nation can ever become "prosperous" in the sense of Swedish or German prosperity, or ever achieve a standard of living roughly equivalent to that of the United States, still remains in serious doubt in view of the limited natural resources with which she has to work. But at long last the leaders of the Mexican nation had come to realize that the greatest natural resource available to any society is its people, who with proper training and stimuli can do wondrous things. With that recognition the battle was half won. . . .

8. DEMOCRACY IN MEXICO

ROBERT SCOTT

Side by side with the negative factors . . . is evidence of a great deal of positive accomplishment in the struggle to establish working democracy in Mexico. As the operations of the political decision-making process become more institutionalized, an effective constitutional system has evolved, even though it does not always follow identically the letter of the law laid down in 1917. Despite obvious weaknesses in this governing system, it does seem to take into account all of the principal and most active interest groups and associations when the highest public officers are being selected and when major policy questions are decided. Moreover, the political system is flexible enough to permit access of new groups and associations representing developing interests which grow out of changes in the social and economic environment.

More important still, from the point of view of the individual, changes in the Mexican environment are both speeding up and proliferating at an almost geometric rate, as Westernization reaches out with roads and radios and schools to embrace all of the Mexicans in a single national life. Not only are the vast majority of Mexicans being exposed to new ideas and the possibility of material change, but the value system within which they operate is being affected by these new concepts. More important in this context is the way in which, as Westernization turns more and more Mexicans into nationally aware and politically conscious citizens, the medium through which it occurs—the Revolution of 1910—has become identified with the values of democratic government.

To date, the propaganda line of the revolutionary governments, that Mexicans live in a democratic environment, has not been fully implemented because . . . the dilemma of the Revolution was that it had to set about providing suitable social and economic conditions before the political goals of democratic

Excerpts from Robert Scott, *Mexican Government in Transition* (Urbana, Ill.: University of Illinois Press, 1959), pp. 300–301; reprinted by permission of the publisher.

government could be achieved. Now that new and more suitable conditions do exist, the minds of many Mexicans are ready to absorb new understandings of the role of the individual in society and of his responsibilities to his fellow man. The seeds of these ideas have been planted in minds already open to change, so that they can take root and bear fruit in the form of socialized action later. In the Mexican world of violently conflicting values, the most consistent and dynamic force of the past half-century has been the Revolution, which does equate with an urge toward democracy, no matter how differently each Mexican may understand the meaning of that word. The social myth can have profound influence over the political activities of men; for Mexico, the myth of democracy, believed by and acted upon by enough citizens, could provide the final tie to bind together the increasingly strong democratic influences into an operative democratic syndrome.

No one who knows Mexico would argue that the country already has attained a working democratic system, or that it is the most democratic country in Latin America today, though one might well argue that in the fifty years since the outbreak of the Revolution more has been done there to solve the real problems hindering development of such a system than in any of the other republics of the area.

9. THE REVOLUTIONARY FAMILY

FRANK BRANDENBURG

Mexico is ruled by an elite to which we may assign the label of the Revolutionary Family. It is composed of the men who have run Mexico for over half a century, who have laid the policy lines of the Revolution, and who today hold effective decision-making power. Five major forces work to keep the Family intact: dedication, friendship, self-interest, fear, and inertia. Its affairs are conducted at the top by the head of the Family, who is usually the incumbent President of Mexico,

Excerpts from Frank Brandenburg, "The Relevance of Mexican Experience to Latin American Development," in Norman A. Bailey (ed.), *Latin America: Politics, Economics, and Hemispheric Security* (New York: Praeger Publishers, 1965), pp. 265–67.

assisted by about twenty favorite sons—a few powerful national and regional political leaders, wealthy individuals, and possibly labor leaders and intellectuals. This inner council keeps the Revolution intact and rolling forward by understanding and defining the relative power of the major vested interests. Since 1952, these interests, which form a second level of the Family hierarchy, have been represented by about 200 spokesmen from finance, commerce, private industry, and agriculture; from cabinet ministries, state-owned industries, federal agencies, and provincial government; from educational, religious, professional, and social organizations; from the armed forces and veterans' groups; from labor unions, cooperatives, communal agricultural groups, and civil servant federations; and from the judiciary, political groupings, and the press. The third level of the Family hierarchy is the formal apparatus headed by the President of Mexico in his immediate capacity as president; it embraces the national bureaucracy, the armed forces, the official political party, captive opposition parties, and state and local public administration.

The Family is thus directed by the undisputed head of the clan, who inherits Hidalgo and Morelos as godparents, Juárez as his grandfather, and Madero as the first father of the Revolution. Either he delivers the definitive word on every matter, or someone else rises to take his place. Aggregation of interests may occur both inside and outside the Family, but in the last instance demands are judged by the head of the Family. When the office of President of Mexico is not held by the Family head, presidential authority is regularly questioned and ignored in his favor. When no single leader is capable of gaining undisputed recognition as head of the Family, or when a leader, on gaining it, proves incapable of being a truly strong father, multiple leadership temporarily results, but only temporarily. Once elevated to the high lordship of Mexico, the Family head constantly must prove that he, and he alone, runs the nation. Within the Mexican milieu, the political sun rises and sets every six years on the presidency, and in identical cycles on gubernatorial offices. Mexicans avoid personal dictatorship by retiring their dictators every six years.

Belief in official party control of Mexico is clearly fallacious. The official party cannot, as some analysts contend, continue to work out a formula for satisfying a majority of the most influential associations in order to retain key aggregating and decision-making functions. It cannot continue because this role in the Mexican political system always has been performed elsewhere. If the decision-making process actually resided in the official party instead of in the Family head and formal govern-

ment apparatus, Mexico probably would have become a
workers' state long ago. Presidents select governors, who in turn
select municipal presidents. A president is selected in the last
instance by the Revolutionary Family head who has no responsibility to discuss his selection with the official party; he in fact
announces to the official party who "its candidate" will be in a
presidential election.

Whether official party sectors cut up the electoral pie for the
designation of state deputies, federal deputies, and (federal)
senators—or the president and governors perform this function—is
peripheral to the exercise of real power in Mexico. No effective
power is at stake anyway; a state legislature obsequiously follows
the state leader, be he governor, regional strong man, or gov-
ernor-designate, just as the federal legislature rubber-stamps the
dictates of the Family head.

There is no "intra-party democracy," "one-party democracy,"
or related system of popular front government. The basic difference between Revolutionary governance and Porfirian governance is that Mexico now has a turnover in dictators every
six years at the national and state levels and every three years
at the local level. This practice also provides a workable formula
for the eternal problem of patronage. From the presidential
office down to municipal governmental organs, from giant state
industries to small regulatory agencies, from the official party
to captive opposition parties, every six-year administration witnesses a turnover of about 18.000 elective offices and 25,000 ap-
pointive posts. The politically ambitious may enter at any place
along the line. The jackpot is six years at the top of the politico-
bureaucratic heap; there, one hardly requires more time to accumulate sufficient resources to retire from political office. The
indefinite terms of office during pre-Revolutionary days have
been replaced by firm adherence to the principle of no re-
election, but this does not mean that the benefits received from
a shorter term today are less than those from a long term yesterday.

The system works. It has helped Mexico accomplish notable
social and economic achievements. Presidents have become less
fearful of the people and people less afraid of their presidents.
This encouraging state of affairs improves tolerance and extends
freedom. Yet there is no effective opposition or effective suffrage. Checks and balances, separation of powers and restraints
by legislative and judicial agents are paper thin. Fifty years of
Revolution suggest that the appearance of effective interest groups
and political parties unimpeded by constant governmental
intervention is wishful thinking. And the future, like the past five

decades, promises little more in the way of improving democratic goals than the expectation of placing in the presidential
office a tolerant, powerful chief executive—of retaining the
"liberal Machiavellian."

10. INTERNAL COLONIALISM AND
NATIONAL DEVELOPMENT

PABLO GONZÁLEZ CASANOVA

The practical and political value of internal colonialism throughout the different stages of social development and social mobilization is clearly perceived when this phenomenon's characteristics are placed within a concrete setting. Mexican social
structure might be usefully examined in this context.

Mexico is a country which obtained its political independence
150 years ago. It has distributed 48 million hectares of arable
land to 2½ million peasants, ending the old latifundist system.
Its rural population was less than 50 per cent in 1960 (the rural-
urban limit being 2,500 inhabitants). In this same year, only 53
per cent of the labor force was in agriculture, and the rest in
secondary or tertiary industrial activities. The rate of integrating
the population into the national development process is very
high. With the triumph of the great liberal and progressive
movements, from independence to the social revolution of 1910,
the *official* and *national* symbols of this "mestizo" country are
the Indians: Cuauhtémoc, who fought against the Spanish
conquerors, and Juárez, who as a child spoke only Mixtec, an
Indian dialect, and who was a full-blooded Indian. In schools
and in secular society generally Indians are objects of venera-
tion. The cementing, symbolic value they have corresponds to a
mestizo society, without racial prejudices in the national orbit
or in the national ideology. The Indian problem of Mexico
is seen—in governmental and intellectual circles—as a cultural
rather than a racial problem. It is linked to the ideology of the

Excerpts from Pablo González Casanova, "Internal Colonialism and National Development," *Studies in Comparative International Development*, I,
No. 4 (1965), pp. 34–35; reprinted by permission.

Revolution. Politicians attribute to the Indian innumerable positive values, pride of a progressive nativist policy.

However, the Indian problem subsists: the number of inhabitants five years of age or over who do not speak Spanish, but only an Indian dialect or language, was more than one million in 1960—that is, 3.8 per cent of the national population over five years of age. The number of inhabitants who speak an Indian language or dialect and garble some Spanish was almost two million in 1960. This constitutes 6.4 per cent of the population. From a linguistic point of view, the Indian problem covers more than 10 per cent of the population. If indicators other than language are used in defining the Indian—work techniques, institutions—the number of Indians "grows to about 20 or 25 per cent," that is, they comprise more or less seven million inhabitants.

The condition of these inhabitants, particularly the least acculturated among them, exhibits many characteristics typical of internal colonialism. These occur despite the period of national independence, the revolution period, the agrarian reform, sustained development and industrialization, civic pride, or even the cultivation of a folk ideology.

The forms internal colonialism takes are the following, as registered by anthropologists in repetitive though unsystematic ways:

A. The "dominant center" or "metropolis" (in Mexico, the cities of San Cristobal, Tlaxiaco, Huauchinango, Sochiapan, Mitla, Ojitian, Zacapoaxtla, etc.). It exercises a monopoly over Indian commerce and credit. The interchange is plainly unfavorable to the Indian communities. It takes the shape of a permanent decapitalization of these communities to the lowest levels. Isolation of the Indian communities with respect to any other center or market is visible. Monoculture, deformation, and dependence of the Indian economy, each coincides with commercial monopoly.

B. An exploitation of the Indian population by the different social classes of the Ladino population exists. "Tlaxiaco," says an anthropologist [Alejandro D. Marroquin], referring to an urban center, "presents heterogeneous forms of social stratification. Its social composition has a pronounced effect on the division of classes. But the characteristic of these social classes is the fact that they rest on the exploitation of the Indian as a worker or producer." The exploitation is combined—a mixture of feudalism, slavery, capitalism, forced and salaried work, partnerships, peonage, and gratuitous "free" domestic services.

The plundering of the Indian communities fulfills two functions, as during the colonial era: it deprives Indians of their land, and it converts them into peons or paid workers. The exploitation of one population by another corresponds to differential salaries for equal work. Such is the case with the exploitation of Indian artisans by the Ladino population (wool, textile, palm, wicker, ceramics). It extends from linguistic discrimination ("I was a worm until I learned Spanish") to discrimination in modes of dress, until higher juridical, political, and trade union discrimination is realized. This coincides with colonial attitudes of local and federal functionaries, and of Ladino political leaders. Finally, this situation corresponds to differences of culture and life style which can be registered according to the type of population: Indian or Ladino.

The following are observed facts: amongst Indian communities a subsistence economy is predominant. Monetary and capitalization levels are minimum. Land is in advanced stages of decay and of low quality (when it can be used at all) for agriculture. Agriculture and cattle-raising processes are deficient; seeds are of poor quality; animals are often diseased and smaller than others of their kind. Techniques of cultivation are backward—pre-Hispanic or colonial—(hoe, ax, windlass). Levels of productivity are low. Life standards are lower than in non-Indian regions (more insalubrity, mortality, infant mortality, and illiteracy). There is an aggravated lack of essential services (schools, hospitals, water, electricity). Prostitution and alcoholism are fomented by procurers and Ladinos. There is aggression of rich communities against poor ones (real and symbolic). The culture is magico-religious. Economic manipulation is based on a prestige economy, while political manipulation (oppression, collective vote) is widely practiced. These characteristics correspond to typical colonial stereotypes in which Indians are considered as "unreasonable people," "lazy, good for nothing," and in which the violation of rules of courtesy, language, dress, tone of voice on the part of the Indians often provokes violent verbal and physical abuse from the Ladinos.

National development and mobilization, the increase of communications, and the size of the market have provided an outlet for the more aggressive members of these Indian communities. As soon as they dress like mestizos, speak Spanish, participate in the national culture, the situation of the Indian corresponds to the different strata they occupy in the society. At the national level the problem is certainly not a racial one. There are two problems that do have national importance. First, the federal government itself maintains a discriminatory policy, consciously or unconsciously. Agrarian reform has much less importance in the Indian regions. The fiscal charge is proportionally higher for these regions, while credits and investments are proportionately lower. Second, if the above characteristics, typical of internal colonialism, are found integrally in a population that comprises only 10 per cent of the total—at the crossroads of Ladino and Indian Mexico—this fact has a natural interaction with the national society as a whole, in which there is a continuum of colonialism —from the society which integrally exhibits all colonial characteristics to those regions and groups in which only residues of paracolonialist manipulatory forms remain.

11. DOCUMENTS ON THE STUDENT REVOLT OF 1968

I. THE STUDENT DEMANDS OF AUGUST, 1968

To Public Opinion, Teachers, Students, and Educational Authorities:

These have been days of anguish and tension for the people of Mexico. The National Polytechnic Institute and the Autonomous National University of Mexico have been brutally and aggressively assaulted. This situation was created by the hysterical and absurd attitude of police force, which is completely opposed to democracy and despised and disrespected for its continual attacks on the whole population. It neither inspires nor possesses the moral authority to impose order. We students have done nothing more than oppose reason to the violence to which we have been subjected.

This is not the first time that the Grenadier Corps has savagely repressed students, nor is it the first time that the army has entered our most noted educational centers. Now the authorities are acting with greater fury and less respect for the Constitution. Every day our liberty is more limited, and we are approaching the complete and absolute loss of freedom of thought, opinion, assembly, and association. We students have had enough of calumny and lies from the national press, radio, and television. We are tired of the climate of oppression. It is

Translated by the editor from *El Día* (Mexico City), August 4, 1968.

clear that the situation is leading the country to reaction . . . .

The latest events have shown that students are not disposed to permit a climate of repression and violence to flourish in the country. We demand of the appropriate authorities immediate action on the following points:

1. Liberty for political prisoners.

2. Dismissal of Generals Luis Cueto Ramírez and Raul Mendolea, as well as Lieutenant Colonel Armando Frías.

3. Dissolution of the Corps of Grenadiers, the direct instrument of repression, and the noncreation of similar corps.

4. Abrogation of Articles 145 and 145b of the Federal Penal Code [the Crime of Social Dissolution], the legal instrumentalities of aggression.*

5. Compensation to the families of those killed and injured as victims of aggression from July 26 forward.

6. Determination of those responsible for the acts of repression and vandalism on the part of the authorities by the police, grenadiers, and army.

---

* Article 145 of the Penal Code reads as follows:

"A prison term of two to twelve years and a fine of 1,000 to 10,000 pesos will be imposed on any foreigner or Mexican national who in spoken or written form, or by any other means, carries out political propaganda among foreigners or Mexican nationals, spreading the ideas, programs, or norms of action of any foreign government that disturb public order or affect the sovereignty of the Mexican state. Public order is disturbed when the acts set forth in this paragraph tend to produce rebellion, sedition, riot, or insurrection.

"National sovereignty is affected when said acts may endanger the territorial integrity of the republic, prevent the functioning of its legitimate institutions, or encourage disrespect on the part of Mexican nationals for their civic duties.

"The same penalties shall be imposed on any foreigner or Mexican national who by any means induces or incites one or more individuals to carry out acts of sabotage, to subvert the institutional life of the country, or to carry out acts of provocation with the aim of disturbing the public order or the public peace; this applies also to those who accomplish such acts. In case the same acts constitute other crimes, the penalties for those crimes shall be applied as well.

"A prison term of ten to twenty years shall be imposed on the foreigner or Mexican national who prepares the way materially or morally for the invasion of the national territory or the submission of the country to any foreign government."—Ed.

II. THE NATIONAL STRIKE COUNCIL: FOR A WORKER/PEASANT/STUDENT ALLIANCE

Our struggle has laid bare not only the repressive character of our government but also the structure of injustice and exploitation on which it rests.

The support that we have received from the popular sectors obliges us to discuss this structure and to let the popular masses know our point of view on how to transform it, as well as the line of action that students, workers, peasants—in a word, the people as a whole—must take in order to banish from our country once and for all exploitation, poverty, abuse, and repression.

Much has been said about the prosperity the country is enjoying. But it has not been pointed out that it is only the prosperity of a privileged minority, which increases its wealth at the expense of the working people. The worker, the peasant, wage earners in general see the cost of living increase while wages and income stay fixed or rise more slowly than prices. Furthermore, increasing numbers of workers are being deprived of the opportunity to work because the innovations in industry, in agricultural machinery, etc., are for the benefit of the bosses alone. Through generalized repression the government has turned the organizations of the people (such as the parties and trade unions) into new means of subjugation and exploitation. The independent trade unions have practically disappeared; the peasants' organizations do not defend the interests of the agricultural workers but are instruments of political control in the hands of the corrupt leaders of the official party. Finally, more and more workers have been forced to work in unproductive and underpaid jobs as their only recourse for obtaining enough income to survive.

The government is not the government of all Mexicans; rather its resources are mainly devoted to increasing the privileges of the big bourgeoisie, consisting of the large industrialists, the large merchants and landowners, the bankers and the corrupt politicals of the "revolutionary family."

Excerpts from *Mexico, '68, The Students Speak,* U.S. Committee for Justice to Latin American Political Prisoners, P. O. Box 2303, New York, N. Y. 10001 (1969); reprinted by permission.

The PRI [Institutional Revolutionary Party] is a political apparatus which forces the masses to act and vote for its candidates by means of deceit, threats, and blackmail. A long time ago it stopped representing any of the popular sectors, which it forces to remain within its ranks for the benefit of the big bourgeoisie.

With the repressions of 1959, those trade unions which used to be controlled by leaders representing the workers ceased being representative in any sense and have become gangs at the service of the bosses and their government.

As time passes, the number of Mexicans who lack education, housing, jobs, etc., increases while, at the same time, part of the national resources are delivered to foreign interests, especially those of the United States.

The peasants are subjected to more arbitrariness every day. They are exploited not only by the landowner, the moneylender, state and private banks, but also by the *ejido* commissariat, trade unions, transportation companies, middlemen, and a whole gamut of corrupt politicians.

These circumstances, and many others too numerous to mention, have led us to the conclusion that we cannot wait any longer. We must begin a general struggle, together with all the workers, in order to demand a minimum of rights that will place us on the road to the final liberation of the Mexican people. The people are our country, not the professional politicians whose only ties with the country are exploitation, treason, and crime.

III. THE NATIONAL STRIKE COUNCIL: THE ATTACK AT THE PLAZA OF THE THREE CULTURES (OCTOBER 2, 1968)

After an hour and a half of a peaceful meeting attended by ten thousand people and witnessed by scores of domestic and foreign reporters, a helicopter gave the army the signal to attack by dropping flares into the crowd. Simultaneously, the plaza was surrounded and attacked by members of the army and all police forces, using weapons of every caliber, up to 9mm.

The local papers have given the following information about the attack, confirmed by firsthand witnesses:

Excerpts from *Mexico 1968, A Study of Domination and Repression*, North American Congress on Latin America (New York, 1968); reprinted by permission.

1. Numerous secret policemen had infiltrated the meeting in order to attack it from within, with orders to kill. They were known to each other by the use of a white handkerchief tied around their right hands.

2. When the National Strike Council itself was attacked, various journalists were hit. Among the victims was the famous Italian writer Oriana Fallaci of *L'Europeo* of Milan, who received four bullet wounds and was left after being robbed of all her personal possessions.

3. High caliber weaponry and expansion bullets were used. Seven hours after the massacre began, tanks cleaned up the residential buildings of Nonoalco-Tlaltelolco with short cannon blasts and machine-gun fire.

4. On the morning of October 3, the apartments of supposedly guilty individuals were still being searched, without a search warrant.

The hospital ambulances had been taken over by members of the army, to ensure preferential treatment for wounded among the military and to impede immediate attention to civilian casualties.

5. Doctors in the emergency wards of the city hospitals were under extreme pressure, being forced to forego attention to the victims until they had been interrogated and placed under guard. Various interns who attended the demonstration for the purpose of giving medical aid have since disappeared.

6. The results of this brutal military operation include dozens of dead (including women and children), thousands of wounded, an unwarranted search of all the apartments in the area, and thousands of violent arrests. Those arrested were taken to various illegal locations, such as Military Camp No. 1. It should be added that members of the National Strike Council who were captured were stripped and herded into a small archaeological excavation at Tlaltelolco, converted for the moment into a dungeon. Some of them were put up against a wall and shot.

7. Onesimo Mason, the general who directed the operation, praised the preparedness of his men, in contrast to the obvious lack of preparedness on the part of the students.

All this has occurred only ten days before the start of the Olympics. The repression is expected to become even greater after the Games, in view of the fact that national public opinion and the protest from the provinces are unified against a regime whose only interest lies in demonstrating its power to control

Already individual liberties have been suspended, and restricted zones have been created where all vehicles are searched at gun point and personal identification is demanded. The Secretary of Defense declared that the friendly disposition of the regime will solve the conflict.

Until now, the Senate and the Confederación de Trabajadores de México [Mexican Confederation of Workers], the latter through the voice of its leader of thirty years, Fidel Velázquez, have been quick to show their support of the president. . . .

WE ARE NOT AGAINST THE OLYMPIC GAMES, WELCOME TO MEXICO

12. STATE OF THE UNION ADDRESS (SEPTEMBER 1, 1968)

GUSTAVO DÍAZ ORDAZ

UNIVERSITIES

We had been provincially proud and candidly complacent that in a world of youthful violence, Mexico formed an unaffected island. Nevertheless, apparently unrelated outbreaks of violence began to appear in different parts of the capital, and in many of our states, with increasing frequency. Suddenly, they became more serious and began to multiply, a low affront to a city devoted to its daily work and which raised its voice in demand of the most basic guarantees. My early warnings and expressions of concern went unheeded.

During my trip to the interior, I issued an invitation to study the facts objectively and to face them serenely. I called for a dialogue . . . a true dialogue, which offers an opportunity to express one's point of view and reasons, and at the same time to hear the opinions of others; its purpose is to persuade, naturally, but it also seeks to understand. Dialogue is never possible when different languages are spoken, when one of the parties stubbornly remains deaf, and it is even less possible when one party insists upon the illogical position of accepting dialogue only when there is no longer anything to discuss. . . .

The Mexican government must protect the university's autonomy, not only respect it; but it is also its duty to uphold the

---

Excerpts from the official English translation published by the Mexican government (Mexico City, 1968).

legally established regime in which we live, and which, in turn, includes the internal juridical order of our universities. It must seek a legal solution for difficulties and avoid endangering our national sovereignty by acts of external or internal violence.

It is obvious that hands other than those of students were involved in the recent disturbances; but it is also a fact that, by their own choice or because they allowed themselves to be swayed, a good number of students took part in the affair.

Consequently, it may be just as well for the well-earned prestige of our universities—their autonomy guaranteed by our laws as is their internal legal system, which is respected by us all—if we make every effort to separate these highly esteemed cultural values from acts of which no one can be proud, many of them legal violations and even crimes that are severely punishable under our penal code. . . .

"Political Prisoners"

I do not admit that there are "political prisoners." A "political prisoner" is one who has been deprived of his freedom *exclusively* because of his political ideas, without having committed any crime. Nevertheless, if I am informed of the name of any person who has been incarcerated without due process of law, in which the required formalities have not been observed, orders will be given for his immediate and unconditional release.

If this demand is limited to those who have frequently been called political prisoners, I must state once more what is already a matter of public record. These are persons who are being tried before the proper legal authorities and in keeping with our Constitution, persons against whom the Public Ministry has formulated a charge, not based on subjective political motives or the ideas they profess, but on acts they have performed that constitute crimes punishable under our Penal Code. Others, whose trials have come to a close, have been sentenced by the proper judicial authorities.

Though I may not invade the sphere of another branch of government, I have requested the Attorney General of the Republic and the District Attorney for the Federal District and Territories, to study with the greatest care, at the request of any interested party, the pending cases in which any doubt could exist concerning the political nature of the charges made. It will thus be possible to decide, in all fairness, whether the Attorney General should withdraw his charges or whether, given the special circumstances of each case, he should maintain his legal action. . . .

"Social Dissolution"

With regard to Articles 145 and 145b of the Penal Code, the first of which refers to the crime known as "social dissolution," the abolition of which is requested, let me make it clear that:

The abolition of a law is not within the powers of the President, even though he is empowered to initiate such action.

This is a situation that has existed for many years and in which public opinion plays no part, since the text of such precepts is not common knowledge.

I shall take the liberty of requesting the honorable Congress of the union to take into consideration the possibility of calling a series of public hearings in which the country's bar associations and all interested parties in general may express their views.

Should it or should it not be considered a crime to affect our national sovereignty, endangering the territorial integrity of the Republic in compliance with the dictates of a foreign government? Should it or should it not be a crime to prepare the invasion of national territory or the submission of our country to a foreign government? Such cases are part of Article 145.

Article 145b defines crimes of a political nature. If it is abolished, no crime will have a political character. Is that what is desired?

These are the questions that must be answered and if, after the text of Articles 145 and 145b of the Penal Code have been studied, public opinion favors abolition and this honorable Congress so agrees, enacting the corresponding law, I shall accept and promulgate it without delay, for, above any other consideration, it is my solemn obligation to heed the will of the people. . . .

Recent Events

. . . The apparently insignificant incident which supposedly originated the problem was not the first of its type, but the culmination of a long series of violent acts infringing upon the freedom and rights of many people.

It is a fact that there have been hundreds of cases throughout the country in which students or pseudo-students have taken violent possession of their schools, imprisoned their rectors, directors, or teachers, resorting to kidnapping, have seized buses, caused destruction, attacked other students or totally innocent persons, etc.

Let us place these events within the framework of international reports of similar bitter experiences of countries in which authorities have been forced, either from the outset or after several futile attempts at conciliation, to employ force as the only means of ending or checking the violence.

Despite the fact that some of these countries are governed by experienced statesmen, they were unable to find persuasive enough arguments.

Now let us examine those aspects of which much has been said, but little has been written: those referring to persons who have suffered damage to their property—at times quite serious—whether these be wealthy owners of bus lines or humble members of the transportation system whose entire patrimony consists of one bus or who are part owners of one; proprietors of large or small businesses which have suffered destruction or looting; drivers of food or soft-drink delivery trucks who have seen their merchandise snatched from their vehicles; factories and labor or farm organizations which have been violently attacked; houses whose walls have been filled with painted scrawls and whose windows have been broken; the quiet rage of so many motorists who have been halted and asked to make contributions of money to "the cause," or see their car windows, antennas, or tires destroyed; the thousands of passengers forced to vacate city buses, and even the financial distress suffered by those to whom fifty centavos constitutes an important part of their weekly budget; the workman or government employee who is penalized for being late to work; the lawyer, the doctor, the engineer, the housewife, who are delayed in arriving at court, at the hospital, at the building site, at the business establishment or at home because city traffic, difficult enough at the best of times, is snarled over a wide area; the distress suffered by completely uninvolved persons held as hostages; all those peaceful passersby who have been insulted, humiliated, or injured and been obligated to resign themselves to it, because of the force of numbers, and not risk their personal safety in an absurd quarrel; so many women assaulted who besides suffering their own shame had a father, a mother, a husband, a brother, or a son also filled with indignation by such attacks. These women could have been the wives, the mothers, the sisters, or the daughters of any Mexican. We must also add to these most recent and serious offenses, gross slander, alarming rumors to provoke panic buying and upset the city's economy. . . .

The Legal System

The general legal system—of which university autonomy forms only a part—is the basis for a propitious working climate for the creation of wealth in order to sustain universities, polytechnical institutes, normal and agricultural schools; it is the basic protection of our freedom, for under anarchy no one is free.

The legal system is not simple theory, or a whim—it is a vital collective necessity; without it, no organized society could exist.

In accordance with this concept, after all measures which good sense and experience dictate have been exhausted, I shall exercise, whenever strictly necessary, the powers vested in me by Article 89, Paragraph VI, of the Constitution of the Republic, which reads as follows: "The powers and obligations of the President are the following: . . . To make use of all permanent armed forces, that is, the army, navy, and air force, for the internal security and external defense of the Federation." This power is also based on the concept of Article 129 of the Constitution.

Our army has been entrusted with various missions, some of them extremely delicate, aimed at the preservation of domestic peace; in these situations, as in others, it has distinguished itself by its spirit of discipline and the calm and measured firmness with which it has fulfilled its duty.

In the name of the nation, I publicly express the gratitude due our soldiers.

When the Mexican Army intervenes to maintain domestic law and order, it must make itself respected and it must be respected. . . .

COURSE OF ACTION

. . . Internally, the nation is working in peace. In a few weeks or months, when time will have given events their perspective, they will no longer be regarded as heroic episodes but as an absurd struggle of mysterious origin and unspeakable aims.

We have caused Mexico to appear in the eyes of the world as a country in which the most reprehensible events may take place; for the unfair and almost forgotten image of the Mexican as a violent, irascible gunman to be revived; and for slander to be mixed with painful truth in the same news reports.

Part of the damage that has been caused will long remain irreparable; that good name for which so many Mexicans worked long and sacrificed so much has been tarnished.

It is the obligation of us all to avoid any further loss of prestige, and, within our borders, to contribute in every way possible to putting an end to unrest, anxiety, and suspicion. . . .

A CALL TO THE PEOPLE

. . . Gratefully I accept the messages of vigorous encouragement from the young worker of the capital and the young farmer from the arid fields of Zacatecas.

Like the first, I believe that the impulses of the new generation should be channeled toward the achievement of the highest destinies of our country, uniting all its will and all its effort in the daily forging of the nation.

Like the second, I know, as he tells me, that the young farmers of the country are fully engaged in a struggle, their weapons in hand, but that their struggle is the work in the fields and that their weapons are the hoe, the pick, the shovel, the plow handle, and the steering wheel of a tractor.

I am filled with emotion as I pay homage to those hands that seldom handle currency, that rarely feel the joy of a caress.

Those same rough and suffering hands raised a cudgel or a lance at the call of Hidalgo and Morelos; those that ignored that immensity of the desert when they hauled the carriages of Benito Juárez's glorious army; the same hands that grasped the rifle or machete under the flag of Madero, Carranza, or Zapata.

YOUTH SUFFRAGE

I shall shortly submit a bill to amend Article 34 of the Constitution.* I remain confident that the rights and duties of citizenship will be honorably exercised and complied with by youth, and that their contribution as citizens to the expression of the electoral will emphasize the real and dynamic meaning of our revolution. . . .

THE MEXICAN REVOLUTION

This step forward in the democratic process is a direct result of the profound social and economic changes brought about by the Mexican Revolution, which have given a new aspect to the country. If present-day Mexicans are more politically aware, and our increasing participation in public affairs gives meaning to the over-all system of our institutions, it is because the changes derived from the revolution have brought us broader liberties, greater material well-being, more education, better conditions in the fields of health, security, communications, and other areas.

The revolution is a long process that renews itself at every stage at great risk and peril and, as a result, demands constant vigilance and strict adherence to its principles and program of action, all the more so by those of us who have reached the higher levels of responsibility.

On assuming the presidency, I stated: "From the broad use

* The amendment lowered the voting age to eighteen.—ED.

of our liberties, our unity is born, and from our unity comes all we have achieved and ought to achieve. What has been won in so many years of effort can be lost if we do not carefully protect it each and every day."

Let us make our unity continue to be the result of the broad use of our liberties and let it go on to mean not resignation, not ambiguity, not surrender, but persistence in one's own firm convictions and respect for those of others, within the law.

II. *Bolivia: The Failure of the Institutionalization of the Revolution*

The second great Latin American social revolution of the twentieth century took place in Bolivia in 1952. The National Revolutionary Movement (MNR), under the leadership of Víctor Paz Estenssoro, united miners, peasants, and middle-class intellectuals in the overthrow of the small group of military men and tin barons who had ruled Bolivia until that time. The revolution decreed the nationalization of the tin mines, extended the suffrage to all citizens, including illiterates (*Selection 1*), and undertook a sweeping agrarian reform that gave lands to any sharecropper or squatter who desired them, although it exempted efficient producers from expropriation (*Selection 2*).

The MNR attempted to dominate the politics of Bolivia as the PRI has dominated that of Mexico. The extension of the vote to illiterates, who constitute about 70 per cent of the population of Bolivia, gave the government an effective electoral machine, especially through the peasant syndicates that were established before and after the agrarian reform. But the government began to encounter difficulties with the miners when efforts were made to run the mines more efficiently, one of the conditions of the considerable American and international aid that Bolivia received after 1952. By 1964, loss of support from the miners, MNR persecution of its political opponents, and, especially, the ambition of Víctor Paz to seek another presidential term (for which it was necessary to amend the Constitution), had greatly increased opposition to MNR rule. In November, 1964, Generals Alfredo Ovando and René Barrientos seized power in a military coup. The new rulers proclaimed their adherence to the ideals of the 1952 revolution, which they claimed Paz and the MNR had betrayed (*Selections 3 and 4*). An analysis of the coup by the American political scientist William Brill, who concludes that the coup took place because the MNR was a revolutionary party gone stale, is included as *Selection 5*. Subsequently, Barrientos built on his political base in the Cochabamba valley, using his personal appeal and his linguistic talents (he spoke Quechua, the major Indian language) to develop the popular support that enabled him to win the presidential elections of 1966.

To one unacquainted with Bolivian conditions, the 1964 coup may appear to have been a reactionary counterrevolution by the military. Yet this view ignores several factors. One was the Bolivian military's express commitment to the ideals of the 1952 revolution. A second was the fact that the continuing massive redistribution of land had transformed the Bolivian peasantry from a revolutionary into a conservative force. (See *Selection* 6 for an evaluation of the Bolivian land-reform experience.)

Ché Guevara, in choosing Bolivia as his guerrilla base (*foco*) in South America, did not take this conservatism of the peasants into account. He also disregarded the weakness and divisions of the Marxist left in Bolivia. Some of these divisions were revealed with the publication of Guevara's Bolivian diary, in 1968, with an introduction by Fidel Castro attacking the Communist Party of Bolivia (PCB) for having sabotaged the guerrilla effort. The polemic was continued with the publication of an article by Inti Paredes, one of the few Bolivian survivors of the Guevara guerrillas,* who criticized the Bolivian Communist Party for its lack of assistance to Guevara and defended the theory of the revolutionary *foco* put forward by the Castroite ideologist Régis Debray (*Selection* 7). The Moscow-oriented Communists replied by emphasizing the need for Bolivian leadership of a guerrilla effort in Bolivia (See *Selection* 8, an interview with Jorge Kolle Cueto, First Secretary of the Bolivian Communist Party.) The Chinese-oriented branch of Bolivian Communism also criticized Guevara for not giving sufficient attention to the building of a political and ideological base, and for cooperating with the "revisionists" of the Soviet-oriented party (*Selection* 9).

In April, 1969, General Barrientos was killed in a helicopter accident. Following a short period of rule by the civilian vice president, General Ovando seized power in September, proclaiming his "ideological affinity" with the radical nationalism of the military regime in neighboring Peru. Ovando's first actions on taking power—especially his nationalization of the Bolivian branch of Gulf Oil—indicate that the revolution of 1952 ˙ continues to influence the course of Bolivian politics in a leftward direction.

---

* Paredes was killed in a skirmish with government troops in September, 1969.

1. THE UNIVERSAL SUFFRAGE DECREE (1952)

(EXCERPTS)

Víctor Paz Estenssoro, President of the Republic,

Considering that it is fundamental to democracy that sovereignty be vested in the people and exercised through a system of representation; that this universally sacred principle has not been applied in Bolivia until now but that instead there has been a system of conditions for voting for public officials established for the benefit of a privileged minority;

Considering that this unjust limitation originated in the contradiction between the ideological principles that encouraged and gave form to the Revolution of Independence and the economic interests of the class that directed this historical process and, controlling political power, organized our first institutions; that this restriction was maintained throughout the life of our republic because the economic interests that established it continued to dominate landholding and increased their control of the mines;

Considering that the feudal mentality characteristic of the organizers of this political regime was unable to recognize the importance of women's participation in the life of all organized societies—a participation that was evident in the last six years in the valiant struggle of the people of Bolivia against the oligarchy;

Considering that the oligarchy denied the vote to the armed forces, members of the regular clergy, and members of the police force in order to maintain these institutions and persons as unconditional instruments of their privileges;

Considering that the national revolution will not fulfill its high and noble ends if it does not correct once and for all a political system that contradicts in practice the democratic ideals on which the revolution is founded;

Decrees:

Article 1. All male and female Bolivians over twenty-one years of age if single, and over eighteen years of age if married, shall have the right to vote, whatever their level of education, occupation, or income.

Translated by the editor from *Ley de Reforma Agraria en Bolivia* (La Paz, 1967).

2. THE AGRARIAN REFORM DECREE-LAW (1953)

(EXCERPTS)

TITLE I: AGRARIAN PROPERTY

Chapter I: Original Rights of the Nation

Article 1. The soil, the subsoil, and the water of the territory of the republic belong by original right to the Bolivian nation.

Article 2. The state recognizes and guarantees private agrarian property when this property fulfills a useful function for the national community. The state plans, regulates, and rationalizes the use of private property and works for the equitable distribution of the land in order to ensure the liberty and the economic and cultural well-being of the Bolivian population.

Chapter II: The Forms of Agrarian Property

Article 3. In addition to the goods recognized as such by law, the following are also in the public domain; highways (even though they may have been built by private persons), lakes, rivers, and all other natural forces capable of economic utilization.

Article 4. The following lands are also part of the domain of the state: fallow lands, lands that revert to the state on the expiration of a concession or by other means, unused lands outside urban areas or population centers, lands that belong to institutions and corporations dependent on the state, forests of a public character, and all lands recognized to be state property by the existing laws. . . .

Article 12. The state does not recognize the *latifundio*, which is defined as a large rural property, depending on its geographic location, which either is not being worked or is worked inefficiently with tools and methods that are antiquated and wasteful of human resources . . . [and] which depends fundamentally on the surplus value that the peasants earn as serfs or tenant laborers, which the landowner takes for himself in the form of rent-labor, thus perpetuating a system of feudal oppression that results in

---

Translated by the editor from *Ley de Reforma Agraria en Bolivia* (La Paz, 1967).

agricultural backwardness and a low level of life and culture among the peasant population. . . .

TITLE II: THE EXPROPRIATION OF PROPERTY

Chapter III: Large Estates [Latifundios]

Article 34. Territorial property defined as a *latifundio*, under the terms of Article 12, is expropriated in full.

Article 35. With respect to the previous article, a property shall not be considered a *latifundio* if the owner has invested capital in machinery and modern methods of cultivation and he or his immediate family works the land. In those regions in which the topography of the cultivable land impedes the use of machines, only work on the land by the owner or his immediate family shall be required. . . .

Chapter IV: Agricultural Enterprises

Article 36. Agricultural enterprises that, upon the promulgation of this decree-law, maintain a system of land tenants and salaried employees shall not be subject to expropriation if profits are reinvested in the amount of at least double the initial capital, and if modern agricultural techniques are employed. . . .

TITLE V: ASSIGNMENT

Chapter I: Preference in the Right of Assignment

Article 77. All Bolivians over eighteen years of age, of either sex, who engage in or wish to engage in agricultural labor shall be given lands where they are available, in accordance with government plans—provided they initiate work on the land within two years.

Article 78. Peasants who have been subjected to a feudal system of work and exploitation as serfs, compulsory workers, indentured workers, attached workers, outside workers and the like, if they are eighteen years of age, or fourteen years if married, and widows with children are hereby declared to be the owners of the plots of land that they now occupy and work until the National Agrarian Reform Service can reasonably assign the respective plots to them in accordance with the definition of small property. The Service may also give these peasants sufficient collectively worked lands to meet their family needs. . . .

TITLE IX: PEASANT ORGANIZATIONS

Chapter IV: Peasant Unions

Article 132. It is recognized that the organization of peasant unions is a means of defending the rights of its members and their

social advancement. Peasant unions shall participate in the implementation of the agrarian reform. They may be independent
or affiliated with a central organization. . . .

TITLE XIV: PAYMENT FOR EXPROPRIATIONS AND THE REDEMPTION OF AGRARIAN INDEBTEDNESS

Article 156. Expropriations that are made under Article 34
shall be paid for, proportionally to the area expropriated, by
agrarian reform bonds, which shall earn a 2 per cent annual non-
compound interest for twenty-five years. . . .

3. THE DECLARATION OF THE MILITARY JUNTA (MAY 17, 1965)

1. The Agrarian Reform Law and the other measures taken for
the benefit of the peasant are in full effect, and the government
of the Military Junta guarantees their permanent execution and
improvement.

The government of the Military Junta is determined to hasten
the legal processing of all the properties of the republic, and in this
concern it has given preferential treatment to the agrarian reform budget, which provides for the extension of this service to
all the rural areas of the nation.

2. It warns ex-latifundists, pseudo-managers, and other pro-
vocative elements that have tried to distort the truth by attempting to re-open proceedings that have been concluded or to divert
the political, social, and economic advancement of the peasants
from its path that the government of the Military Junta will
drastically crush any abuse and will defend with the utmost vigor
and energy the acquired rights of the national majority, applying
the Agrarian Reform Law without exceptions. Cases decided and
titles issued for the benefit of the peasants have full legal value
and cannot be altered, annulled, or corrected by any social or
juridical authority. The matter is decided and defined.

3. It instructs the general population and decrees that the regional, provincial, and departmental authorities shall report any
person who extracts extortion from the peasant, collects an il-

Translated by the editor from *Ley de Reforma Agraria en Bolivia* (La Paz, 1967).

legal sum as compensation for land, or exploits him in any way, so that the sanctions established by law may be applied to that person. The incorporation of the peasant into national life is the only road to national progress.

4. A MESSAGE TO THE NATION
(AUGUST 6, 1965)

RENÉ BARRIENTOS ORTUÑO AND
ALFREDO OVANDO CANDIA

On April 9, 1952, a decisive date in our history, the people tried to take political power, and fundamental changes in the political, economic, and social structures followed: the nationalization of the large mines, an agrarian reform, universal suffrage, educational reforms, and the diversification of the economy. Unfortunately, this common effort of Bolivians, which in its initial phase had a wholesome direction and was supported by all the people, was later distorted and ended in frustration, as a result of misgovernment due to the immorality, ineptitude, economic disorder, and the delusions of an arid one-partyism, as well as the political bossism that finally divided and destroyed the MNR, once the hope and later the shame of the Bolivian people.

We do not deny the past. We accept it with its successes and its errors. To criticize it, to evaluate it with justice is a duty. . . .

WHO ARE WE? WHERE ARE WE GOING?

. . . As children of the Bolivian revolution, which demands dynamic leadership in politics, solid advances in economics, and positive results in ethnic and social integration, we must assume the position of dissatisfied critics and reject the prevailing inertia, the old practices, and the dominant disorder. We must build a more rational society that will be capable of confronting the tensions of modernity.

Who are we? A young nation that is in the process of formation, surrounded by the difficulties of its setting, and torn by contradictory internal drives.

Translated by the editor from *Mensaje a la Nación* (La Paz, 1965).

We have defended our natural riches with valor, but we did not know how to exploit them intelligently. Agriculture is at the subsistence level. Mining, until a few years ago, operated solely to export capital. Industry is only beginning and needs to be protected by the state. Commerce has not developed, due to small internal markets. We have a high illiteracy rate and a permanent imbalance between our needs and our resources for educational services. Although several attempts at economic diversification have been made, principally in the east, we remain essentially an underdeveloped, one-crop producer, with huge masses anxious to be incorporated into the life of effective citizenry and to share in domestically produced consumer goods. Surrounded by mountains, deprived of direct access to the sea and to international commerce, we are not moving decisively toward the large plains of the northwest and east. Sociogeographic divisions adversely affect national unity. There is a lack of internal communication, ethnic separation, and a division of languages and communities that are not integrated in a true national state. National capital is limited and needs to be complemented by international capital. The working class, generally ill paid, was cast adrift by a policy of lies and deceit; the sacred rights of unions were turned to the wicked ends of brutal partisanship and oppressive bossism. Improvised laws were distorted in application, so that the worker was abandoned in misery. The middle classes lost their savings because of inflation. They have neither the security nor the opportunities that better organized countries can offer. Few are those who have faith in Bolivia and reinvest their earnings; they prefer to put their money in American or European banks. Until recently, lack of confidence and fear were the earmarks of the Bolivian situation.

We continue. In the countryside, things have not changed much. Landownership, to which we recently gave legal confirmation, and the abolition of serfdom are not enough to liberate the peasant and to incorporate the great Indian majorities into effective citizenship. It will take us many years to complete an integral agrarian reform, that is to say, to adapt the peasant ethically and educationally to modern life through an integrated process of planning, socioeconomic transformation, and a rise in his standard of living. In addition, the state programs for public health and social security in the countryside are dramatically weak; much has been wasted and little accomplished.

To all this we must add an antiquated juridical structure, economic disorder, and politico-social blundering that consume the best Bolivian energies in idleness, discord, and desperate struggles for government jobs. An archaic institutional regime that the post-Chaco governments altered at their whim.* Ancient codes that are often inoperative. An administrative system that is heavy and slow and cannot keep pace with the accelerated tempo of modern life. And beneath these defects of organization there is what we might call the physiology of Latin irresponsibility: public office is viewed as a means of sustenance and of gain; the common welfare and the interests of the community are disregarded, and it is not realized that government means serving, not being served.

Old flaws of ethics and of methods. Pernicious habits. A heritage of softness, of intrigue, of violent passions. A lack of adaptation of both leaders and masses—with the exception of a gifted minority—to the technological and scientific spirit, to the commerce and dynamism of the modern world.

We bog down and retrogress materially. Spiritual degeneration. This is what we encountered on November 3, aggravated by a general immorality and a profound lack of confidence in the capacity of the nation to change for the better.

Where are we going, what must we do with this picture of general confusion, retreat, and the breakdown of modern methods of social organization?

There is only one path: to advance toward a new order of things. To destroy the harmful, to eliminate the archaic, to correct the errors and omissions of the past. To move the men of Bolivia toward the goal of a vast transformation in the national organism. The ideal of a better nation, which began with Chaco, now means the urgent necessity of change in the political, social, and economic structures of Bolivia, which will give the state a new form and a more efficient administration.

We desire—and it is a desire supported by all honest citizens— a better-organized nation for a better life.

We are marching toward the Second Republic because the First has left us a terrible heritage of misfortune and frustration.

The nation wants to be reborn from the debris. And it shall be reborn!

Bolivians: Help us in this enterprise!

Before referring to the new Republic, it is necessary to review in broad strokes why the armed forces had to assume power on November 3, 1964.

If the great nationalistic ideals of 1952, when the MNR took over the government, had been fulfilled, surely the army would

---

* The Chaco War with Paraguay (1932–36) began the process of social change in Bolivia that resulted in the 1952 revolution.—Ed.

still be in its barracks. Yet when the high objectives of social progress and economic reorganization were replaced by misgovernment of unrestrained privilege and appetite, the people, led by their armed forces, determined to end the despotic regime that had destroyed human dignity and brought the country to ruin.

No one denies the nobility of the original nationalist policy or the vigor of its initial effort: the nationalization of mineral resources, an agricultural revolution to liberate the peasant, universal suffrage, economic diversification, promotion of workers' unions, the direct participation of the people in public life, educational reform—these were and continue to be the guide lines of the Bolivian revolution. Unfortunately, as our Investigating Commission has proved with irrefutable data, this great program of socioeconomic transformation was turned, in recent years, into an arid and oppressive party monopoly: politics, economics, administration, all the elements of national life, fell under the iron dictatorship of the governing class. Three hundred million dollars of American aid were largely squandered, and only a small sum benefited the people. Inflation impoverished people by wiping out their savings. Industry and commerce suffered continual extortion by the political bosses and their aides. The concentration camps, the police inquisition, the tortures and outrages to human dignity have been described in frightening books and in testimony that cannot be dismissed, that affirms the apocalyptic horror of the twelve years from April, 1952, to November, 1964.

Not social peace, not political stability, not advancement for the majority, not economic order. Instead, chaos, anarchy, a decline in the gross national product and in per capita income. Money undermined. The gold reserves of the Central Bank risked in dubious investments. Some isolated successes in the production of sugar and of rice, the handing of incomplete land titles to the peasants, universal suffrage, and educational reform—which remained a piece of paper and was not put into practice—all this meant nothing compared to the general results; fraud in the Comibol * and total failure in the nationalized mines; fraud in the agrarian reform, which did not raise the peasant from misery and backwardness but only made use of him in union demagoguery and as a source of votes for the governing party; fraud in the economy, which instead of increasing production diminished it in the principal areas, as is illustrated by the closing of mines, the failure of commercial firms and the small number of new industries; fraud in the administration of the social security laws, which

---

* The national mining corporation that operates the Bolivian tin mines, the principal source of foreign exchange.—Ed.

raised charges intolerably and produced paid idleness and banditry in union circles, which in turn engaged in deceit and abuse. Atrophy in the private sector, which saw itself vassalized and the target of constant extortion by the cliques of negotiators and businessmen of the MNR that controlled 80 per cent of all transactions. The plans for economic and social development, more theoretical than real, meant little compared to the flood of administrative ineptitude and bureaucratic corruption. The common good, the intensive development of sources of production, the creation of new elements of wealth for the nation—these were ignored in favor of more money for favorites and cabals, who came to constitute a financial "circle" [*rosca*] * more powerful than the one displaced in 1952: the plutocracy of the MNR replaced the plutocracy of the mine owners.

To all this must be added the internal split· in the governing party; misfits and puppets replaced the statesmen and politicians of the earlier era. The caprices of Paz Estenssoro reigned over the standards of dignity and decorum in the nation. The reversal of values was complete: The most capable were dismissed, and rogues and flatterers were promoted.

Political crime became the order of the day. Political bosses and opportunists operated with impunity in the cities. Law was the law of the strongest.

Wherever one looks, wherever one makes an impartial judgment of the situation, one realizes that the period of MNR rule constitutes a gigantic fraud, the "great swindle" of the Bolivian people, as one writer described it.

Paz and Lechín left only ruins, tears, corruption, and disaster.† This is the heritage that we received in November, 1964.

It is for this reason that, given the great frustration of the original movement, we again took up the pure banner of the Bolivian Revolution, in order to rectify the errors committed, to punish the crimes against the state and against humanity, and to make possible a resurgence of the national community.

* *Rosca* is the term used to describe the small elite associated with the mining companies that dominated Bolivia before 1952.—Ed.

† Juan Lechín is a leftist leader of the Mining Union. He broke with the MNR shortly before the 1964 coup.—Ed.

5. THEORIES OF MILITARY INTERVENTION AND THE BOLIVIAN CASE

WILLIAM H. BRILL

One set of reasons which leads a military establishment to intervene in politics has been advanced by S. E. Finer. These reasons
are class interests, regional interests, perception of national interest, the corporate self-interest of the military, and the self-
interest of individual officers.[1] In the Bolivian case, all of these
motivations were operating to some extent. Class interests may
have played a small role in that most officers were from the middle class, rather than from the ranks of the peasants and workers
—those elements which the MNR claimed to represent. This
middle-class orientation may in part explain the military's objec-
tion to the MNR, especially in light of the MNR's condemnation of all who had supported the pre-1952 regime. Yet it should
be emphasized that the military in 1964 was not reactionary or
linked to other opposition elements on the basis of class, and had
even come to support all of the MNR's basic reforms.

Regional interests, along with purely class interests, must also
be judged to have played a minor role in the military's intervention. Although Barrientos was able to establish a political stronghold in the Cochabamba Valley, the place of his birth, there is
no evidence that his supporters there were motivated by a desire
to secure dominance over any area in Bolivia; and although Barrientos had the overwhelming support of officers stationed in
Cochabamba, this allegiance was not regionally determined. Indeed, one of the central features of the Bolivian military, like
the military of other underdeveloped nations, is that it is less
subject to regional pressures than other institutions.

Considerable importance, however, can be attached to the military's perception of national interest as a factor influencing its

[1] Samuel E. Finer, *Man on Horseback: The Role of the Military in Politics*
(New York: Praeger Publishers, 1962).

Excerpts from William H. Brill, *Military Intervention in Bolivia: The Over-
throw of Paz Estenssoro and the MNR* (Washington, D.C.: Institute for the
Comparative Study of Political Systems, a division of Operations and Policy
Research, Inc., 1967), pp. 59–64; reprinted by permission of the publishers.

decision to intervene. This motive was evident in Barrientos' charge that Paz had corrupted the Bolivian National Revolution; and in the last months of Paz's regime, when riots and demonstrations were sweeping Bolivia, many officers may have viewed military rule as the only alternative to chaos or to a possible takeover by the left.

The military's corporate self-interest appeared to be less of a factor than might have been expected. For although the military undoubtedly had some old scores to settle with the MNR as a result of the humiliating treatment it received following the revolution of 1952, and although it deeply resented the existence of the militias and a well-armed police force as well as being required to take an oath to the MNR, it is important to note that the military was receiving substantial rewards in terms of prestige, influence, and budgetary allocations during the last year or so of the MNR regime. The motive of defending itself against a threat of status-deprivation, which was found to be an important factor in the military's intervention in Brazil, Guatemala, and Paraguay in 1954,[2] could not be cited as an active factor in the Bolivian case, although the military did have many latent objections of this type to the MNR, which surfaced as Paz's position weakened in the civilian political community.

It is for this reason that considerable importance should be given to the fifth motive cited by Finer, the self-interest of individual officers. For the ambitions of Barrientos, and his particular skills and talents—so well suited to the situation—were critical in mobilizing and giving expression to the latent discontent within the officer corps. Because Barrientos presented a respectable, promising alternative to Paz, he was also able to capitalize on the machinations of those civilian elements opposed to Paz. He thus emerged as the one man acceptable to such powerful groups as the students, the military, the FSB,* and he was also popular within the ranks of the MNR and among various peasant groups. Only the left, which was too intent upon overthrowing Paz to concern itself about his successor, failed to support Barrientos.

Although Finer's set of motivations offers a framework or typology broad enough to encompass many of the factors which influenced the Bolivian military to intervene, other considerations cited in the literature were also in evidence. Certainly McAlister's point that military intervention is most fundamentally a com-

---

[2] Ross K. Baker, "Military Intervention and Status Deprivation in Post War Latin America" (unpublished Ph.D. dissertation, University of Pennsylvania, 1966).

* Falange Socialista Boliviana, the strongest opposition party.—Ed.

mentary on the whole political system—and may indeed be a functional imperative of the system—is particularly relevant.[3] For it will be remembered that the breakup of the MNR directly preceded the military's move against Paz. Had the MNR remained intact, and managed to cross that threshold which separates a revolutionary party gone stale from a modern, aggregative party, then it is unlikely that the military would have ever considered a *golpe*. The risk would not only have been unacceptable in the absence of widespread civilian support, but as became the case in Mexico, the incentive would have been reduced as the military would probably have continued to be rewarded in its own terms by increasing pay, prestige, and a feeling of involvement in a nation that was politically stable and making headway economically.

This leads to still another reason advanced for military intervention in Latin America. Namely that it is the result of certain historical processes that have left the armed forces with the impression that they are the ultimate guardian of their country's integrity and honor. This was noticed by Needler in his study of the intervention in Ecuador in 1963,[4] and this self-image was certainly present in Bolivia. Many officers emphatically pointed out to the present author during his stay in Bolivia in 1963–1964 (well before Paz faltered), that the military had a mission to lead Bolivia toward modernity—a task that they considered it well equipped to perform because of its traditions, organization, dispersal, and predisposition to think in national terms. Even though other groups also claimed a special mandate in Bolivia—the students by virtue of their privileged position and training, the miners because of their economic importance—the military's "guardian mentality" had special importance, in that it was backed by force of arms. As Paz weakened, this self-image was reinforced by civilian groups anxious to provoke the military to move against the government.

And finally, parts of Needler's "swing man" theory [5] appeared to be operating in the Bolivian case. This theory holds that the military's decision to intervene consists of its officers' crossing a series of "thresholds of interventionism." The instigator has the lowest threshold, while the last man to join, the one whose sup-

[3] Lyle McAlister, "Changing Concepts of the Role of the Military in Latin America," *The Annals*, CCCLX (July, 1965), 85–98.

[4] Martin C. Needler, *Anatomy of a Coup d'Etat: Ecuador, 1963* (Washington, D.C.: Institute for the Comparative Study of Political Systems, 1964).

[5] Martin C. Needler, "Political Development and Military Intervention in Latin America," *American Political Science Review*, LX (September, 1966), 621–24.

port is necessary to assure the success of the attempt, has the highest threshold. This latter individual, usually a high-ranking officer, is thus the "swing man," and because of the significance of his support, he then receives a high post in the new government, even though he was not committed to the move in its earliest stages. In these terms, the "instigator" in Bolivia would be General Barrientos, and the "swing man" would be General Ovando.

The second component of this theory is less in evidence, however. This holds that because the "swing man" was least committed to the coup, he is therefore most desirous of returning to civilian rule. While General Ovando is unquestionably anxious to assure the participation of civilians in the leadership of Bolivia,[6] there is no evidence that he was any more anxious for elections than any other member of the junta.

Although many factors contributed to the military's move against Paz in November of 1964, two motives, frequently cited in the literature, did not seem to be present. First, the military did not justify its actions in terms of saving the country from Communism, as Lieuwen found to be the case in the interventions he studied.[7] To be sure, the Bolivian armed forces were decidedly anti-Communist, yet this was not at issue in the fall of 1964. The target of the intervention was the government that had broken with its left sector—a group thought to contain many Communists.

And secondly, the military was not motivated by any basic aversion to democratic procedures, for it regarded the civilian-led riots and demonstrations against Paz as nullifying the efficacy of his election. Nor was the military motivated by a desire to restore a deposed class or oligarchy, or to maintain the status quo, as is so often thought to be the case in instances of military intervention.[8] Evidence that it was not can be found in the relative speed with which new elections were called and in their proper administration as determined by OAS [Organization of American States] observers. Also relevant is Barrientos' claim that he really led a "revolution within a revolution"—one designed to cleanse

[6] Interview with General Ovando in Washington, March 20, 1967.

[7] Edwin Lieuwen, *Generals vs. Presidents* (New York: Praeger Publishers, 1964).

[8] That military intervention is generally designed to maintain the status quo and resist social and economic change is the general conclusion of both Lieuwen and Needler. See Edwin Lieuwen, "The Military: A Force for Continuity and Change," in John TePaske and Sydney N. Fisher (eds.), *Explosive Forces in Latin America* (Columbus: Ohio State University Press, 1964), p. 77; and Martin C. Needler, "Political Development and Military Intervention in Latin America," p. 618.

and purify the revolution of 1952 which had been led astray by Víctor Paz. Notwithstanding the other motivations which were also present and the several reasons that would make such a claim politically expedient, this position is an important component of the Bolivian military, and, as such, provides an example for Johnson's observation that the military in Latin America is becoming increasingly reform-minded.[9]

[9] John J. Johnson, *The Military and Society in Latin America* (Stanford: Stanford University Press, 1964), p. 152.

6. LAND REFORM AND SOCIAL REVOLUTION IN BOLIVIA

DWIGHT B. HEATH

LAND REFORM: LAW AND REALITY

My conclusions concerning agrarian reform are based on the premise that land cannot be considered as an isolated entity but has meaning only in the context of general economic and social development.

In summary, the idea of Bolivia's land reform as having been the product of grass roots action on the part of the illiterate Indian majority is not supported, but claims by the MNR that they instituted it as part of a deliberate program of social revolution must be honored in the light of historical evidence.

Furthermore, it is clear that the evaluation of the accomplishments of any land reform program must include multiple perspectives—at least distinguishing between psychological and economic aspects. Having learned what local people feel and believe, I am convinced that, in the opinion of the rural majority, Bolivia's experiment in land reform and social revolution has been enormously successful—at least in psychological terms. Increased morale and active political involvement among *campesinos* are only two of many indications of this. By contrast, an articulate but powerless minority dismisses the whole program as a culturally and

Excerpts from Dwight B. Heath, "Conclusions and Implications for Action," in Dwight B. Heath, Charles J. Erasmus, and Hans C. Buechler, *Land Reform and Social Revolution in Bolivia* (New York: Praeger Publishers, 1969), pp. 371–87.

economically disastrous triumph for a few unscrupulous demagogues. Each of these extreme views contains some truth; the
advantage of an anthropological perspective is that it allows us to
gain an awareness of both, and to weigh them against other more
objective bases for evaluation. Some of the more important successes and shortcomings, after a decade's attempt to achieve the
objectives set forth in the decree, follow.

Reallocation of Land

Officials of the National Agrarian Reform Service pride themselves on having completed what they call "the first stage of the
reform," breaking up latifundia and granting land to *campesinos*,
at least on the altiplano in the western provinces of La Paz department, throughout most of the temperate valleys in the department of Cochabamba, and in the small populated portion of
Santa Cruz in the tropical lowlands of the east. . . .

If we assume an average of only five members in each family
that received a new title to land, it is noteworthy that nearly
one-third of the total population of the country appears to have
benefited from the agrarian reform in the immediate sense of
land reallocation. It is also clear . . . that the administrative machinery for expropriation and reallocation started very slowly, and
has continued effectively ever since the ouster of MNR.

Application of the law has been colored by political considerations, so that partisans of the MNR did not lose even excess land,
whereas members of the opposition often lost land even when
they had less than legally allowable. Elaborate conditions for indemnification were spelled out too, but no one has received or
expects to receive any payment for expropriated land. The net
effect has been the granting of token plots to an enormous number of *campesinos*; the symbolic value of even a sub-subsistence
fraction-of-an-acre has evoked grass roots support among *campesinos* who were also given the vote.

Development of Indian Communities

A second major objective, development of the indigenous *com-
unidades*, autonomous traditional communities, has received almost no attention.

Revision of Agricultural Labor Relations

This third objective reflects the lawmaker's concern with effecting a thoroughgoing social revolution as well as revising land tenure patterns. In effect, the traditional social system has been
crushed; cash wages have become commonplace; and many *campesinos* enjoy a heady sense of having been "liberated" from

feudal oppression. The very denomination *campesino* [peasant]
is important, replacing the odious term *indio* [Indian], which
has become taboo.

Stimulation of Agricultural Development

The fourth "fundamental objective" of the agrarian reform was
"to stimulate greater productivity and commercialization of the
agricultural industry." Although detailed data are not available,
it appears that there was an abrupt and general drop in agricultural production in the early years after enactment of the reform. In the eastern lowlands, there has recently been a marked
increase in rice and sugar cane, the two large-scale cash crops. . . .

Implications for Action

In brief, then, the land reform must be viewed as a success if
we speak in terms of "social justice"—the back of the old quasi-
feudal order has been broken and *campesinos* are, in their own
terms, "becoming human beings." Clearly this has been achieved
at no little cost to some other human beings, but history shows
little sympathy for dethroned oligarchs. In cold economic terms,
by contrast, the reform is a mixed bag of a few dramatic successes
and several dismal failures, with very little information at all on
far too many crucial subjects. . . .

THE SOCIAL REVOLUTION

No one can deny that Bolivia has undergone a profound transformation since the National Revolutionary Movement came to
power in 1952. On the contrary, it is difficult to comprehend the
breadth and depth of changes which have revolutionized the social
order. Methods used by the party in effecting change were controversial, but there is no longer any doubt about the pervasive-
ness of change, and the durability of many innovations seems
assured. Whatever new directions may emerge, it is unthinkable
that there might be a return to the previous system. . . .

If we speak in terms of "social justice" for the masses, we must
credit MNR with having utterly destroyed the old quasi-feudal
order in most areas, by emancipating many *campesinos* from traditional economic and social bondage. It is difficult to overesti-
mate the impact of the revolution, even recognizing the fact that
a *campesino* used to spend as much as two-thirds of his time doing
unpaid and often demeaning work for a landlord, and now has
no such obligations. It is equally true, and perhaps more dramatically impressive, that *campesinos*, who had been legally forbidden to bear arms until 1952, were then given rifles, machine-guns,

and mortars so that they soon constituted a force stronger than the Army. They who had had no voice in even local administration were given the vote and became the major bloc in national politics. They who had been required to get police permission to walk on the streets of La Paz could roam through the city at will, and even use the sidewalks. Bolivia's *campesinos* were not merely admitted to citizenship in 1952; that marked virtually their induction into the status of human beings, and many have phrased it in just such terms. . . . *Campesinos* are generally proud to have the vote and their own parcel of land, however tiny; even more important appears to be a cherished intangible, *dignidad de la persona* (individual dignity). . . .

The redistribution of wealth has been more pervasive in Bolivia than many had expected. The nation still ranks with Haiti among the lowest per capita incomes in the New World, but most *campesinos* are *relatively* much more affluent now than a decade ago. On the altiplano, this is readily apparent in the prevalence of consumer goods such as bicycles, radios, and accordions, which were virtually unknown before, and in the increase in Western dress, metal roofing, and two-story houses. In some other areas it is apparent in better tools, utensils, dress, and other improvements. For many *campesinos*, personal participation in the market and money economy is a new experience, but it has become general in recent years. Furthermore, most *campesinos* appear to be eating more of the produce which they cultivate, even if their diet is no more varied than before. . . .

In sum, we have a situation in which the former elite has been virtually stripped of power and wealth. In part, these have been distributed among the rural masses, but the emergence of a new elite demonstrates the unevenness of this redistribution. The institution of a new social structure is epitomized in the MNR's semantic victory over the negative connotations of the word *indio*, which has been replaced by *campesino*. Although demagogy is still a powerful force in the countryside, one of the most striking (and, to me, frankly surprising) features of Bolivia's land reform and social revolution is the degree to which *campesinos* have begun to assume the roles of citizens and to participate in social systems that were not only closed, but virtually unknown, to them a decade ago. These achievements appear to be irreversible, so that the social revolution will probably survive subsequent changes in national administration.

7. BOLIVIAN COMMUNISM, THE GUERRILLA *"FOCO,"* AND THE DEATH OF CHÉ GUEVARA

INTI PAREDO

Our critics conclude, from circumstantial evidence, that it is our method that is wrong. They do not take into account, nor do they want to analyze, the causes that induced our partial and momentary failure. And they do not want to do it because they would have to pass judgment on themselves.

They regarded our struggle from afar. And what is more: they isolated it completely, they denied us cooperation, and they made anti-guerrilla propaganda in place of militancy. Then, to save "anti-imperialist" appearances, they issued statements of "solidarity" with the guerrilla struggle. But, in reality, this "solidarity" was no more than a few words of obligatory moral support for a small group of "romantic dreamers."

Dreamers! Yes! But dreamers who constituted, and constitute, the only force in Bolivia that is working for the taking of power by and for the people.

The leaders of the PCB [Bolivian Communist Party] speak of the preparation of the Party for the taking of power by "all means." All the people should and must participate in the taking of power. In this respect, the people must be prepared for the assumption of power, and one cannot speak to them of "all" means when one method is being used and is effective. When a party or group decides to take power, it chooses one particular method: to hold the contrary is not to think seriously of assuming power.

They have graciously decided to give up on the guerrilla method after its first defeat and to insist on the possibility of the "democratic" or reformist means, in spite of the permanent defeats this method has suffered.

Let us discard the electoral method! It cannot be the road to power for any serious revolutionary in Bolivia, or in any other Latin American country.

How many peaceful demonstrations, participated in by thousands and thousands of workers and citizens, have been violently broken up by the repressive apparatus of government, inflicting

---

Translated by the editor from *El Diario* (La Paz), July 16, 1968.

innumerable casualties. The events of May and September of 1965 are still fresh; factory workers and miners were brutally killed, almost without resistance. There is also the San Juan bloodbath of 1967, in which humble and defenseless miners were assassinated in cold blood, while our guerrilla operation, at the same time and with scarcely forty men, was launching strong blows at the same massacring army, causing it many casualties and demoralizing it internally.

We are not enemies of the people's struggles for their demands. But we are sure that these struggles will be much more fruitful if they confront a government threatened and weakened by the actions of a guerrilla *foco*.

This guerrilla *foco* shows the people, by deeds, that it is possible to confront the power of imperialism and its puppets, and not only that it is possible to confront them but that it is possible to defeat them.

The people, and especially the peasants, will not support something that does not exist for them. To expect the support of the peasants for armed struggle, when that struggle does not exist, is to play at insurrection, like those "technicians" of armed conflict who demand massive support from the peasant population before doing anything. The peasants will give concrete support to the guerrilla *foco* only when it shows them that it has power.

For this reason, the object of the struggle in its first stage is to become strong and to survive in the territory of operations; the question of aid from the cities is essential. In our case, this aid was denied us by political forces that knew of the existence of our movement.

The parties that claim to be in the vanguard of our people in the anti-imperialist struggle have the duty to be honest and to give an accounting of their actions to the people. They also have the duty to recognize their errors if they feel they have erred, or to explain their conduct if they consider it correct.

How can they explain the fact that they paid homage to the fallen guerrillas, but attacked them when they were preparing for battle?

How can they explain that Monje alerted the militants of his party to a "faction" that strayed from the "line" and that for the same reason Zamora expelled his compatriot Moises Guevara from the pro-Chinese PCB for joining the guerrilla struggle with his group? *

* Mario Monje was First Secretary of the pro-Moscow Communist Party of Bolivia. Oscar Zamora held the same post in the pro-Chinese branch of the Bolivian Communist Party.—Ed.

The people expect and demand an explanation for this dual conduct. . . .

We are certain that when the guerrillas are established in this country, and when the regular army proves incapable of destroying them, it will quickly receive the assistance of the armies of neighboring countries, in the form of both war equipment and soldiers. The revolutionary war will then spread to those countries, producing insecurity and incapacity within their own armed forces. That will be the moment at which the Pentagon will be obliged to change its policy of "advising" for one of "direct participation" by its troops, in ever increasing numbers, as happened in Vietnam.

Some pseudo-revolutionaries tremble at this prospect. They want to avoid such a "tragedy" for the people. They do not realize that to act this way is not to avoid tragedy but to maintain the people permanently under the scourge of misery, hunger, and death, immolating them on the sacrosanct altar of conformism.

This "tragedy" is not a tragedy if we compare it with what the people will suffer if they are obliged to remain indefinitely under the yoke, with the noose being continuously tightened around their neck.

Nor is it a tragedy compared to the cruel life that our people presently lead.

The mining camps are concentration camps whose inhabitants have no rights, not even that of simple relaxation, much less the right to protest.

Systematically organized massacres are the reply of the tyranny to the just requests of the people, who support the economy of the country and the luxury of the military.

No movement of protest or demand by the people is tolerated by the military, the pillar of the ruling "democratic" regime. Such movements are violently punished to serve as a lesson and to maintain the principle of authority. Anyone who rebels against these principles will feel on his own flesh the brutality and force of the military regime.

In the face of this crude reality, can we perhaps consider the sacrifices of a just war? Our struggle would not impose greater sacrifices than those our people suffer under the present tyranny.

For this reason, to create another Vietnam would not be a "tragedy." It is a duty and an honor that we will not refuse.

8. THE BOLIVIAN COMMUNIST PARTY ON THE DEATH OF CHÉ GUEVARA

JORGE KOLLE CUETO

The Bolivian revolution must be directed by Bolivians. . . . Politics must direct the revolution, as opposed to the militaristic conception of the rifle barrel over politics. From the point of view of the struggle, the facts will judge men, organizations, and their conceptions . . . . The leaders of the [Bolivian Communist] Party feel that the publication of the diary of Commander Guevara, as well as of the other materials on the guerrilla movement that took place in Bolivia, is an invaluable aid in the historical evaluation of the facts and of the role played by the Communist Party—its concepts, its principles, and its revolutionary methodology in the face of the presence and actions of the *"foco*-centered" conceptions of the revolution. . . . The information published by the foreign news agencies and the local press is insufficient for a definitive judgment. Nevertheless, we consider that basically it confirms what the Communist Party of Bolivia has been maintaining publicly since March, 1967—that the experience of Nancahuazu * serves to demonstrate to revolutionaries in Bolivia which is the best method for the victory of the revolution, and that the Communist Party of Bolivia enunciated in its Second Congress the concept and method applicable to our country. . . .

Foreign correspondents have commented on the "chauvinistic" attitude of Mario Monje because he dared to discuss with Ché who would be the political and military leader of the movement. For the revolutionary who accepts Leninism as a guide to revolutionary action, the national character [of the revolution] is unavoidable. In other words, the Bolivian revolution will have to be led by Bolivians. The international solidarity of revolutionaries is another matter. They can volunteer their advice, participating to the extent of their experience and capacity. International participation does not mean the replacement of the national by the international but the identity of the two. . . .

When Mario Monje demanded the leadership of the movement

* The location of Guevara's guerrilla activity in Bolivia.—ED.

Translated by the editor from *La Presencia* (La Paz), July 7, 1968.

if it was to take place on Bolivian territory, I think that he was considering not only the national problem but also the concept that politics should direct the revolution, as opposed to the militaristic conception that the "gun barrel should direct politics," to use the formula of Mao Tse-tung. We declare that this claim of leadership took place three months before the guerrilla action broke out, and that the leaders of the Communist Party of Bolivia were informed of the presence of Ché on Bolivian territory and his plans only after the interview of Guevara and Monje on New Year's night, 1967. . . .

9. THE DIFFERENCES BETWEEN MAOISM AND GUEVARAISM

OSCAR ZAMORA

My Party [Bolivian Communist Party] never wanted to follow the road developed by Ché, because, in the light of Marxism-Leninism, it has, in all honesty, proclaimed its differences with him over the strategy and tactics to be followed in liberating the Bolivian people from the imperialist yoke. Our point of view with respect to armed struggle in Bolivia is the following:

1. Politics must be placed at the first level in the direction of the people's war. This means that it is essential to maintain a firm Marxist-Leninist ideology and to eliminate all counterrevolutionary currents, such as contemporary revisionism.

The Party, the popular front, and the people's revolutionary army must be united in the Marxist-Leninist ideology.

2. A people's war is a political struggle of the masses, by armed means, for their liberation. Political work with the masses, particularly the workers and peasants, is inseparable from military activity. This political effort must be carried out before and during the armed struggle.

3. A people's war is developed through the three following phases: (a) war of movements, (b) war of guerrillas, allied with peasant uprisings, and (c) war of positions—that is, the taking of cities throughout the country. We consider that the bases of support, with different characteristics at each stage, are fundamental

Translated by the editor from *El Diario* (La Paz), July 14, 1968.

to victory in a prolonged war, such as the people's war, that would carry the Bolivian people to their liberation.

Our differences with him have not led us to underestimate the intrinsic value of the revolutionary personality of Ernesto Guevara. Neither has it caused us to refrain from pointing out that his grave error was to have agreed to cooperate with the revisionists in the struggle. . . .

The Bolivian Communist Party, guided by Marxism-Leninism and by the thought of Mao Tse-tung, will pursue the revolutionary line to the total liberation of our nation. Our duty is to develop the people's war to secure the liberation of Bolivia.

III. *Cuba: The Revolution Turns to Communism*

The third and most influential model of revolutionary change in Latin America is Cuba. Mexico, despite the rhetoric of its leadership and the fact that it is a country where major changes are still taking place, is no longer regarded as a revolutionary regime. The Bolivian revolution failed to maintain its original dynamic, and the present military regime, although asserting its allegiance to the ideals of 1952, is not considered a model for imitation by others. But Cuba exerts a continuing, if in recent years somewhat diminished, fascination for Latin Americans as a regime that has broken with the United States and reorganized its economic, social, and political order along the lines of its own brand of revolutionary Marxism-Leninism.

Despite the assertions of some of its critics, the Cuban revolution was not originally Marxist-Leninist. The intensely personalistic quality of the revolution is best shown by tracing the evolution of the policies and ideology of Fidel Castro, as expressed in his speeches and writings. When he came to power at the beginning of 1959, Castro repeatedly denied that the Cuban revolution was Communist (*Selection 1*). However, as a result of United States policy (and lack of policy) toward the new Cuban regime, as well as his sensitivity to the whole issue of American influence in Latin America (especially its role in the overthrow of the leftist Arbenz regime in Guatemala), Castro pursued an increasingly anti-American course, beginning in the late spring of 1959 (*Selection 2*). The United States reaction to Castro's closer ties with the Soviet Union—notably, the termination of the Cuban sugar quota in July, 1960, and the Bay of Pigs invasion of April, 1961—accelerated Castro's movement toward Communism, which he publicly embraced in a speech in December, 1961 (*Selection 3*). At that time, he announced that the various Castroite groups were being united in the Integrated Revolutionary Organizations (ORI), in preparation for their fusion in a United Revolutionary Socialist Party (PURS), organized along Marxist-Leninist lines. In 1965, the PURS was reorganized under the name of the Communist Party of Cuba. The regime, however, continues to be dominated by the personality and policies of Castro, and the Party remains distinctly secondary (*see Selection 4*). After 1961, the Cuban agrarian reform program was also revised so as to follow the Soviet model more closely. In 1963, the agricultural cooperatives established by the agrarian reform law of 1959 were reorganized into collective and state farms. (For Castro's views on the agrarian reform, see *Selection 5*.)

Cuba has become identified with a theory of revolution based on the experience of the Cuban struggle against the Batista dictatorship and calling for the export of guerrilla warfare to the rest of Latin America. In an article published in April, 1961, Castro's principal counsellor, Ché Guevara, emphasized the atypical aspects of the Cuban revolution, including the personality of Castro and the "confused" reaction of the United States (*Selection 6*). In an article published in 1963, however, Guevara outlined a general theory of guerrilla warfare, based on the Cuban experience, that was applicable to the other countries of Latin America (*Selection 7*). Castro's support of anti-government guerrillas in Venezuela led the Organization of American States, in 1964, to sever diplomatic and commercial relations with Cuba, on the grounds that it was engaged in aggression and intervention in the affairs of other states (*Selection 8*).

Despite heavy financial support from the Soviet Union (estimated at about $500 million a year), Castro has become increasingly critical of Moscow's lack of support for Latin American revolutionary guerrillas. In March, 1967, he openly attacked the Communist Party of Venezuela for its abandonment of guerrilla tactics and for its expulsion of the guerrilla leader Douglas Bravo (*Selection 9*). In a speech before the Latin American Solidarity Organization (OLAS), in August, 1967, Castro derided those Latin American Communists who support the *via pacifica*, the peaceful road to social change, and attacked the Soviet Union for giving aid to the government of Colombia rather than to the Colombian guerrillas (*Selection 10*). At the time of the conference, *Pravda* printed an article by a leading proponent of the *via pacifica*, Luis Corvalán, the General Secretary of the Chilean Communist Party. Without mentioning Castro by name, Corvalán criticized as "petty bourgeois" and "adventurist" those "Latin American revolutionaries" who were guilty of "anti-Sovietism" and who tried to create a revolutionary movement "arbitrarily and artificially around a leader" instead of around the Party (*Selection 11*). The most sophisticated and detailed expression of Cuban revolutionary ideology, Régis Debray's *Revolution in the Revolution?*, published in 1967, was also attacked by orthodox Latin American Communists for its elevation of the guerrilla over the party, the countryside over the city, and revolutionary activism over careful examination of the proper conditions for revolution. A criticism of Debray by the Argentine Communist Party is included as *Selection 12.*

The divisions on the left and, in particular, the death of Ché Guevara in October, 1967, have dimmed the prospects for Cuban-style revolution in the immediate future in Latin America. Cuba, however, still provides an alternative model of development along Marxist-Leninist lines. Whether that model is worth the price of an estimated 300,000 exiles, 30,000 political prisoners, and dependence on the Soviet Union for economic survival continues to be a subject of debate. Manuel Urrutia, President of Cuba from January, 1959, until his break with Castro in July, 1959, has expressed the opinion that Castro could have introduced reforms and promoted development in Cuba without destroying political and personal freedoms, mortgaging the economy, and saddling Cuba with an expensive military establishment. In Urrutia's view, Castro "has damaged Cuba and the free world and benefited only Russia" (*Selection 13*).

1. THE ACCUSATION OF COMMUNISM (1959)

FIDEL CASTRO

I do not know whether the calumny against the revolution—that it is Communist and infiltrated by Communism—is due solely to the fact that we do not persecute the Communists and do not shoot them. I do not know how the ideas of the revolution can be defined in such a way that there will be no more intrigues or lies than there are at present, and that the infamous attacks against our revolution will finally cease. Is it perhaps because we have a firm conviction of the freedom of mankind and the rights of man, and of equity and human equality, that we cannot conceive that anyone would desire to have rights that he keeps from others? Is it because we have pledged to carry out our ideals, not by force, but by reason and justice? On the contrary, if the theory is accepted that someone has a right to suppress others' rights, the easiest thing for the revolution would be to suppress the right to speak of everyone except those who are members of the revolutionary government. But that would not be democratic, nor is it our philosophy, for clearly the right to think and to speak belongs to all equally. Is it because we think this way, because this is our political philosophy, that the fear of Communism is being aroused, in order to incite division in the country and to unite the enemies in other countries against us? Can our revolution be accused of being Communist? Can the ideals of our revolution be confused? Have we not spoken with sufficient clarity on the doctrine of the 26th of July Movement? Are our purposes not clearly defined? Then why are these fears and fantasies pursued? Are they not trying to create obstacles for the path of our revolution? If our ideas are very clear, if the majority of the people are behind those ideas, and we are all at the command of that movement and that revolution, do the people not trust us? Can someone perhaps maintain that we have ever lied to the people? Can anyone think that we have lacked courage to speak to the people? Can anyone think that we lack the necessary sincerity to speak what we think to the people? Can anyone perhaps think that we

Excerpts from a speech delivered by Castro in the Plaza Civica, Havana, on May 8, 1959; translated by the editor from the text in *Guía del Pensamiento político económico de Fidel* (Havana: Diario Libre, 1959).

are hypocrites or cowards? Then why do we say that our revolution is not Communist? Why, when we prove that our ideals are different from Communist doctrine, that the revolution is not Communist or capitalist, that it is a revolution of its own . . . that it has its own ideology—entirely its own—which has a Cuban basis and is entirely Cuban, entirely Latin American, why then, do they start to accuse our revolution of being something it is not? It is necessary to explain once and for all that if our ideas were Communist, we would say so here, and that if our ideas were capitalist, we would say so here. We do not give anyone the right to decide for our conscience what we are and what we have a right to be.

2. A CUBAN DIALOGUE—MAY, 1959

DANIEL M. FRIEDENBERG

"Do you really think the Americans will help us?" Fidel asked sarcastically. "How can they? The Yanquis are thinking of their billion-dollar investment and we are thinking of the needs of our people. The two aims are incompatible. They are already calling us Communists, just as Ché said they did in Guatemala before they found Castillo Armas under a rock and armed him to overthrow Arbenz. Ché gave me the *Fábula del tiburón y las sardinas,* by Juan José Arévalo.* Did you ever read the book? It shows how the American Pentagon, the State Department, and Wall Street work hand in glove to suck us of our wealth. If their small investment in Guatemala forced them to invade the country for what they call democracy, what won't they do to us?"

. . . I replied † . . . "Cuba stands behind you. You are the *Jefe Máximo,* the new José Martí. The first thing we should do is have elections. We will win by such an overwhelming vote that

* *The Shark and the Sardines* (New York: Lyle Stuart, 1961) was written by a former president of Guatemala, Juan José Arévalo, following the overthrow of his leftist successor, Jacobo Arbenz, by a Central Intelligence Agency–assisted military coup in 1954.—ED.

† The dialogue represents an account by a Cuban exile of an earlier conversation with Castro.—ED.

Excerpts from an article published in *Dissent,* IX, No. 4 (Autumn, 1962); reprinted by permission.

the American people—if not their government—will see that our 26th of July Movement is the only voice of the Cubans. Then we can advance more securely to the social measures necessary to destroy the old order."

"Arbenz was elected by popular choice, and that did not prevent the American State Department from crushing him," Fidel said with a snort.

"Our case is different [I answered]. The Army was never with Arbenz and the power of the oligarchy was untouched in Guatemala. But the old Cuban Army is shattered and our militia unbeatable. Most of the corrupt plutocracy has fled and what remains can be turned to our will. We have a golden chance in Cuba, perhaps the first in the entire history of all Latin America. Let us call elections and show the Yanqui that Cuba is a *frente unido!*"

"And let Grau San Martín, Carlos Prío Socarras,* and that collection of *chivatos* [rascals] return, supported by more American dollars, to twist and confuse the minds of the people! No, thank you, Manuel, even you are naive on the question of American power. You think the good will of the Americans can help us. But it is not good will, it is *interest*, that motivates Yanqui policy. Only through destroying the roots of United States control on Cuban soil can our people recover their soul. Look at Puerto Rico. The standard of living may have risen since the Americans stole the island. And what is the result? The schools teach American culture, not Hispanic. The native customs are dying. The Negro is a degraded citizen. Even the Spanish language is being corrupted. We did not fight the revolution for that!"

Teté spoke up.

"Fidel, you are exaggerating. I lived over ten years in exile in Mexico. American investment is strong there too but it has not destroyed the Mexican spirit. Lázaro Cárdenas told the Yanquis where to get off and ever since then they have been forced to accept the autonomy of Mexico."

"But Mexico is forty million and we are six," Fidel answered. "And American investment is greater on our small island than throughout all Mexico. Besides, Lázaro Cárdenas had the exceptional luck of being president at the same time as Franklin Roosevelt, the smallest of the sharks after Lincoln, while this Eisenhower is the worst of reactionaries. No, I tell you, the Americans will try to break our revolution and the first step will be to corrupt the people against us. Let us not play into their hands with the legal *porquería* [rubbish] of elections when we have already voted

* Presidents of Cuba in 1944–48 and 1948–52, respectively.—Ed.

with our own blood and sacrifice. Ché can tell you about Americans! In Argentina the Yanquis bitterly opposed Perón because they thought their investments threatened. But Perón ended up actually proposing more concessions to Standard Oil of California! When the Americans can't buy elections, they buy the elected. If we yield one inch, the whole gang of thieves, the electric and telephone companies, the petroleum and the sugar and the mining outfits will manipulate us just as they did after the fall of Machado." * . . .

Fidel answered. . . . "According to a report Ché recently drew up, the so-called premium we get on sugar could easily be compensated by a combination of cutting off the flow of dollars to the American owners, buying goods cheaper than what we overpay them now, and selling unlimited sugar on the world market. We will do just what Lázaro Cárdenas did. We will sell elsewhere, we will crush the *pulpo americano* [American octopus] by developing new markets."

"And tobacco?" I asked.

"And tobacco, and tomatoes, and mineral ores and petroleum and manufactured goods of all kinds," Fidel answered gaily. "You classical economists get me sick. You have no vision of the energy that will flow forth from a liberated people. The underdeveloped countries are being strangled by the imperialists. Their wealth is being sucked out like a sponge. Break the chains that bind us and we can produce like they do. Are we so different? Can we not learn the industrial skills of the Yanqui? Our Cuba is the richest country of its size in the world. We have incredibly fertile soil. We have great resources of iron, copper, manganese, nickel, chromium, and cobalt. The Yanquis have built enormous petroleum refining plants here. Good! we will use them for ourselves instead of letting the profits go north."

"And whose petroleum will we refine?" I asked.

"We can import from Venezuela, from Mexico, even from the Arab states."

"But what if the international cartels block the passage?"

"Then we will defeat the capitalists!" he roared. "We will go elsewhere. We will buy petroleum from the Soviet Union, we will sell sugar to the Soviet Union! An enemy of an enemy is *un amigo*. If the United States tries to strangle us, we shall know who our friends are. And don't tell me I am a Communist. President Cárdenas sold petroleum to Hitler when he was blocked by the Yanquis, even though he loathed the Nazi system. I don't

* Gerardo Machado (1871–1939), Cuban dictator overthrown by a popular revolt in 1933.—ED.

have to be a Communist to know that I buy and sell where I can to save the Cuban revolution." . . .

"Wait a minute, Fidel," I said. "Do you mean that you agree a system should be imposed on a people even if they don't want it, because you feel it is superior and disregarding whether the people agree with your definition of superiority? But that is the reverse of democracy; it is tyranny in its old form cloaked by a new vocabulary. For it must then imply a secret police, a powerful army, a totalitarian press and propaganda machine, even torture cells—only now a man who calls himself a socialist will do the torturing instead of a man who calls himself a fascist. That is the very system we fought to destroy."

Fidel glared at me. "Manuel, you talk like a counterrevolutionary. Never lose sight of the prime enemy and don't be led astray by a lot of *intelectuales estúpidos*. Our enemy is the imperialist forces flowing from America and linking themselves with the reactionaries in Cuba that want to perpetuate the old order. These people care nothing for economic democracy or the rights of the workers for a better life. To break their chain of repression is the goal to which I am dedicating my life. And to achieve this I am willing to seek support from the progressive forces, wherever they come from. Do you realize we are the only people in all Latin America who say No to the Yanquis? Who tell the Americans that we will no longer be inferior, puppets, *sardinas* ready to be eaten by the shark? This demands strength and will, a united Cuba. And to create this unity we have to forge our own organization of iron. It may take twenty or thirty years of struggle to win. I may even fail. The Yanquis may invade us and destroy our revolution, as they did in Guatemala and, with more subtle means, in Bolivia. But we, Manuel, *we* are the future and not they. And how glorious to be able to fight for the right, knowing that the right is on our side and that history will record us, if not conquerors, at least martyrs for the truth!"

Celia turned and kissed Fidel. She was crying like Teté, but for a different reason. "*Viva Fidel! Viva el Jefe!*" she cried out. "*Patria o muerte!*"

I looked at Fidel. His mouth was clamped in a vise, his lips thin and curled in a hard line. And I shuddered. For Fidel had the absolute truth of a Loyola or Stalin, of the dedicated fanatic who creates a new set of torture chambers and concentration camps, of large armies and the eternal cycle of hunger and war. The truth, I thought! Judges, what for? Justice, what for? Truth, what for? And what is truth? But I knew that Fidel's truth, true or false, could no longer be for me. . . .

3. I AM A MARXIST-LENINIST (1961)

FIDEL CASTRO

THE REVOLUTION AND SOCIALISM

This was the method the revolution had to follow, the method of anti-imperialist struggle and of socialism—that is, the nationalization of all the large industries and businesses, the nationalization and social ownership of the basic means of production, and the planned development of our whole economy at the pace permitted by our resources and by the aid we have been receiving from outside. There is something else very favorable to our revolution: the fact that we can count on aid and solidarity, which enable us to carry our revolution forward without the enormous sacrifices that other countries are required to make.

We have had to carry out an anti-imperialist and socialist revolution. The anti-imperialist and socialist revolution had to be a single revolution because there is only one revolution. This is the great dialectic truth of humanity: imperialism, and, opposed to imperialism—socialism. The result of this opposition is the triumph of socialism, the supremacy of the epoch of socialism, the overcoming of the stage of capitalism and imperialism, the establishment of the era of socialism and, after that, the era of Communism.

If there are still any anti-Communists here, they need not be afraid. We will not have Communism in less than thirty years. This is the way it is with Marxism. One cannot simply leap over a historical stage. Perhaps the historical stage that some underdeveloped countries can omit today is the construction of capitalism—that is, they can begin the development of the economy of the country by way of planning and socialism. What cannot be skipped is socialism. The Soviet Union itself, after forty years, is beginning to construct Communism and hopes to have advanced considerably in this direction at the end of twenty years.

Thus, we are in a stage of construction of socialism. What is

Excerpts from a speech delivered by Castro on December 1, 1961; translated by the editor from the text printed in *Revolución* (Havana), December 2, 1961.

this socialism that we should apply? Is it utopian socialism? Clearly, we must apply scientific socialism. On this subject, I had to begin by saying with complete frankness that we believe in Marxism, that we believe it is the most correct, most scientific theory, the only true theory, the only true revolutionary theory. I say this here with complete satisfaction and confidence. I am a Marxist-Leninist, and I will be a Marxist-Leninist until the last day of my life. . . .

PAST ATTITUDE TOWARD COMMUNISTS

. . . This is the way it was at the first stage—the conflict between two things, in reality between prejudices, between a series of things. If a Communist was working on anything, his Communism had to be clandestine. But immediately there were the UPI, the AP, and all the American newspapers crying out "ten, twelve, fifteen Communists." It was curious in those days that they called all the comrades Communists, and there were a number of comrades who were not members of the Communist Party but members of the 26th of July Movement. They called them that already, and published their Communist antecedents to all the world. They began a campaign that, in many areas, had a response influenced by the propaganda of anti-Communism and imperialism. Fortunately for all our efforts, these stages have passed.

I think that one of the bad aspects of those first days was the lack of greater interchange among the various organizations. Each of us was going somewhat on his own. It was the same revolutionary struggle that should have been more and more in contact, in discussion, and in interchange, to promote more and more unification.

I should mention one of the things in our terrible experience. Someday, when historians write about this stage and want to describe some characteristic of [the Cuban] revolution, they may say that we were establishing a socialist revolution without socialists. At that time, there was so much anti-Communist prejudice that when a Communist functionary was assigned to the smallest matter, a wave of protest arose, followed by numerous intrigues on the subject. At that time, our methods were socialist —a collective farm, a cooperative, a nationalized industry—those were all socialist institutions. We had good comrades for those jobs—wonderful comrades of the revolutionary movement of the 26th of July—but they did not succeed. If those men did not succeed, how were we going to succeed?

One of the most difficult things, then, was to carry out a social-

ist revolution without socialists. Later, when the process of unification of the revolutionary forces and the revolutionary organizations had begun, when anti-Communism was being defeated
and destroyed, a stage came in which it was easier for a number
of the members of the [Popular] Socialist Party * to carry out
numerous functions without so much intrigue and divisionism.

THE INTEGRATED REVOLUTIONARY ORGANIZATIONS (ORI)

What was the meaning of this union? What was the significance of this moment in which the unification of all the
revolutionary organizations took place? It meant, among other
things, hundreds, thousands of cadres, of trained people, of
people who had passed through sacrifices, through hard and
difficult tests, and had a political education. On this point, I
remember that some people came to me and said, "When are
we going to carry out the program of the 26th?" And I said,
"What program of the 26th are we going to carry out? Why not
a Marxist-Leninist program?" And, "Why are we going to carry
out two Marxist-Leninist programs?" This is reality. Anything
else is a figment of the imagination.

Therefore, it meant the addition of thousands of trained
leaders, who were indispensable, fundamental, and necessary for
the creation of socialism. It signified the addition of all the
cadres of the Revolutionary Directorate.† They did not have the
number of experienced leaders that the Socialist Party had, because there were people who said that, no, they would rather do
this or they would rather do that. You have to be a complete ig-
noramus with regard to the facts of revolution to think that a
revolutionary can choose to do this or that. What we know about
all revolutions is that work is divided today among all, and it is so
great that it cannot be carried out; that many comrades, if they are
in the army, would prefer to go to a military academy; if they are
civil servants, they would prefer to go for something like a vaca-
tion to a school of revolutionary instruction. That is, the revolutionary considers it a rest—compared to the work which he must
do—to be a pupil in school.

The revolution today can count on all the cadres of all the
revolutionary organizations. The important addition of the Socialist Party has brought the cadres of the old militants educated

* The Popular Socialist Party (PSP) was the name of the Cuban Communist Party under Batista and in the first years of the Castro regime, until it
was integrated into the ORI.—ED.

† The student movement of opposition to Batista, located principally in
Havana.—ED.

in socialism by the Socialist Party. The addition of the Directorate has brought young people. The 26th of July Movement could not bring older, politically educated people but has brought many young persons who were enthusiasts and revolutionists by vocation. It has also added all the experience acquired in the seizure of power. That is, we all have brought something, one way or another, and we represent the basic forces.

These forces were asked to unite in one single organization, and they have, therefore, joined together in the ORI. It was not easy. It took a long time, and at the end they joined together into the Integrated Revolutionary Organizations (ORI). . . .

THE PARTY OF THE VANGUARD

. . . Thus, I think that the ideal system, the most perfect encountered by man for governing a country (a system that does not aspire to be eternal but simply transitory, as are the stages that the history of a country is destined to realize) is a system of government with a revolutionary, democratically organized party under collective leadership. This means that this party ought to exercise the functions of leadership.

This is the best system if democratic standards function, if the standards of collective leadership function. If democratic standards of collective leadership do not function, then the system can be very bad, like any other system. But if the fundamental principles of internal democracy maintain a collective leadership, this is without any doubt the most perfect method of government, especially for a country in a stage of revolutionary transition. . . .

So what can the party of this revolutionary people do? This party will be the great instrument of merit, the instrument of revolutionary calling and revolutionary intelligence. This party should be above individuals, because it is the party that is going to include not the value of one intelligence but the value of tens of thousands, of hundreds of thousands of intelligences; not the value of one hero, but the value of the heroism of all; not the value of one spirit of sacrifice, but the value of the spirit of hundreds of thousands of citizens and the spirit of combat, of love of the revolution. This is what the United Revolutionary Socialist Party of Cuba must be.

4. LEADER AND PARTY IN CUBA (1965)

FIDEL CASTRO AND LEE LOCKWOOD

LOCKWOOD: It is a commonly held view in my country that you are a dictator with absolute power, that the Cuban people have no voice in their government, and that there is no sign that this is going to change.

CASTRO: I think we have to state the ideas a little more precisely. We are Marxists and look upon the state as an instrument of the ruling class to exercise power. What you people call "representative democracy" is, in our opinion, the dictatorship of the capitalists, and the North American state is an instrument of that class domination, from the domestic point of view as well as from the international point of view. . . .

On the other hand, we think of the revolutionary state as an instrument of the power of the workers and peasants, that is, of the manual and intellectual workers, directed by a party that is composed of the best men from among them. We organize our party with the participation of the workers of all the centers of labor, who express their opinions in a completely free way, in assemblies, proposing and supporting those whom they believe should be members of the party or opposing those whom they believe should not be.

Our party is the representative of the workers and peasants, of the working class, in the same way that the Congress of the United States is the representative of the capitalists. So that our system is a class system too, in a period of transition. Ultimately, we will go even a little further and proclaim the non-necessity of the state, the disappearance of the state with the disappearance of social classes. When Communism is a reality, that instrument will no longer be necessary as a coercive force by which one class maintains its domination over another, since neither exploiters nor exploited will exist. As Engels said, "The government over the people will be replaced by the administration of things and by the conduct of the processes of production."

Reprinted with permission of The Macmillan Company from Lee Lockwood, *Castro's Cuba, Cuba's Fidel*, pp. 134–38. Copyright © 1967 by Lee Lockwood.

You ask about power concentrated in one person. The truth is that, although I perform certain functions inherent to the office that I hold within the state and the party, my authority to make decisions is really less than that of the President of the United States. If we are going to speak about personal power, in no other country in the world, not even under absolute monarchies, has there ever been such a high degree of power concentrated in one person as is concentrated in the President of the United States. . . .

We honestly consider our system infinitely more democratic than that of the United States, because it is the genuine expression of the will of the vast majority of the country, made up not of the rich but of the poor.

LOCKWOOD: How do the majority express this "will"?

CASTRO: By struggling and fighting against oppression. They revealed it in the Sierra Maestra by defeating the well-equipped army of Batista. They revealed it on Girón Beach [the Bay of Pigs] by destroying the mercenary invaders. They revealed it in the Escambray [mountains] in wiping out the counterrevolutionary bands. They reveal it constantly, in every public demonstration that the revolution organizes with the multitudinous support of the masses. They have revealed it with their firm support of the revolutionary government in the face of the economic blockade, and by the fact that there are hundreds of thousands of men ready to die defending their revolution.

LOCKWOOD: But if Cuba is not a dictatorship, in what way are your people able to effectively influence the leadership?

CASTRO: I believe that there is a mutual influence of the people over the leaders and of the leaders over the people. The first and most important thing is to have a genuine affection and respect for the people. The people can feel that, and it wins them over. Sometimes the leaders have to take responsibilities on their own; sometimes they have to walk at the head of the people. The important thing is the identification of the leaders with the necessities, the aspirations, and the feelings of the people. There are many ways of establishing this identification. The best way of all is to maintain the most immediate contact possible with the masses.

LOCKWOOD: Ché Guevara, in his book *Socialism and Man in Cuba*, characterizes the manner of communication between the leaders of the revolution and the people as "almost intuitive." Do you agree that there is this intuitive element in your leadership of the people?

CASTRO: At certain moments, under certain circumstances, when there is a great sense of confidence between the leaders and the masses, yes. Especially in such a convulsive process as a revolution, the intuitive element can be necessary at the beginning, but not later on, when the revolution advances and is consolidated, because in such a process millions of men raise their political culture and their revolutionary conscience; thousands of capable men arise from the masses to take on the tasks of organization, of administration, and of policy-making; and all this creates a developed culture, a powerful and organized force. Individual men begin to have less importance to the degree that the whole social task becomes more and more a collective undertaking, the work of millions of persons and the responsibility of tens of thousands of men.

LOCKWOOD: But do you feel that a kind of intuitive communication between yourself and the masses during these first years has kept you from making bad mistakes?

CASTRO: I don't know how a leader can arise or how a revolution can be led without a great sensitivity for understanding the problems of the people and without the ability, too, of formulating the means of confronting and resolving those problems. A revolution is not an easy process. It is hard, difficult. Great errors can cost the life of the revolution. Not only the leadership of the revolution, but its very life.

There must be not only intuition, an emotional communication of the leaders with the people, but there are other requisites. One has to find solutions, one has to put them into operation, one has to go forward, one has to choose the path correctly, the way of doing what has to be done. The leaders in a revolutionary process are not infallible receptacles of what the people think. One must find out how the people think and sometimes combat certain opinions, certain ideas, certain points of view, which, in the judgment of the leaders, are mistaken. One cannot conceive of the leader as a simple carrier of ideas, a simple collector of opinions and impressions. He has to be also a creator of opinions, a creator of points of view; he has to *influence* the masses. . . .

LOCKWOOD: Is the party fully organized yet?

CASTRO: It is virtually organized at the base. The leadership cadres are being organized now.[1] By the end of 1967 we will hold the First Congress, with delegates elected by the members of the party throughout the entire country. Later on, we will be in a position to promulgate the Constitution of the Socialist State.

[1] Shortly after this conversation took place, Castro announced that the name of the Party had been changed from the United Revolutionary Socialist Party of Cuba (PURSC) to the Communist Party of Cuba (PCC), and presented the names of a new one-hundred-man Politburo.

You must understand that during these years we have had first of all to defend the existence of the revolution in a bitter struggle against a powerful enemy, the United States. We have not had all the time we would have liked to occupy ourselves with dressing the revolution in its legal clothing. It was necessary first to survive, then to philosophize.

Lockwood: When will the Constitution be ready?

Castro: We have given ourselves a time limit: before 1970. And certainly it will be long before that.* We are also working on something else that is very important: the institution of decentralized local administrations. By the end of 1966 they will all be organized, and we will hold a kind of congress of local administrations that same year. It will be a great step forward.

Lockwood: These local institutions will be administered by the party?

Castro: The party does not administer. The party, acting as a kind of parliament of workers, will select the local government officers, who will have to give an accounting of their administration to all the people every six months, in popular assemblies, with the participation of all the workers of the locality.

Lockwood: And submit themselves to their questions?

Castro: To questions and proposals about all matters. And in the regions, there will be the same thing, an assembly once a year, before the delegates elected for the municipal districts.

Lockwood: What is a region?

Castro: The level intermediate between the municipal district and the province.

We think it is going to be a great school of government. It will require the party to select competent officials, and it will require the officials to do their best work, because of the constant control that there will be over their activities. We believe that in this way we are developing entirely new democratic forms, and very effective ones.

Lockwood: Would you explain what the party is and how it functions?

Castro: First, it is the revolutionary vanguard, the political organization of the workers who, manifesting the power of the state, mobilize the masses to the accomplishment of the tasks and functions of the revolution. It educates them, it organizes them, it directs and controls the administration, it draws up the plans of work and controls the carrying out of those plans. It is, in short, the political power. There is no duality, neither of powers nor of functions.

When we hold the First Congress we will be in a better posi-

---

* As of January, 1970, no constitution had been adopted.—Ed.

tion to map out all the tasks of the party; we will have a much better idea about what we have to do and how to do it. It will be a real congress which will discuss economic, social, and political problems, but it won't be an assembly of a formal character. We have always refused to fall into ceremonies and institutions of a formal type. For that reason we have chosen to go slowly and not to do things simply by formula in order to fill a vacuum without essential content. We could have drawn up a socialist constitution from the beginning, and it would possibly have been saturated with faults, with errors; whereas now, with the experience acquired during these years, we are in a position to work out a constitution that really is responsive to all the new realities of the revolution.

5. A DIALOGUE ON AGRARIAN REFORM IN CUBA (1965)

FIDEL CASTRO AND LEE LOCKWOOD

LOCKWOOD: What exactly is a people's farm [*granja*]?

CASTRO: It's an agricultural production center whose lands are the property of the nation and which is operated as an enterprise of the nation.

I will give you a more concrete example. The United Fruit Company owned some three hundred and twenty-five thousand acres of land. Its stockholders lived in the United States and received a profit there, an income, without ever having visited those lands. The company assigned an administrator—naturally they tried to assign a good one—who ran things like a huge agricultural enterprise. Today, the substantial difference is that there are no foreign stockholders who own the business and receive the profits. Today, the enterprise belongs to the nation, which uses its profits for economic and social development for all—for schools, hospitals, roads, housing for workers, the acquisition of machinery, etc.

Thus, our success consists in having a good organization, designating good administrative groups, with a further advantage that the North American company could not have. The North

Reprinted with permission of The Macmillan Company from Lee Lockwood, *Castro's Cuba, Cuba's Fidel*, pp. 90–92. Copyright © 1967 by Lee Lockwood.

American company was in constant social conflict with the workers, while the *granja* acts in permanent cooperation with the workers, who have their party organizations, their union organizations, their youth organizations, their women's organizations, who work there, who study, who receive the greater part of the profits and many benefits they did not receive before, who have the possibility of progressing in accordance with their level of experience and preparation, since from their own ranks come the men who occupy the posts of management and of responsibility.

And this also allows us to introduce mechanization. The company could not introduce mechanization. Why? Because there was a lot of unemployment in the country. If they had gone ahead and put in a machine to cut the sugar cane, the workers would not have permitted it, because that would have meant a shortening of the three or four months of the year in which they worked, a reduction of their incomes. Today, since there is work for all, no laborer fears the machine or looks upon it as an enemy, but on the contrary he sees the machine as a friend, because he is changed from a manual worker to a mechanical worker who is going to have better living conditions, more income, and easier work.

Finally, the company had to limit production because the country had limited markets. It had no reason for introducing fertilizers, irrigation, or methods of extensive production. Today, we are able to apply all these methods and increase production as much as we want, because we have the markets. We maintain full employment, and at the same time we considerably improve the living conditions of the workers and their families.

Alongside the system of people's farms there still exists the system of small landowners who own their own farms. The small farmers can hold up to one hundred and sixty acres of land. Of course, in a country like Japan, one hundred and sixty acres would be considered a vast estate, but in Cuba they are considered small farms. Also, there are some exceptions made for very efficient farmers who have always completely fulfilled their obligations to the state. Under the policy adopted by the Second Agrarian Reform Law toward the most competent, dependable, and hard-working farmers, there are some unusual cases of holdings up to nine hundred acres.

The revolutionary government sustains these individual landowners; it gives them credit and resources and buys their surplus produce, whatever they do not need for their own consumption. They can even sell individually, provided it is not in wholesale quantities. A neighbor who wants to buy from them, individual people, thus can go and buy.

Obviously, there are some exceptions. A product like sugar cane, which requires an industrial process, can only be bought by the sugar mill. But many other things, like eggs, chickens, and milk, can be traded freely on a small scale. Sales in large amounts are made only by the state.

LOCKWOOD: There is a limit on how much they may sell?

CASTRO: They cannot sell over a certain quantity in each case. They can sell to any family as much as they wish to buy for their own consumption.

What happened, for example, with regard to eggs? Before, when production was limited, the small farmers sold eggs at an exorbitant price, at thirty cents an egg. When the government's program of egg production was developed, the price was reduced to six, seven, and eight cents. They can now consume the eggs they produce or sell them at that price, which is a fair one. The best way to fight speculation, in our experience, is not by taking measures of a legal nature, but by increasing production.

Although some small farmers have organized their own co-operatives, we do not exert pressure on them to do so. In fact, we are not even interested in organizing them into cooperatives. Why? First of all, out of respect for their traditions, for their habits as small individual property owners. Any effort to organize cooperatives could have clashed in part with those feelings. Second, because we believe that with the passage of time every one of these small farms will progressively become a part of the National Common Lands Fund. How? Through expropriation? No. Through new agrarian reforms? No; we have promised them that the era of agarian reform laws is already ended. How, then? By buying the land whenever there is a farmer who wishes to sell out. . . .

LOCKWOOD: How many small farmers are there in Cuba now?

CASTRO: There must be, I believe, some one hundred and fifty thousand, counting the smallest. But actually, considering only those with any kind of economic productivity, I figure that there must be around one hundred thousand.

At present, 70 per cent of the land is nationalized, 30 per cent is privately owned. It does not matter to us if within twenty years 20 per cent of the land is privately owned, if within forty years 90 per cent is nationalized and 10 per cent is privately owned. It doesn't matter how long it takes. It will be a completely evolutionary process.

6. CUBA, HISTORICAL EXCEPTION? (1961)

CHÉ GUEVARA

We accept the fact that there have been exceptional factors that have given our revolution peculiar features, and it is an established fact that each revolution depends on such special factors. But it is no less established that all revolutions will follow laws than cannot be violated by society. Let us therefore analyze the factors of this so-called special case.

The first, and perhaps the most important, the most original, is that massive force called Fidel Castro—a name that in just a few years has attained historic significance and whose merits we consider worthy of comparison with those of the most outstanding figures in Latin American history. Fidel is a man of tremendous personal magnetism, destined to assume the role of leader in any movement in which he takes part. He has all the characteristics typical of a great leader: audacity, force, the desire to keep his ear attuned to the will of the people. But he has other important qualities: the capacity to absorb knowledge and experience, a grasp of the over-all picture in a given situation, boundless faith in the future. . . . Fidel Castro did more than anyone else in Cuba to construct the now formidable apparatus of the revolution.

Nevertheless, no one can affirm that there were political and social conditions in Cuba that were totally different from those in any other country of the hemisphere, that it was precisely because of such difference that the revolution came about. Nor can it be charged that Fidel Castro made the revolution. Fidel directed the Cuban Revolution, interpreting the profound political unrest that was preparing the people for the great leap along the road to revolution. Certain conditions also existed that were not peculiar to Cuba but that could, with difficulty, be utilized again by other peoples, for the reason that imperialism—unlike some progressive groups—does learn from its mistakes.

The condition that we might describe as exceptional is that

From Luis Aguilar (ed.), *Marxism in Latin America* (New York: Alfred A. Knopf, 1968), pp. 173–79. Copyright © by Alfred A. Knopf, Inc. Reprinted by permission of the publisher.

North American imperialism was confused and was thus never able to assess the true extent of the Cuban revolution. By the time imperialism wanted to react, when it realized that the group of inexperienced young men who were parading the streets of Havana in triumph were clearly aware of their political responsibilities and had an iron resolve to carry them out, it was already too late.

We do not consider that there was anything exceptional in the fact that the bourgeoisie, or a large part of this sector, showed itself in favor of the revolutionary war, while at the same time it sought solutions that would make possible the replacement of the Batista government by elements that would be disposed to hold the revolution in check. Nor was there anything exceptional in the fact that some of the latifundist elements adopted a neutral attitude, or at least one of nonbelligerency toward the insurrectionist forces. In this way, nonrevolutionary forces in effect helped smooth the road to political power for the revolutionary forces.

By going one step further, we can point out another exceptional factor: In the majority of the localities in Cuba, the peasants had become proletarianized by the demands of the great capitalist, semimechanized farms and had attained greater class consciousness. But we must add that, throughout the original territory first dominated by the rebel army, there was a rural population of a different social and cultural origin from that which was to be found in the settlements around the large semimechanized farms in Cuba. In effect, the Sierra Maestra is a place where the peasants go to seek a new plot of land, where they wrest land from the state or from some greedy landholder, to find a refuge. The soldiers who constituted our first guerrilla army of peasants came from the latter group, a group that had already demonstrated in the most aggressive manner a love for the land and a desire to possess it, a group that displayed what might be termed "the spirit of the petty bourgeoisie." The peasant fights because he wants land, for himself, for his children, and wants to control it, to be able to sell it, and to improve his lot by working it.

Regardless of that spirit, the peasant quickly learns that he cannot satisfy his desire to possess the land without breaking up the latifundia system. Radical agrarian reform, which is the only way to give land to the peasant, runs counter to the interests of the imperialists, the large landholders, and the sugar and livestock magnates. The bourgeoisie is afraid to go against such interests; the proletariat is not afraid. Thus, the progress of the revolution unites the workers and the peasants. . . .

There are also conditions that will make the struggle more difficult in other countries of America. Imperialism has learned its lesson, and it will not let itself be taken by surprise in any corner of the hemisphere. The bourgeoisie of the various countries, despite their differences with imperialism, are in general incapable of maintaining a coherent position of opposition to imperialism: They fear the revolution more than they fear the despotic domination of the imperialists. The upper middle class is openly opposed to the revolution and does not hesitate to ally itself with imperialism and the feudal landowners in order to block the revolution's path.

Even when there exist great urban concentrations, it may be advisable to base the campaign outside the cities. The presence of a nucleus of guerrillas in the mountains maintains a continuing focus of rebellion.

7. GUERRILLA WARFARE: A METHOD (1963)

CHÉ GUEVARA

We consider that the Cuban revolution made three fundamental contributions to the laws of the revolutionary movement in the current situation in [Latin] America. They are: Firstly, people's forces can win a war against the army. Secondly, we need not always wait for all the revolutionary conditions to be present; the insurrection itself can create them. Thirdly, in the underdeveloped parts of America the battleground for armed struggle should in the main be the countryside. . . .

In all the countries in which oppression becomes unbearable, the banner of rebellion must be raised, and this banner of historical necessity will have a continental character. As Fidel said, the Andes will be the Sierra Maestra of America, and all the immense territories that make up this continent will become the scene of a life-and-death struggle against the power of imperialism.

We cannot tell when this struggle will acquire a continental character, or how long it will last; but we can predict its advent

Excerpts from an article published in *Cuba Socialista* (Havana), No. 25 (September, 1963); translated in a pamphlet published by the Foreign Languages Press, Peking, 1964.

and its triumph, because it is the inevitable result of historical, economic, and political conditions and its direction cannot be changed. It is the task of the revolutionary force in each country to initiate [the struggle] when the conditions are present, regardless of the situation in other countries. The general strategy will emerge as the struggle develops. The prediction of the continental character of the struggle is borne out by analysis of the strength of each contender, but this does not in the least exclude independent outbreaks. Just as the beginning of the struggle in one part of a country is bound to develop it throughout its area, the beginning of a revolutionary war contributes to the development of new conditions in the neighboring countries.

The development of revolution has normally produced high and low tides in inverse proportion; to the revolutionary high tide corresponds the counterrevolutionary low tide, and conversely, at moments of revolutionary decline, there is a counterrevolutionary ascendency. At such moments, the situation of the people's forces becomes difficult, and they should resort to the best defense measures in order to suffer the least loss. The enemy is extremely powerful, continental in stature. Therefore, the relative weaknesses of the local bourgeoisie cannot be analyzed with a view to making decisions within restricted limits. Still less can one think of an eventual alliance of these oligarchies with an armed people. The Cuban revolution has sounded the alarm. The polarization of forces is becoming complete: exploiters on one side and exploited on the other. The mass of the petty bourgeoisie will lean to one side or the other according to their interests and the political skill with which it is handled; neutrality will be an exception. This is how revolutionary war will be.

Let us consider the way in which a guerrilla *foco* may start.

Nuclei of relatively few persons choose places favorable for guerrilla warfare, sometimes with the intention of launching a counterattack or to weather a storm, and there they begin to take action. But the following must be made clear: At the beginning, the relative weakness of the guerrilla fighters is such that they should endeavor to pay attention only to the terrain, in order to become acquainted with the surroundings, establish connections with the population, and fortify the places that eventually will be converted into bases.

The guerrilla unit can survive only if it starts by basing its development on the three following conditions: constant mobility, constant vigilance, constant wariness. Without the adequate use of these elements of military tactics, the unit will find it hard to survive. It must be remembered that the heroism of the guerrilla fighter at such times consists in the scope of the planned objective and the long series of sacrifices that must be made in order to attain it.

These sacrifices will not mean daily combat or face-to-face struggle with the enemy; they will assume forms more subtle and difficult for the individual guerrilla fighter to endure physically and mentally.

The guerrillas will perhaps suffer heavily from the attacks of enemy armies, at times be split up while those taken prisoner will be martyred. They will be pursued like hunted animals in the areas they have chosen to operate in, with the constant anxiety of having the enemy on their track, and on top of all this with the constant doubt that in some cases the terrorized peasants will give them away to the repressive troops in order to save their own skins. They have no alternative but death or victory, at times when death is a concept a thousand times present and victory a myth that only a revolutionary can dream of.

That is the heroism of the guerrilla. That is why it is said that to be on the march is also a form of fighting and to avoid combat at a given moment is another form. Faced with the general superiority of the enemy, the way to act is to find a form of tactics with which to gain a relative superiority at a chosen point, either by being able to concentrate more troops than the enemy or by making the best use of the terrain to secure advantages that upset the correlation of forces. In these conditions tactical victory is assured; if relative superiority is not clear, it is preferable not to take action. As long as one is in a position to choose the "how" and the "when," no battle should be fought that will not end in victory.

Guerrilla forces will grow and be consolidated within the framework of the great politico-military action of which they are a part. And within this framework they will go on forming the bases that are essential for their success. These bases are points that the enemy can penetrate only at the cost of heavy losses; they are bastions of the revolution, both shelters and starting points for bolder and more distant raids.

Such a time will come if the difficulties of both tactical and political discipline have been overcome. The guerrillas must never forget their function as the vanguard of the people, the mandate entrusted to their care, and therefore they should create the necessary political conditions for the establishment of a revolutionary power based on the full support of the masses. The main demands of the peasantry should be met to the degree and in the form that circumstances permit, so as to bring about the unity and solidarity of the whole population.

If the military situation is difficult from the first moments, the political situation will be no less delicate; and if a single military error can wipe out the guerrillas, a political error can check their development for a long period.

The struggle is politico-military; so it must develop, and so it must be understood.

In the course of its growth, guerrilla fighting reaches a point at which its capacity for action covers a given region, for which there are too many men and too great a concentration. Then begins the beehive action, in which one of the commanding officers, a distinguished guerrilla, hops to another region and repeats the chain development of guerrilla warfare, but still subject to a central command.

Now, it is necessary to point out that one cannot hope for victory without the formation of a people's army. The guerrilla forces can be expanded to a certain size; the people's forces in the cities and in other enemy-occupied zones can inflict losses, but the military potential of the reactionaries would remain intact. It must always be remembered that the final outcome should be the annihilation of the enemy. Therefore, all these new zones that have been created, as well as the penetrated zones behind the enemy lines and the forces operating in the principal cities, should be under a unified command. It cannot be claimed that there exists among guerrilla forces the closely linked chain of command that characterizes an army, but there is a strategic command. Within certain conditions of freedom of action, the guerrillas should carry out all the strategic orders of the central command, which is set up in one of the safest and strongest areas, preparing conditions for the union of the forces at a given moment.

The guerrilla war, or war of liberation, will generally have three stages: First, the strategic defensive, when a small force nibbles at the enemy and makes off, not to shelter in passive defense within a small circumference but rather to defend itself by limited attacks that it can carry out successfully. After this comes a state of equilibrium, during which the possibilities of action on the part of both the enemy and the guerrillas are established; then comes the final stage of overrunning the repressive army, ending in the capture of the big cities, large-scale decisive encounters, and the total annihilation of the enemy.

After reaching a state of equilibrium, when both sides are on guard against each other, in the ensuing development guerrilla war acquires new characteristics. The concept of maneuver is introduced: Big columns attack strong points, and there is mobile warfare, with the shifting of forces and of considerable means of attack. But owing to the capacity of resistance and counterattack that the enemy still retains, this war of maneuver does not entirely replace guerrilla fighting; it is only one form of action taken by the larger guerrilla forces until finally they crystallize into a people's army with army corps. Even at this time, the guerrillas will play their "original" guerrilla role, moving ahead of the actions of the main forces, destroying communications and sabotaging the whole defensive apparatus of the enemy.

We have predicted that the war will be continental. This means it will be protracted; it will have many fronts, and will cost much blood and countless lives over a long period. But besides this, the phenomena of polarization of forces that are occurring in America, the clear division between exploiters and exploited that will exist in future revolutionary war, mean that when the armed vanguard of the people seize power, the country or countries that attain it will at one and the same time liquidate both their imperialist and national exploiting class oppressor. The first stage of the socialist revolution will have crystallized; the people will be ready to staunch their wounds and begin to build socialism.

8. CUBAN INTERVENTION IN THE HEMISPHERE

THE ORGANIZATION OF AMERICAN STATES

I. EXCERPTS FROM THE REPORT OF THE INVESTIGATING COMMITTEE APPOINTED BY THE COUNCIL OF THE OAS, ACTING PROVISIONALLY AS ORGAN OF CONSULTATION, FEBRUARY 18, 1964

V. Conclusions

A.

In formulating its conclusion, the committee considers it pertinent to make some general observations on the policy of intervention in the hemisphere of the present government of Cuba, which has been substantiated in the investigation of the charges made by Venezuela:

Reprinted from U.S. Department of State, *American Foreign Policy, Current Documents, 1964* (Washington, D.C.: U.S. Government Printing Office, 1967).

1. The present government of Cuba since its institution in 1959 has carried on, supported, and directed in various ways a policy of intervention in the hemisphere through propaganda methods, provision of funds, training in sabotage and guerrilla operations, and the supply of arms to support those movements that seek to subvert national institutions through force in order to install Communist regimes.

2. This support of subversion, which generally takes the form of political aggression, has had positive application in the Republic of Venezuela, the primary objective in Cuba's policy of expansion and ideological penetration in the hemisphere. The vast natural resources of Venezuela, its strategic importance in the hemisphere, and its status as a democratic country were factors that motivated the present government of Cuba to make use of the subversive action of organizations that employ force and violence to overthrow that democratic government.

B.

1. The Republic of Venezuela has been the target of a series of actions sponsored and directed by the Government of Cuba, openly intended to subvert Venezuelan institutions and to overthrow the democratic Government of Venezuela through terrorism, sabotage, assault, and guerrilla warfare.

2. A characteristic manifestation of this policy of aggression has been the systematic and hostile propaganda campaign carried out through information organs that are under the control of the government of Cuba and that are directed against Venezuelan institutions, the President of the Republic, and other high government officials, inciting the people of Venezuela to rebellion and, in addition, giving direct support to subversive movements.

3. Other manifestations of this policy of aggression are found in the supply of funds and the indoctrination and training in Cuba of numerous Venezuelans who later returned to their country to participate in subversive movements.

4. An important element in this intervention in Venezuela, directed by the government of Cuba, was the shipment of arms that was found on the Peninsula of Paraguana in the state of Falcón on November 1, 1963, close to the date of the general elections. The shipment was made up of arms originating in Cuba that were surreptitiously landed at a solitary spot on the coast, for the purpose of being used in subversive operations to overthrow the constitutional government of Venezuela.

With respect to this shipment, the following facts are noteworthy:

a. The perforations and obliterations that were made on the various weapons in places where the Cuban coat of arms and other identifications marks had been stamped, in an effort to hide their well-known Cuban origin.

b. The conditioning and packing of the arms for immediate use, the quantity and quality of the arms, and the instructions for their use, which were found in the hands of Communist groups. These arms were to be used to support subversive activities and guerrilla action by organizations disciplined and trained for such purposes.

c. The discovery, at the same spot where the shipment of arms was found, of a boat with an outboard motor, which motor was sent from Montreal, Canada, to Havana by air on October 1, 1963, for delivery to the National Institute of Agrarian Reform of Cuba, an official institution of that country.

5. The policy of aggression on the part of the government of Cuba was confirmed by the discovery on November 4, 1963, by Venezuelan authorities, of a plan of operations, the "Caracas Plan," prepared for the subversive action of the so-called Armed Forces of National Liberation. This plan anticipated the use of arms similar in type and numerical proportion to the shipment of arms mentioned in the preceding paragraph. The objective of the plan was to capture the city of Caracas, to prevent the holding of elections on December 1, 1963, and to seize control of the country.

6. Consequently, the acts of intervention that have been outlined, and in particular, the shipment of arms, constitute a policy of aggression on the part of the present government of Cuba against the territorial integrity, the political sovereignty, and the stability of the democratic institutions of Venezuela.

II. EXCERPTS FROM THE FINAL ACT OF THE NINTH MEETING OF CONSULTATION OF MINISTERS OF FOREIGN AFFAIRS OF THE AMERICAN REPUBLICS (WASHINGTON, D.C., JULY 21–26, 1964) *

I

Application of Measures to the Present Government of Cuba

The Ninth Meeting of Consultation of Ministers of Foreign Affairs, serving as Organ of Consultation in application of the Inter-American Treaty of Reciprocal Assistance,

Having seen the report on the investigating committee designated on December 3, 1963, by the Council of the Organization of American States, acting provisionally as Organ of Consultation, and

Considering:

That the said report establishes among its conclusions that "the Republic of Venezuela has been the target of a series of actions sponsored and directed by the government of Cuba, openly intended to subvert Venezuelan institutions and to overthrow the democratic government of Venezuela through terrorism, sabotage, assault, and guerrilla warfare," and,

That the aforementioned acts, like all acts of intervention and aggression, conflict with the principles and aims of the inter-American system,

Resolves:

1. To declare that the acts verified by the Investigating Committee constitute an aggression and an intervention on the part of the government of Cuba in the internal affairs of Venezuela, which affects all of the member states.

2. To condemn the present government of Cuba for its acts of aggression and of intervention against the territorial inviolability, the sovereignty, and the political independence of Venezuela.

3. To apply, in accordance with the provision of Articles 6 and 8 of the Inter-American Treaty of Reciprocal Assistance, the following measures: (a) that the governments of the American

---

* The Final Act, signed on July 26, 1964, was adopted by a vote of 15–4, with Bolivia, Chile, Mexico, and Uruguay casting negative votes. Venezuela, a party to the complaint, was not eligible to vote.—ED.

states not maintain diplomatic or consular relations with the government of Cuba; * (b) that the governments of the American states suspend all their trade, whether direct or indirect, with Cuba, except in foodstuffs, medicines, and medical equipment that may be sent to Cuba for humanitarian reasons; and (c) that the governments of the American states suspend all sea transportation between their countries and Cuba, except for such transportation as may be necessary for reasons of a humanitarian nature.

4. To authorize the Council of the Organization of American States, by an affirmative vote of two-thirds of its members, to discontinue the measures adopted in the present resolution at such time as the government of Cuba shall have ceased to constitute a danger to the peace and security of the hemisphere.

5. To warn the government of Cuba that if it should persist in carrying out acts that possess the characteristics of aggression and intervention against one or more of the member states of the Organization, the member states shall preserve their essential rights as sovereign states by the use of self-defense in either individual or collective form, which could go so far as resort to armed force, until such time as the Organ of Consultation takes measures to guarantee the peace and security of the hemisphere. . . .

II

Declaration to the People of Cuba †

Whereas:

. . . The present government of Cuba, identifying itself with the principles of Marxist-Leninist ideology, has established a political, economic, and social system alien to the democratic and Christian traditions of the American family of nations and contrary to the principles of juridical organization upon which rest the security and peaceful harmonious relations of the peoples of the hemisphere; and

The exclusion of the present government of Cuba from participation in the inter-American system, by virtue of the provisions of Resolution VI of the Eighth Meeting of Consultation of Min-

---

* At the time of the meeting, only four Latin American countries still maintained diplomatic relations with Cuba. As a result of this resolution, Chile, Bolivia, and Uruguay broke off relations, leaving Mexico as the only American republic maintaining diplomatic relations with Cuba.—ED.

† Adopted by a vote of 16-0-3, with Bolivia, Chile, and Mexico abstaining. —ED.

isters of Foreign Affairs, by no means signifies any intention to deny the Cuban people their rightful place in the community of American peoples;

The Ninth Meeting of Consultation of Ministers of Foreign Affairs, serving as Organ of Consultation in application of the Inter-American Treaty of Reciprocal Assistance,

Declares:

That the free peoples of the Americas are convinced that the inter-American system offers to the Cuban people unequalled conditions for the realization of their ideals of peace, liberty, and social and economic progress;

That the peoples belonging to the inter-American system are in complete sympathy with the Cuban people in all their sufferings, in the face of the total loss of their liberty both in the spiritual domain and in the social and economic field, the denial of their most elementary human rights, the burden of their persecutions, and the destruction of a legal system that was open to improvement and that offered the possibility of stability; and

That, within this spirit of solidarity, the free peoples of America cannot and must not remain indifferent to or uninterested in the fate of the noble Cuban people, which is oppressed by a dictatorship that renounces the Christian and democratic traditions of the American peoples; and in consequence

Expresses:

1. Its profound concern for the fate of the brother people of Cuba.

2. Its deepest hope that the Cuban people, strengthened by confidence in the solidarity with them of the other American peoples and governments, will be able, by their own endeavor, very soon to liberate themselves from the tyranny of the Communist regime that oppresses them and to establish in that country a government freely elected by the will of the people that will assume respect for fundamental human rights.

3. Its firm conviction that the emphatic condemnation of the policy of the present Cuban government of aggression and intervention against Venezuela will be taken by the people of Cuba as a renewed stimulus for its hope that there will come to prevail in that country a climate of freedom that will offer to man in Cuba a favorable environment for the development of his personality and the realization of his just aspirations.

9. THE ERRORS OF THE VENEZUELAN COMMUNIST PARTY (1967)

FIDEL CASTRO

There is no doubt that the Venezuelan revolutionaries, like all revolutionaries everywhere, committed mistakes in both strategy and tactics. The fact that the revolutionary movement was strongest in the capital while, as in the case of many other Latin American countries, it was very weak in the countryside, due to the inactivity of the Communist Party, contributed to those mistakes. Why? Because the [Latin American] Marxist parties preferred to concentrate their attention on the cities and in many cases (although there are exceptions to this generalization) greatly underestimated the importance of the peasantry as a revolutionary force. . . .

The revolutionary leadership of the [Venezuelan Communist] Party tried to direct the guerrillas from the capital. It did not do what it should have done, what a bold and truly revolutionary leadership would have done, what the leaders of all successful contemporary historic movements have done—go to the mountains and join the guerrillas, direct the war from the field of battle, direct the war from the mountains.

It is absurd and almost criminal to try to lead the guerrillas from the city. The city and the countryside are two things so different and distinct, two scenes so completely dissimilar, that it is madness to wish to lead the guerrillas from the city. And the guerrillas were not really considered as a force that could develop and take revolutionary power in countries like ours but as a tool to exert pressure, an instrument for political maneuvering or negotiation. . . .

For us, the international Communist movement is first of all a movement of Communists, or fighters, for the revolution. And whoever is not a fighter for the revolution cannot be called a Communist. We conceive of Marxism as revolutionary thought and action. Those who do not possess a true revolutionary spirit cannot call themselves Communists. . . .

Excerpts from a speech delivered by Fidel Castro, March 13, 1967; translated by the editor from *Punto Final* (Santiago, Chile), April 1–15, 1967.

The international Communist movement, as we understand it, is not a church or a religious or Masonic sect that obliges us to sanctify every weakness, to consecrate every error, to be associated with every kind of reformist and pseudo-revolutionary. Our position with respect to the Communist parties is based on strictly revolutionary principles. Above all, we support those parties that hold a line without vacillation or weakness, the parties that in our judgment follow a consistently revolutionary line. But parties which think that because they have the name "Communist" or "Marxist" in their title they have a monopoly on revolution, when in reality they only represent reform, we do not consider as revolutionary parties. And if those who call themselves Communists in any country do not know how to fulfill the requirements of Marxism, we will support those who, although they do not call themselves Communists, act like true Communists in action and struggle.

Every true revolutionary who has within himself the spirit of revolution and a vocation as a revolutionary will end up as a Marxist. It is impossible for a man with a revolutionary calling who is on the road to revolution not to end as a Marxist. Every consistent revolutionary on this continent will arrive at the Marxist conception of society. And they are the ones who matter, the revolutionaries who are able to make revolutions and to develop in the revolutionary struggle.

Often, practice comes first and theory afterward. Our [Cuban] people are an example of this, for the immense majority of those who today proudly proclaim themselves to be Marxist-Leninists came to Marxism by way of the revolutionary struggle. . . .

The revolution that arose out of nothing, the revolution that arose out of a small group of men who lived for years surrounded by forces through which nothing could pass, is a revolution with its own right to exist, and a revolution—hear this, you puppets, oligarchs, vacillators, and pseudo-revolutionaries of all types—that nothing and nobody can destroy or delay. And this revolution will maintain its own absolutely independent position with that independence that belongs by right to people who know how to fight, who possess dignity. And we proclaim it to the world, this revolution will follow its course, this revolution will follow its own line, this revolution will never be a satellite of anybody, and it will never seek permission from anybody to maintain its own ideological position domestically and internationally. With head held high and a proud heart in its breast, this people will face the future, whatever it may be.

10. SPEECH TO THE CONFERENCE OF THE LATIN AMERICAN SOLIDARITY ORGANIZATION (OLAS) (1967)

FIDEL CASTRO

What distinguishes the true revolutionary from the false revolutionary is precisely this: One acts to move the masses, the other waits for the masses as a whole to acquire awareness before starting to act.

A whole series of principles exists that one should not expect to be accepted without an argument, but which are essential truths, accepted by the majority, but with reservations by a few. This Byzantine discussion about the ways and means of struggle, whether it should be peaceful or nonpeaceful, armed or unarmed —the essence of this discussion, which we call Byzantine because it is like an argument between two deaf and dumb people, is what distinguishes those who want to promote revolution from those who do not want to promote it, those who want to curb it from those who want to promote it. Let no one be fooled.

Different terms have been employed: Whether this is the only way, or not the only way; whether it is exclusive, or not exclusive. And the Conference has been very clear about this. It has not used the term "the only way," although it could be called the only way; it has referred, instead, to the fundamental way, to which the other forms of struggle must be subordinated. And, in the long run, it is the only way. To use the word "only" —although the sense of the word is understood, and it is the right word—might lead to erroneous thinking about the immediacy of the struggle.

That is why we understand that the Declaration's * reference to [revolution as] the fundamental way, as the road· that must be taken in the long run, is the correct formulation.

If we wish to express our way of thinking, that of our Party and our people, let no one harbor any illusions about seizing power by peaceful means in any country of this continent. Let no one harbor any such illusions. Anyone who tries to sell such an idea to the masses will be deceiving them completely.

* The Second Declaration of Havana, adopted at the Conference.—ED.

Reprinted from *Granma* (Havana) (English ed.), August 20, 1967.

This does not mean that tomorrow one has to go out and grab a rifle, anywhere at all, and start fighting. That is not the question. It is a question of ideological conflict between those who want to make revolution and those who do not want to make it. It is the conflict between those who want to act and those who want to hold back. Because, essentially, it is not that difficult to decide if it is possible, if conditions are ripe, to take up arms or not.

No one can be so sectarian, so dogmatic, as to say that, everywhere, one has to go out and grab a rifle tomorrow. And we ourselves do not doubt that there are some countries in which this is not an immediate task, but we are convinced that it will be a task in the long run. . . .

There are those who believe that a peaceful transition is possible in some countries of this continent; we cannot understand what kind of peaceful transition they refer to, unless it is to a peaceful transition in agreement with imperialism. As if in practice such a thing were possible, considering that the mechanisms of the bourgeoisie, the oligarchies, and imperialism control all the means for peaceful struggle. . . . And then you hear a revolutionary say: They crushed us; they organized 200 radio programs, so-and-so many newspapers, so-and-so many magazines, so-and-so many TV shows, so-and-so many of this and so-and-so many of that. And one wants to ask him: What did you expect? That they would put TV, radio, the magazines, the newspapers, the printing shops, all this at your disposal? Or are you unaware that those are the instruments of the ruling class designed explicitly for crushing the revolution?

They complain that the bourgeoisie and the oligarchies crush them with their campaigns, as if that were a surprise to anyone. The first thing that a revolutionary has to understand is that the ruling classes have organized the state so as to dedicate every possible means to maintaining themselves in power. And they use not only arms, not only physical instruments, not only guns, but all possible instruments to influence, to deceive, to confuse.

Those who believe that they are going to win against the imperialists in elections are just plain naive, and those who believe that the day will come when they will take over through elections are even more naive. It is necessary to have lived in a revolutionary process and to know just what the repressive apparatus is by which the ruling classes maintain the status quo, just how much one has to struggle, how difficult it is.

This does not imply the negation of forms of struggle. When someone writes a manifesto in a newspaper, attends a demonstration, holds a rally or propagates an idea, he may be using the famous so-called legal means. We must do away with the differentiation between legal and illegal means; methods should be classified as revolutionary or nonrevolutionary.

The revolutionary employs various methods to achieve his ideal and his revolutionary aim. The essence of the question is whether the masses will be led to believe that the revolutionary movement, that socialism, can come to power without a struggle, that it can come to power peacefully. And that is a lie! . . .

In Venezuela the revolutionary movement was growing. The revolutionary movement there has had to pay dearly the consequences of the absurd concept of trying to lead the guerrillas from the city, of trying to use the guerrilla movement as an instrument for political maneuvering, of trying to use the guerrilla movement as a tool of dirty politics: the consequence that can arise from incorrect attitudes, from wrong attitudes and, on many occasions, from immoral attitudes. . . .

Naturally, we publicly expressed our condemnation—after a series of statements had already been issued by that rightist leadership against our Party—of the treacherous ways in which they were slandering and attacking the revolutionaries. . . .

Logically, that provoked the irate and indignant protest of that rightist leadership, which made us the butt of a series of tirades. They did not answer a single one of our arguments; they were unable to answer even one, and they wrote a maudlin reply to the effect that we were ignoble, that we had attacked an underground Party, that we were fighting a most combative, a most heroic anti-imperialist organization. And they drafted a reply against us. . . .

I am going to read this answer, if you'll pardon me, even though it is rather lengthy. Of course, it is an answer full of phrases which are not at all kind to us, but if you'll permit me I would like to read this answer, which has been made public, the so-called "Reply of the Communist Party of Venezuela to Fidel Castro." And may this be a starting point for refuting some things that have been said about Cuba and about the revolution.

It reads:

"Fidel Castro, Secretary General of the Communist Party (in power) of Cuba, and Prime Minister of the Socialist Government of Cuba, taking advantage of his comfortable position, has attacked the Communist Party of Venezuela [CPV], an underground Party, with hundreds of its militants in prison, dozens of them having been killed in the mountains and streets of the cities; and now subject to relentless persecution daily, while new victims fall even as Fidel Castro speaks. . . .

"We are Venezuelan Communists, and we do not accept the tutelage of anyone, no matter how great his revolutionary merits may be.

"If there is any revolutionary group in Venezuela that submits with pleasure to the tutelage and patronage of Fidel Castro, that is its business. The CPV will never do so. If Fidel Castro does not like it, so much the worse for him. Now then: Why does Fidel Castro intervene precisely at this time against the CPV? Because the CPV has already begun to defeat in practice, and not only ideologically, the anti-Party faction of Douglas Bravo; because the Party and the Communist Youth have attained great political and organizational successes in applying their policy; because our recent feat, the rescue of comrades Guillermo and Teodoro Pompeyo has filled all the militant Communists of the country with enthusiasm and renewed energy; and because, finally, the anarchistic, adventurous policy of the anti-Party group has shown the inevitability of its failure and has helped enormously in the clarification of problems under discussion.

"That is precisely why Fidel Castro has thrown all the weight of his prestige against the CPV in a desperate attempt to help the anarchistic group of adventurers, which he sponsored and urged on so that the CPV would go under.

"Nevertheless, our policy and the facts prove daily what the adjectives 'hesitant,' 'halting,' and 'opportunist'—which Fidel Castro applies to the leadership of the CPV—are worth. And that is proved here in Venezuela, even in spite of the things Fidel Castro has done to us, and, surely, will continue doing to us. . . .

"In his speech, Fidel Castro shows that he wants to assume, once more, the role of a sort of arbiter of the revolutionary destiny of Latin America—a superrevolutionary who, if he had been in the place of all the Communists of Latin America, would have already made the revolution.

"On another occasion we referred to the characteristics of the Cuban struggle and to the place where Fidel Castro would still be if it had occurred to him to hoist the red flag in the Sierra Maestra. At the moment we only want to reject the role of revolutionary 'papa' that Fidel Castro adopts.

"We firmly reject his presuming to believe that he and only he can decide what is and what is not revolutionary in Latin America. In Venezuela, this question is judged by the CPV, before itself and its people, before no one else. But of this Fidel Castro—highest dispenser of revolutionary diplomas, who asks what North Vietnam would say if Cuba were to trade with South Vietnam—we only want to ask if he thinks about what the

Spanish people have to say about his trading with Franco and the Spanish oligarchy, or what the Negro peoples of Zimbabwe, Rhodesia, and the patriots of Aden might say about his trading with imperialist Britain. Or is it that what Fidel Castro considers as opportunism in others would be washed away in himself by the holy waters of his own self-sufficiency?

"Sixth: This is an unpleasant polemic and one that makes the enemy jump with joy; but it evidently cannot be deferred any longer. Fidel Castro himself forces us to the limit with his speech. All right, then. We will argue. And just as we claim our descent from Simón Bolívar and the fathers of our homeland in our anti-imperialist struggle, so we tell Fidel Castro that the descendants of Simón Bolívar and Ezequiel Zamora will never tolerate anybody's using language as insolent and provoking as that which he used in his speech on March 13.*

"The Venezuelan believes himself neither above nor below anybody else; but if there is one thing that will provoke his fiery militant pride, it is an insult.

"And already Fidel Castro must have started to realize that he has stumbled against something different, that he has come up against the Venezuelan Communists.

"Seventh: We realize that such acts as Fidel Castro's will cause us difficulties but we do not despair.

"We have the calm conviction of those who know they are right, and we have the revolutionary passion to defend it.

Political Bureau of the Central
Committee of the Communist Party
of Venezuela
March 15, 1967"

. . . They are lying when they state that Cuba is opposed to trade. In every international body, in every economic conference, in all organizations in which Cuba has taken part as a state, we have constantly denounced the imperialist policy of blockade, and we have denounced the acts of the government of the United States against our country as a violation of free trade and of the right of all countries to trade with one another. Cuba has inflexibly maintained that position at all times; that has been a policy pursued by our country and the entire history of the commercial relations of our country bears it out. Our position does not refer to trade; it has never referred to trade. And our position is known by the Soviet Union; we have stated our viewpoint to them.

---

* See *Selection 9.*—Ed.

We were talking about financial and technical help given by any socialist state to the Latin American oligarchies. These things must not be confused; one thing should not be confused with the other: Some socialist states even offered dollar loans to Sr. Lleras Restrepo * because he was in difficulties with the International Monetary Fund.

And we asked ourselves: How can this be? This is absurd! Dollar loans to an oligarchic government that is repressing the guerrillas, that is persecuting and assassinating guerrillas! And the war is carried out with money—among other things, because the oligarchies have nothing with which to wage war except money, with which they pay mercenary forces.

And such things seem absurd to us—as does everything that implies financial and technical aid to any country that is repressing the revolutionary movement, to countries that are accomplices in the imperialist blockade against Cuba. That we condemn. . . .

If solidarity is a word worthy of respect, the least that we can expect of any state of the socialist camp is that it refrain from giving any financial or technical aid to those regimes.

* President of Colombia, 1966–70.—Ed.

11. THE ALLIANCE OF REVOLUTIONARY ANTI-IMPERIALIST FORCES IN LATIN AMERICA (1967)

LUIS CORVALÁN

The principal contribution of revolutionaries to the cause of the worldwide liberation of the peoples and the victory of the working class on an international scale consists above all in the struggle for this cause in their own countries and in the manifestation on this basis of maximum moral and material solidarity with the revolutionary struggle of other countries. . . .

In this national struggle it is precisely the revolutionaries of each country who determine in all aspects the direction and specific tasks arising on the path of their own revolution. They

Excerpts from an article published in *Pravda*, July 30, 1967. Translation from *The Current Digest of the Soviet Press*, published at the Ohio State University by the American Association for the Advancement of Slavic Studies. © 1967 by the *Current Digest*. Reprinted by permission.

know better than anyone else the reality and conditions in which they are struggling, and they possess the greatest opportunities for correctly defining the goals of the struggle and the methods of their attainment. They can make mistakes, but the probability of the commission of errors is minimal. At any rate, the revolutionaries of each country can work out a correct line only by assuming responsibility and studying primarily their own experience, their own successes and failures. This, of course, does not exclude an exchange of opinions and, in certain cases, of fraternal advice.

The Cuban revolution is graphic proof of how life breaks through all schemata and is one more reminder that one cannot engage in generalizing the unique, specific features of one experience or another. However, it would be incorrect on this basis to deny that the specific features of one revolution—in this case the Cuban revolution—may be repeated in another place (although not in an exactly analogous form). . . .

Any attempt on the part of Communists to impose their viewpoint on other detachments of the anti-imperialist forces—and the same is true of attempts by the latter to impose their views on others—does not promote the attainment of the very important unity of action or the imparting of a broad character to the struggle against the common enemy. It is precisely for this reason that tasks which unite and do not disunite should be placed in the forefront, i.e., concrete tasks whose realization we all agree is essential. In this connection, we think the Latin American Solidarity Organization [OLAS] and the corresponding national committees of each country should focus their activities on the development and coordination of international solidarity, on the achievement of unity of action in the struggle for the solution of common tasks. . . .

Experience has shown that open polemics lead only to needless label-fixing and arbitrary appraisals. The principal result of this type of polemics is the exacerbation, not the overcoming, of difficulties. Sometimes parties under certain circumstances are compelled to express their opinions publicly on one question or another. We are not against this. But we are convinced that the best method of achieving mutual understanding is through direct contacts, bilateral and multilateral meetings, fraternal, nonabusive dialogues, and, most important, the uninterrupted development of joint actions. . . .

The proletariat is the most powerful social class on our continent, and it is now in the process of rapid development.

There are Communist parties in all the countries of the continent. The ranks of the Communist parties contain the advanced segment of the working class and the best representatives of the Latin American intelligentsia. . . .

Opportunities for the development of Communist parties and the transformation of small parties into large ones materialize as the parties take their places in the vanguard of social battles. The proletarian masses accumulate a diversity of experience. Ultimately they unite around the Communist parties.

However, we also run into another objective phenomenon which must constantly be taken into account; this is the fact that not only the class-conscious proletariat but also substantial numbers of the petty bourgeoisie are shifting to revolutionary positions, selflessly fighting for the liberation of the Latin American countries and advancing as their goal the building of socialism. This has manifested itself with special force in Latin America since the victory of the socialist revolution in Cuba. . . .

A revolutionary current springing from a petty-bourgeois foundation usually underestimates the proletariat and the Communist parties; it is more inclined toward nationalism, adventurism, and terrorism and sometimes is guilty of anti-Communism and anti-Sovietism. It also sinks more easily into despair and subjectivism. Nonetheless, it is a revolutionary current with respect to which the revolutionary proletariat should take a position more of unity than of struggle. . . .

It can be affirmed that in most Latin American countries the question is not only one of the necessity of joint action of the Communist parties and other revolutionary forces but also one of the necessity of implementing this cooperation on the level of the joint leadership of the liberation struggle of each people by the revolutionary forces, which in a certain sense share the function of the vanguard.

It is impossible to create a vanguard arbitrarily or artificially around a leader or people who individually occupy the most radical—at least in their opinion—positions and who are preparing to undertake one or another revolutionary action. Exceptions to this rule do not rescind it. . . .

The Communist parties in Latin America spring up at different times; they operate in varying situations and in diverse social and political conditions. Some parties are making efforts aimed at shifting from the stage of the propagandizing of the ideas of scientific socialism to the stage of strengthening ties with the masses, to the period of organizing and guiding the mass struggle, to the period of intensive social and political work with the people; this will enable them to open the way to the gaining of power. At the same time, this is the path to the rapid development of all the Communist parties of Latin America, to their

transformation into the guiding force of the revolutionary movement.

12. A "REVOLUTION IN THE REVOLUTION"
IS IMPOSSIBLE (1967)

CENTRAL COMMITTEE OF THE COMMUNIST PARTY
OF ARGENTINA

Régis Debray, the author of *Revolution in the Revolution?*, is
described in the introduction to his book as "one of the most
lucid interpreters of Latin American problems." He proposes one
common revolutionary method for all the countries of Latin
America except Uruguay: struggle by force of arms, without
which "there is no definitive vanguard." He recommends beginning with a guerrilla *foco*, disregarding any situation that does
not have to do with the guerrillas and ignoring altogether the
existence and role of the Party and mass organizations, the
independent organization of the working class, trade union formation, ideology, and even the concrete examination of the relationship of forces—so that at any time and in any place one can
and should follow the course indicated.

What this amounts to is a militarist interpretation of the
revolution, in the sense that it underestimates the role of mass
movements, leading the author to condemn "political leaders
who prefer to spend day after day in the activities of world
trade unionism and involve themselves in a thousand and one
democratic international organizations that are concerned with
maintaining themselves in existence rather than becoming seriously
and concretely informed on the military questions related to
the war of their people." This assertion shows a strange conception of such groups as the World Federation of Trade Unions,
the World Federation of Democratic Youth, the Women's
International Democratic Federation, which seem to be those
referred to.

Then, after establishing the subordination of strategy to tactics
and criticizing the "political leaders" for refusing "to choose one
form of struggle as fundamental and others as subordinate," he

---

Translated by the editor from the pamphlet "No Puede Haber una 'Revolución en la Revolución'" (Buenos Aires, 1967).

enlarges on the single solution that he recommends—armed struggle through the establishment of a guerrilla *foco*. He adds that "today in Latin America a political line that cannot be expressed effectively in a clear and coherent military policy cannot be considered as revolutionary."

The *foco*, as the author has said in an earlier work, is considered as the "matchstick," the "oil stain," which results in the conversion of an "isolated minority" into a "national tidal wave," the nucleus of the national revolutionary front. This *foco* must be established in the countryside—not in just any part of the countryside but in areas where there are feudal property relationships and which lie near the frontier and are mountainous. It is not even necessary that the place where the *foco* is established have a growing peasant mass movement. The *foco* will produce this, and, by itself, without the action of Party or ideology, will engender a socialist conscience.

Marxist-Leninists have a well-known position on the question of the way to revolution, since the question of the possibility of revolution without an earlier civil war is not new to them. Already in 1916, Lenin admitted that this was possible in exceptional circumstances, and for several months in 1917, between the February and October Revolutions, he re-emphasized it at various times. This was an historically concrete question, which occurred before the appearance of the first socialist state.

Synthesizing the results of the revolutionary experience of world Communism, the Declaration of the [Moscow] Conference of Representatives of Communist and Workers Parties in 1960 expressed the unanimous point of view of Marxist-Leninists, this time in the conditions produced by the existence of a world socialist system: "The working class and its vanguard—the Marxist-Leninist party—seek to achieve the socialist revolution by peaceful means. This would accord with the interests of the working class and the people as a whole, with the national interests of the country.

"Today, in a number of capitalist countries, the working class, headed by its vanguard, has the opportunity, given a united working-class and popular front or other workable forms of agreement and political cooperation between the different parties and public organizations, to unite the majority of the people, win state power without civil war, and ensure the transfer of the basic means of production to the hands of the people. Relying on the majority of the people and resolutely rebuffing the opportunist elements incapable of relinquishing the policy of compromise with the capitalists and landlords, the working class can defeat the reactionary anti-popular forces, secure a firm majority in parliament, transform parliament from an instrument serving the class interests of the bourgeoisie into an instrument serving the working people, launch an extra-parliamentary mass struggle, smash the resistance of the reactionary forces, and create the necessary conditions for the peaceful realization of the socialist revolution. All this will be possible only by broad and ceaseless development of the class struggle of the workers, peasant masses, and the urban middle strata against big monopoly capital, against reaction, for profound reforms, for peace and socialism." But, it adds, this does not depend solely on the proletariat; if the exploiting classes resort to violence, "the possibility of a nonpeaceful transition to socialism should be borne in mind." In each country the way depends on "concrete historical conditions."

Debray does not appreciate in any way the role of the working class, the vanguard force of every democratic and popular movement, in the struggle for national and social liberation. This is no accident. His revolutionary *foco* must be based in the countryside.

The lack of appreciation of the city, where the majority of the working class lives and works, is part of the author's thesis regarding the contradiction· between the city and the mountains. The contrast is not geographical but social. Essentially, the mountains are the peasants and the city is the workers, so that the thesis of the author results in the affirmation of an opposition between the workers and the peasants. In place of the basic thinking of Marxism-Leninism concerning the worker-peasant alliance and the hegemony of the proletariat, he expounds a thesis that calls on the countryside to redeem the city proletariat, which has been corrupted by the bourgeoisie.

The author does not doubt that the city is the corruptor of revolutionaries, that it weakens them and turns them into members of the bourgeoisie, that "we have seen the mountains proletarianize the bourgeoisie and peasants while the city can even turn workers into members of the bourgeoisie," that the city endangers the revolution, that "all the contemporary experience of Latin America confirms and establishes as a law this disharmony and division between the forces of the mountains and those of the plains."

The anti-proletarian attitude of the author enables us to understand his hostility toward the world trade-union movement and his opposition not only to the notion of the worker-peasant alliance but to the principle, which cannot be renounced by Marxist-Leninists, of the leading role of the working class in this alliance. It leads, as we shall see, to a total revision of Communist theory all over the world on the role of the Marxist-

Leninist party. The author does not appreciate "the evangelical role of penetrating one or another factory," since for him the guerrilla *foco* will determine the fate of the city.

The author is also opposed to the conception of Marxist-Leninists on the function and importance of the city under capitalism. Lenin affirmed "the historical importance of great cities"—those cities that Debray sees only as centers of parasitism. If, for Lenin, "in capitalist societies the great cities constitute an element of progress," for the author the city is the death of the revolution. . . .

The author puts forward the idea that it is necessary to rejuvenate the party—an idea that he expresses by a comparison to biological rejuvenation: "In Latin America there is a profound link between biology and ideology wherever armed struggle is the order of the day. Absurd and shocking as this may appear, it is no less important." From this basic concept he concludes that the adult in the city is not adapted to the mountains or to underground work in the city. Moreover, if "a perfect Marxist training is not an essential condition at the outset, physical preparation is fundamental."

The author declares that his statement may appear shocking and "a somewhat theoretical triviality," but he concludes triumphantly: "Armed struggle may have reasons that theory does not know."

Evidently, Debray is abandoning social science in favor of biology. The march of history depends on the age of the individuals who act in it and especially on those who, because of their youth, are able to go to the mountains and breathe the air at higher altitudes. This surprising attempt at social biology, which claims to order the march of social phenomena on the basis of the physical age of the persons involved, testifies to a complete divorce between his view and that of Marxism-Leninism, historical materialism, and the class struggle, confusing the laws of biology with those of social development and denying the fact that the laws of society are specifically and qualitatively different. . . .

In the year of the fiftieth anniversary of the Great October Socialist Revolution, the event that transformed once and for all the course of history, opening the era of socialism, the author acts as if the movement of social and national liberation in both Latin America and Asia and Africa is taking place independently of world conditions and especially of the presence, existence, and action of the Soviet Union and the socialist states. He writes as if the October Revolution meant nothing for the emergence, development, and future of that movement, although it was the dividing line between two different periods—the period of heroic but unsuccessful struggle before the victory of the first socialist revolution, and the period of the revolutions that triumphed, first in Russia and then in a series of other countries. Nor do his reflections take into account the enormous role of the proletariat in the advanced capitalist countries and their respective Communist parties in the world anti-imperialist front. As is known, this neglect leads Maoism to deny the leading role of the working class of all countries, whose greatest accomplishments is the creation of the world socialist system in a single world anti-imperialist front.

Debray tries to justify his views by referring to the peculiarities of Latin America. Certainly, Latin America has peculiarities that must be taken into account—not to depart from Marxist-Leninism but to apply it more correctly to given concrete conditions.

If Debray speaks of the peculiarities of Latin America when he develops his deviationist conceptions, he ignores them when he discusses the countries that make it up. He closes his eyes to their special characteristics, their specific national traits, their different degrees of development, which makes it easy for him to give a common recipe for them all. And proceeding thus, he forgets something essential—that it is the task of Marxist-Leninists in each country to draw particular conclusions by analyzing the reality of each country and deciding the method and form of the struggle for each given moment. No one can say from the outside if one should begin armed struggle or not, or when, where, and how.

13. THE CASE AGAINST CASTRO

MANUEL URRUTIA

After Batista, Cuba, for the first time in many years, presented a potential for continuous development under an honorable and efficient administration. But the confidence of investors in Cuba was dissipated by the government's stupid and ambitious Communist policy of despoilment.

The revolutionary government could have obtained capital, for

Excerpts from Manuel Urrutia Lleó, *Fidel Castro and Company, Inc.* (New York: Praeger Publishers, 1964), pp. 174–79.

instance, by means of the so-called "management contract," under which a foreign firm agrees to establish and manage a factory in the country for a fixed period of time. The government owns the plant but the firm helps to finance it by providing a fixed interest loan for the duration of the management contract, that is, for several years. This contract obviates permanent foreign ownership and control and, at the same time, provides foreign capital and technical assistance.

When the management contract expires, the government can denationalize the enterprise in a democratic way—the way in which the German Federal Republic denationalized the Volkswagen corporation, by establishing a corporation whose capital is represented by shares of nominal cost for distribution among people of low income, with an express prohibition against selling shares to one person in quantities that would permit him to corner the market.

However, in place of foreign investment capital, the government of the Soviet Union has provided precarious and meager aid that entails the complete subordination of the economy of the recipient to that of the lender, equivalent to the degree of political subordination. Examples of this are only too well known, and the international policy of the Soviet socialist government proves it clearly.

The Soviet Union, of course, does not *lend* money but rather *grants credits* for the acquisition of low-quality products that it can market nowhere else in the world. And under the terms of agreements signed by Cuba, Russian technicians direct our economy and are paid by us. Our submission is, in short, complete. . . .

Cuba's entrance into the cold war has brought as a consequence a scale of military arming that reveals our subordination to the interests of Russia. It came about at a time when although the entire economic resources of the nation were needed for our complementary development, we were converted into a Russian stronghold. The Communists say they have turned barracks into schools, but in reality, they have made a military barracks of the entire island—or more precisely, a mixture of prison and garrison.

Intolerable sacrifices have been imposed on Cuba: suppression of all freedoms; of the right to choose the political, social, and economic system it prefers; of choosing its governing officials freely and periodically; using energies according to its own desires and interests; of guiding institutions according to its own preference. Cuba has been subjected to an implacable political police joined to an immense net of informers—those so-called Committees for the Defense of the Revolution that operate in every office, street, labor center, university, school, etc. Accusations by members of these committees send their neighbors, school companions, and fellow workers before the firing squads. The people have been subjected to an intolerable labor regime, and blood has flowed profusely. The right of free expression has been suppressed along with religion, choice of dwelling, location and class of labor, type of children's education—and the new governing class has wrested private schools from their legitimate proprietors to be used for Communist indoctrination.

The population has been taught to read in order to poison their souls with Marxist venom; thus that vile, hate-filled indoctrination is disseminated in offices, centers of labor and instruction, barracks, police stations, and militia encampments. A work norm is imposed, together with low salaries and free labor. A single voice—the government's—is heard in controlled propaganda calling for war with the free world and subordination to Red Russia. Misery, sorrow, and privations have choked the land.

Every hope of freedom has been extinguished, every hope of free choice in political, syndical, social, ideological, religious, and philosophical matters. Workers labor in Cuba at a frantic pace to forge their own chains and solidify their status as slaves.

The Constitution of 1940 proscribed unduly large landholdings but, at the same time, fully protected private property and legally guaranteed the producer's security.

The Agrarian Reform, the work of Communist specialists in hatred, was imposed less to provide land for the working farmer than to wrest it from its old proprietors. The accompanying demagogy was nourished more by hatred for the landowner than by sympathy for the unfortunate *campesino*. A badly planned agrarian program undertaken at dizzying speed has disorganized production, destroyed the existing agricultural economy, and, in consequence, brought hunger to the entire country.

"Cooperatives" and "People's Farms" have failed because they are instruments of exploitation that disregard the initiative and self-interest of the *campesino*, who knows that he works *for* the government. The Agrarian Reform has been robbery, pure and simple. The landholder has been expropriated without compensation—in many cases unnecessarily, but in others for the calculated destruction of flourishing agriculture. The impoverished *campesino* has been given an all-powerful master, "the Company," whose symbol in this case is INRA [National Institute of Agrarian Reform].

A reasonable agrarian reform, with equitable compensation and without destruction of the existing economy, would have provided a powerful stimulus for the economy of the country. Indemnification in the form of bonds would have been a just and honest compensation, and the development of the country, accelerated by agrarian reform, would have guaranteed full and prompt payment of capital and interest on the bonds.

In underdeveloped countries, the state may take a larger role than private initiative in economic action. A rule of thumb is that the less developed a country is, the greater the action by the state should be in order to complement the private sector. In Cuba, which needs only to complete its economic and industrial development, action by the state should be complementary to the initiatives and undertakings of free enterprise. A state economic policy is undoubtedly essential in order to plan development and assure equitable distribution.

One must not confuse economic planning—and this must be emphasized—with the formation of totalitarian absolute monopolies, which, under the *pretext* of planning economic development, create new classes whose dominion over the population is absolute and unyielding.

Castro consciously impoverished the Cuban middle class, especially merchants, with a cruel, unnecessary, and detrimental policy. This class has performed an important role in the development of advanced countries and as [Walt W.] Rostow says, it is easy to forget that the industrial revolution in Western Europe and the United States was preceded by several centuries of commercial and industrial development that created a class of entrepreneurs morally, intellectually, and technically prepared to exploit the potentials of the innovations that were developed. In one sense, the middle class was the most important economic innovation of modern times.

In Cuba, the middle class should have been preserved, and its enterprising spirit stimulated, while the state assumed the initiative in economic development. A just and equitable agrarian reform, without Communist plunder, plus democratic economic planning to complete the industrialization of the country, would have been sufficient to make Cuba prosperous. In addition, the cooperation of the working class is indispensable if economic development is to be accelerated. Democracy obtains this cooperation by properly compensating the extra efforts of those who are engaged in production. But the totalitarian absolute monopoly drives the laborers, imposing such sacrifices upon them that they react with extraordinary violence in countries where there is a deeply democratic tradition.

Castro has established a controlled economy planned in purely national terms, ignoring an independent variable—the international market, which he cannot control, yet which is indispensable to the economy of the country. Cuba was a country with an "open" economy whose international commerce represented almost 50 per cent of its national income. Given the immense dificulties of coordination, it is far easier to plan the economy of countries with a "closed" economy, such as Russia, whose international commerce represents only 5 per cent of its national income. The worst of Castro's sins is that he forced Cuba into complete isolation. If war broke out between the free world and the slave world, Cuba would collapse because the precarious economic relations which Castro maintains with the latter would be totally severed. The Communists have cost Cuba the United States market, which, together with the other markets of the free world, is the most satisfactory in terms of our national economy. The United States *needs* our sugar and other products, but open economic warfare has resulted from Castro's irreconcilable Russian policy, which is anti-Cuban as much as it is anti–North American. In short, the policy of the Communists has damaged Cuba and the free world and benefited only Russia.

PART TWO

IV. *Brazil: The Military vs. the Radical Left*

In the early 1960's, there was reason to believe that the influence of the military in Latin American politics was declining. One after another of the military oligarchs of the 1950's—Juan Perón in Argentina, Gustavo Rojas Pinilla in Colombia, Marcos Perez Jiménez in Venezuela, Manuel Odría in Peru, Fulgencio Batista in Cuba, and Rafael Trujillo in the Dominican Republic—had been overthrown, and with the exception of Cuba on the left and Paraguay on the right, constitutional democracy seemed to be everywhere on the advance. Yet, by the end of the decade, a new wave of military rulers appeared to be emerging in many countries of Latin America. These new military rulers were concerned with national development and economic growth, and impatient with what they considered the "corruption," "compromises," and "demagogy" of civilian politicians.

The most important of these new military regimes, because of the size and strategic location of the country, is that of Brazil. Following the surprise resignation of President Jânio Quadros, in August, 1961, and the succession of João Goulart to the presidency over military opposition, Brazilian politics rapidly became polarized into two groups. On one side were those supporting Goulart— left-wing students and intellectuals, the illegal Communist Party, and the government-sponsored labor unions, which had been organized by former dictator Getulio Vargas—who shared a commitment to a socialist-oriented economic nationalism. (For a leftist criticism of the influence of foreign capital in Brazil, see *Selection 1*.) The National Union of Students (UNE), which included representatives of most of the university students of Brazil, was dominated by a group of radical Catholics from the Acão Popular (Popular Action) movement, who combined the thinking of Teilhard de Chardin and Karl Marx in their denunciation of "neo-capitalism" and their demands for a revolutionary transformation of Brazilian society (*Selection 2*). Opposed to the left coalition was a Western-oriented, conservative group, backed by the middle class and the military. After a period of vacillation, Goulart appeared to adopt the leftist program, but inflation and corruption undercut his political support, and on March 31, 1964, he was overthrown by a coalition of military officers and state governors. Under pressure from the military, the Brazilian Congress installed General Humberto Castelo Branco as president. Castelo Branco's inaugural address is included as *Selection 3*.

The new military regime governed under a series of Institutional Acts, which allowed it to suspend the political rights of many of Brazil's leading politicians, to limit the powers of the Congress, and to reorganize the national political parties. In the economic field, President Castelo Branco gave considerable power to his Minister of Planning, Roberto Campos, to reduce the rate of inflation, which at the time of the coup was approaching 100 per cent a year. Campos' austerity program limited wage and price increases and actively encouraged foreign investment, which had been frightened away by the Goulart regime (see *Selection 4*). The inflation rate was cut back to less than 25 per cent and economic growth, which had stagnated under Goulart, took a sharp upward turn. However, the alliance of pro-Western military men and orthodox economists and businessmen was denounced by some Brazilians, including the academician Hélio Jaguaribe, who described it as "colonial fascism" (*Selection 5*).

By 1966, the regime was opposed by most of the politicians who had supported it in 1964. In September, 1967, Carlos Lacerda, one of the architects of the 1964 coup, formed a "Broad Front" of civilian opposition, which included his former political opponents Juscelino Kubitschek, Brazilian president in 1955–60, and João Goulart (*Selection 6*).

In March, 1967, General Artur Costa e Silva succeeded to the presidency, under a new Constitution, and promised a liberalization of the regime. But increasing opposition to military rule on the part of university students and members of Congress led the "hard line" faction of the military to force the adoption of a Fifth Institutional Act, in December, 1968. The act gave the president the power to recess the Congress indefinitely (which he immediately proceeded to do), to suspend the political rights of opponents of the regime for ten years, to deny habeas corpus and other rights, and to confiscate the property of those suspected of "illicit enrichment" (*Selection 7*). In October, 1969, after Costa e Silva suffered an incapacitating (and as it proved, fatal) stroke, the Brazilian Congress was reconvened and elected General Emilio Garrastazú Médici as president. The election, however, was a mere formality, ratifying the choice of the leaders of the armed forces.

The principal organized opposition to military rule that still enjoys freedom of expression is in the hierarchy of the Catholic Church. Dom Helder Camara, the Archbishop of Recife, is one of the most vocal opponents of the regime, as well as an internationally known critic of rich individuals (and nations) who do not share their wealth with the poor. Although as a Christian he is opposed to violence, he has expressed his admiration for the guerrilla leaders Ché Guevara and Camilo Torres (*Selection 8*). Partly as a result of Camara's influence, the National Conference of Brazilian Bishops, meeting in secret in São Paulo, in February, 1969, issued a declaration criticizing the Fifth Institutional Act and the excesses of military rule (*Selection 9*). The declaration, signed by twenty-two members of the Central Committee of the Conference, including two cardinals and eleven archbishops, has never been published in Brazil.

General Aurelio de Lyra Tavares, Minister of War under Costa e Silva, has written that the 1964 coup was in the Brazilian tradition of military intervention for the sole purpose of defending the nation, and that the present regime is not a military dictatorship (*Selection 10*). In fact, however, real political debate, as well as all decision-making power, continues to be restricted to the military. The regime has promised a return to at least a partial democracy, but the immediate prospects of redemocratization seem dim.

1. A DAY IN THE LIFE OF A BRAZILIAN
(1961)

PAULO GUILHERME MARTINS

A Brazilian, his name does not matter, who lives in an apartment, in Santos, for example—

This Brazilian, like all good city-dwellers, begins his day in this way: He gets up still sleepy in order to get to work on time.

The Brazilian pushes the button at the head of the bed, thus using up electricity that comes from Light* —the Brazilian therefore begins his day by paying dividends to *Foreign Capital*. But the Brazilian does not know this, and he begins his day, happy!

He opens the door. Martha, the maid, enters with his breakfast: coffee, milk, bread, butter, a little jelly, and the newspaper—*O Estado do São Paulo*. The Brazilian, like all good bourgeois, reads only good, sound newspapers.

While he reads the news, he eats his breakfast. The Brazilian doesn't know that the milk he drinks came from a cow that was fed Refinazil stock-feed from the Refineries of the Mill of Brazil (Brazil with a "z," not an "s"), which is American, and that the flour, too, with which the bread was made came from Santos Mills, which is not owned by natives of Santos but by Englishmen. Therefore, in order to have his breakfast, the Brazilian has to pay dividends to *Foreign Capital*. But the Brazilian does not know this . . . and he eats his breakfast, happy!

Finishing his breakfast, the Brazilian lights his first cigarette of the day: Minister, or Hollywood, from Companhia Souza Cruz, which isn't run by a Sr. Souza, much less a Sr. Cruz, but by the British-American Tobacco Company, the Anglo-American smoking monopoly. And so, in order to smoke his cigarette, the Brazilian pays dividends to *Foreign Capital*. But the Brazilian never thinks of this, but only savors his cigarette, happy . . . happy . . .

Now the Brazilian goes to his bathroom to wash. He lights the gas waterheater, the gas coming from City Company, and therefore from Light, and, while the water warms, he picks up his

---

* A Canadian-owned electric company in Brazil.—ED.

Translated by the editor from *Um Dia na Vida do Brasilino* (São Paulo, 1961).

toothbrush marked TEK by Johnson and Johnson of Brazil (which is American) and his Kolynos toothpaste, with chlorophyll, from Whitehall Laboratories of New York, and so, in order to brush his teeth, the Brazilian pays dividends to *Foreign Capital* . . .

But the Brazilian never thinks about this . . .

The Brazilian does not know what chlorophyll is, or what he is doing when he enters a pharmacy and chooses this toothpaste. He is unaware that his choice was conditioned by costly advertising campaigns in the newspapers, on radio, and on television, and that in the same way that he chose his toothpaste he also chose his candidate for the presidency of the republic.

Then the Brazilian begins to shave: He takes his shaving brush, made with nylon filaments, by Rhodia—which is French—lathers it with Williams Shaving Cream, which is American. Applying the lather to his face, the Brazilian takes his Gillette razor, inserts a Gillette blade, both made by Gillette Safety Razor of Brazil, and happily shaves, little knowing that, in order to shave, he had to pay dividends to *Foreign Capital*.

Finishing his shave, the Brazilian dries himself with a fuzzy towel from Fiação da Lapa, which is not from Lapa because it is Swiss, and then applies Johnson talcum powder to his body, another product of Johnson and Johnson of Brazil.

And . . . he begins to dress.

Here he encounters a tragedy! A button pops off the Brazilian's shirt. He rings again, and Martha runs to aid our hero, bringing her needle and thread. In a very few seconds after Martha has made the button secure, the Brazilian feels happy again. Happy because he doesn't know that Martha, the maid, in order to sew the button on his shirt, had to use thread of the Current brand from Companhia Brasileira de Linhas para Coser, which is English, and that, in order to have his button sewn on, the Brazilian had to pay dividends to *Foreign Capital*.

Once dressed, the Brazilian says goodbye to Martha, telling her not to fix either lunch or supper because he will be going to São Paulo on business. . . . He closes the door, takes the elevator, which is a Schindler of Schindler of Brazil, which is Swiss, which operates on electricity generated by Light, and then arrives on the ground floor. He says "Good morning" to the caretaker, goes to his Volkswagen, manufactured by Volkswagen of Brazil, which is German, with Firestone tires of Firestone of Brazil, which is American, running on gasoline refined by Petrobrás * but distributed by Esso Standard of Brazil, which is American. In order

* The national Brazilian oil company.—ED.

to use gas refined by Petrobrás, the Brazilian pays dividends to *Foreign Capital!* He doesn't know that although Brazilians are able to refine petroleum and produce their own gasoline, they still don't undertake the "difficult" task of distribution. For this simple service, the distributors (Esso-Shell-Gulf-Texaco, etc.) get much more profit than Petrobrás. But the Brazilian does not know all this . . . and the Brazilian is happy!

The Brazilian arrives at the offices of Crescinco Investment Company, belonging to Mr. Rockefeller. The Brazilian feels proud to lend his money to one of the world's richest men, who prefers to finance his industries by using Brazilian capital, attracting it with a 2 per cent monthly rate of interest and no income tax. The Brazilian doesn't know that, from the day he invests his money to the day it is returned, the currency is devalued by 4 per cent a month, and so he is worse off. And that the interest and the income of the Investment Company is derived from profit—that is, from the exploitation of Brazilians. But the Brazilian does not know this and accepts his money and interest, happy!

Finishing his business, the Brazilian goes to lunch. He enters a restaurant, where he is served appetizers: coldcuts by Armour of Brazil, which is American; Clay-Bon margarine, by Anderson Clayton, which is American; he drinks Coca-Cola and savors a dish of pasta, prepared with flour from the São Paulo Mill, which is English; later he has a steak with french fries. The meat was supplied by Frigorifico Wilson and the potatoes were fried in Mazola oil from Corn Refineries of Brazil (Brazil with a "z," not an "s"). For dessert he has a pudding topped with Duryea Cornstarch, also from Refineries of Brazil, and so, when he eats, the Brazilian has to pay dividends to *Foreign Capital.*

After lunch, the Brazilian decides to see a movie; he walks through the city wearing down the soles of his shoes, which are made of Goodyear rubber, therefore paying dividends to *Foreign Capital.*

The Brazilian enters the theater, where he spends the afternoon, enjoying an American film. And so, in order to have a good time for a few hours, the Brazilian pays dividends to *Foreign Capital.*

When he comes out of the theater, the Brazilian feels slightly indisposed. He goes into a pharmacy and takes an Alka-Seltzer. Thus even to prevent indigestion the Brazilian has to pay dividends to *Foreign Capital.*

He then takes his car and returns to Santos. Arriving home, he freshens up again and turns on a table radio marked General Electric of Brazil; he lies down on a couch made of Fomex rubber by Firestone of Brazil and puts his head on a pillow of the same material, sleeping happily a dream of innocence.

I don't know the reason, but the history of Brazil always brings to my mind fhe Sermon on the Mount: "Blessed are the poor in spirit, for theirs is the kingdom of heaven."

But one thing a Brazilian will never be is: KING IN HIS OWN HOMELAND.

Therefore, reader, if anyone says that imperialism does not exist in Brazil, it is either because he is deceived or because he is deceiving you.

2. BASIC DOCUMENT OF AÇÃO POPULAR (1963)

Our unique commitment is, then, to man. To Brazilian man, above all. He is born with the shadow of early death stretching over his cradle. He lives with the specter of hunger under his miserable roof, inseparably accompanying his uncertain steps, which trudge through life without hope and without aim. He grows up brutalized and illiterate, alienated from the benefits of culture, from creative possibilities, from the authentic human ways of genuine freedom. He dies an animal, anonymous death, stretched out on the hard floor of his misery. . . .

WORLD-HISTORICAL PERSPECTIVE

The fact of socialization unquestionably dominates human history and reveals itself as the fundamental matrix for the interpretation of its evolutionary process. Man—who is not viable historically as an isolated individual, or within the static and rigid forms of animal societies—creates ever more complex forms of social relations; it is in the internal dialectic of these communitarian structures of life that history finds the proper rhythm of its development. This development does not occur by chance. It obeys laws. But the laws of historical development are not formulated according to the deterministic model of the laws of nature. They are dialectical laws, which means that they express concrete possibilities presented to human freedom in each historical

Translated by Thomas Sanders from *Ação Popular, Documento Base* (São Paulo, 1963).

epoch—which may be realized or lost—within the social complexes that are the necessary surroundings of man. Socialization is not opposed to personalization; the communitarian is not opposed to the free. They are conditioned dialectically. . . .

When we speak of *capitalism* and *socialism,* we are not interested in abstract systems of economic relations but in the concrete possibility of the realization of man within the process of socialization that is irresistibly developing in history. Beginning from such a perspective, we discover that modern history is marked by the appearance of social structures that are based on the capitalist relations of production and conditioned by them. Powerful forces and gigantic instruments for the exploitation of nature, vast and headlong accumulations of wealth: these are the characteristics that emerged in the context of the new economic structures of the European West when feudal property disappeared. The cycle of exchanges expanded into the dimensions of a genuine world market; artisanal production was absorbed by large industry; investment and credit were projected into ventures of great risk and great profit.

The appearance of capitalism propelled the march of socialization in a rhythm and proportion that history had not known until then. Unified economically, the world entered into a process of political and cultural unification. From this point of view, the appearance of capitalism represents an enormous forward leap of history. But from the point of view of man, it underlines the presence of structures of domination and alienation that bring tensions and impediments to the process of socialization in its capitalist form. It is these that led historically to the socialist outcome. . . .

Indeed, it is in a world-historical perspective that the evolution of capitalism reveals the profound significance of its internal dialectic of separation and opposition and of its iron law of the relation of man to man in terms of domination: It shows us the march of socialization, the fundamental movement of history, encountering the risk of a definitive impasse in the proportions of an effectively universal phenomenon, the phenomenon of the worldwide expansion of capitalism. It is in this perspective that it is convenient to place the advent of socialism, first as an immanent criticism of capitalism, afterward as an historical necessity of [capitalism's] certain defeat.

As a critical attitude, socialism emerged at the very time that capitalism was developing its ideological justification in classical economic theory. Socialism signified fundamental opposition to the basic thesis of this ideology: the belief that an unrestricted right to property was in accordance with the laws of nature, and the optimistic assumption that an ideal distribution of goods would result from the free functioning of the laws of the market-place. In sum, [socialism], whatever its ideological forms, stood for the claim that man, as the subject of the process of socialization, should be the measure and the end of socioeconomic reality. As an historical demand to replace capitalism, the socialist movement produced a revolutionary consciousness, which was soon translated into schemes of political action among the elements of humanity that had been dominated and alienated from progress by the global historical process and internal dialectic of capitalism. The movement began in the laboring class, in the centers where capitalist structures originated, expanded, and consolidated—that is, in the countries of Western Europe, extending itself to new areas where capitalism was penetrating and absorbing the traditional economies. Afterward, it spread to the peasant masses, gradually proletarianized by the integration of agricultural economies into the system and dynamic of capitalist production. Finally (and this is the present stage in the march of socialist revolution), the immense human masses of the countries subjected to the aggression and domination of colonialism and political and economic imperialism developed a consciousness and revolutionary action that give the popular movements of liberation in the areas of the underdeveloped world a decisive importance in the historical overcoming of capitalism and the worldwide advent of socialism. . . .

But the world crisis of capitalism in 1929, which resulted in World War II, produced new conditions, usually revolutionary in effect, that came to mark all the Third World and, in particular, Latin America. From the economic point of view, they were expressed in the sudden fall of the prices of basic agricultural products and their permanent depreciation, which sporadic increases (as, for example, during the Korean conflict) were unable to check. The underdeveloped areas, including Latin America, began to oscillate under the impact of the changes in the world market and the economic crises of the industrialized areas. Trade relationships are systematically unfavorable to [the underdeveloped countries], and the cycle of their impoverishment takes the form of a descending spiral.

The reaction to this state of affairs appeared in the form of an initial effort at industrialization, which attained a relative development in a few countries of Latin America (Mexico, Brazil, Argentina, Chile). But the weakness of the over-all economic structure, together with the instability of the social structure, opened an unprotected flank to imperialistic domination, with predatory and vicious foreign investments (almost exclusively

North American in Latin American areas), which, by denationalizing industry, transported excessive profits to the home office, increased the idleness or paralyzed the development of less profitable sectors, even though they might have had greater priority, and ended by creating conditions of open intervention in the social, political, and even cultural life of the nation. Domination extended in a chain reaction: economic, political, ideological. . . .

If man, as a conscious being, is a human person, he can understand and transform nature. He can overcome its determinism; he is free. As such, he is elevated to the universal, to the free encounter with the Other. He is socialized. It is from the human person, then, that the three master directions of history radiate: liberation, universalization, socialization.

The historical consciousness of the modern world has as its fundamental characteristics: the discovery of the individual, which marked the advent of the new cultural cycle that began with the Renaissance and the expansion of capitalism; the discovery of the social and the historical, which was linked to the acceleration of the technical-scientific domination of nature and social organization and produced the crisis of capitalism in its cultural world; and the emergence of socialism. . . .

POLITICAL-IDEOLOGICAL CONSEQUENCES

The process of socialization, which characterizes the evolution of humanity only since 1917, expressed itself in socialist experiments. These experiments, despite the deficiencies characteristic of the period of implantation, and despite some errors of political orientation and sectarianism, are progressively being perfected and are creating better conditions for human realization.

Socialism is the immediate consequence of the negation of capitalism, a negation which, dialectically, is not pure negativity but the concretization of a new mode of existence. In fact, the socialist system creates economic and social conditions that break down relations of domination, increasing the possibilities of the communication of consciousnesses and control over nature. Socialism is an important stage in the struggle against the process of domination and the search for the conciliation of consciousnesses.

The Brazilian reality, like that of all underdeveloped countries, includes structures of exploitation that condemn a large part of the world population to a state of total backwardness in the process of socialization. . . .

We are interested in guaranteeing the free development of the human person and the possibility of his self-expression and free choice. Liberty, as the expression of the human person, is not the ability to do anything that one wishes, but rather to do that which expresses a fundamental human need, from the point of view of reason. Liberty, being personal, is essentially social and is judged by its social function. Therefore, to guarantee liberty is to provide that the state may act as the point of convergence of decisions socially assumed.

The socialization of property is the process of democratizing the distribution and use of goods proceeding from human labor, to prevent their being used for purposes of domination, and thus to create the basis for a real democratization of power. With respect to property, power, and the state, it is technically possible to change the social order so as to resolve men's problems and attend to their necessities, but in a way that can be reconciled with a social morality that affirms that the basic relationship for man cannot be that of domination.

It is not our responsibility to anticipate the form in which the concretization of this revolutionary process will take place. Nevertheless, it can be said that there is no record in history of a breakdown of structures in which violence was not generated by those same structures. . . .

The unbalanced growth of the economy led the laboring class to express itself, through pressure, for the redistribution of the products of development.

Inflation and disequilibrium have helped to create an awakened urban proletariat with a revolutionary outlook, a fact that is expressed in the progressive integration of the organizations of the proletariat and in the recent political movements in which it has participated. . . .

The bourgeoisie have successively presented, through representative groups, different "ideologies" of correction for development. Such corrective schemes are represented sometimes by political moralizing, which is proposed in place of the consolidation of an authoritative state; sometimes by plans of monetary stabilization and financial discipline; and sometimes by reformism, which sees the solution of the tensions in unstructured conceptions of so-called basic reforms. Fundamentally, these schemes constitute an attempt at setting up a system of neocapitalism, to permit bourgeois development to succeed while avoiding the radicalization of the masses that can bring about an alteration in the social structure and in the prevailing system of exploitation.

This outlook finds support in the imperialistic scheme to which our ruling groups are linked through the Alliance for Progress, which proposes to modernize the Latin American economies, adjusting them to a new phase of international capitalism and lessening the conflicts that are capable of generating the revolutionary struggle. . . .

We define our revolutionary struggle as a struggle against international capitalism, including opposition to the effort to implant in Brazil a neocapitalist economic system. This fact should not convey the naive vision of an immediate possible revolution but should make us direct our efforts toward an active preparation of that process.

Ação Popular has thus chosen a policy of revolutionary preparation, consisting in the mobilization of the people through the development of the level of their consciousness and their organization in the struggle against the dual domination of capitalism (international and national) and feudalism. Progressively strengthening its ranks, Ação Popular will gradually fulfill the role of promoting and orienting this mobilization, supporting it through direct action and through the coordinated activity of its militants within the present structures of power.

We propose this [policy] for ourselves, as the task of our militants in the exercise of power to which we may be called, but we ought also to engage in permanent dialogue with other anti-imperialist and revolutionary sectors and to work for the radicalization of contradictions in the present power structure.

Our work will be directed first to workers and peasants organizations. If we recognize the essential character of the phenomenon of imperialism, and the integration of the present diverse forms of domination in the ranks of international capitalism, this does not fail to impose upon us the necessity for a method of awakening consciousness and for an organization that proceeds from the concrete exigencies of the masses.

3. INAUGURAL ADDRESS OF APRIL 15, 1964

HUMBERTO CASTELO BRANCO

In the special significance of this civic ceremony, and while millions of our compatriots encourage us with their trust and their hopes, I want to assure you that the oath I have just taken before

Translated in Max Manwaring, "The Military in Brazilian Politics" (unpublished Ph.D. thesis, University of Illinois, 1968), Appendix IX; reprinted by permission.

the august representatives of the nation embodies much more than the ritual form: it contains the reiteration of the sentiments and ideals that have accompanied and inspired us since our youth. I will preserve with honor and loyalty the Constitution of Brazil, including the Institutional Act that is a part of it.

I shall observe and maintain the laws of the country and I will remain watchful to see that all obey them with exactitude and zeal. Mine will be a government of law, of the traditions and moral and political principles that represent the soul of Brazil. It will be a government firmly set on the future, since it is also true that a permanent striving for progress and advancement is the hallmark as well as the general trend of our social and political history. It is no exaggeration to say that in this march to the future we shall engage ourselves with ardor in a crusade in which all Brazilians will be called to participate. In this journey I expect, through energy and above all through my own example, to count on the participation of all the citizens in an endeavor that will be the supreme guarantee of every man and woman in this country. My behavior will be that of a head of state who will permit no delay in the process of electing the Brazilian to whom I shall transfer my office on January 31, 1966.* I will uphold with all my ability the union, integrity, and independence of our country, within and without its territorial frontiers. And by this I mean not only the admirable heritage of national unity but the harmony of all Brazilians. I shall be the president of all of them, not the head of a faction.

The independence of Brazil will be the paramount principle of our international policy. All friendly nations can rely on the loyalty of the Brazilian people, who will honor treaties and covenants entered into. All democratic nations will be our allies, and at the same time all those people who wish to be free through representative democracy will have the support of Brazil in their [desire for] self-determination. The historical alliances that bind us to the free nations of the Americas will be preserved and strengthened. We shall respect the independence of nations throughout the world in regard to their domestic affairs, and we shall demand equal respect toward our own, not brooking the least interference, however subtle or discreet.

I shall do whatever lies within my means to consolidate the ideals of the civic movement of the Brazilian nation in these memorable days of April, when it rose united and resplendent in courage and determination, to restore democracy and liberate it from the frauds and distortions that were rendering it unrecog-

* Congress later extended Castelo Branco's term until March 15, 1967. —ED.

nizable. Not through a *coup d'état* but through a revolution that, born in our homes, expanded in public opinion and in our institutions, and decisively supported by the armed forces, expressed the firmness of our convictions and the depth of our concepts of life—convictions and concepts which come to us from the past and which we must transmit in ever more perfect form to future generations. It was a revolution to ensure progress without reneging the past. We have thus seen the nation stand up to vindicate its freedom and its will, finally affirmed under constitutional provisions, through the Congress as the lawful representative of the ideals and aspirations of our people. We advocate democratic freedom through government by the majority, with the collaboration and respect of the minorities. The citizens—civilians and soldiers, men and women of Brazil—in an expressive attitude, one of the most beautiful and single-minded impulses recorded in our history, rose up against the debasement of the regime.

Tirelessly and without discouragement, I shall work for the general well-being of Brazil. I shall spare no sacrifice in order that this well-being may be extended as swiftly as is reasonably possible to all Brazilians, and particularly to those who toil and suffer in the less-developed regions of the country. The takeoff toward economic development through moral, educational, material, and political elevation will be a central object of the government's attention. With this end in view, the government will not be an impediment to private enterprise, without detriment, however, to the imperatives of social justice due to the worker, who is an indispensable factor in our prosperity. I am, indeed, one of those who believe in the benefits of constant evolution, capable of reaching an ever growing number of our people, many of whom are unfortunately still far from being able to share in the conquests of civilization. We shall forge ahead in the assurance that the remedy for the evils of the extreme left does not lie in the rise of a reactionary right, but rather in the execution of the necessary reforms.

I firmly believe in the compatibility of development with the democratic processes, but I do not believe in development through an inflationary orgy, the delusion and scourge of the less-favored by fortune. Inflation and backwardness must be attacked now and at once; and no one can hope to destroy them without doing his part in the work and sacrifice that lie ahead, the only source whence the well-being and prosperity of all can flow. Let each and every one do his part and carry his own weight in this task of national recovery. Each laborer and each entrepreneur—the latter especially, to whom I repeat these words of Ruy Barbosa: *

* Brazilian writer and statesman (1849–1923).—Ed.

"It is among the more cultured and well-to-do classes that re-
generative agitations must have their starting point. If we set an
example for the people, they will follow us." Therefore, let
Brazilians who are happier or better served by fortune do their
duty toward the nation, and they will see that the whole of Brazil
will imitate them, to the glory and concord of this privileged
homeland.

The votes of the representatives of the nation who chose the
head of government at this difficult moment are assuredly the
greatest honor a citizen can receive. To me, however, they also
convey a clear idea of the magnitude of the task with which I am
charged: to fulfill the hopes of the nation. I shall go further and
say that the humility of my entire life has become greater in this
moment: never has a man been more in need of understanding,
support, and assistance from all his fellow citizens. Let the
Brazilians come to me and I will go with them, so that with God's
help and with serene confidence we can together seek better days
ahead.

4. ECONOMIC POLICY AND POLITICAL MYTHS

ROBERTO CAMPOS

. . . A second fallacy is *the confusion of the means and the end.*
The intervention of the state in certain sectors of the economy is
certainly a means to attain specific economic objectives. It should
not be an end in itself. How many of us are aware of this subtle
difference?

A third fallacy is that of *false options.* It is imagined, for example, that when the government eliminates subsidies on fuel
and opts for more realistic prices for transportation and electricity, it does so out of a kind of masochistic tendency, taking
pleasure in its disregard for the suffering of the people, the people
whom the demagogues claim to love but whom they know so
well how to deceive. . . . Nothing could be more incorrect. The
real options were and are between financing the necessary investments in roads and electricity through correct prices and realistic

Excerpts from *Política econômica e Mitos políticos* (Rio de Janeiro, 1965);
translated by the editor.

exchange rates as the basis for the taxation of fuel—and, on the other hand, either ceasing to invest or doing so at the price of printing more paper money. Ceasing to invest means economic stagnation, rationing, and ultimately the perpetuation of poverty. Printing more money means an acceleration of inflation with the greater sacrifices being made by the poor, when the illusory goal of maintaining some prices stable forces an increase in all the others. That would be so futile and ignorant an effort that it reminds me of the ancient Chinese proverb, "It is useless to go to bed early in order to save money on light, if the result is twins." . . .

Let us turn for a moment to consider what the government is trying to do, attempting to evaluate its successes and failures and assessing its future. The government does not fear self-criticism or objective analysis, since it believes, as [John Kenneth] Galbraith has said, that "Without public criticism, governments appear much better and are really much worse."

Perhaps the best way to achieve an effective assessment would be to indicate what the government proposes to do rather than accuse it of not doing what it never intended to do. The [Castelo Branco] government has proposed the following objectives. First, the gradual containment of inflation. The objective for 1964 will be only to alter the nature of the inflation, transforming it from a cumulative to a corrective process, terminating the tendency to hyperinflation which reached crisis proportions in the first four months of 1964 and was leading us to an annual inflation rate of 150 per cent.

For 1965, the government proposes to complete the process of correction of the distortions of the economy in the first three months of the year and to concentrate its efforts on limiting the inflationary process, reducing it to tolerable levels in the second half of the year. Finally, it has planned a return to a near equilibrium in 1966. I say "near-equilibrium" because complete stability would be reached in Brazil only with the nation contemplating its navel in a state of Buddhist impassivity.

This is what the government proposes. Only this. I do not promise miracles. . . . We hope that the inflation rate in 1964 will not exceed that of the previous year, despite the strong inflation in the first four months before the revolution and the vast and painful corrections that were necessary in the exchange system, in the cost of public services, and in the subsidized prices, which acted as a kind of morphine for the consumer, in some cases discouraging the producer and in others undermining our capacity to invest.

More important, much more important, than the rate of inflation, in my view, is its nature. No one in good faith will deny that the prices that have gone up the most are exactly those that should have gone up in order to correct the artificial patterns of the past, which were leading us into the blind alley of rationing and stagnation that we are already confronting face to face. What good is it to keep the price of electricity cheap when in a short time it leads to rationing because of a lack of investment? What good is it to maintain artificial prices for gasoline so as to keep transport cheap if we lessen our capacity to build and pave highways, the only realistic way to reduce transportation costs? . . .

[In 1965] external aid will begin to flow in on a more substantial scale, since in 1964 Brazil has tried to help herself, making the necessary sacrifices to appear before the financial world not as an irresponsible beggar but as an austere partner ready to sacrifice and aware of its responsibilities.

On the matter of reforms, the government plans to initiate a process of institutional modernization. It would be difficult to deny it credit for having confronted problems that are both controversial and fundamental: agrarian reform, fiscal reform, housing reform, and reform of the banking system.

President Castelo Branco declared recently that 1965 would be the year of modernization of our obsolete and inflexible administrative system, joining with it a determined effort to democratize the business firm, so that we can finally enter into the era of democratic capitalism. . . .

To initiate industrial recovery we must have a fundamental change in the attitude of our businessmen. They must abandon the psychology of low volume and high prices; they must abandon their propensity for excessive indebtedness through recourse to officially subsidized credit. They must abandon their morbid aversion to competition. . . .

The problem is less one of scarcity than of discipline—less a failure of natural resources than of character and human capital. In summary, we should have a passion for development but also sufficient rationality to organize it. We must purify our own qualities rather than engage in the infantile sport of transferring to others—the monopolies, the United States, the angels, or the devil—the blame for our poverty. We should apply ourselves to correcting our defects rather than cultivating our prejudices, for, as the poet says, the fault is not in the stars but in ourselves. No one will resolve the problems that we ourselves leave unresolved because of incompetence or cowardice.

A long and bitter road separates us from our goal; a dangerous and difficult period separates us from the day when we will have a just and prosperous society where everyone will have the right to enjoy riches because we have succeeded in eliminating poverty. But to attain that goal and to see that day, it is clear that the government must proceed with the resolution of those who will brave the storm and the patience of those who do not seek to be loved.

5. COLONIAL FASCISM IN BRAZIL

HÉLIO JAGUARIBE

Another way of dealing with the structural distortions would lead to the preservation of the social order, at the expense of the national structures and the national individuality. This model can be described in terms of three major requisites.

In the first place, this model would require . . . a substantial reinforcement of the state. Such reinforcement, however, would not be for permitting a greater intervention in the economic sphere, but for preserving stability.

In the second place, it would require the promotion of the tightest possible economic and political integration of the country into the Western system, under United States leadership—the Atlantic Community. This integration would consolidate the parties, generally in terms of their existing functions. This integration would also ensure maximum use of foreign assistance, which would compensate for the lack of internal dynamism caused by the preservation of the status quo. A third result of integration would be enlargement of markets, with a new emphasis on the Latin American Common Market, thereby incorporating the whole of Latin America (under expected Brazilian regional leadership) into the Atlantic Community.

In the third place, this model would re-establish, under state supervision, a free market, assuring private enterprise full control and management of the economy, along with the transference of most of its productive activities from the public to the private sector.

Excerpts from Hélio Jaguaribe, "Political Strategies of National Development," *Studies in Comparative International Development*, III, No. 2 (1967–68), pp. 43, 45–46; by permission.

The most appropriate name for such a model is colonial fascism. Indeed, in the last analysis fascism is simply a model for promoting economic development without changing the existing social order. The German and Italian examples, however, were characterized by the fact that in each of these countries there was an important industrial complex, owned and managed by a dynamic bourgeoisie. In the alliance between the middle class and the bourgeoisie, the German and Italian bourgeoisies let the middle class take over the political leadership of their respective countries, in exchange for preserving their ownership and management of industry. In the Brazilian case, however, this solution would be doubly impossible. Internally there is the dependence of the model on the West in general and the United States in particular, due to its need for foreign assistance and foreign markets. The adjustment of a fascist model to dependence on foreign metropolitan centers transforms it into colonial fascism. This is, therefore, why that designation has been given to the model which can deal with the Brazilian structural distortions in terms of the existing social order. . . .

The military coup which overthrew President Goulart in April, 1964, was originally an expression of a very broad opposition to his government. This opposition acquired a militant counterrevolutionary character at the end of 1963. The unexpected ease with which the first rebel troops carried with them the rest of the armed forces, and the ease with which the armed forces took full control of the country, led the coup to a fast and increasing radicalization by the right. On the other hand, these same facts led the army, as the core of the armed forces, to concentrate all power in the military as a corporation, reducing to nominal or dependent participation the politicians who had taken part in the anti-Goulart counterrevolution—a counterrevolution aware of its meaning and unsatisfied with it, which felt the compensatory necessity of labeling itself a "revolution." Carlos Lacerda, a veteran and the ablest of the Brazilian counterrevolutionists, rapidly found himself in a marginal position, long before he decided to openly recognize this and to oppose the Castelo Branco regime for its pretense of an authentic "revolutionary" message. He would, later in 1966, once again shift his position, this time to assume—in complete contradiction with all his political past—a center-left, national-laborism posture, fiercely opposed to the Castelo Branco regime.

The message of the Castelo Branco regime, however, although originally reduced to the simplistic terms of a middle-class and conservative moralism and anti-Communism, was reformulated in a very elaborated form by the new minister of planning, Roberto Campos. Diametrically opposed to Celso Furtado,* Campos prepared for the Castelo Branco regime a model for social stability, with strong colonial-fascist propensities. This model he succeeded in bringing into existence.

The total control of the state by the military and its self-legitimation by Institutional Acts provided the most formidable reinforcement of the state ever attempted in Brazil and equipped the government with means of coercion seldom paralleled even in the most authoritarian regimes. With socio-political stability thus assured, the Campos policies were oriented toward achieving financial stability. He had the advantage, in his attempt to control inflation, of not being encumbered by the usual difficulties. The tough military dictatorship eliminated working-class resistance to the more than proportional reductions of their real wages. The bourgeoisie, although alarmed by the recession caused by the anti-inflationary policies, was still too frightened by the last tendencies of the Goulart government and too concerned with the imminent risk of hyperinflation not to accept the sacrifice of a period of bad business. The middle class, although enjoying its former influence, was the least patient. Its most influential sector, the military, was, however, given a fair pay raise and compensated by many other advantages resulting from its now direct and unchecked control of the state.[1] On the other hand, insofar as the loss of autonomy and internal development of the economy was concerned, with its gradual denationalization, there was no actual problem from the point of view of the new model, oriented toward the maximum use of foreign participation. Great strides were made, therefore, in the direction of financial stability. The rate of inflation was reduced by the end of 1965 to about 45 per cent per year, half the rate of 1964, although this trend was sensibly slowed down in 1966.

The second requirement of the model, the total realignment of Brazil with the United States, was constantly proclaimed as the government's major external goal and was in all forms actively pressed forward. New facilities for foreign investment and capital movement were rapidly provided. Foreign aid, which had been practically suspended during the Goulart government, was again

---

* Celso Furtado was an economic advisor to President João Goulart and head of SUDENE, the Northeast Development Agency—Ed.

[1] The pre-existing tendency in Brazil of appointing the military to manage state-owned corporations was led to a new height by the Castelo Branco regime. Another relevant technique for increasing military pay and influence was the setting up of innumerable military commissions of inquiry (Enquerito Policial-Militar—IPM), endowed with the widest and judicially uncontrollable powers

channeled to Brazil with larger amounts promised. The political aspects of the new Brazilian foreign policy were also made visible in a fast pace of participation in the occupation of the Dominican Republic.

A third basic feature of the model, the emphasis on private capital and free enterprise, has also been put into practice. In that respect, however, due to the resistance of the military nationalists, the selling out of state-owned concerns could not be seriously contemplated. The government was even forced to restate its loyalty to Petrobrás and its policy of state oil monopoly.

6. THE BROAD FRONT (SEPTEMBER 25, 1967)

JOINT COMMUNIQUÉ OF
JOÃO GOULART AND CARLOS LACERDA

We have met together in Montevideo, convinced of the urgent necessity of promoting the redemocratization of Brazil. We know what privation and frustration the [Brazilian] people are suffering, especially the workers, who are the ones who feel the effects of the suppression of democratic freedoms most severely. We know the meaning of the silence of the workers, who are subjected to a permanent threat of violence and deprived of the opportunity to demand their rights. The archaic institutional structures, which do not respond to the desire of the country for development, must be changed by democratic and open means. We must assure Brazilians that their national riches will be used for the people and not for external and internal groups who exploit their labor.

No one has the right to use secrecy, the usurpation of civil power, or hatred to suppress the hopes of the country for the peaceful resolution of the great problems of our time. We think that it is our duty to use all the resources at our disposal to seek a peaceful solution of the current crisis of Brazil, without personal resentment or a spirit of revenge. We have not reached agreement in order to promote disorder but to assure the establishment of a true democratic order that does not consist in silence and submission.

Now more than ever, a just wage is a requirement for the

Translated by the editor from *La Nación* (Buenos Aires), September 27, 1967.

worker oppressed by poverty, and for the whole country, if it is to develop its internal market. The re-establishment of the democratic process by direct elections is essential to return the right to make decisions to the people and to produce national peace, the prerequisite for the mobilization of Brazil in the effort to develop under conditions of social justice and national independence. We want peace with liberty, law with legitimacy—not as mere words but to advance the people to power.

The Broad Front [*Frente Amplio*] is the way to fulfill, in a responsible fashion, this commitment to the popular desire for the restoration of civil and personal liberties, for the participation of all Brazilians in the establishment of the organs of government, and for the definition of the constitutional principles that will be necessary to return Brazil to the democratic process.

Motivated exclusively by our concern for the future of our country, we did not make any agreements nor did we plan new parties or future candidates for the presidency of Brazil. We spoke with objectivity and mutual respect about the present political, economic, and social situation in the country. We do not have any personal ambitions or hatred. We are animated solely by the everlasting ideal of the struggle for the liberty and greatness of Brazil and a better life for all its children. Thus, only thus, will we avoid the terrible necessity of choosing between submission and rebellion, between peace in slavery and civil war.

7. INSTITUTIONAL ACT NO. 5
(DECEMBER 13, 1968)

Considering that the revolution of March 31, 1964, and the acts by which it was institutionalized were intended to give the country a governmental system that, while respecting the requirements of a political and juridical system, would ensure an authentic democratic order based on liberty, respect, and the dignity of the human person, the fight against subversion and ideologies contrary to the traditions of our people, and the struggle against corruption, seeking in this way "the indispensable means for the economic, financial, political, and moral reconstruction of Brazil so as to face directly and immediately the

---

Translated by the editor from *O Estado de São Paulo*, December 14, 1968.

grave and urgent problems on the solution of which depend the restoration of internal order and the international prestige of our country" (Preamble to Institutional Act No. 1, April 9, 1964);

Considering that the government of the republic, which is responsible for the attainment of those objectives and for order and internal security, will not and cannot permit anti-revolutionary persons and groups to work, plot, and act against it, or it would be failing to fulfill the promises that it made to the Brazilian people, since the revolutionary power, when it issued Institutional Act No. 2, declared, "this does not mean that the revolution has taken place but that it will continue," and, therefore, that the revolutionary process cannot be restrained in its course;

Considering that the same revolutionary power, exercised through the President when he convened the national Congress to discuss, vote, and promulgate the new Constitution, stated that the Constitution, besides representing "the institutionalization of the ideas and principles of the revolution," should "assure the continuity of the work of the revolution" (Institutional Act No. 4, December 7, 1965);

Considering, nevertheless, that clearly subversive acts on the part of different political and cultural sectors prove that the legal instruments that the victorious revolution granted to the nation for the defense, development, and welfare of its people are being used as means to combat and destroy it;

Considering that it is essential that measures be adopted that will prevent the frustration of the high ideals of the revolution and preserve order, security, tranquility, economic and cultural development, and the political and social harmony of the country, which would be destroyed by subversion and revolutionary warfare;

Considering that all such disturbances of order are contrary to the ideals and the consolidation of the movement of March, 1964, and oblige those who are responsible for the movement and who have sworn to defend it to adopt the means necessary to avert its destruction, the following is decreed:

Article 1. The Constitution of January 24, 1967, and the state constitutions remain in force with the modifications contained in this Institutional Act.

Article 2. The President of the Republic may decree the recess of the national Congress, the state legislatures, and the municipal councils, by means of a Complementary Act, whether in a state of emergency or not, which bodies shall reassume their functions when convened by the President of the Republic.

Paragraph 1. When the parliamentary bodies are in recess, the appropriate executive is authorized to legislate in all matters prescribed by the Constitution or the Organic Law of Municipalities.

Paragraph 2. During the period of recess, the senators, federal and state representatives, and municipal councillors shall receive a fixed part of their salaries.

Paragraph 3. In the case of recess of municipal councils, the financing and budgetary review of the municipalities that do not have courts of accounts shall be carried out by the respective states, including hearings and review of accounts of administrators and others responsible for public property and finances.

Article 3. The President of the Republic, in the national interest, may by decree take over the government of states and municipalities, without observing the limitations specified in the Constitution.

Paragraph 1. "Interventors" in the states and municipalities shall be named by the President of the Republic and shall exercise all the functions and powers, respectively, of governors or municipal prefects and enjoy the prerogatives, perquisites, and benefits attached to those offices.

Article 4. In the interest of preserving the revolution, the President of the Republic, with the advice of the National Security Council and without observing the limits specified in the Constitution, may suspend the political rights of any citizen for a period of ten years and may nullify federal, state, and municipal electoral mandates.

Paragraph 1. The members of federal, state, or municipal legislatures who have their mandates nullified shall not be replaced so long as a parliamentary quorum remains in the legislature involved.

Article 5. The suspension of political rights as described in this act means the following: (1) termination of parliamentary immunity; (2) suspension of the right to vote or to run in union elections; (3) prohibition of actions or public statements on matters of a political nature; (4) application, when necessary, of the following security measures: (a) surveillance of liberty; (b) prohibition against frequenting specified places; (c) assignment of domicile.

Paragraph 1. The act that decrees the suspension of political rights may fix restrictions or prohibitions on the exercise of any private or public rights.

Paragraph 2. The security measures listed in Item 4 of this article shall be applied by the Minister of Justice, and no appeal of his action to the judiciary shall be permitted.

Article 6. The constitutional or legal guarantees of life tenure, nontransferability, and security, as well as the guarantee of the exercise of office for a fixed time, are suspended.

Paragraph 1. The President of the Republic may by decree dismiss, remove, retire, or place on the inactive list anyone who is subject to the guarantees mentioned in this article as well as employees of public corporations, enterprises, or mixed companies and may dismiss, transfer to the reserve, or reorganize military personnel or members of the military police, maintaining when applicable the perquisites and benefits proportionate to the period of service.

Paragraph 2. The provisions of this article and Paragraph 1 also apply to the states, the municipalities, the territories, and the federal district.

Article 7. The President of the Republic may, in any of the cases specified by the Constitution, declare a state of siege and establish the period for which it will be applicable.

Article 8. The President of the Republic may, after investigation, decree the confiscation of the property of all those guilty of illicit enrichment in the exercise of public office, including public corporations, enterprises, and mixed companies, without prejudice to the appropriate legal penalties.

Paragraph 1. If the legitimacy of the acquisition of the property confiscated is proven, restitution shall be made.

Article 9. The President of the Republic may issue Complementary Acts for the execution of this Institutional Act as well as adopt, if necessary for the defense of the revolution, the measures provided in lines (*d*) and (*e*) of Paragraph 2 of Article 152 of the Constitution.*

Article 10. The guarantee of habeas corpus is suspended in cases of political crimes against national security, the economic and social order, and the popular economy.

Article 11. All acts carried out in accordance with this Institutional Act and its Complementary Acts and their effects are exempt from judicial review.

Article 12. The present Institutional Act shall take effect on this date, all contrary legal dispositions being revoked.

* Sections of the 1967 Constitution that provide for the suspension of the right of assembly and the establishment of censorship in cases where the president declares a state of siege.—ED.

8. IS VIOLENCE THE ONLY OPTION?

DOM HELDER CAMARA

It is easy to speak about violence when it is a question of condemning it from afar, without identifying it, distinguishing its
various types, or analyzing its deeper causes; or of praising it
from afar, in the manner of a living room Ché Guevara. . . .

An initial observation that is fundamental to a real understanding of the problem of violence is this: The whole world is
in need of a structural revolution.

In the underdeveloped world, this truth seems evident; but as
one examines the underdeveloped world from many perspectives
—economic, political, social, and religious—one begins to understand that a superficial alteration will not suffice. We must attempt a total change in depth, a profound, and rapid change, a
structural—let us not fear the word—revolution. . . .

From the economic point of view, who is not aware that a
system of internal colonialism exists in the underdeveloped
countries? That is to say, there is a small group of the privileged
in those countries whose wealth is maintained at the expense of
the misery of millions of their fellow citizens. It is still a semifeudal system: In some ways the life appears patriarchal, but in
reality the absence of individual rights creates a subhuman condition of real slavery. The rural workers—real pariahs—have no
access to most of the land, which the owners of the great estates
keep uncultivated for future speculation.

When this situation exists in a continent such as Latin America, which is entirely Christian—at least in name and tradition—
one can appreciate the enormous responsibility of Christianity.
Without ignoring the great examples of abnegation, of sacrifice,
even of heroism, we must recognize that in the past—and this
danger persists into the present—we Latin Americans bear a large
responsibility for the injustice that exists in this continent. We
accepted the slavery of Indians and Africans: And even now,
have we spoken in a clear and straightforward fashion to the
owners of the large estates, to the great and the powerful? Or

---

Translated by the editor from "La Violencia: Opción Unica?," in *DC
Avanzada* (Bogotá), No. 14 (July, 1968).

have we closed our eyes and helped them to have an easy conscience, so long as they cover up their frightful injustices with alms for the construction of churches (frequently scandalously large and ornate, in shocking contrast with the surrounding misery), or with contributions for our social programs? Have we perhaps made Marx appear to be correct, presenting a passive Christianity to the pariahs—one that is both alienated and alienating, truly an opiate of the masses . . . ?

If we Christians of Latin America assume our responsibility regarding the underprivileged nations of the continent, we can and should help to promote profound changes in social life, particularly in politics and in education.

Politics cannot continue to be the property of the privileged classes, which impede basic reforms, distort them, or leave them only on paper.

Education is so far removed from the requirements of technology, which is always progressing, that one begins to comprehend the unhappiness of our university students, who ridicule the university reforms imposed on them as shallow, flimsy, and unchallenging.

What I am saying about Latin America can be said about almost the entire undeveloped world: Everywhere there is real need of a structural revolution. . . .

Now, we ask ourselves if the structural revolution that the world needs necessarily presupposes that violence be exercised at times, even unconsciously, by the same people who condemn it as a plague on society.

Violence exists in the underdeveloped world: The oppressed masses are abused by small groups of the privileged and powerful. It is well known that if the masses try to become human beings and make an effort at education or popular culture, if they organize themselves into syndicates or cooperatives, their leaders are described as subversives and Communists. It has been said very accurately: "They appear to be rebels against the established order—they are put outside the law . . . they must be removed for order to reign." . . . Disorderly order!

As for "law," very often it is an instrument of violence against the less powerful, or it is reduced to platitudes in the text of declarations like the Universal Declaration of Human Rights, whose twentieth anniversary the world is about to commemorate. A good way for the United Nations to celebrate this anniversary would be to determine whether any of these rights are really respected in two-thirds of the world. . . .

Violence also exists in the developed world, as much on the

capitalist as on the socialist side. In this respect, there are signs of disquiet that speak very clearly.

In the face of this threefold violence—in the underdeveloped countries, in the developed countries, and by the developed countries against the underdeveloped countries—one can understand why people think, talk, and act in terms of liberating or redeeming violence.

If those who have the power in the underdeveloped world do not have the courage to rid themselves of their privileges and to do justice to the millions of people living in a subhuman condition, if governments make reforms that remain only on paper, how can one restrain the youth who are tempted by radicalism and violence? How will it be possible to control the youth of the developed nations on both sides, if the signs of disquiet and of violence are multiplied? How can nuclear bombs be more powerful than the bomb of misery that is being prepared in the womb of the Third World?

Allow me the small favor of expressing my position:

With respect to those who, in conscience, feel obliged to opt for violence, not the easy violence of the guerrillas of the living room, but the violence of those who have proved their sincerity by the sacrifice of their lives, it seems to me that the memory of Camilo Torres or of Ché Guevara merits as much respect as that of the Reverend Martin Luther King.

I accuse as the real promoters of violence all those, whether of the right or the left, who have hurt the cause of justice and impeded peace.

My personal vocation is that of a pilgrim of peace, following the example of Paul VI: Personally, I would prefer a thousand times to be killed than to kill.

This personal position is founded on the Gospel. A lifelong effort to understand and live the Gospel has led me to the profound conviction that the Gospel can and should be called revolutionary, in the sense that it demands a conversion in each of us. We do not have the right to enclose ourselves in our own egoism. We should open ourselves to the love of God and the love of mankind. And it is enough to think of the beatitudes— the quintessence of the Gospel's message—to discover that the choice for Christians seems clear: We Christians are on the side of nonviolence, which is a choice neither of weakness nor of passivity. Nonviolence is believing in a higher power than the power of war, of death, and of hate—it is believing in the power of truth, justice, and love.

If this seems moralistic to you, wait one moment. The option of nonviolence is rooted in the Gospel; it is also based on reality.

Do they want realism? Then I say to them: If there should appear in any part of the world, but above all in Latin America, an outbreak of violence, they can be certain that, immediately, the great powers will arrive—even without a declaration of war—and we will have a new Vietnam. If they want more realism: Precisely because we must carry out a structural revolution, it is necessary first to promote, but in a new sense, a cultural revolution, because if attitudes are not changed, then the structural reforms, the basic reforms, will remain only on paper, ineffective.

I direct myself particularly to the young.

To the young of the underdeveloped countries, I say: Why get power if you still have no models adapted to your own countries, because until now you have been taught solutions that are perhaps valid, but valid for developed countries. While we try to exert moral pressure, with increasing animosity, on those responsible for the situation in our countries, try to prepare for the responsibilities that will be yours tomorrow, to aid the masses to become human beings. You know very well that material and physical underdevelopment causes intellectual, moral, and spiritual underdevelopment.

To the young of the developed countries—of both the capitalist system and the socialist—I say: Instead of going to the Third World in order to try to activate violence there, stay home in order to help develop the consciences of the affluent countries, which also need a cultural revolution that will lead to a new hierarchy of values, a new view of the world, a global strategy for development, the revolution of mankind. . . .

Only men who achieve in themselves interior unity, only men with heavenly vision and universal hearts, will be valid instruments for the miracle of being violent as the prophets, sincere as Christ, revolutionary as the Gospel, but without offending against love.

9. DECLARATION OF THE CENTRAL COMMITTEE OF THE BRAZILIAN EPISCOPATE (FEBRUARY 18, 1969)

PRESENCE OF THE CHURCH

This is the first meeting of the Central Committee of the National Bishops' Conference of Brazil (CNBB) since the serious national crisis that began on December 13th of the past year. The Committee considers that it has a strict obligation to make public its thinking and its concerns. We, the undersigned, are citizens of this country, which we deeply love. We are not moved by partisan political motives but by a concern for the common good and by our pastoral responsibility for the mission of the Church, which is one of service, solidarity, and communion with the sufferings and aspirations of our fellow citizens, as well as by a desire to promote the efforts that are being made to develop the nation.

The orthodoxy and activities of the Catholic Church in Brazil are our responsibility. The Church has been present in a positive and beneficial way throughout our national history, and it cannot refuse at this time to give its loyal collaboration to the government in every area in which it is sincerely working for truth, justice, liberty, and love.

Reforms for the Benefit of Man

It is this sense of service and conscious collaboration that obliges us to apply the social doctrine of the Church, an important aspect of the preaching of the Gospel, to demand the reforms which the government itself has frequently affirmed as necessary and which it can now carry out because of the exceptional powers that it possesses.

These reforms do not signify the subversion of order but a change in the archaic structures that are flagrant obstacles to development. These reforms do not in any way accept Marxist and Communist postulates, but neither can they consist in the defense and incidental improvement of a status quo in which profit is the supreme value of economic progress, competition the sole law of the economy, and private ownership of the goods of production an absolute right.

It is not by reason of a materialistic conception of life—the belief that efficiency, economy, productivity, and technical competence are central—but it is to man that we consider an authentic development must be directed. Every man has the right to realize himself as a person; that is to say, to assume his vocation in society and to carry out his responsibilities in the field of work for which he is qualified.

A reform aimed at the development of the whole man can only be carried out in solidarity. Man must see his fellow man as a brother and a son of God, in order to construct a just, fraternal

---

Translated by the editor from NADOC (Lima), No. 35 (March 12, 1969).

society in which the progress of a few is not an obstacle to the development of the rest. In this connection, we would hope that certain ambiguous terms would no longer be used, such as "subversion," "socialization," "democracy," *"conscientização,"* * "security," and "development."

The Mission of the Church

In November, 1967, we wrote:

"Although the teachings of the Church, based on the message revealed in a perfect manner by Jesus Christ, refer essentially to truths that relate to the eternal destiny of man, they are also concerned with the human values that are the unavoidable basis of a transcendent life. We repudiate the Marxist thesis that religion alienates man by offering the consolation of a future happiness as compensation for the inevitability of earthly frustration. To assert that the religious mission of the bishops should not go beyond the limits of the so-called spiritual life is to accept in practice the Marxist conception of religion. To proclaim the defense of Christian civilization, and at the same time to limit the teaching mission of the Church in the defense of human values, is a disguised form of paganism.

"We therefore profoundly regret the distorted interpretations and the misunderstanding of the actions of the Church in our country—even if there may have been some lack of prudence, which we likewise regret. In fact, we are against true subversive movements; that is to say, those that produce social disorder and seek anarchy in order to impose the interests of one group. However, we also think that it is subversive of the social order to abuse one's political and economic power for one's personal benefit."

We reaffirm what we said in 1967. We are determined to apply the principles of the Second Vatican Council, of the social encyclicals, and now of the Second General Conference of the Latin American Episcopate in Medellín.† Even if this causes us bitter personal difficulties, this is our response to the request of the Holy Father, to the needs of our people, and to the outcry of civilization.

* *Conscientização* refers to programs of radical Catholics to develop political consciousness among peasants and slum-dwellers.—Ed.

† The social encyclicals are papal declarations of the social teaching of the Church, especially *Rerum Novarum* (1891) of Leo XIII, *Quadragesimo Anno* (1931), of Pius XI, and *Mater et Magistra* (1961) of John XXIII. The meeting of the organization of Latin American bishops (CELAM) at Medellín, Colombia, in September, 1968, was concerned with social questions.—Ed.

Position of the Church

The present situation, given institutional form last December, is an open invitation to arbitrary action and the violation of fundamental rights, such as the right of defense and the right to the legitimate expression of thought and information. It threatens human dignity both physically and morally. Power has been established in a way that makes it very difficult to have an authentic dialogue between governors and governed and leads many Brazilians to dangerous underground activity. We recall the words of Pius XI, "Some human laws which are clearly opposed to the natural law are vitiated from the outset and cannot be improved by pressure or intensification of external force."

A Call and An Exhortation

Our ardent desire, in the form of an appeal to all men of good will, especially to those who are presently responsible for the destiny of the nation, is that a re-democratization of the regime be carried out as soon as possible. We are fulfilling our pastoral duty in recalling that those who have absolute power of decision in their hands assume an enormous responsibility before God and history.

In the charity of Christ we exhort the clergy and the faithful, including those who exercise public responsibilities, to an increasingly generous fidelity to the Gospels and to the teachings of the Church, especially to those of our Holy Father, Paul VI, with whom we feel firmly and affectionately united. We hope for perseverance from all and effective action, guided by prudence and inspired by respect and love for our country.

May the Virgin, Our Lady of the Apparition, Queen and Patroness of Brazil, lead us to the Prince of Peace and grant the peace that is the fruit of justice and love (as Paul VI recalled in his last Christmas Message), harmony of spirit, true security, and the attainment of the means which will lead to "the development of the whole man and of all men."

10. THE BRAZILIAN ARMY AND POLITICS

GENERAL AURELIO DE LYRA TAVARES

THE ARMY AND THE IDEOLOGICAL STRUGGLE

As a national institution in a democratic state, the Army cannot be an organization apart, autonomous, and immune from changes in the government, particularly since the government has the power to select, promote, and assign military leaders as serves the interests and purposes of those in power. This means that, both in the past and at present, the Army is less political and more professionalized where the democratic structure of the state is the most stable and developed.

Two forces, which sometimes converge, are capable of weakening the cohesion and discipline of the Army, compromising its role as a supporter of democracy: an external one, directed by international Communism, and an internal one, resulting from distortions and fluctuations in the policy of the government. The first of these forces, which possesses vast means and resources, is directed from abroad but also makes use of domestic agents. It exploits the discontent of the poorer sectors of the civilian population and incites the worker in the city and the countryside against the Army; it tells him that one of the principal causes of his low standard of living is the large unproductive expenditure for the maintenance of the armed forces, which are depicted as an instrument of oppression in the service of the priviliged classes. At the same time, it lends the Communist name to the worldwide movement for peace through the brotherhood of the workingmen of all nations.

This ideological effort is directed at the minds of men without civic education, and it attempts to persuade them to become revolutionaries and potential instruments of subversion. It is important to be aware of this fact and to consider it in military recruiting, so that the Army is not infiltrated by elements capable of compromising its unity of spirit and action.

Translated by the editor from O Exercito Brasileiro visto pelo seu Ministro (Recife, 1968).

To neutralize the effects of this propaganda, it is necessary to demonstrate the popular character of the democratic army by explaining to the man of the less favored classes the meaning of free government and the dignity that it assures him, in contrast to life under a Communist regime. This effort is most convincing when it points to the participation of the army in constructive civic-action and aid programs, especially in areas that are vulnerable to Communist propaganda.

In the case of Brazil, this kind of orientation has proved to be beneficial. I could see this as Commander of the Fourth Army. The area of jurisdiction of the Fourth Army stretched from Maranhão to Bahia; it included the nine states most influenced by Communist propaganda before the democratic revolution of March 31, 1964, and the areas that were most vulnerable in the defense of the continent, because of the strategic location of the Northeast and the shocking contrast between the wealth of a small minority and the poverty of the general population. Under the influence of a government that was involved in subverting the social order, the country was rapidly moving toward Communism through the organization of the peasants and the progressive weakening of the cohesion and discipline of the Army.

At that time, I could see for myself the firm commitment to democracy of our military officers, including the noncommissioned officers, who were the particular objects of subversive teachings. Because of its hierarchical structure, the Army could therefore resist this effort and at the appropriate time rise up to preserve our traditional institutions.

In this effort, the Brazilian military had the support and confidence of the people of the Northeast. These feelings resulted from the great influence of the Army, in civic education, in aid and training programs, and, especially, from the substantial support that the Corps of Engineers enjoys in the interior of the Northeast because of the essential public works it undertakes for the improvement of the living conditions of the people. The Army's involvement in this and other types of civic action is a longtime tradition in Brazil.

This does not mean that the Army is immune to Communist propaganda, especially when the political and administrative structure of the government is open to the infiltration and activities of Communist elements, as was the case in Brazil prior to the revolution of March 31, 1964. Against the possibility that this second force may develop because of the internal weakness of the governmental structure, it is important to preserve the morale of the armed forces. In extreme cases of action, or inaction, by the government, which may compromise the security of our democratic institutions, the armed forces face a grave dilemma, caught between violating what appears to be the legal structure and betraying the country of which they are supposed to be the ultimate guardian. . . .

We have a horror of militarism. Dictatorship? Never. Much less a military dictatorship. History proves what I am saying. You may recall that the only dictator this country ever had was not a military man.* The Brazilian Army's tradition of respect for civil power has been uninterrupted throughout our national history. This demonstrates the unalterably civilian orientation of the military in Brazil and illustrates the role it has played in guaranteeing and strengthening our democratic structure. In Brazil, we have never had the figure of the military strong man [caudillo], nor has the military power usurped the functions of the civilian power in order to assume direction of the nation.

In exceptional circumstances, on the rare occasions in which the continuity of the democratic process was threatened in Brazil and the very survival of its institutions and sovereignty was in peril, the strictly legalistic spirit of the Army had to give way; the Army then rose up to intervene among the parties and to take power, for the sole purpose of re-establishing the democratic order. It has been led to that extreme by its inalienable and lofty duty. This is a mission that it has exercised at various points in the democratic development of the nation, in order that Brazil might advance with determination and security. This is the great desire of all true democrats, both military and civilian. As I said during Army Week in Recife, the Army has tried to remain invulnerable to the repeated appeals and attempts of groups that invoke the prestige of the uniform as a magic solution to the problem of strengthening political power in Brazil. But that prestige derives precisely from the aversion of the Brazilian military man to any kind of dictatorship. . . .

[The movement of March 31] once again demonstrated the Army's fidelity to democracy. It was a proof of its vitality and represented a general and forceful reaction by the democratic spirit of the Brazilian people. And the Army, as well as the other branches of the armed forces, had to demonstrate its solidarity with the people. It does not have an attitude different from that of the people. The Revolutionary Command took power into its hands for the minimum period necessary before

---

* Getulio Vargas, provisional president after the Brazilian revolution of 1930, was elected by the constituent assembly in 1934 to serve until 1938. He seized power in a coup in 1937, ruling as dictator until 1945. He won the 1950 presidential elections and served as constitutional president until his suicide in 1954.—ED.

transferring it to the President of the Republic. When the nation invests the presidency in a military man, it is clear that his role as a citizen overshadows his role as a soldier, for that is what the term "civil power" means to him. No one is more of a civilian than the Brazilian military man invested with civil office. No force in Brazil is more vigorously opposed to military dictatorship, as well as to the dictatorship of any class, than the civic conscience of the soldier. . . .

[The opponents of the restoration of Brazilian democracy], because they do not find the climate suitable for subversion and corruption, seek to present the revolution of March 31 as a military movement to establish a military dictatorship. The very liberties that they use and abuse constitute a convincing public refutation of their position, the proof that invalidates the basis of the argument to which they appeal. The Brazilian Army never was and never will be a militaristic army, or one subject to any party that arrogates to itself the right to select its membership, to prescribe the attitudes and even the thinking of its men, as is the case in politicized armies. Our Army does not take part in politics because it is not a party but a national institution. Power is for it a temporary responsibility, which cannot be refused in moments of national crisis or prolonged beyond that period, for the Army is aware that power is justified only when it is exercised in order to overcome a crisis, and for no other purpose. . . .

We are individuals and interested citizens who favor development. We were the forerunners in this field, for Brazil was born when the Army Engineers marked off and guaranteed our frontiers. The Army is a force for the dynamic development of the interior, particularly through the construction battalions, which are building highways and opening up distant regions. How can they help but rush to the defense of our petroleum and other subsoil resources? . . . .

Is there a "hard line" faction [within the armed forces]? I realize that it exists in the newspaper columns, but it does not exist within the military family. There is simply a pyramidal hierarchy, a homogeneous structure in spirit and action, under the direction of the President of the Republic. Everything else is pure speculation. . . .

V. *Argentina: The Military vs. Peronism*

In the case of Brazil, inflation, corruption, and Communism were the issues that led the military to take power in 1964. In Argentina, the democratic regime that was overthrown in June, 1966, had also failed to solve the problems of inflation and corruption. But the most important element in the decision of the Argentine military to stage a *coup d'état* was the fear of the return to power of the followers of former dictator Juan Perón. Since Perón's overthrow in 1955, the Argentine political system had been unable to incorporate the third of the electorate, principally the organized workers, who consistently voted Peronist. The military who intervened in 1966 were not defenders of oligarchic rule; in fact, a struggle within the armed services had recently been won by the *Azules* faction, which favored constitutional democracy. But when the government of President Arturo Illia appeared incapable of dealing with the economic and political problems facing the country (especially that of Peronism), the military commanders removed the president and replaced him with General Juan Carlos Onganía, the prestigious former Army Chief of Staff. A Statute of the Revolution superseded the Constitution (*Selection 1*), and political parties, the Congress, and democratic self-government were indefinitely suspended. Onganía himself spoke of remaining in power for ten years.

As in Brazil, the military made an alliance with orthodox economists in order to reduce the rampant inflation and promote economic development. (A description of this "Bismarckian formula," by the Argentine sociologist José Luis de Imaz, is included as *Selection 2*.) The Minister of Economics, Adalberto Krieger Vasena, had considerable success in holding down prices and in attracting foreign investment; his economic liberalism competed for Onganía's favor with the "corporatist" philosophy of the Minister of the Interior, Guillermo Borda, who called for greater state control of the economy and the incorporation into the governmental structure of organized social groups (*Selection 3*). The government also won the support of traditional Catholic conservatives, such as Alfredo Rueda, because it promised "order, discipline, and hierarchy" (see *Selection 4*). The strong support Onganía received from the Argentine middle class, the largest in

Latin America, led some observers to question the earlier assumption that the Latin American middle class favors democracy over authoritarianism. The Argentine political scientist José Nun has argued that their fear that the lower classes will be mobilized by such leaders as Vargas and Goulart in Brazil, and Perón in Argentina leads the middle class to support military intervention (*Selection 5*).

The Peronist labor leaders were at first divided in their attitude to the military government; the majority, however, soon joined the opposition to the regime. A criticism of the labor policies of the Onganía regime, by John W. Cooke, Secretary General of the left-wing Acción Revolucionaria Peronista, is included as *Selection 6*. A year after the coup, the Onganía government was also attacked by a group of democratic socialists, led by Américo Ghioldi, for its infringement of the democratic process (*Selection 7*). By mid-1969, labor and student opposition had undermined the image of stability that the military sought to project. After violence swept several provincial cities, Onganía reorganized his cabinet, dropping both Krieger Vasena and Borda. In June, 1969, even the business-oriented mass magazine *Primera Plana* deplored the lack of functioning democracy in Argentina (*Selection 8*). (Shortly thereafter, *Primera Plana* was suppressed by the regime.) A viable alternative to military rule has yet to emerge, however, and Argentina remains deeply divided.

1. THE STATUTE OF THE REVOLUTION
(JUNE 28, 1966)

Bearing in mind the Official Proclamation of the Revolution, and considering:

That the government represents all the people of the republic, whose sacrifice and collaboration are indispensable to attain the ends of the revolution and re-establish our national greatness;

That the government is backed by the armed forces and other security and police forces, and therefore has sufficient power to guarantee peace and public order and protect the lives and property of the population;

That it is necessary to give an efficient and flexible structure to the various governmental offices, with power to do whatever is necessary, including acts of a legislative character;

That the government intends to promote the participation of representative sectors of the Argentine people in the preparation of initiatives of great importance;

That the principle of judicial tenure must be maintained as an essential way to ensure the full rule of law, the violation of which has been one of the principal causes of the evils that afflict the republic;

That since the government must be guided by the goals of the revolution, the Statute of the Revolution, and the national Constitution, it is indispensable to have a Supreme Court whose members have sworn allegiance to the above norms;

That the republic will strictly observe its contractual obligations;

That, in the case of the President's inability to exercise his office, it is necessary to establish the manner in which he will be replaced;

For these reasons:

The Revolutionary Junta, in order to attain the objectives of the revolution and in exercise of its constitutional power, decrees:

Article 1. The executive power shall be exercised by the citizen whom this Revolutionary Junta designates as President of the Argentine nation.

Article 2. A law shall establish the number of ministers and

Translated by the editor from *Ordenamiento jurídico y básico de la Revolución* (Buenos Aires, 1967).

secretaries of state who will handle the affairs of the nation, and it shall also establish their functions and interrelationships.

Article 3. The government shall carry out its activities in accordance with the Articles of this statute, the principles of the national Constitution, and the laws and decrees that follow them, insofar as they do not oppose the goals enunciated in the Official Proclamation of the Revolution.

Article 4. The government shall respect all the international obligations undertaken by the Argentine republic.

Article 5. The President shall exercise all the legislative powers that the national Constitution assigns to the Congress, including the powers that are exclusive to each chamber, with the exception of those defined in Article 45, 51, and 52, concerning cases of the impeachment of judges of the national courts.

Article 6. In order to receive the best advice concerning legislative matters, the President shall be able to convene permanent or transitory bodies that are established by law.

Article 7. The judges designated to form the Supreme Court and the present members of the lower tribunals shall be protected by the guarantees of Article 96 of the national Constitution.

Article 8. To comply with Articles 45, 51, and 52 of the national Constitution, referring to the members of the Supreme Court and lower tribunals, the government shall promulgate a law establishing a special jury of judgment for judges of the national courts.

Article 9. The government shall tend to the needs of the provincial governments and shall designate the governors, who shall exercise the powers defined in the provincial constitutions with respect to the executive and legislative branches, and shall carry out their responsibilities in accordance with the principles expressed in Articles 3 and 5 of the present statute and the instructions of the national government.

With reference to the judiciary, the governors may propose, on one occasion only, the total or partial replacement of the present members of the superior courts of each province. With respect to the other judges, they shall observe the guarantees of tenure contained in each provincial constitution. For the removal of these judges, the governors shall establish a special system in line with the principles established for national judges.

Article 10. When the President is absent from the country, his office shall be exercised by the Minister of the Interior. In the case of the incapacity or death of the President, his successor shall be designated by the unanimous decision of the Commanders in Chief of the Armed Forces.

2. NEO-BISMARCKIANISM AND THE ARGENTINE REVOLUTION

JOSÉ LUIS DE IMAZ

It is possible that in Argentina we shall find a new example of the "Bismarckian formula." The "Bismarckian formula" is a well-known sociopolitical formula that can serve as a basis for true national development. This model is often opposed to the models of classical liberal-capitalism and state socialism.

The "Bismarckian" model calls for the state to promote the development process through state action, although the actual implementation is left to private interests. In this model, the state is controlled by a strong man with powerful military backing, who launches a long-range development program. This strong man, who comes from the traditional sectors, is able to mediate between traditionalism and modernism; he is surrounded by a "concentrated elite" and imposes his plan through the centralization of power.

The plan makes an appeal for national unity; it makes a nationalistic plea to the various sectors and supports the dynamic industrial sectors instead of the traditional ones. Businessmen, and not the state, sustain the economy. They recognize that the state provides stability and social peace, and this social peace is the result of the trust that the labor force has in the head of state and the actions of the head of state who, despite his different origins, listens to them and satisfies their expectations. We say that this model may be reproduced in Argentina because some of the a priori preconditions are present.

Whether this happens or not depends not only on the personality of the man who assumes the role of Bismarck, but also on the capacity of the "elite" that surrounds him to develop a "Bismarckian imagination." A "Bismarckian imagination" entails the ability to discern, among the conflicting groups, those sectors in the country that favor modernization and human progress and those that support the status quo.

Once it is known which are the immobile interests and which

Translated by the editor from La "Revolución Argentina" (Buenos Aires: Ediciones Depalma, 1966), pp. 187-90; by permission.

are the dynamic ones, which ideologies are stunted in their development and where the perceptive analysts may be found, their incorporation into the government elite becomes a matter of strategy. The strategy is easy to carry out when one has a monopoly of political power.

This is essentially the "Bismarckian model," with an immovable center that is in no danger of being dominated by private interests.

The preconditions are favorable: The re-emergence of a paternalistic image, the proclivity of the masses to adhere to authoritarian systems of government, the hopes of our compatriots for providential solutions, all create a favorable climate for the popular support of the new elite.

What is lacking can be obtained through authenticity—a relationship of authenticity between the theoretical image and the practical results. Bismarck was not charismatic, but even the lower classes were loyal to him because of the close relation between his accomplishments and the image of authority.

Here in Argentina, perhaps, we have another chance to produce this model.

3. THE REVOLUTION AND PARTICIPATION

GUILLERMO BORDA

When we say that we hope that well-organized labor unions will participate in the revolutionary process, we should be taken at our word. Since the head of the revolution [Juan Carlos Onganía] assumed the presidency, there have been no demagogic concessions, nor have we been guided by political considerations. But we want the support of the community, and we know that we will not attain it unless we give each of the vital sectors the degree of participation it deserves in a democratic and coherent society.

This participation is inherent in the concept of an organized society, which is opposed to the individualistic concept that a

Excerpts from a speech to the Foreign Press Association, published in *Cinco Discursos y una Revolución* (Buenos Aires, 1968); translated by the editor.

relationship exists only between the state and the individual citizen. According to the individualistic conception, the citizen completes his political role on election day by voting for one of the lists that are offered to him. The complexity of modern society, however, demands the permanent participation of the citizen in the multiple functions that make up the service and government of the country. Pierre Mendès-France has said: "Democracy means the continuous influence of the citizen not only on governmental affairs, but also on religious, communal, and cooperative affairs. . . . Movement and progress are possible only if democracy permeates the social structure and constantly rejuvenates society." "The national will"—he concludes—"can only triumph if the people exercise their will directly, through countless local and national organizations where all the questions concerning public life are raised."

We must add, in order not to be misunderstood, that communal participation does not replace or exclude traditional political rights, such as elections and political parties. On the contrary, it affirms, rejuvenates, and strengthens them.

Participation perfects democratic life because it organizes the citizen's activity in fields other than the electoral one and develops a civic involvement that is receptive to the needs of the municipality, province, region, and nation. It is the proper way to change structures and to seek more liberty and justice for men and nations.

The constitutional principle that the people deliberate and govern only through their representatives, which in the orthodox liberal conception involved excluding the citizen who does not hold office from any governmental function, has acquired a new and more productive sense. It is right that only the representatives of the people should govern; this brought about the fall of the previous regime, when the political parties, and consequently the men chosen by them, ceased to be representative. We now want the people involved in government in many ways, through authentic representatives. We do not want to limit popular participation simply to the right to vote in elections. We want associations, corporations, cultural centers, affecting all aspects of national life, to flourish with the involvement of those who govern and those governed, thus permitting the most valuable elements of society to participate in community life and in everything that affects its development.

The lack of true representativity in those who were in power generated a crisis of authority and, as a consequence, impotency in government. One of the most obvious examples of this situation was the lack of legislative capacity on the part of Congress.

In a changing society, which required that legislation keep pace with the times, Congress was alarmingly stagnant. Aside from the budgetary law, and other laws forced upon them by impending elections, Congress was unable to accomplish the most minimal reform of our legislative system. . . .

The philosophy of liberalism was imbued with a basic optimism about the natural evolution of men and society. It believed that progress would be spontaneous and that all that was needed was to liberate personal initiative from all restraint and intervention. This school of thought has reached a crisis in our time. Our society is highly technical and complex; its development cannot be left to chance and unorganized individual efforts. An efficient directing power is needed as an indispensable means to promote social, economic, educational, technological, and political change and to develop and extend it to the whole society. It would be a costly error to resist such a leadership for fear that it would affect the democratic style of life. On the contrary, the real menace to modern democracy consists of weakness and ineptitude in the leadership. An energetic and intelligent direction, based on a solid plan, makes change possible. . . .

Today, I have presented many arguments against those who describe us as corporatists. I have spoken of the need for a change in structures, for communal participation, and for energetic leadership of the development process. For much less reason than that, we were given that label [corporatist] last year. But words wear thin, and this accusation no longer disturbs us. In a revolution that seeks to modernize the country, no one can reasonably hope to establish an outmoded political system that is based on the false and dangerous premise of the division of the people into [separate] sectors and that, still worse, has totalitarian connotations.

4. ORDER, DISCIPLINE, AND HIERARCHY

ALFREDO RUEDA

The philosophy of the West recognizes order in the universe as a basic principle. In the physical world, much of this order is obvious; it is governed by laws of regularity and proportion that can be confirmed by experimentation. (There is also order in other fields, as in mathematics, where we find many examples that impress us with their regularity.) Furthermore, physical and mathematical order are related in a way that can be discovered and described. This vision of order is not limited to these two fields or to their combination; it also includes the ethical field—that is, the rules that govern the relations among men, that determine a way of living and life itself.

To live within a framework of order like the one that exists in the universe should be the aspiration of any nation that hopes to create, build, and progress. This subject is a very timely one. If, in every generation, youth has been the object of criticism, those who judge the youth of today find greater reason for concern. Though comparisons with other generations are impossible, there is a strong feeling that at least a part of today's youth is very disturbing in its refusal to conform, its propensity to rebel, and its pretensions.

Since the young are hostile and incomprehensible, any circumstance can lead to a conflict, which is almost always violent and contrary to public order. The [May, 1968] student demonstrations in Paris, a paramount example of so many other demonstrations in various parts of the world, culminated in a state of anarchy and the destruction, so to speak, of the whole structure of France. They offer one more proof that the world seems to disown the rule of law, aspiring to destroy our Western civilization with its principles, precepts, moral structure, and religion.

The wave of violence unleashed in the United States—represented by the murders of Martin Luther King and Robert Kennedy—although limited to the United States, is a terrible condition, the causes and origins of which are subject to conjecture, much of it ill intentioned and therefore destructive. Let this essay be in memory of Martin Luther King, winner of the Nobel Peace Prize, and Robert F. Kennedy, young politician with the makings of a true statesman and the merits and qualifications to occupy the presidency of the United States.

The word "order" includes many different aspects of life, and it is impossible for me to cover all of them here. From our point of view, order is the established and harmonious disposition of all things. When public order is disturbed, peace and tranquility are destroyed. Our definition of order is a very ambitious one, since if it were achieved the world would be perfect. But this only serves to make its attainment all the more desirable.

Without downgrading the creative capacity of the individual, we must recognize man's need to live in society. His worth is developed on the basis of his cultural and social heritage. Over

Translated by the editor from *La Nación* (Buenos Aires), July 28, 1968.

time, his habits, customs, conventions, and knowledge form different civilizations. We are part of one of the most prodigious of all—that of the West.

Yet two tendencies aspire to alter the established order and destroy peace and tranquility by resorting to force: the anarchists, who in their extreme individuality do not recognize social order and try to destroy it; and those diametrically opposed to them, the Communists, who recognize the social aspect but reject the individual as a source of creative activity. They employ force, destruction, and chaos, to appear later as "saviors." They use this method because of their inability to attain power by means of persuasion and reflection.

The political and social heritage of our civilization, along with its corollary of justice, is such a portentous thing that it is difficult to conceive of movements that wish to change it by utilizing the unbridled passion of the ignorant mob, whose uncontrolled actions can produce a wave of oppression and enslavement.

It is up to Argentines, who are distinguished by their industriousness and their adherence to principles based on knowledge, to try to find the methods and forms to protect the rule of law that links us to our ancestors; that rule of law is based on the recognition of the creative capacity of free men within the framework of a social order in which discipline and hierarchy are respected for the sake of the general welfare. Our definition of order demands, first of all, the defeat of all those who promote the authoritarian statism to which we have referred above. All methods are permissible in combating these groups, even their own, since we cannot offer protection under our flag to those who are disloyal to Argentina.

There will be little to do if Argentines in all the different walks of life understand the concept and idea of order. Private enterprise must respect and obey all the directives of the government; it should order the various competing functions and, while demanding a return, also promptly reward services rendered. On the executive level, private enterprise must seek to train the individual in the performance of his tasks as a primary condition of the maintenance of order. Furthermore, everyone must be urged to perform his duties by following the example set by the leadership. Private enterprise must respect other activities, however humble, that contribute to national goals, and directors, executives, and workers must feel that they are participants with one objective: the national interest.

The state is what completes this new organization. We must bear in mind that the Argentine revolution inherited an institutional regime riddled with interventionism. It controlled business,

exporting, importing, transportation, investment, mining, telephones, and railroads, in addition to subsidizing and regulating
agricultural, industrial, and commercial activities. Under these
conditions, no attempt was made to stop inflation, and the
situation was worsened by falsely humanitarian social legislation,
which merely served to increase production costs and lower productivity and, ultimately, the abundance that is necessary to
distribute goods to all.

In this unstable situation, the Argentine revolution has unquestionably greatly improved the national picture. There have
been no strikes, stoppages, or similar hostile actions against the
governmental order, and the stock market and monetary exchange
rates have been stabilized as a consequence of the new economic
policy—an undeniable indication of order.

In the political arena, the anarchical situation created by numerous political parties seeking popular support through lies
and demagogy has been ended, thus creating the peace of spirit
so important for the calm and dispassionate establishment of the
basis for a restructuring of the system.

The Argentine revolution must establish order and the sphere
of action of our traditional institutions, at the center of which is
the national Constitution, which can be perfected in time through
an evolutionary process but never through revolution.

The Argentine revolution, as represented by the chief of state,
cannot be accused of arbitrariness or usurpation of power. It
complies with the fundamental principles of the Constitution
and guarantees the basic rights of the citizens. The fact that all
civilized countries have recognized the government as guardian
of order shows their belief in the rule of law. It is thus our decision
to unite under God's protection to implant order, discipline, and
hierarchy in public and private life, understanding that this is the
only way to prevent [in Argentina] the state of disorder and unrest
that has become common the world over.

5. THE MIDDLE-CLASS MILITARY COUP

JOSÉ NUN

A good deal of the American sociopolitical literature about Latin
America is based on a three-legged conceptual system: political
instability, size of the middle classes, and militarism. The scheme

has two alternatives which I will call *traditional* and *modern*. According to the *traditional* analysis, militarism—conceived as a typical Latin American phenomenon—is the principal cause of political instability which in turn victimizes the recently emerging middle classes. Only through the consolidation of these middle classes will the army men go back to their headquarters and a stable democracy be established south of the Rio Grande. From the *modern* point of view, even though militarism—conceived as a typical phenomenon of developing countries—is a factor in political instability, it can promote economic development which in turn will foster the growth of middle classes and allow in this way the democratization of Latin America. In both perspectives, value connotations go beyond the cognitive meaning of the concepts in use: democratic stability and the growth of middle classes are *a priori* positive and interdependent phenomena, while militarism has an ambiguous conceptual status: from being a total misfortune to being a partial misfortune and even a commendable inconvenience.

In my judgment, the simple reading of those works and of the sparse empirical data they present authorizes a completely different ordering of the above-mentioned conceptual system. I leave aside the doubtful convenience of taking Latin America as a unit of analysis, and I accept provisionally the narrow definition of democratic stability as a periodical renewal of authorities through constitutional elections. But, inverting the equation, I consider that, in many cases, Latin American middle classes are threatened by the oligarchy or by the working classes and *voting is one of the principal instruments of this threat*. Therefore, the army—that in the majority of the countries represents the middle classes with all their contradictions—comes to the defense of the threatened sectors and *allows for political instability in the defense of a premature process of democratization*. Middle classes are, then, confronted with a dilemma, which . . . constitutes a double fear: fear of the problem and fear of the solutions. In other words, I suggest that there are enough reasons to see the Latin American middle classes as factors of political instability, whose instrument is the army, and whose detonator is precisely the democratic institutions which those sectors appear to support. This is a peculiar Latin American phenomenon that may be called the *middle class military coup*. . . .

I want to explain why both perspectives [traditional and modern], even though they aim to remain at the phenomenon

Excerpts from *Trends in Social Science Research in Latin American Studies*, Institute of International Studies, Berkeley, Cal., 1964, pp. 55-56, 63-65, 85-86; reprinted by permission.

level, are based on implicit models uncritically transferred to the Latin American context. The first perspective is connected with the European anti-militarism of the nineteenth century. This tendency takes form in the Comtean contraposition between military and theological societies on the one hand, and industrial and scientific societies on the other, and it strengthens itself in Spencer's work. American thought was fed by the anti-militarist tradition; this tradition offered an appropriate frame for a "business pacifism" which managed to conceive military landings in Cuba, Nicaragua, or Santo Domingo as outposts of progress. The explanation was relatively coherent: Latin America did not develop, and in Latin America military interventions in politics were a daily phenomenon. Therefore, it was a repetition of the European problem: backwardness and militarism were synonymous. The weak points of the scheme are evident: from the simple fact that Latin America is *not* Europe to the more or less explicit assumption that progress and civilian rule are in turn synonymous.

This scheme—not even valid for the European context (remember the revolutionary role of the Napoleonic armies)—was not only partially disproved by a reiterated experience of more or less progressive military governments and of overtly reactionary civilian governments, but received the theoretical impact of a system of interpretation that was elaborated for African and Asian countries. The emphasis has been displaced from liberal anti-militarism to a kind of pro-technical militarism. According to the happy phrase of Seton-Watson, when one talks about a military dictatorship it is necessary to distinguish between "the order restorers" and "the intelligentsia-in-uniform." In this respect the analysis of Lucian Pye of Afro-Asian militarism is a meaningful starting point: in the context of underdevelopment the army can be conceived as a modern organization and as a modernizing agent at the same time.

This approach finds an echo in the work of John Johnson about the military problem in Latin America. He adopts an apparent *realistic* position: if military intervention is an undeniable fact in Latin American political life, and if it is a "deterrent" to the violence that extremism can cause, it is necessary to try to transform the army forces "into more socially constructive institutions." . . . In this way, through what the Department of State has called "civic action," the army would be transformed into an effective agent of modernization. Here again the attempt is made to analyze an aspect of Latin American reality making use of implicit models elaborated for other contexts.

The European anti-militarist conception of the nineteenth

century had in sight an army which represented the last shelter of a displaced traditional aristocracy and was, therefore, a potential threat for the industrial bourgeoisie. The analysis of Africa and Asia deals with *new* countries, characterized by "the introduction of institutions from outside, with a minimum concession to the values and behavior of the people," the army being a modern organization "that has been somewhat artificially introduced into disorganized transitional societies." [1]

According to these points of view, Latin American armies are conceived more as external forces that interfere with "normal" historical processes than as integral elements of those processes. . . . What eventually changes in both perspectives is the direction of that interference: negative in the first case—when they appear as obstacles to progress—and positive in the second case—when they are introduced as agents of change. But in none of these assumptions is there an answer to the key questions: Why do army men intervene in Latin American politics? What will be the orientation of this intervention? I believe that the answer can be sought at the level of the armed forces as institutions, or in terms of the society as a whole. . . .

What is seen as exceptional is that a government (*a constitutional government chosen through normal elections*) could maintain itself for a long period in an ambiguous situation. To come out of that situation *it has to make a choice, and in making a choice it will unavoidably alienate some of its supporters.* This is exemplified by the famous "historical half-turns" of a Frondizi or a González Videla.* . . .

When the moment of decision finally arrives, the working and upper classes *may or may not* be affected by the decisions adopted by the government. It depends on whether the solution is an overt labor policy or an oligarchic one. But, due to their position in the sociopolitical space, certain sectors of the middle classes will always be affected whatever the decision may be. And, as I have noted before, the capacity for defense of these sectors is reduced by their lack of such organizations as the unions of the working class, and their lack of traditional representative instruments like the ones efficiently used by the oligarchy.

It is here that the army intervenes. Bourricaud says with reference to developed countries with a socially organized pluralism:

[1] Lucian W. Pye, "Armies in the Process of Political Modernization," *European Journal of Sociology*, II, No. 1 (1961), 82–83.

* The reference is to the governments of Arturo Frondizi in Argentina (1958–62) and Gabriel González Videla in Chile (1946–52), both of which pursued a centrist economic and social policy after coming to power with a leftist program and support.—ED.

"The *appel au soldat* has no possibility of being heard *in normal times*; even though many sectors of public opinion are always ready, they only will succeed in mobilizing the rest of the population in those circumstances in which the resource of the sword appears to the majority as a kind of *ultima ratio*." [2] But, what are *normal times* for the middle classes in the countries we are concerned with? In the best case, for the more middle-of-the -road groups, they are times of exhausting activity, an activity of Sisyphus, for they are trying in vain to conciliate and unite the extremes. The typical representatives of these groups in the political arena are the Latin American Social-Democrats, revolutionaries and pacifists, supporters of adjustments more than of changes of structure, leaders of an imaginary working class "in the European way," in frequent alliances with traditional groups, and attempting to become the "loyal opposition." A socialism, defender of private property and free enterprise, that, confronted with the threat of social revolution (not shaped precisely in Fabian terms), becomes a supporter of coups and angrily asks—as in Argentina —for the intervention of the army. The answers of the army can vary within certain limits. If my reasoning thus far is correct, *the army being today an institution representative of the middle classes in the countries I am considering,* the contradictions of these classes will be reflected in its internal cleavages mediated by some peculiar traits of the institution itself. . . .

[2] François Bourricaud, "Democratie et polyarchie: une forme nouvelle de pouvoir," *Esprit*, May, 1959, p. 788.

6. PERONISM AND THE COUP D'ÉTAT OF 1966

JOHN W. COOKE

Other classes, when they acquire economic power, gain possession of the state, but the workers can eliminate the economic injustices of which they are victims only by taking political power. At the present time, this is a patriotic necessity, because the proletariat is a class whose interests are identified with the aspirations of the nation.

For its part, Peronism is not something outside the workers, an instrument they can use when they need it. In spite of all its

Translated by the editor from John W. Cooke, *El Peronismo y el Golpe de Estado* (Buenos Aires, 1966).

mistakes—in spite of all the things that we have denounced in the political and trade union leadership—Peronism is the proletariat. Peronism is a movement that is outside the factory, acting on it through its directives and connecting it with the rest of the workers, but it is also a movement within each factory. It bases its power on them, and it exists because the workers give it vital strength. Peronism has not succeeded in organizing itself on a theoretical and practical plane. It suffers the divisive effects of bureaucracy. It is too large, and its organic structures are proportionately too small. But, in the midst of crisis and confrontation, Perón is not only the highest leader but he is the point to which all look, the unifying element of all wills. Everything converges on the figure of Perón, because he is the orienting element in the confusion of the regime and the unfavorable conditions to which the masses are subjected.

This decisive role is what the [trade union] bureaucrats do not understand and, in any case, are not interested in. Perón has charismatic appeal and thus he will attain power, and they can benefit from this power as contenders for trade union or political offices. Therefore, they are with Perón, but they take any attitude, hold any ideological position, any nauseating mixture of populism and orthodoxy, and they do not oppose the military, the perfumed clergyman, or the dogs who are the defenders of the regime. Perón has for them a magical quality without any relation to concrete social phenomena. He is an idol to which they make offerings of unconditional adoration, and then each one gives Peronism the meaning that is convenient at the time.

The bureaucrats are now seeking any pretext to gain power in the government. If a revolution is going on, there is no obligation to make one, or to make excuses for not trying to do so. Some explain that Onganía is near and Perón is far away. There is always time to explain one's tactics after the fact. Others know what the real situation is, and they prudently maintain silence, but the people, who can hope for nothing from them, have been deprived of a relationship with leaders who can serve as a point of reference in political torment and symbolize the opposition to the oligarchy. Hatred of the regime and support for the people are the same phenomenon manifested in two different ways. The two nourish each other and are charged with the same emotional voltage and social significance. Now, some letters are circulating that indicate that a messenger has arrived [from Perón], but the military regime has ensured that this will have no effect on political action. Political action is not possible; trade union activity can take place but parties are forbidden. Neither the Peronist nor the left-wing press can publish. Against that enemy

[Perón], against that permanent disturbing factor, the coup was directed—against an exiled chieftain who was able to produce political effects by remote control. When General Onganía and other members of the regime announced that the dissolution of the political parties was temporary, they did not give any estimate of the duration of this transitory phase, as if to say that it would last until Perón died. The plans for a government lasting eight to ten years are not based on any technical considerations; they are based on the estimate that this should be a sufficiently long period for a depoliticization that will end the influence of Perón. . . .

The present government is a mixture of the worst of every system. From liberalism, it borrows free enterprise. From Fascism and its feudal variants, it takes authority and hierarchy considered as a divine right. From Christianity, it borrows ultramontanist morality, clericalism, and the use of religious sentiments to support the established order. Any kind of authority is considered good because it exists.

They are going to modernize the country with a mixture of the twelfth century, the nineteenth century, and Western technology. The country will have machinery, monopoly capital, efficiency, productivity, patriarchalism, immovable hierarchies, lists of saints, order, monotony, censorship, excessive patriotism, modesty in dress, puritanism, and uniformity. They want productivity in a country characterized by boredom, barrenness of spirit, and conservative stolidity—without Peronism, without a people, without opposition, without brilliant leaders in the public plazas. This marvel is what they wish to create in our name. Mummified ecclesiastical putrefication appears today to contribute its syllogistic metaphysics to support the liberalism that was its executioner and that is, in its turn, condemned by history.

We know that the bureaucratic realist smiles at our opposition. What can one do against a monopoly of force? But as revolutionaries we know that no overwhelming power is permanent, that the dialectic of the historical and social future has destroyed more overwhelming power. We can add that Caamaño of Santo Domingo, the guerrilla chiefs of Guatemala such as Turcio and Yon Sosa, the commander of the FALN of Venezuela, and others were also military men—some of them educated in counterinsurgency; today, they are in the forefront of the struggle and of popular hopes.* But we also know that nothing will take place favorable to the people if there is not action, insofar as conditions

* Colonel Francisco Caamaño Deno was the leader of the Constitutionalist forces in the 1965 civil war in the Dominican Republic. FALN (the Armed Forces of National Liberation) is the guerrilla movement in Venezuela.—ED.

permit it. We know that a correlation of forces can change, but only if it is not considered definitive and invincible. . . .

We do not wish to be martyrs. We would prefer peaceful solutions. But we are not the ones who have made this impossible. It is the oligarchy, imperialism, the gendarmes of exploitation. We will not watch in silence the sacrifice of our people to the idols of the witch hunters, to the cohort that impels them to greater errors by the manipulation of patriotism. Peronism is more than a party; it cannot be dissolved by decree nor destroyed by intimidation. . . .

This Argentina, where children and dreams die of malnutrition, where the exploiters dictate the conditions of survival, this Argentina we do not want. This pseudo-patriotic unity, obedience to privilege, and submission to force is not ours; against it we proclaim the unity of all patriotic, anti-imperialist forces that will not bow before the status quo and its iron-fisted guardians.

We seek liberty, and we begin by proclaiming our lack of liberty. We call for liberation in the name of a national awareness that we are a country unable to determine its own future. If material force is monopolized by the regime, moral force and values that are not based on the material are on our side, the side of the people, and militance will transform them into a powerful force. Militant fervor, the sense of a fatherland in need of liberation, solidarity among men to struggle for a society free of humiliation or exploitation, this is the expression of our love for humanity and loyalty to our Argentine and Latin American destiny.

7. THE COUP OF JUNE 28, 1966

AMÉRICO GHIOLDI

People of Argentina: There is no need for a judgment on the administrative record of one year of military revolution, but it is a civic necessity to form an opinion of the activities that have taken place without the knowledge of the nation, which suffers and pays but is resigned to its plight.

The country has been deprived of a republican, representative, and federal form of government. The "regime," a system that casuistically dictates its own laws, has once more replaced the historical rule of law. Constitutional titles were usurped and

Translated by the editor from *Ejército y Política* (Buenos Aires, 1967).

proper functions abused. The titles of president and governor were given to those who are only provisional officials. The word "provisional," if it is not insulting, would at least serve to remind the aforementioned officials of their transitory function and the precariousness of their offices.

The revolution, or military coup, did not lack causes or background. Among these we must mention the conduct of national organizations, parliamentarians, and labor unions, who played at revolution, believing that they could thus satisfy the various desires of the masses. They did not understand that the only possible outcome of such a policy was military power, prejudiced against democratic policies and with affinities for clericalism, Francoism, and a nebulous ideology that would soon manifest itself. The disorder created by forces demanding the impossible and dangerous return [of Perón], backed demogogically by other factions to hide their weakness, laid the groundwork for the military coup. The legal government, in spite of opportune and insistent advice, did not adopt the necessary measures for its preservation and institutional consolidation.

The coup took place, and its makers committed errors that soon alienated public opinion, thus depriving the government, at present and in the future, of popular consent. The ambiguity, obscurity, and lack of definition of its ideas appear in the original documents of the revolution. References were made to structural "failures," which led to the "application of systems and techniques that were inadequate for contemporary reality." These were slogans common to anti-democratic forces and had a totalitarian and dictatorial ring. The fundamental structural change that was sought was the destruction of democracy and its replacement with a syndical corporativism protected by military force. The deliberate reticence of those who were supposed to convey the official view, and the silence of the heads of government on such vital subjects, lead us to believe that we are in the presence of a regime whose purposes and duration cannot be publicly acknowledged, although the people are intuitively aware of them.

The Statute of the Revolution was given precedence over the Constitution; legal organs were dissolved, including the Supreme Court; but other structures, considered to be friendly, were maintained, among them the Church, the Army, and the General Confederation of Labor, which was opposed to democracy but eventually had to be repressed.*

* The Peronist General Confederation of Labor (CGT) was at first favorable to the 1966 coup, or at least neutral; it later opposed the Onganía government, which then took repressive measures against some of its more militant unions.—Ed.

On the economic level, the government introduced the so-called free-enterprise policy, which maintained technical and economic backwardness and protected the monopolies by means of anti-social measures. No attention was given to a positive, real, and productive competition; this system was annulled, more by the trusts than by governmental action. When those upholding free enterprise concern themselves with the eradication of the slums, a social disgrace for Argentina, they will have proved the honesty of their intentions to those of us who wish the state, without upsetting essential economic mechanisms, to act as an organ of stability, justice, and social security. . . .

The peso has been devalued from a rate of 205 to the dollar in 1966 to 350 in the third devaluation of the revolution. It is expected that in the immediate future production costs will increase, and then prices will follow.

Never has there been a devaluation so high as that of 40 per cent decreed on March 13, as a consequence of which one peso was worth less than three-tenths of a [U.S.] cent, the final result of the prolonged debacle that began with the delirious economic policy inaugurated in 1945.

8. ARGENTINA, 1930–69: "WE ARE ALL COUP SUPPORTERS"

PRIMERA PLANA

Already three years. Half a presidential term. If Arturo Illia had not been overthrown, the country would be about to elect a new president: the unbeatable candidate, Juan Carlos Onganía. With an overwhelming majority, he would have been able to govern without difficulty until 1975.*

"Was it necessary that winter night for the troops to go into the streets?" millions of Argentines ask. Have the changes been so profound that they justify the temporary elimination of democracy? The two most perceptible changes are a rapid increase in subversion and a cruel deterioration in the public atti-

* Illia was elected in 1963 for a six-year term. Under the Argentine Constitution, he could not have succeeded himself.—ED.

Translated by the editor from *Primera Plana* (Buenos Aires), No. 339 (June 24, 1969); by permission.

tude toward the armed forces. The ending of inflation? In three years, the circulation of money has doubled. The image of the country abroad? The rioting in Córdoba, with its numerous deaths, has stupefied the world. . . .

Juan Carlos Onganía in 1966 was the man called upon to de-politicize the Army once and for all and to save it from dissension. The Army—or better, one part of it—is today his sole support. There is now no doubt that only his enemies would have advised him to do what he did.

The facts say much, but they are also deceptive. In the fourteen years since the fall of Perón, seven were dominated by the *Colorados* [1955–62] and seven by the *Azules* [1962–69] but, as we remember, in 1962 and 1963, the group in the Army that favored elections [the *Azules*] won out over those who did not. That same sector abolished them in 1966 for an indefinite period. Halfway through their seven years, the *Azules* have turned into *Colorados*, and those who glorified despotism are now the ones who pine for elections.

This is the way politics is. When the military play politics, they do not cease to be political. The only problem is that, educated as they are in certain elementary virtues, they are not very expert in the art of political mystification.

Perhaps it would be useful to think on this third 28th of June about the new sense of frustration that oppresses the Argentines and see if it is not due to the same causes as others in the past.

In the course of one generation, the vote of the citizens has elected only five presidents. Of these, only two—[Augustín B.] Justo [1932–38] and Perón [1946–52]—finished out their term. Both were military men. No civilian was able to hand over the badge of office to a regularly elected successor.

This seems to indicate that the institutions created, or better, imported, by Argentina a century ago—when it was a land of a million and one-half inhabitants, without railways or highways, when to travel from Salta to the coast required a month by stage-coach—ceased to operate forty years ago and have not been re-placed by others more modern and more related to our own historical experience.

One kind of state based on law disappeared at that time, and no one has tried to replace it with another with the same basis. And one can say that, until the Argentines seriously try to do something about this situation, they will be wasting their time in truculent adventures and sterile plotting.

This Latin American republic, whose presidential succession functioned regularly for eighty years [1853–1930], has lived since that time in a state of siege or internal war, deprived of constitutional guarantees, with its citizens counting tanks, planes, and cruisers in place of votes. Argentina competes in this respect (and only in this, because its economic and social indices are the only ones that are declining in the continent) with its tropical sister republics inhabited by mulattoes. It does them one better, in fact, since here the enemies of one de facto government plan to replace it with another de facto government. . . .

All this has taken place in our country at a time when Chile and Uruguay, with ethnic and social structures similar to ours, and even Mexico and Venezuela, which were traditionally unstable, have maintained stable civilian governments limited by constitutional mechanisms. The experience of those countries, as well as that of Colombia, suggests that such governments are not fatally condemned to impotence and failure. Perhaps the Uruguayan case leads one to doubt, yet a clear majority of opinion would be convinced that theirs is the better system. . . .

The problem is militarism, say some foreign observers, whose discussions seem to us picturesquely unrealistic. This same view is shared by a few Argentines, who have a monomania on the subject. If the term *militarism* means the intervention of the armed forces in politics, there is militarism in Argentina. It is not exactly foreign to the contemporary world, yet it has not produced an anti-militarist attitude on the part of Argentines. Why, if this is the correct diagnosis, does the country reject it?

Perhaps because every Argentine knows that, in all honesty, he cannot cast the first stone. At one time or another, each of us has favored military intervention—either because we did not like the "conservative fraud" of the 1930's, or the demagogy of Perón, or the class vengeance of Aramburu and Rojas,* or the consistent insincerity of Frondizi, or the parsimony of Illia. Each one claims that the Army is doing the right thing when it does what he wants, the wrong thing when it does not. If the politicians do not mention their own incursions into the barracks, it is because for a long time there has been no real intellectual debate in this country. But the Argentine has a conscience that will not permit him to lie to himself. It is easy to blame the military as a group, just as it is easy to imitate them and blame everything on the politicians. The problems of the nation cannot be explained by the perversity of men. Militarism is not a vice of the military but of a whole society. It is a belief throughout the society that its problems do not have any peaceful and rational solution by way of the free decision of its members. . . .

The military try to demonstrate that they follow the rules,

*Generals Aramburu and Rojas were the leaders of a "de-Peronization" campaign that followed Perón's overthrow in 1955.—ED.

while the others are involved in "politics." The fact that they are convinced of this does not mean that it is true. Politics is a word that provokes odium on the part of everyone in the military. This is understandable, because politics divides people, and the Army does not wish to be divided. But in this way, the normal process of politics—that is, the hazardous process by which a country rules itself—has become obscured in Argentina for forty years by direct action, by military politics just as dangerous as the other—or more dangerous but less rational.

Less rational because military politics is naturally extremist, because their education leads military men to think in terms of all-or-nothing, to trust blindly in simplistic recipes, to demand that the entire society react with the certainty and promptness of a regiment. There are no skeptics among the military, but skepticism is essential in politics, where every idea loses 90 per cent of its force in practice. . . .

We Argentines are among the most conservative people in the world, but we practice permanent revolution with the same enthusiasm as the supporters of Mao Tse-tung. It is interesting that the government attributes the disturbances in Córdoba to extremists. Extremists are those who, like Fidel Castro, take power by force, conceal their intentions, and say that they will remain in power as long as they wish. . . .

Onganía has handed over economic policy to the liberals. They have demonstrated by their absurd results that they cannot do anything, even readjust the economy. Now he is talking about homogenizing the government. But, meanwhile, he has had to put down a social uprising that has profoundly impressed the Army. The Army today remembers that it is not a praetorian guard, that it is not automatically at the service of any government, even a government of military origin. It is talking about legitimacy, but it is a little late to try that. Are we in for another restoration?

Argentina is acting out an historic drama that needs a generous but decisive solution. The systematic use of military force has postponed it. It is still not able to establish a responsible government elected by a majority. Other nations have overcome horrible catastrophes and created new forms of self-government. We have avoided catastrophe by handing over our discords to the Army. Perhaps the hour has come when the Army, which is still seeking to avoid problems, will allow civilians to resolve the historic drama that affects the country today.

VI. *Peru: The Military vs. Aprismo*

The military intervened in Peruvian politics twice in the 1960's: in 1962 and again in 1968. In both cases, it acted in order to prevent the possible election of a president from the American Popular Revolutionary Alliance (APRA, or Aprista party), founded in 1924 by Víctor Raúl Haya de la Torre. The APRA was intended as a continent-wide alliance of workers and the middle class, which would initiate Mexican-style revolutions throughout Latin America. In reality, it became the strongest political party in Peru, with a mass base in the trade unions and in the north (Trujillo). Haya gave the APRA a strongly anti-capitalist, anti-militarist program and sought to advance the Indian cause in a country in which Indians constitute about half the population (*Selection 1*). Today, however, the Indians are still effectively excluded from political life by the literacy requirement. A criticism of the domination of Peruvian politics by the white ("creole") element, by the Peruvian sociologist José Varallanos, is included as *Selection 2*.

By the 1960's, the APRA had moderated its program and was no longer the revolutionary threat of the 1920's and 1930's. Its strong organizational structure and its influence in the labor unions, however, meant that it was a serious electoral contender. In 1962, APRA cooperated with the outgoing president, Manuel Prado, a representative of the Lima upper class, in order to secure support for Haya. The military, however, had become a self-conscious interest group (many of them mestizo racially) that could no longer be controlled by the politicians or by the old families; they remembered the Aprista massacre of the military garrison at Trujillo in 1932, and Haya's well-known anti-militarism. Haya won the 1962 election, although his vote fell short of the constitutional one-third necessary for direct election, thereby necessitating election by Congress; the military leaders then seized power, claiming that there had been electoral irregularities. (For a description of the seizure of power, by a colonel who participated in it, see *Selection 3*.) Many of the leaders of the coup were American-trained, and the intervention increased pressure in the U.S. Congress for a reduction of military aid to Latin America (*Selection 4*). One of the results was a provision in the Foreign

Assistance Act, reducing American aid to all countries buying unnecessary "sophisticated" weapons (*Selection 5*).

During their year in office, prior to new elections held in June, 1963, the military gave evidence of a reformist nationalism that had not characterized earlier military regimes in Peru (*Selection 6*). In the 1963 elections, they supported the victorious candidate, Fernando Belaúnde Terry, and his reformist Acción Popular party (*Selection 7*). The Belaúnde government adopted a mild agrarian reform law, which was aimed principally at inefficient producers and exempted the cotton and sugar plantations on the coast. Belaúnde also promoted community development, expanded education, and attempted to open up the interior through the construction of highways. But in 1967, budgetary imbalances led to inflation and devaluation, and resulted in a loss of popular support for Acción Popular. In August, 1968, the settlement of a long-standing dispute with the International Petroleum Company (IPC), a subsidiary of Standard Oil, over its holding in northern Peru, proved to be Belaúnde's downfall. The settlement provided for transfer of the oil fields to Peru but gave marketing and exploration concessions to the company. Acción Popular split over the agreement, and the nationalist military leaders, denouncing the settlement as a surrender of national sovereignty, used it as a pretext for once again taking power to prevent a seemingly certain victory by the Apristas in the 1969 presidential elections. The goals of the military government are set forth in *Selection 8*.

One of the first acts of the new government was to seize the IPC oil fields and refinery (*Selection 9*). In the ensuing controversy over compensation, the military government refused to pay the IPC, arguing that the company should first pay Peru an amount equal to its total profits since it began its "illegal" operations in the country in 1924. This action brought Peru into conflict with the United States. Following the Cuban nationalization of American property in 1960–61, the U.S. Congress passed two amendments aimed at discouraging similar actions in the future. The first of these was the Hickenlooper Amendment to the Foreign Assistance Act, which provided for the termination of aid to countries nationalizing American-owned property without compensation (*Selection 10*). The second was a clause in the the 1962 Sugar Act that authorized the United States to suspend the quota in its lucrative sugar market of any nation expropriating American property (*Selection 11*). Peruvian-American relations have been adversely affected on two other counts. Claiming a 200-mile territorial limit, Peru has seized several U.S. fishing boats off the Peruvian coast, thereby making possible the application of the provision of the 1967 Fishermen's Protective Act reducing U.S. aid to governments that seize and fine American fishing boats outside the twelve-mile limit (*Selection 12*). Finally, Peru's purchase of supersonic jet planes from France meant that the United States could limit aid under the provisions of the ban on sophisticated weapons (*Selection 5*). So far, however, the United States has made only half-hearted attempts toward implementing these various provisions, fearing that to do so would only make relations with Peru more difficult and encourage an anti-American reaction throughout Latin America.

The Peruvian military regime has thus far followed a radical nationalist and populist course. (For an analysis of its characteristics by the American political scientist Luigi Einaudi, see *Selection 13*.) Like those in Brazil and Argentina, the Peruvian military regime is nationalistic and development-oriented. Unlike those regimes, however, it does not face a real or imagined threat from the left. It is also less sympathetic to the business community. If anything, in fact, the Peruvian military regime has been more radical in its approach to development than its principal civilian antagonists; in June, 1969, for example, it decreed an agrarian reform that initiated a massive nationwide redistribution of large landholdings to the peasants and peasant cooperatives (*Selection 14*). The Peruvian example of radical, development-minded nationalism under military auspices has sometimes been described as Latin American Nasserism. It has already begun to influence other military regimes in Latin America to make use of nationalization of foreign interests and the promotion of social reform as a way to gain legitimacy.

1. THE APRISTA IDEOLOGY

VÍCTOR RAÚL HAYA DE LA TORRE

I. INDO-AMERICA

In my opinion, the term "Spanish America" corresponds to the colonial epoch, the term "Latin America" corresponds to the republican period, and the term "Pan-America" is an expression of Yankee imperialism. "Indo-America" is the expression of the new revolutionary conception of America which, having passed through the period of Spanish and Anglo-Saxon conquests, will create a definite political, economic, and social organization on the national base of its workers, who represent the tradition, and the race of the exploited indigenous masses who, throughout the economy of [Central and South] America (the unity of which is indestructible) have formed the basis of our productivity and the core of our collective life from the time of the period before Columbus.

It is true that the terms are used at the same time. Some say Pan-America, others Spanish America, some Latin America, and others Indo-America. But this coexistence has a social and economic significance. Up to the present day in America, there has also been both a coexistence and opposition between the various periods of historic evolution that followed after one another in other continents. In America, we have, living together and at the same time in opposition, within the frontiers of our continent or even within the frontiers of each country, all forms of social organization and every level of economic development—savagery, barbarism, and civilization, communal primitive agriculture, feudalism, manufacturing, industrialism, and imperialism. Indians who have never known the use of a wheel as a means of locomotion see swift airplanes in the skies above their mountains. The young gentleman of Buenos Aires who plays golf and visits London has as compatriot and fellow citizen the half-naked Indian in the Chaco. The same thing is true in Peru and Mexico and Colombia and Central America.

This and the following excerpt are from Víctor Raúl Haya de la Torre, ¿A Dónde Vá Indoamérica? (Santiago de Chile: Biblioteca América, 1936); translated by the editor.

This lack of definition, this contradiction, this historic juxta-position, if the terms are appropriate, describes in great part the dialectic of our educational development. America has been and is a land that has experienced invasions—as Europe once did. From the immigrations and transmigrations of the period before Colum-bus . . . from Asia, from Indo-America, from Oceania, from the North to the South and back, America has been the site of in-vasions and countless conquests. Three centuries of Spanish dom-ination represent a long period in our history. It seems to us almost an eternity because it was so recent, but it is less in time than the eight centuries of Arab domination over Spain, for example. The Arabs gave Spain a great civilization and formed a southern racial mixture. They left behind 10 per cent of the word-roots in the language, according to the philologists. The Arabs would have the right to demand, as thanks from the Spaniards, that they call Spain Ibero-Arabia or something similar. But the Arab invasion was just that—an invasion—and historically it created a movement of independence in which many Hispano-Arabs fought to free themselves from the tutelage of their racial ancestors. The re-ligious factor in this struggle corresponds to the period and is less clear than in the struggle of the natives [of Latin America] against Spain. Yet, in both conquests and "reconquests," we can see eco-nomic causes which are the basis of all great historic phenomena.

In America, after suffering the inroads of feudalism and mercantilism along with the conquest and Spanish colonization, we now have been suffering the invasion of industrialism or capi-talism. . . . It may be that this new invasion will be less extensive in this period, when everything proceeds at a faster pace, but it *is* an invasion with its own particular characteristics, its own parti-cular politics, and with formidable social effects. The question for the future is whether we will undergo further invasions. Under-neath these conquering influences from outside, there persists one economic fact—the conqueror always seeks wealth. And the In-dian or his decendants, in the great majority, work to create this wealth. It has been calculated by experts that there are more than 75 million Indians in America. This means approximately 75 per cent of our total population.* Those Indians, with their own traditions, their own languages, their own suffering and aspira-tions, with their own great problem, constitute in their immense majority a work force, "productivity," the hand that creates the riches. This is the way it has been from the social point of view until now and, relatively speaking, always in America. . . .

We in the vanguard, the Apristas, the anti-imperialists of Amer-

* The present population of Latin America is more than 200 million—double Haya de la Torre's 1936 estimate.—Ed.

ica, who are inclined to interpret history economically, have adopted the term Indo-America as a fundamental expression. The invasions of the Anglo-Saxon, Spanish, and Negro races have come to us, are coming to us, and will come to us; they have contributed and continue to contribute to the context of a new America. Yet there survives underneath all these the force of the labor of the Indian. If in Cuba he has been wiped out and in Argentina and Costa Rica absorbed, the Indian continues to be the ethnic, social, and economic basis of America. This is true both for those who live in the framework of modern civilization and for those who in great number are still grouped in primitive tribal organizations. Many other races are mixed with the Indian race, but this America of ours will find its identity and its course before those 75 million natives have disappeared. Every immigration, every conquest has partially modified the Indo-American race, but the ethnic basis of our people is still definitely native.

Those who live in this period struggle against the Yankee capitalist imperialism just as those who lived 100 years ago struggled against feudal Spanish, French, and Portugese imperialism. Yankee domination, if it lasts, will also leave its profound traces on us, just as the Spanish domination did. The "Latin American" period, which historically replaced the "Spanish American" period can be succeeded also by a "Pan-American" stage. We are working against this, especially as regards its imperialist implications. After these three stages, which result from ethnic, political, economic, and spiritual invasions, will come the Indo-America which is to be established and defined. The new revolution in Latin America will be a revolution with an Indian base and orientation, with the native conscience and subconscious expressed in an economic and social renaissance, The Mexican Revolution is a symptom of this great movement. The countries where the Indian does not predominate in Latin America cannot withdraw from his influence.

II. THE *APRISTA* THESIS

For the fulfillment of *Aprista* doctrine, a party has been created which, like the work it hopes to accomplish, is [Latin] American in character. The base of this party is in the producers in alliance with other middle classes,which are also involved in the struggle against imperialism, The party attempts to form an "anti-imperialist consciousness" in the working classes—a consciousness that they are the ones who produce for imperialism, and they alone are those who can place conditions upon it and constitute a force of liberation—without hoping that the proletarians of Europe and the United States will destroy the capitalist system, the origin of imperialism. The alliance with the middle classes reinforces the action of the working classes, especially those that are specifically laborers—new in their role as controlling forces in the state, just as the [economic] system in Latin America which determines their existence as a class is new.

Aprismo already has opened the doors to the future because, following the economic independence of Latin America—an independence that will have to be based on equality in the exchange of raw materials and finished products and the investment of capital according to the principle of progressive nationalization of the sources of production under the control of the state—it will bring about the industrialization of our countries. As a result, a working class will be formed, and favorable conditions will be created for the rapid total direction of the economy and the abolition of the capitalist system. While this revolutionary process is being carried out, *Aprismo* will utilize the anti-imperialist forces of today, not excluding the middle classes, which are threatened with extinction by imperialism. It will seek to defend them through the anti-imperialist state which, by nationalization and progressive socialization of the sources of production, will be definitely oriented in the direction of state capitalism, preventing the middle classes from tending toward large private capitalism, which would mean a return to imperialism.

Aprismo thus presents a complete doctrine and a realistic method of realistic action—that is, an integral economic, social, and political program to secure the economic independence of Latin America. . . .

III. THE CRISIS OF MILITARISM IN INDO-AMERICA

I have always maintained that political militarism, carried out by generals who assault civilian power while disguising themselves as providential saviors in order to conceal their personal ambitions and odious intentions against liberty, is the cancer of our politics. The false assertion of political generals or would-be politicians that the citizens of Indo-America are incapable of living in a civilized democracy has no more basis than the morbid obsession of the military to overthrow legal government and enjoy the sensual pleasure of dictatorial control. History shows that democratic

Translated by the editor from Víctor Raúl Haya de la Torre, *Indoamerica* (Lima, 1961).

coexistence is possible in our continent. Whenever the armed forces in a country have respected the constitutional civil order and carried out their basic duty to be its servants and not its destroyers, we have had democracy. We have it, for example, in Uruguay, in Costa Rica, in Chile, and in the British and Dutch possessions in the Caribbean. . . .

The "pre-atomic age" military man knows nothing [about modern warfare]. This is how we can explain that when he is useless for modern war he turns to make old-style war on the unarmed people. He opts for the politics of adventurism and applies his reactionary concepts of how to run a barracks to running the government of a modern state. Thus the native "pre-atomic age" general turned stateman is nothing but a displaced person who leaves his proper function and invades another to suppress by force the civilized right of all nations to govern themselves in freedom.

Thus it is that the military regimes in our countries take on the characteristics of Nazi and Fascist totalitarianism. They combine with their terrorism a deceptive socialism and support for the poorer classes. Invoking order and justice, they strangle liberty. Asserting their patriotism, they provoke a hostile jingoism and chauvinistic nationalism which leads their people astray at a time when the world is moving toward larger continental communities and finally to the establishment of a universal superstate.

This America of ours, if it is not to remain behind in the path of history, must shake off the domination of anachronistic forms of anti-democratic domination. And the "pre-atomic age" military men who transgress the civilian field of politics—which belongs to parties educated in civic discipline—should return to their barracks or join with the people. A union of the whole continent and the establishment of a common army, such as Bolívar suggested, which will serve only power that is based on the sovereignty of the people and the common security of America, will save us from the military danger. The case of Perón demonstrates the disastrous outcome of armed dictatorship, but at the same time it announces the end of an epoch of barbarism which the resolute will of our united peoples must now overcome.

2. THE CASTE SYSTEM, THE MIXED BLOOD (*CHOLO*), AND PERUVIAN POLITICS

JOSÉ VARALLANOS

The bankruptcy of our social morality and our lack of civic culture are primarily the result of the dictatorial governments that Peru has suffered, or, more accurately, of the system of corruption that has become entrenched and that even the so-called democrats practice (for example, the already classic system of securing "recommendations" for any legal step). These governments are supported, directly or indirectly, by international economic imperialism which exploits our natural wealth and works with the bourgeoisie and wealthy Peruvian conservatives—puppet governments, serving the interests of the Anglo-Saxon capitalists while they claim to exercise sovereignty and represent the nation.

These rulers generally acquire power through fraudulent elections or through a military coup financed by oligarchical groups. Calling themselves "constitutional presidents," "saviors of the country," "restorers of order, of the rule of democracy, of social peace," etc., they have brought morality and politics to their present evil state. Lacking a program of action, their financial plans consisting of contracting loans, they have had all authority in their hands. As a result, republican institutions and the legislative and judicial powers of the state are fictional bodies, subject to the executive and dependent, in the final analysis, on the all-powerful will of the dictator.

Surrounded by a veritable court of flatterers and corrupt politicians—experts in legal chicanery—they trample all our liberties and punish with prison or exile any opposition criticism, appeal to civil rights, defense of the national interests, or insistence on social and human rights. Instead, they reward courtier servility and adulation of their persons and family with diplomatic and public positions and extravagant expenditure of favors and property.

For these "desk or highway dictators," for these "republican monarchs" with a totalitarian court, democracy is a meaningless term and constitutional government a mere form. That is why they

Translated by the editor from José Varallanos, *El Cholo y el Peru* (Buenos Aires: Imprenta Lopez, 1962), pp. 216–24; by permission.

have put their personal friends and groups of supporters in parliament, to be able to rely on a congress with a submissive majority. They have appointed and installed their successors, establishing an ad hoc machinery for that purpose to carry out fraudulent elections to which they give an apparent legality, thanks to regulations and laws written by our Peruvian jurists. They have awarded credentials to those on the "official list" formulated by the government palace, without giving attention to moral quality, qualifications, or even place of birth but only to the candidate's willingness to support them unconditionally.

The so-called plans for progress of these usurpers were conceived so that their close friends might build fortunes or increase the ones they had, making deals or taking graft in the execution of supposedly necessary public works. Their simple procedure was to double or triple the cost, or to use materials of the lowest quality, which led to their almost immediate collapse. All these crimes continued to be committed with impunity, because of the complicity of the civil service and because of a political "bossism" that was characterized by concealment, complacency, and friendship, where favoritism takes precedence over law.

Added to this is the presence of [political] parties and caudillist groups encouraged or directed by demagogic leaders who, far from raising the civic-cultural level of the citizens, have turned them into unconditional slaves. Thus there is a repetition of the pattern of the nation's political life in the last century, when the masses gave transitory emotional support to any audacious or ambitious man but were unaffected by political ideology, class considerations, or the national interest.

The crisis of democracy and the evil dictatorial governments in our country are due in the final analysis to the "whites," who have established a caste system, maintaining undiminished their colonial mentality and methods.

Our independence from Spain was an historic deed that benefited only the sons of Spaniards or whites born in Peru. Since then, government, culture, law, and the advantages deriving from them, have been in the hands of an aristocratizing conservative oligarchy that feeds on a pride based on the family coat of arms and the color of the epidermis. (It will be said that some *cholos* [mixed bloods] became presidents of Peru, for example. As we have said before, even these exceptional cases were at the service of the oligarchical castes, shared their mentality, used their methods, and were their allies or collaborators.)

It is true that there is no difference of persons under our Constitution. We are all equal before the law. Yet this equality is theoretical rather than real, because there still exist privileges for

certain families who maintain the power of their ancestors from
the period of the [Spanish] viceroyalty.

The colonial oligarchy, deaf to human problems and insatiable
for wealth, has promoted and supported dictatorships to its economic benefit, facilitating the delivery of our riches, such as oil,
to foreign enterprises in return for the payment of "commissions"
or the acquisition of shares. This is the reason why Peru is losing
its *Peruanidad,* to the detriment of our national character. Peru
appears to foreign eyes as an amorphous country that has left its
historic path. The oligarchy has attempted to identify this over-
whelmingly Indo-mestizo nation with Europe, under the pretext
of progress. From this mistaken outlook, which has even per-
meated education, we have a sickly eagerness for things foreign,
even for foreign heroes, denying, despising, and neglecting those
of our own soil and race. It is the oligarchy that practices a
curious democracy with the trappings of the viceroyalty, replete
with protocol and ostentation in a country whose immense majority is illiterate and miserable. . . . At this hour in universal
history, ours is a "republican monarchy."

3. A DESCRIPTION OF THE SEIZURE OF
POWER IN 1962

COLONEL E. P. GONZALO BRICEÑO ZEVALLOS

July 19, 1962

Director of *La Prensa*
Lima, Peru

Dear Sir:

I address this note to you on behalf of the Governing Junta,
with reference to the article entitled "How the Palace Was Captured and Doctor Prado Overthrown," which is published on
page four of today's edition.

It is the opinion of the government, undoubtedly shared by the
directors of *La Prensa,* that though the press has many clear rights
it also has the duty to tell the truth in an objective fashion and
without distortion. The government further believes that your

Translated by the editor from a letter to *La Prensa,* July 19, 1962; reproduced in General Felipe de la Barra, *Objectivo: Palacio del Gobierno* (Lima,
1967).

own and other publications have strict ethical principles that serve as the only censorship acceptable to newspapermen.

The exact version of the events as recounted by Colonel Gonzálo Briceño Zevallos, Chief of the Army Commandos, will demonstrate to you the inaccuracy of the article in *La Prensa*.

The government does not wish to limit in any way the freedom of the press, which permits differences of opinion, but it zealously defends objectivity in the service of the high principles of true journalism.

I would be very grateful, sir, if you would publish this note and the enclosed article.

Sincerely,
Julio Vargas Prada
Secretary of the Governing Junta

The Facts

1. Colonel [Briceño] and his officers stand in front of the tanks facing the government palace.

2. The ultimatum is read twice, with a time limit of two minutes after the last reading.

3. Commander Lombardi, presidential aide, indicates that the President will receive the Colonel but that the palace troops will not open the front or side doors.

4. The Colonel orders a tank to open one of the front gates of the palace.

5. General Ciriani, Chief of the [presidential] Military Household, without his aides, stands in the center of the ceremonial patio of the palace.

6. The Colonel enters, followed by eight officers in a double column.

7. The Colonel salutes the General, as do his officers, and identifies himself as Chief of the Army Commandos and Representative of the Joint Command of the Armed Forces, wishing to speak to the President of the Republic.

8. The General and the Colonel, followed by their officers, enter the palace, led by the Chief of the Military Household, using the street door. Thereafter, they enter the presidential office.

9. The President is standing behind his desk, surrounded by ministers, relatives, friends, and other people, among whom is Sr. Pedro Beltrán.*

10. The Colonel salutes the President, identifies himself, and says: "I am ordered by the Joint Command of the Armed Forces to invite you to please accompany me."

* The Prime Minister, and also publisher of *La Prensa*.—Ed.

11. The President addresses the Colonel, his officers, and the public, nervously at first, but always correctly and with decorum in his actions and words.

12. Cheers are heard, some get angry, others shout, and the national anthem is sung; but there are no acts or gestures that are not in keeping with the momentous occasion.

13. After the President has put on his overcoat and scarf, the Colonel sends for his baggage. The Colonel assures those present that the President will receive courteous treatment, in keeping with his high office, and that he guarantees his life. These words are pronounced calmly and firmly in the midst of absolute silence.

14. The Colonel then speaks to the President and says: "Mr. President, please accompany me," and the President answers: "I am ready, Colonel," and walks toward the [palace] guard.

15. Those who wish to accompany the President are told that they may do so up to the ceremonial patio of the palace.

16. When the group arrives at the place where the station wagon is parked, the Colonel addresses the President and invites him to sit where he pleases. The President chooses the center seat and lends a helping hand to the Chief of the Military Household. At that moment, the officers are ten steps away from the President and the gentlemen who accompany him. The Colonel is beside one of the doors and a captain is behind the steering wheel. At no time have enlisted men intervened, since they had not yet entered the palace.

17. Many people, among them ministers, aides, and relatives, wish to enter the vehicle but are stopped by the Chief of the Military Household, who is authorized by the Colonel to enter the car and, together with Commander Rivero Winder and the Minister of Aeronautics, to be transported to its destination.

18. In the struggle to enter the vehicle the Colonel is pushed, and as a result is forced to raise his voice in order to be heard; he warns of the imminent danger to the life of the President and others present should one of the ten security latches on the eight hand grenades and two charges of TNT that he carries be accidentally loosened. Commander Mezett is one of those closest to the Colonel, who keeps pushing him; despite his technical knowledge, [Mezett] is obviously unaware of the grave danger to those present.

19. It is common among commando teams to carry grenades and TNT on the belt in this fashion, with very sensitive security latches in position.

20. The Colonel permits the relatives of the President to follow in their own cars, which they do in the company of his aides and

Interior Minister Elias Aparicio, who was permitted to follow in spite of the ordering of his arrest.

21. In the station wagon, the seating order is as follows: in the front seat, the Captain driving, and General Ciriani and Colonel Briceño; in the center seat, the President and the Aeronautics Minister; in the back seat, the aide with two commando officers; standing on the right running-board, a captain of the commandos.

22. The station wagon is escorted by two armored vehicles, one in front and one behind, followed by two cars.

CONCLUSIONS

The correct attitude and behavior on both sides was remarkable. In accordance with their education and dignity, neither the President, the Colonel, nor the others present acted in a discourteous or insulting fashion.

Any other account of the events, especially if told by a witness, is an evil and ill-intentioned act and an attack on the prestige of the armed forces.

The events that took place did not ruffle the calm of the commandos, since such situations are routine in the light of their training, as is proved by the weapons they each carried, in spite of which no one was harmed. This is proof of the self-control, confidence, and responsibility with which the army commandos acted.

4. THE 1962 PERUVIAN COUP

ERNEST GRUENING

SENATOR [ERNEST] GRUENING: The military assistance program also has had a bad psychological impact upon our relations with Latin America. Military aid and training grants to dictatorial governments in Latin America have done the United States much harm. Despite clear provisions of the Mutual Security Act that aid would not be used for internal security purposes, a number of Latin American tyrants, when hard pressed, did not hesitate to

Excerpts from a speech by Senator Ernest Gruening, delivered before the U.S. Senate on August 2, 1962; reprinted from *The Congressional Record*, August 2, 1962, pp. 15, 420–22.

use against their own people U.S. grants of military hardware. No matter how long and hard we protest our innocence and good intentions, such acts have helped identify the United States, in Latin American public opinion, with the maintenance of dictatorships.

Another question which troubles me deeply is where the funds come from for the purchase of weapons from other nations.

All of the Latin American countries suffer from severe shortages of capital and foreign exchange. Under the Alliance for Progress, the United States has agreed to provide $1 billion a year in order to spur Latin American economic and social development. Ironically, it is estimated that the Latin American countries spend about $1 billion a year for the purchase of military materiel and its maintenance. . . .

Where, Mr. President, did the millions Peru spent to purchase unnecessary British Canberra jet bombers come from? Is the American taxpayer indirectly paying for the purchase in England of British Canberra jets?

I am concerned, Mr. President, that indirectly through our economic aid, just as much as through our military aid, to Latin America we are enabling those nations to step up their arms race.

Take the case of Argentina.

Here is another case of a civilian government having been overthrown by a military junta.

Last Saturday's *New York Times* carried a story of a $500 million loan to Argentina, $200 million of it from the United States. The same day's *Washington Post and Times Herald* reported that Argentina's cattlemen were receiving tax cuts and government cash subsidies.

Yet the case of Argentina parallels that of Peru.

In both Peru and Argentina, the military overrode and nullified the result of a nationwide election.

In both Peru and Argentina, the military seized the President and imprisoned him.

If there is a distinction between these two actions of these two military *coups d'état*, the Argentine case was worse, for in Peru President Prado was finishing his term, whereas in Argentina President Frondizi was not.

In Peru President Prado, shortly to be ex-President Prado, has been released; in Argentina President Frondizi—the rightful President of Argentina—is a prisoner of the military on Martín García Island. In his place the Argentine military have installed their own creature, José Guido, in the presidential office.

So why the difference in our treatment of Argentina and Peru?

In the case of Peru we rightly suspend our financial aid. In the case of Argentina we continue to pour it in.

Such inconsistency does not help our purpose to have the Alianza para el Progreso operate successfully. I am talking only about economic aid. I am not talking about withdrawal of recognition which I do not approve of in either case. . . .

So long as we are pouring millions of dollars in economic aid into these countries we have a right to exact certain reciprocal conditions from them. These were the things predicated by President Kennedy when he launched the Alianza para el Progreso. It was said that we would give help if these countries would make certain social and economic reforms. In very few cases have they done so. One of those social and economic reforms would be not to squander their substance on an arms race.

That would be the answer I would give.

Mr. President, in the ten years since the inception of the Latin American military assistance program, we have provided over one-half billion dollars in military assistance to Latin American governments. . . .

It is interesting to note, Mr. President, that when the program of military assistance to Latin America was first instituted in 1952, total military aid that year totaled only $200,000. It has climbed—indeed soared—steadily since that time.

The figures for the intervening years are:

Latin American Military Aid

Fiscal year	
1952	$ 200,000
1953	11,200,000
1954	34,500,000
1955	31,800,000
1956	30,400,000
1957	43,900,000
1958	47,900,000
1959	54,000,000
1960	53,700,000
1961	91,600,000

I am informed that it is expected that $63.6 million will be the total of the military assistance to all Latin American countries in the 1962 fiscal year. For the new fiscal year, the United States is budgeting an additional $84 million in military aid. . . .

Mr. President, a re-examination of U.S. military assistance to Latin America is sorely overdue. None of the goals of the program have been achieved—not hemisphere defense; not standardization; not modernization; not a reduction in forces; not even that much-to-be-desired by-product, indoctrination of the military in their role in a modern democracy. Instead, we have witnessed some tragic results.

I am convinced that the evils of the military assistance program in Latin America far outweigh whatever benefits we hoped to achieve when first the program was started.

I call for an end to this unsuitable and fruitless venture. I am suggesting to the Senate Committee on Appropriations that its AID appropriations bill for fiscal year 1963 shall contain a prohibition against the expenditure of any funds appropriated for military assistance to Latin America either directly or indirectly through bailout payments to take the place of funds spent unnecessarily on armaments.

Mr. President, I yield the floor.

Exhibit 1
The Puzzle in Peru: Junta, After U.S. Amity and Aid, Is Shocked by Response Over Coup [From *The New York Times*, July 21, 1962]

Lima, Peru, July 20.—The U.S. military assistance program to Peru provided the Sherman tank that rammed through the iron gates of the Pizarro Palace when President Manuel Prado y Ugarteche was deposed and taken prisoner Wednesday.

The officer, who carried out the capture of the palace, Col. Gonzálo Briceño, was trained at the Ranger School at Fort Benning, Ga. After his instruction, he returned to Peru to develop a crack anti-guerrilla commando unit that was a showpiece of the U.S. military mission here.

A son of former Navy Minister Guillermo Tirado Lamb, who spearheaded the armed forces' resistance to accepting the results of last month's presidential elections, was graduated from the U.S. Naval Academy in June.

When the *coup d'état* took place, Mrs. James Loeb, wife of the U.S. Ambassador, was on a Peruvian Navy gunboat in the Amazon region. The boat had been provided by Admiral Tirado to carry a string quartet, in which Mrs. Loeb plays viola, on a concert tour of riverfront communities.

Hundreds of Peruvian officers and enlisted men of the three services have attended the specialized training schools maintained by the Pentagon in the Panama Canal Zone.

The three commanding officers of the armed forces who form part of the military junta that has taken control of Peru have autographed photographs of their U.S. counterparts or of the U.S. Caribbean-area commanders, with whom they are on a first-name basis.

Of all the Latin American military establishments, there was probably none that had higher marks in the U.S. book than Peru's in the period after Fidel Castro had seized power in Cuba.

With the help of the mutual security program which began here in 1952, and the U.S. missions to the 3 services, involving more than 40 officers and men, the Peruvian military made great strides.

The progress involved the modernization of equipment, anti-Communist indoctrination, the development of anti-guerrilla forces and the adoption of economically productive programs such as roadbuilding and the vocational training of recruits.

Because of the record of friendship and aid, the swift reaction of the Kennedy administration to the overthrow of President Prado has come as something of a shock to the Peruvian military leaders. The White House severed relations with Peru and suspended all U.S. assistance except for certain humanitarian programs.

The surprise over these stern steps was evident despite the fact that the military leaders had been warned repeatedly by Ambassador Loeb and the U.S. military attachés that military interference in the Peruvian elections would produce severe consequences.

The leaders of the armed forces here do not feel that they have done anything wrong. On the contrary, they say the ineptitude and duplicity of the politicians, including President Prado, had produced a situation in the presidential succession in which their interference was a "moral duty."

There is little doubt, even among the critics of the coup, that the military leaders were convinced that a fraud was perpetrated in the June 10 elections and that President Prado had participated in political manipulations to bring to power the American Popular Revolutionary Alliance (APRA Party) and its presidential candidate, Dr. Victor Raúl Haya de la Torre.

The military gave repeated evidence that they were willing to accept any solution arrived at by the politicians that would have resolved the inconclusive presidential vote by excluding Dr. Haya de la Torre.

The APRA leader won the most popular votes in the seven-man election but failed to capture the constitutionally required one-third of the total. Congress was to meet July 28 to select a President to succeed Dr. Prado. . . .

The APRA Party today is a moderate anti-Communist Party with a leadership that has given luster to its democratic image by 6 years of participation in the government of President Prado, which was basically conservative. But this cooperation has not wiped out long-standing military resentments toward the party or the suspicion that APRA is basically anti-military.

In the two major services—the Army and Navy—there is a mistrust of the APRA Party that it is difficult for an outside observer to appreciate fully. The military conserve these memories stubbornly.

In the early days of the party, when APRA was a leftist revolutionary movement, it clashed head on with the armed forces in an uprising in Trujillo in 1932 when a group of army officers was killed. Several thousand APRA followers were shot by firing squads.

In 1948 the APRA Party participated in another abortive uprising, in which the naval base of Callao was briefly seized. Enlisted men and civilians organized by the party rose against their officers. This subversion of naval discipline has never been forgotten by Admiral Tirado.

There is an almost desperate lack of communication between the APRA leaders and the military commanders.

Observers here believe that a bridge of understanding, or at least of tolerance, between the party and the Peruvian armed forces must be established if Peru is to enter a period of full representative democracy. . . .

5. UNITED STATES BAN ON "SOPHISTICATED" WEAPONS SYSTEMS

Countries with excessive military expenditures; termination of assistance. In furnishing development assistance under this chapter, and in making sales under the Agricultural Trade Development and Assistance Act of 1954 as amended, the President shall take into account (1) the percentage of the recipient or purchasing country's budget which is devoted to military purposes, and (2) the degree to which the recipient or purchasing country

Excerpts from the Foreign Assistance Act of 1967; reprinted from the *United States Code*, Supplement IV, 1965–68 (Washington, D.C.: U.S. Government Printing Office, 1969), p. 1558.

is using its foreign exchange resources to acquire military equipment. When the President finds that the development assistance under this chapter, or sales under the Agricultural Trade Development and Assistance Act of 1954, as amended, are being diverted to military expenditures, to a degree which materially interferes with its development, the President shall terminate such assistance and sales until he is assured that such diversion will no longer take place. No other provision of this chapter shall be construed to authorize the President to waive the provisions of this subsection.

Withholding of assistance to countries with expenditures for sophisticated weapons systems; Presidential determination of importance to national security; report to Congress. The President is directed to withhold economic assistance in an amount equivalent to the amount spent by any underdeveloped country for the purchase of sophisticated weapons systems, such as missile systems and jet aircraft for military purposes from any country, unless the President determines that such purchase or acquisition of weapons systems is important to the national security of the United States and reports within thirty days each such determination to the Congress.

6. APRA AND THE IDEOLOGY OF THE MILITARY IN PERU

LIISA NORTH

In Peru, the military structures remained closely associated with the oligarchic ruling groups until the mid-1950's. The army maintained its identification with the interests of the upper classes. However, this identification was to change as middle class opposition groups were organized and social conflict increased.

During the long dictatorship of Augusto B. Leguía (1919–30), conflicts within the upper classes and between them and newly organized groups became intense. Favoring newer sectors of the social hierarchy, particularly commercial and middle class groups, Leguía was opposed by the more traditional sectors of the oli-

Excerpts from Liisa North, *Civil-Military Relations in Argentina, Chile, and Peru* (Berkeley, Calif.; Institute of International Studies, 1966), pp. 48–49, 52, 54, 56–57; reprinted by permission of the publishers.

garchy. However, opposition to his regime arose not only from those upper class groups which were increasingly denied access to governmental favors, but also from lower middle and lower class elements. APRA, the Alianza Popular Revolucionaria Americana, was organized in the mid-1920's, followed by the foundation of the Peruvian Communist Party. APRA's proposed program of national development included land reform and social legislation, nationalization of foreign enterprises, and the elimination of the army from the political process. If this constituted a direct threat to oligarchic power, the subversive activities of both APRA and the Communist Party were a direct threat to Leguía's regime. Leguía was therefore threatened from "above" and "below." Faced with such a situation, Leguía turned to the army. In addition, he created special new armed forces directly dependent on himself to suppress the opposition. Within the army, promotion laws were ignored to elevate loyal officers into command posts. Politicization and institutional discontent was sufficient to provoke rebellions among junior officers and even among noncommissioned officers.

Whereas in both Chile and Argentina, the new middle class parties and reform programs influenced the officers and oriented them politically, in Peru APRA's influence on the military was largely negative. The military's alienation from APRA, which by the early 1930's may have had the support of the majority of the electorate, was intensified by the revolt in the city of Trujillo in July, 1932. APRA militants in that town captured the local army garrison during an attempted revolt and assassinated all men and officers stationed there. Since then, the army has held yearly ceremonies in commemoration of the military personnel killed in the Trujillo revolt; officers receive anti-Aprista ideological indoctrination in military schools. APRA's later attempts in the 1930's to conspire with noncommissioned and low-ranking officers were considered especially noxious for their effects on military discipline and subversion of hierarchy. The cleavage between the two middle class organizations—APRA and the army—was of course to the advantage of the upper class groups, who consequently fomented and nursed the already existent division.

This alienation of the military from APRA, the only significant anti-oligarchic political organization, made it possible to maintain discipline and standards in the army while it was used as an instrument for maintaining the power of the upper classes. Favoritism in promotion patterns continued, its extensiveness depending on the specific administration, and officers continued to play political roles. But such practices did not permeate the structure as a whole, and the trend toward increasing professionalization. President (General) Benavides contracted for a German military mission in the late 1930's which aided in the further reorganization of the army. Military revolts became less frequent in the 1940's and 1950's, and tended increasingly to be conducted by the highest-ranking officers.

All this did not, however, mean apoliticization of the army. In fact, the political nature of the army has been given legal sanction. In the Constitution of 1933, there is a section on the nature and function of the armed forces which begins with the following clause:

> The purpose of the armed forces is to assure the rights of the Republic, the fulfillment of the Constitution and the laws, and the preservation of public order. . . .

While Peru's military organization has been increasingly professionalized, in terms of institutional cohesion, respect for formal universalistic norms in promotion patterns, and the maintenance of discipline, it has also begun to develop an independent ideology toward Peruvian social and political phenomena. If alienation from APRA is a continuing factor, the military has also become alienated from the oligarchy and the latter's political policies. . . . The military's new political position includes many of the early APRA proposals on land reform and development of the national economy, social legislation, and nationalization of foreign holdings. It is on the whole expressed in the language of technology and planning, although some concepts of political dynamics and mobilization also have appeared. . . .

. . . The new institutions, concerns, and ideological positions are promoted by the Centro de Altos Estudios Militares, a military planning and educational institute which employs civilian advisors of leftist sympathies.

The Centro has published a statement of the new principles of action for the armed forces, which includes an imperative for all national administrations:

> The final end of the State being the welfare of the nation, and the Armed Forces being the instrument which the State uses to impose its policy . . . in order to arrive at collective prosperity, the Armed Forces has as a mission to watch over the social welfare, the final end of the State.

In accordance with the above enunciated principles, the Centro has embarked on ambitious studies of demography, national productivity, and economic development. . . .

The Peruvian armed forces until the 1950's were an instrument of oligarchic power. Because the military was alienated from the only opposition group with a significant popular following, the upper class governments were able to use this middle class institution essentially for police work in the suppression of civilian opposition. However, this situation did not last. As the military was professionalized and made into a modern organization, it took a more independent position. As the army was modernized, the officers began to apply the rational standards of their own organization to the society as a whole. The articles appearing in the *Revista Militar* offer evidence for this hypothesis. Modernization of the army essentially signified the imitation of Western military models; in recent Peruvian military history this has specifically been the adoption of standards of organization developed in the United States. The rationalized military institutions were introduced into a society which was still patrimonial with reference to social and political relationships, and which had an underdeveloped agricultural economy. Appointments to office in the civilian bureaucracy were still based on personal affiliations with important and powerful personages, and the recruits that the army received were illiterate Indians who often did not speak Spanish. The officers recognized that the social structure and the economy could not sustain the type of military structure posited by the modern model. They came to feel that the oligarchy was using the army for the continued maintenance of an out-dated system in a context of rising conflict.

The contradictions between the ideal posited through modernization and the actual situation has led to the emergence of the military's present orientation. Developed in isolation from political groups, the new ideology reflects its bureaucratic origin: it can "be reduced to a faith, not blind, but simplistic, in the possibility of a technological solution" for Peru's developmental problems. However, to the extent that political manipulators appear within the officer corps and the cohesiveness of the institution is retained, there remains the possibility that the "technological solutions" may be coupled with political ones. The Peruvian military is a possible modernizing agent and source of a modernizing leadership.

7. THE IDEALS OF ACCIÓN POPULAR

Acción Popular is a new state of collective consciousness on the part of the Peruvian people. It is a living force that transforms the concerns of our time and offers a permanent possibility of renovation and adaptation to the demands of society. As the expression of a new generation in Peru, it is a party committed to democracy, nationalism, and revolution. Within this historical and political conception, we affirm the following ideals:

1. Peru as doctrine—a search for inspiration in the national reality, in the territory and the people of Peru, a revival that combines the basic principles that our great past has given us with the ideas and techniques of our time; a return to the idea of an adequate relation of man and nature based on the organizational structure of ancient Peru; the re-establishment of the principle of cooperation and mutual aid.

2. Emancipation of the food supply—the effort to liberate the country from its dependence on foreign sources for its basic supply of such essential products as wheat, milk, and meat, through irrigation and transformation of the uninhabited regions of the Punas.

3. Land and water, the double name of reform—agrarian reform, with the use of machinery in the development of land and water; the stimulus of cooperatives and increase of sources of credit in the service of the peasant; the creation of a rural community in place of a countryside of large landholdings.

4. The emancipation of the villages—the stimulation of local initiative through works of Acción Popular and the establishment of fiscal cooperation to promote efforts in this direction.

5. Planning instead of improvisation—stimulation of techniques for the direction of public investment; national planning with a fixed order of priorities, the application of which will not be affected by the political calendar or by improvised programs without public support or consultation.

6. The revolution of credit—the development of national plans that can attract the largest international credit possible for development institutions, in equitable conditions and without specu-

Translated by the editor from *Ideario, Principios, Programa de Acción Popular* (Lima, 1963).

lation; the channeling of resources to generate employment; the use of savings, social security, etc., for credit at low interest and long terms for the benefit of the family; credit for the artisan and small businessman; a policy of low interest rates for money to be used to increase employment possibilities.

7. Social solidarity for justice—the stimulation of a spirit of cooperation and fraternity; the promotion of agricultural and industrial planning aimed at the creation of the community and the dignity of man and of the family, without underestimating purely material goals; the solution of social conflicts not through a sense of social fear but through a sense of social justice without restriction.

8. The protection of human capital—the organization of public health programs that give first consideration to children and mothers; a struggle against sickness in general and against those ailments created by work in particular; coordination of assistance programs with plans for economic development—in particular, education and social security.

9. Education and those to be educated—a struggle against cultural centralism; planning that brings the school to the scholar and the university to the student; efforts to avoid the uprooting of the youth from his native soil, and especially the exodus of Peruvian students to foreign countries.

10. The conquest of Peru by Peruvians—civil-military cooperation for the development of regions of potential wealth; the use of the Army's experience and knowledge of the territory and men of Peru; the use of [the Army's] technical and scientific potentialities, both for the defense of the country and for planning and development.

8. THE STATUTE OF THE REVOLUTIONARY GOVERNMENT (OCTOBER 3, 1968)

Article 1. The Armed Forces of Peru, duly heeding the desire of the citizenry and conscious of the immediate necessity of putting an end to economic chaos, to administrative immorality and improvisation, to the surrender of our natural resources of wealth and their exploitation for the benefit of privileged groups, as well as to the loss of the principle of authority and [the government's]

Translation by Esso International (Coral Gables, Fla., n.d.).

inability to achieve the urgent structural reforms demanded for the well-being of the Peruvian people and the development of the country, assume responsibility for the direction of the state with the purpose of moving it ahead definitively toward the achievement of the national objectives.

Article 2. The Revolutionary Government of the Armed Forces has for its principal goal the attainment of the following objectives:

   a. to transform the structure of the state, making it more dynamic and effective for better government action;
   b. to promote higher standards of living, compatible with the dignity of the human person, for the less favored sector of the population, carrying out the transformation of the economic, social, and cultural structures of the country;
   c. to impress upon the acts of the government an independent national purpose in the firm defense of national sovereignty and dignity;
   d. to improve the moral fiber of the country in all the fields of national activities and to re-establish fully the principle of authority, respect for the law, and the rule of justice;
   e. to promote union, harmony, and integration of Peruvians, strengthening the national consciousness.

Article 3. The Armed Forces of Peru, identified with the aspirations of the Peruvian people and represented by the Commanders of the Army, Navy, and Air Force, constituted as a Revolutionary Junta, accept the obligation to comply and enforce definite compliance with the Statute and the Plan of the Revolutionary Government. To this end, the Commanders of the three branches of the Armed Forces will be at the same time Ministers of State in the portfolios of War, Navy, and Air, respectively.

Article 4. The Revolutionary Junta shall designate unanimously one member of the Armed Forces to be President of the Republic.

The Ministers of State, with the exception of those of War, Navy, and Air, shall be designated by the President of the Republic with the agreement of the Revolutionary Junta, and these ministers may be members of the Armed Forces or civilians. The Minister of War shall serve as Prime Minister.

Article 5. The Revolutionary Government shall act in conformity with the provisions of the present Statute and those of the national Constitution, laws, and other dispositions, insofar as they may be compatible with the objectives of the Revolutionary Government.

Article 6. The President of the Republic shall exercise the functions that the Constitution grants to the executive and, with the approval of the Council of Ministers, those of the legislature, through decree laws issued jointly with the members of the Revolutionary Junta.

Article 7. The Revolutionary Government will respect international treaties entered into by the Peruvian Republic.

Article 8. Each Minister will have a technical assistant [*asesor técnico*], who will be his immediate collaborator with the purpose of assuring continuity in the execution of the plans and programs of the respective ministry.

Article 9. The Commanders of the branches of the Armed Forces will continue to be governed, insofar as their military situation is concerned, by legal provisions presently in effect. Upon [vacancies due to] retirement, the senior general officer of the respective branch shall succeed.

Article 10. The President of the Republic shall swear to comply with the present statute in the presence of the Revolutionary Junta; the Ministers of State shall do so in the presence of the President.

Article 11. The present Statute may not be modified and shall be signed by the General Commanders of the Army, Navy, and Air Force, constituting the Revolutionary Junta.

9. DECREE OF EXPROPRIATION OF LA BREA AND PARIÑAS OILFIELDS AND REFINERY (OCTOBER 9, 1968)

The Revolutionary Government of the Armed Forces, *Considering:*

That by Decree Law No. 3, the contract between the state and the International Petroleum Company, Ltd., of August 12, 1968, the Act of Talara of August 13, and all the administrative acts relating to said instruments have been declared null and void; *

That, as a consequence the so-called contracts for the sale of gas and of crude oil, which though made on August 13 appear to be dated August 12, are also held null and void and without any effect, and equally null the so-called concessions of August 14, 1968;

---

* The agreements between the International Petroleum Company and the Belaúnde government.—ED.

Translation by Esso International (Coral Gables, Fla., n.d.).

That the La Brea and Pariñas oilfields recovered by Law No. 14,696 belong to the state in conformity with Article 37 of the Constitution and are areas of national reserve, because there has never been a mining claim regarding same, much less a concession in favor of International Petroleum Company, Ltd., or its legal predecessors;

That Law 16,674 authorizes the executive power to carry out expropriations in conformity with Article 29 of the Constitution and taking into account the debts of International Petroleum Company, Ltd., and that this expropriation must be applicable to the installations, plants, systems of transportation, camps, storage tanks, the refinery and other implements making up the industrial complex, as well as the land area of the La Brea y Pariñas estate, previously called Máncora, excepting the public lands that are the property of the state;

That the Revolutionary Government is not attempting to obtain for the state unlawful benefits from said expropriation but must jealously guard the national interests so that they suffer no impairment, in accordance with the Constitution and the Mining Code;

That the exercise of the power to expropriate, prudently employed, does not militate against foreign investment, much less against private property in general;

That at the same time the Revolutionary Government, as defender of the assets of the state, must proceed to take possession of the oilfields owned by it, as well as the industrial complex, to ensure the administrative collection of the outstanding debts of the International Petroleum Company, Ltd.;

That, moreover, it is essential, in conformity with Article 16 of the Constitution, to put an end to the private monopolistic condition of the oil industry;

That the Empresa Petrolera Fiscal [National Oil Company] must take charge of the functioning of the installations to be expropriated, and which are necessary for the proper development of the state's oilfields because they constitute an industrial complex unit;

That it is the duty of the Revolutionary Government to prevent the workers presently employed by International Petroleum Company, Ltd., from being prejudiced in any way in the rights they have acquired;

In conformity with the faculties vested in it

Decrees:

Article 1. The expropriation of the so-called Industrial Complex of Talara is declared to be a matter of public necessity, utility, and security; this complex includes the Talara Refinery, with its

annexes and the storage tanks of the Talara Tablazo; the installations of Verdún Alto, including the distillation plants, the electrical plant, and the water plant of Portachuelo; the gas and
analogous hydrocarbon transportation systems; the port installations; the camps; the surface area of the La Brea y Pariñas estate,
which is privately owned; and everything that may be an annex of
or accessory to said Industrial Complex. The Ministry of Development and Public Works is authorized to commence and
carry out the procedure of expropriation, it being necessary to take
into account, for the purpose of payment, the debts that the
International Petroleum Company, Ltd., owes to the state, whose
collection shall be effected.

Article 2. Possession shall be taken this day by the Armed
Forces of the La Brea and Pariñas oilfields, which are the property
of the state and of the Industrial Complex of Talara, to which
the previous article applies.

Article 3. The Empresa Petrolera Fiscal is charged with the
administration of the oilfields and of said Industrial Complex, so
as to ensure its uninterrupted functioning, as well as the functioning of all of its economic activities.

Article 4. The present workers of International Petroleum Company, Ltd., shall enjoy all the benefits applicable to them, in no
case losing the rights and guarantees that they presently enjoy.

10. THE HICKENLOOPER AMENDMENT TO
THE FOREIGN ASSISTANCE ACT

(EXCERPTS)

The President shall suspend assistance to the government of any
country to which assistance is provided under this or any other
Act when the government of such country or any government
agency or subdivision within such country on or after January 1,
1962,

A. has nationalized or expropriated or seized ownership or
control of property owned by any United States citizen or by any
corporation, partnership, or association not less than 50 per
centum beneficially owned by United States citizens, or

Excerpts from the Foreign Assistance Act of 1961 as amended 1962 (Public Law 87-565, 76 Stat. 255), from *U.S. Code, Congressional and Administrative News,* No. 12 (July 27–August 10, 1962), p. 1761.

B. has taken steps to repudiate or nullify existing contracts or agreements with any United States citizen or any corporation, partnership, or association not less than 50 per centum beneficially owned by United States citizens, or

C. has imposed or enforced discriminatory taxes or other exactions, or restrictive maintenance or operational conditions, or has taken other actions, which have the effect of nationalizing, expropriating, or otherwise seizing ownership or control of property so owned,

and such country, government agency, or government subdivision fails within a reasonable time (not more than six months after such action, or, in the event of a referral to the Foreign Claims Settlement Commission of the United States within such period as provided herein, not more than twenty days after the report of the Commission is received) to take appropriate steps, which may include arbitration, to discharge its obligations under international law toward such citizen or entity, including speedy compensation for such property in convertible foreign exchange, equivalent to the full value thereof, as required by international law, or fails to take steps designed to provide relief from such taxes, exactions, or conditions, as the case may be; and such suspension shall continue until the President is satisfied that appropriate steps are being taken, and no other provision of this Act shall be construed to authorize the President to waive the provisions of this subsection. . . .

11. THE SUGAR ACT AMENDMENT

(EXCERPTS)

In any case in which the President determines that a nation or a political subdivision thereof has hereafter (1) nationalized, expropriated, or otherwise seized the ownership or control of the property of United States citizens or (2) imposed upon or enforced against such property or the owners thereof discriminatory taxes or other exactions, or restrictive maintenance or operational conditions not imposed or enforced with respect to property of a like nature owned or operated by its own nationals or the nationals of

Excerpts from the Sugar Act of 1948, as amended 1962 (Public Law 87-535, 76 Stat. 156), from *U.S. Code, Congressional and Administrative News*, No. 11 (June 30–July 26, 1962), pp. 1357–58.

any government other than the Government of the United States, and has failed within six months following the taking of action in either of such categories to take steps determined by the President to be appropriate and adequate to remedy such situation and to discharge its obligations under international law toward such citizens, including the prompt payment to the owner or owners of such property so nationalized, expropriated, or otherwise seized, or to arrange, with the agreement of the parties concerned, for submitting the question in dispute to arbitration or conciliation in accordance with procedures under which a final and binding decision or settlement will be reached and full payment or arrangements with the owners for such payment made within twelve months following such submission, the President shall suspend any quota, proration of quota, or authorization to purchase and import sugar under this Act of such nation until he is satisfied that appropriate steps are being taken.

12. THE FISHERMEN'S PROTECTIVE ACT OF 1967

(EXCERPTS)

Reimbursement of owner for any direct charges paid to secure the release of vessel and crew. In any case where a vessel of the United States is seized by a foreign country under the conditions of Section 1972 of this title and a fine, license fee, registration fee, or any other direct charge must be paid in order to secure the release of the vessel and crew, the owners of the vessel shall be reimbursed by the Secretary of the Treasury in the amount certified to him by the Secretary of State as being the amount of the fine, license fee, registration fee, or any other direct charge actually paid. . . .

Action by Secretary of State on claims for amounts expended because of seizure; withholding amount of unpaid claim from foreign assistance funds. The Secretary of State shall take such action as he may deem appropriate to make and collect claims against a foreign country for amounts expended by the United States under the provisions of this chapter (including payments made pursuant to Section 1977 of this title) because of the

From the *United States Code*, Supplement IV, 1965–1968 (Washington, D.C.: U.S. Government Printing Office, 1969), pp. 1525–26.

seizure of a vessel of the United States by such country. If such country fails or refuses to make payment in full within one hundred and twenty days after receiving notice of any such claim of the United States, the Secretary of State shall withhold, pending such payment, an amount equal to such unpaid claim from any funds programmed for the current fiscal year for assistance to the government of such country (as shown in materials concerning such fiscal year presented to the Congress in connection with its consideration of amendments to the Foreign Assistance Act of 1961). Amounts withheld under this section shall not constitute satisfaction of any such claim of the United States against such foreign country.

13. PROFESSIONALIZATION AND THE POLITICAL ROLE OF THE MILITARY IN PERU

LUIGI EINAUDI

Professionalization, therefore, has obviously not taken the military out of politics. On the contrary, by giving officers an interest in economic development and Peruvian political integration, it has promoted a new interest in governmental affairs and a sense of technical and perhaps political leadership. Incomplete data even suggest a positive correlation between military education and political activism: ever since the opening of the Military Academy, the more advanced the education of a particular officer, the more likely he has been to participate in national politics when compared to his less-trained fellow officers.

But professionalization has also contributed to the bureaucratization of the military, to the reinforcement of hierarchical relationships, and to underscoring the importance of preserving the profession and the institution from excessive individual adventurism. Generals, not colonels, take command of coups in Peru, and not since 1932 has there been a general under forty-six years of age.

The *second* new development, partly related to the first, is that

Excerpts from Luigi Einaudi, *The Peruvian Military: A Summary Political Analysis* (Santa Monica, Calif.: The RAND Corporation, 1969), pp. 12–17; reprinted by permission.

the military has shifted from the role of temporary warden to that of policy-maker. The continued loosening of the military's ties with the elite, increasing self-consciousness at having been maneuvered in the past into an automatically conservative and repressive role, and improved knowledge of political and social problems have helped to move the military toward a politically independent position, which enables it to look in a relatively disinterested fashion at the claims and policies of competing groups.

Clearly, the role of policy-maker (or even merely of policy-supporter) is more complicated than that of a simple warden who acts sporadically in a limited sphere. If the powers of the state are to be expanded and used to direct national development, as most officers would now prefer, the problems become much more complicated and may require continuous intervention or participation of a relatively sophisticated variety.

It is at this point that most fears about the military's future role arise. Some observers argue that the military's interest in social problems is potentially dangerous to established political patterns. Specifically, there is talk of the emergence of the military as a nationalist or revolutionary force expressing social, provincial, and racial antagonisms in a heavy-handed authoritarian effort to remake Peruvian society. In 1962, prior aspects of military behavior—caution, diversity, and aloofness from the corrupt civilian world—ultimately dominated. Will the same hold true after the 1968 coup?

What lies behind the coup of October 3, 1968, in which the military, acting as an institutional unit, replaced Fernando Belaúnde Terry, the reformist civilian President they had helped to elect in 1963, with General Velasco Alvarado, until then the little-known Chief of the Joint Staff?

This question holds particular urgency because the seizure by the military government of the assets of the International Petroleum Company (registered in Canada, but in fact a wholly owned subsidiary of Standard Oil of New Jersey), threatened to set in motion the Hickenlooper machinery and disrupt the economic fabric (as well as the weakened political and military framework) of relations between the United States and Peru.

Already in 1962–63, the governing junta was more than a little influenced by a combination of nationalism and a desire to bring about basic social reforms. In the end, the normal patterns of military caution dominated policy: the military junta contented itself with establishing a basic law for agrarian reform, founding the National Planning Institute, and ensuring the election of the one civilian politician, Fernando Belaúnde Terry, who seemed most closely to represent their views (and who had most assiduously courted military favor). . . .

The 1963–68 period, with its political temporizing and the executive jettisoning of social and economic programs that could not be supported by a Congress dominated by opposing civilian political parties, therefore led to increasing military disenchantment with civilian politicians and perhaps with the procedures of liberal democracy as well. Belaúnde thus appears to have been viewed by some military men as a last chance for moderate civilian reform. If the military's previous strategy of acting as a policy-supporter for a broad program of change under civilian leadership was frittered away, then what alternatives remained to taking over directly? As in Brazil, the more the military developed a clear consciousness and commitment to social and political development, the less likely they were to find civilian politicians competent to carry them forward and implement their goals, and perhaps also the more likely to underestimate the difficulties of governing that had sapped the energies of Belaúnde.

Although it will be some time before all the motivations for the actual coup of October 3, 1968, become clear, it is therefore apparent that both military opposition to APRA (which might have won the presidential elections scheduled for 1969 and now cancelled) and the famous "missing page" (used to symbolize civilian corruption) in Belaúnde's proposed IPC settlement, are but fragments of a complicated set of deteriorating relations between important elements within the Army and some leaders of the civilian political elite. The collapse of Belaúnde's Acción Popular Party, and the President's use of the national police to retain control of his own party headquarters against his followers' opposition was probably of considerable significance in undermining Belaúnde with the military. . . .

In the absence of external pressure, these factors may with time be enough to permit the civilian political elite to take advantage of the political inexperience of the military as a whole to drive a wedge between them and their current supporters, thereby reducing them to their normal state of isolation. Should this happen, the military's choice between withdrawal and the attempt to develop new allies, perhaps by Peronist-style populism, may well hinge on whether or not there is a graceful avenue open for institutional withdrawal that does not appear to be a retreat.

14. THE AGRARIAN REFORM DECREE-LAW (JUNE 24, 1969)

(EXCERPTS)

TITLE I: BASIC PRINCIPLES

*Article 1.** Agrarian reform is a global process, an instrument for the transformation of the agrarian structure of the country aimed at replacing the *latifundio* and *minifundio* systems by a just system of property, landholding, and agricultural development that will contribute to the economic and social growth of the nation and to the creation of an agrarian order that guarantees social justice in the countryside, increases production and productivity in the agrarian sector, and raises and guarantees the income of the peasant, so that land constitutes for the man who works it the basis of his economic stability, the foundation of his well-being, and the guarantee of his dignity and liberty.

Article 2. Agrarian reform, as an instrument of national transformation, shall be part of a national development policy. It shall be closely related to the planning of the state in other essential fields for the advancement of the rural population of the country, including the organization of effective rural schooling, generalized technical assistance, mechanisms of credit, research in agriculture and cattle raising, the development of natural resources, city planning, industrial development, the expansion of a national health system, and state marketing mechanisms.

Article 3. In harmony with the purposes mentioned above, the legislation for agrarian reform should (a) regulate the right of property so that it is used in harmony with the social interest, and indicate the limits to which rural propery is subject; (b) distribute and consolidate small and medium property worked directly by its owners; (c) guarantee the property rights of present communities to their land and grant them any further extensions they require to meet the needs of their population; (d) promote cooperative organization and regulate community systems of working of the land; (e) ensure adequate conservation, use, and

---

* Articles so marked are repeated from the 1964 Agrarian Reform Law. —ED.

Translated by the editor from *La Prensa* (Lima), June 26, 1969.

restoration of natural resources; (f) regulate agrarian contracts and eliminate forms of indirect exploitation so that the land may belong to the one who works it; (g) establish rules for the system of rural labor and social security, taking into account the particular requirements of agricultural workers, and abolish any relationship that de facto or de jure links the use of land to the furnishing of personal services. . . .

Article 8. Lands abandoned by their owners shall be taken over by the nation. The abandonment of a rural property takes place when its owner leaves it uncultivated for three consecutive years. . . .

Lands shall also be considered abandoned that are cultivated and exploited for more than one year by peasants who have no contractual link with the proprietor, if he has not taken any judicial action with respect to that situation.

Article 9. The state, by administrative action, can declare that all or part of a rural property has been abandoned, regardless of whether or not it is located in an agrarian reform zone. . . .

*Article 15.** For purposes of compliance with Article 34 of the Constitution, the usage of a rural property shall be considered as not in keeping with the social interest in any of the following cases: (a) abandonment of the land or its inefficient exploitation, as well as bad management and deterioration of natural resources; (b) the continuation of sharecropping or of anti-social forms of utilization of the land; (c) unjust conditions or those that are contrary to the Labor Relations Law; (d) concentration of the land in such a way that it constitutes an obstacle to the distribution of small and medium rural property and creates extreme or unjust dependence of the population on the landowner; (e) the *minifundio*, or the fragmentation of rural landholding so as to produce misuse or destruction of natural resources, as well as a low return on the factors of production. . . .

Article 22. Corporations and companies may not be proprietors of rural landholdings. A period of six months is granted from the date of publication of the present law for the conversion of these corporations into legal associations of persons and for the transfer of the rural properties to their possession. Once this period has expired, the estate or estates belonging to the company may be expropriated with a fine of no less than 50 per cent of the cost of expropriation. . . .

Article 28. The agricultural estates in the region of the coast that are operated directly shall be expropriated to the extent that they exceed 150 hectares [approximately 375 acres] of irrigated land. The area exempt from expropriation may be increased to 200 hectares if the proprietor demonstrates that he has complied with all of the following conditions: (a) that the estate has irrigation works necessary for the total area exempt from expropriation; (b) that more than two-thirds of the cost of the operation of the enterprise, including costs of the harvest, general costs, and any other cost that is not capital in nature, comes from personal resources or private credit sources; (c) that the wages and salaries paid individually amount to 10 per cent above the minimums fixed by the labor legislation and that the permanent and temporary workers receive the indispensable services for health, housing, education, and family needs that the applicable legislation provides; (d) that the taxes on the value of the rural property and the irrigation tax and social security contributions are paid up to date; and (e) that the permanent workers of the enterprise receive a share in the gross annual profits of not less than 10 per cent. . . .

Article 30. The area exempt from expropriation of irrigated lands directly operated and located in the regions of the mountains and the tropical forest is the following: [There follows a list of provinces with limits ranging from fifteen to fifty-five hectares.] . . .

Article 31. The area exempt from expropriation of the land referred to in the preceding article may be increased by a multiple of two if the proprietor demonstrates the fulfillment of the first three of the following conditions, and by a multiple of three if he fulfills all of the following conditions: (a) for irrigated land, that the estate has irrigation works sufficient for the total area exempt from expropriation or for land not subject to irrigation, that the cultivated area in the last three years has been no less than 75 per cent of the area capable of cultivation; (b) that the salaries and wages paid to individuals are 10 per cent higher than the basic minimums fixed by the labor legislation and that permanent and temporary workers receive the indispensable services for health, housing, education, and family needs, as established by the applicable legislation; (c) that the taxes on the value of the rural property, the estate tax, the contributions for social security, and the irrigation tax, when applicable, are paid up to date; and (d) that the permanent workers of the enterprise receive a share in the gross annual profits of not less than 10 per cent.

Article 32. For purposes of exemption from expropriation, a hectare of irrigated land is equivalent to two hectares of unirrigated land. . . .

Article 37. When an estate is expropriated whose principal cultivation is intended for a specific industrial plant, which constitutes a single economic unit with the land, the expropriation shall include the totality of the economic complex—that is, the land, the plants that benefit from it, and industrial installations for its processing, even when they are located outside the estate and belong to other owners.

In these cases, the General Directorship of Agrarian Reform and Rural Settlement shall expropriate the businesses, taking over all the shares in the enterprises. . . .

Article 50.* Once an agrarian reform zone has been declared, the transfer of proprietorship of the rural estates in private ownership shall be carried out according to the following procedure: (a) the zonal Director of Agrarian Reform and Rural Settlement shall make known to the public and to the owners the initiation of procedures of expropriation in the zone, so that the owners, within a period of sixty days beginning from the notification, may make a sworn declaration of the rural property that they own in the entire country, providing the data specified in the forms used for this purpose and presenting their titles and future plans. . . .

Article 63. The value that shall be fixed as the just price for the land, buildings, installations, and other integral parts expropriated shall be that determined by the General Directorship of Taxes in computing the rural census.

While the rural census is being prepared, the following shall be considered as a just price: (a) for estates worked directly, the value indicated in the self-evaluation made by the proprietor for the tax paid on the value of rural property in 1968. The increase or reduction in the value of the expropriated estate for improvements or deterioration that occurred after the date of the declaration of self-evaluation, or the official evaluation for 1968 for the payment of the tax on the value of rural property, shall be the only item on which the evaluations of experts may be used. . . .

Article 74. Assignment of lands, cattle, installations, equipment, and other items in the agrarian reform zones shall be made to Agricultural Societies of Social Interest, which shall be governed by the basic principles of legal associations. To be a member of an Agricultural Society, natural persons must fulfill the requirements for beneficiaries of the agrarian reform, members of cooperatives, or of peasant communities. . . .

Article 76.* In the case of lands occupied at the time of expropriation by sharecroppers and small renters, these persons shall have absolute priority for the awarding of the lands they have been working. . . .

Article 78.* When awards are made to natural persons, the settlement of the beneficiaries of agrarian reform shall be made in family agricultural units.

Article 79. A family agricultural unit is defined as the land area that, when worked directly by the agricultural worker and members of his family in efficient conditions, fulfills the following requirements: (a) it absorbs the entire labor force of the family and does not require the use of external labor, except during periods of harvest and in a proportion no greater than one-fourth the capacity of the annual labor of the family; (b) it provides the agricultural worker with a net income sufficient to support his family, to comply with the obligations required for purchase of the land, and to accumulate a certain margin of savings. . . .

*Article 83.** The assignment of land shall be carried out through a contract of sale containing a provision concerning eminent domain for a price that is fixed proportionately to the ability to pay of the relevant agricultural unit.

The land shall be paid for in twenty annual installments, beginning with the date of the award. The beneficiary may pay this price in a shorter time. The General Directorship of Agrarian Reform and Rural Settlement is empowered to grant, in special cases, a number of payment-free years, which in no case may be greater than five, as well as to establish the rate of interest that the remaining installments shall require. . . .

Article 84. An applicant for the assignment of family agricultural units must be: (a) Peruvian; (b) no less than eighteen years of age or civil status; (c) the head of a family; (d) a peasant; (e) not a proprietor of land, or else own land less than that of a family agricultural unit (in the latter case, the applicant shall be obliged to surrender it to the General Directorship of Agrarian Reform and Rural Settlement if so required); and (f) preferably a resident of the land area assigned, or of a neighboring location. . . .

*Article 86.** Beneficiaries shall agree contractually to fulfill the following essential conditions: (a) to work the land directly; (b) to have their housing in a place compatible with the personal working of the lands; (c) not to sell, borrow on, or transfer in any way their rights over the unit assigned without authorization from the General Directorship of Agrarian Reform and Rural Settlement before they have paid for the land; (d) to contribute personally or financially in proportionate form to the labors and services of common interest; (e) to pay at the assigned periods the installments for the purchase of the unit assigned, so as to fulfill the obligations they have contracted with the institutions authorized by the General Directorship of Agrarian Reform and Rural Settlement; (f) to belong to a cooperative or society of social interest when, at the moment of assignment, this obligation has been established; and (g) to observe the technical and administrative directives that are issued by the General Directorship of Agrarian Reform and Rural Settlement. . . .

Article 98. Beginning from the date of promulgation of the present law, rural estates may not be divided into units smaller than that specified for the family agricultural unit. In no case may such units be smaller than three hectares. As a result, for legal purposes, rural properties of such size that their division would result in one or more units of less than three hectares are now considered indivisible. . . .

Article 127. Once an agrarian reform zone is declared, rental contracts for rural properties located in that zone shall be prohibited, with the exception of those that belong to minor children, while they remain minors or are engaged in study for professions strictly linked to agriculture or cattle-raising activities, for a period not exceeding six years.

Rural rental contracts in zones not declared subject to agrarian reform shall be subject to limitations and determinations provided for in the present law. Renting of areas of land of a size less than that of a family agricultural unit is prohibited. . . .

Article 174. The agrarian reform bonds shall be of three classes. . . . Class A bonds shall receive an annual interest of 6 per cent on the remaining debt outstanding and shall be redeemed by annual payments in cash and/or in stock certificates, as the present law provides, for a period of twenty years beginning from the date of their issue.

Class B bonds shall receive annual interest of 5 per cent on the remaining debt outstanding and shall be redeemed through annual payments in cash and/or stock certificates, in accordance with the present law, for a period of twenty-five years beginning from the date of their issue.

Class C bonds shall receive an annual interest of 4 per cent on the outstanding debt and shall be redeemed by annual payments in cash and/or in stock certificates, in accordance with the present law, for a period of thirty years beginning from the date of issue. The agrarian reform bonds and their interest shall be exempt from all taxes.

Article 177. . . . Indemnification for expropriation shall be paid in the following form: (a) lands directly operated by their owners, in which all the conditions provided by Articles 28, 29, 31, and 34 of the present law are fulfilled, when their value does not exceed 100,000 gold *soles*,* shall be paid for in cash; (b) when their value exceeds 100,000 gold *soles*, they shall be paid for by

* Approximately $2,300.—Ed.

100,000 gold *soles* in cash and the remainder in Class A bonds.

2. Rented lands and those worked directly, which do not fulfill all the requirements listed in Articles 28, 29, 31, and 34 of the present law, when their value does not exceed 50,000 gold *soles* shall be paid for in cash, and when the value exceeds 50,000 gold *soles*, shall be paid for by 50,000 gold *soles* in cash and the remainder in Class B bonds.

3. Unused and sharecropper lands, as well as the installations located on them (a) when their value does not exceed 25,000 gold *soles* shall be paid for in cash, and (b) when their value exceeds 25,000 gold *soles* shall be paid for by 25,000 gold *soles* and the remainder in Class C bonds.* . . .

Article 180. Annual payments of principal and interest of agrarian reform bonds shall be made in cash up to an amount equivalent to one hundred and fifty times the monthly minimum wage in the province of Lima and the remainder in stock certificates at market value in enterprises that the Bank of Industrial Development deems appropriate for the payment of agrarian reform bonds.

Article 181. Agrarian reform bonds of Classes A, B, and C will be accepted at 100 per cent of their value by the State Development Bank when they are used to finance up to 50 per cent of the value of a duly qualified industrial enterprise to which the holder or holders of the bonds contribute the other 50 per cent of the value of said enterprise. The stock certificates of the enterprise may not be transferred for a period of ten years, unless the income from the sale is invested in another enterprise that is also duly qualified.

*Article 182.** Since, from the date of the promulgation of Law 15,037 [the Agrarian Reform Law of 1964], contracts that link the granting of use of land to personal service have been abolished, even when the services are paid for in money, all granting of personal services is subject in full to labor legislation. . . .

Final Provision. Law 15,037 and all other laws and provisions that are not in keeping with the present law are annulled.

---

* The 1964 Agrarian Reform Law provided eighteen, twenty, and twenty-two years until maturity for Class A, B, and C bonds. Cash payments were double those of the 1969 law—ED.

VII. *Venezuela: The Victory of Constitutional Democracy*

It is appropriate that Venezuela should be placed first in this section, immediately following the discussion of military rule, because it offers a striking example of a country whose political pattern has only recently changed from one dominated by military strong men to what is apparently a strong and stable constitutional democracy. After a period of nearly one hundred and fifty years in which no constitutional government ever completed its term of office, Venezuela has held three free elections for president—in 1958, 1963, and 1968. In 1968 an opposition candidate was elected president and took office without difficulty, the first time in the history of the country that the government had handed over power peacefully to the opposition.

The earlier Venezuelan political pattern was characterized by the rule of a series of military caudillos, among them General Antonio Páez (1830–48) and Juan Vicente Gómez (1908–35). In 1919, during the Gómez dictatorship, the Venezuelan historian Laureano Vallenilla sought to explain the frequency of military rule in Venezuelan history by ascribing it to the need for a "democratic Caesar," a personal ruler who based his legitimacy on the loyalty of the free plainsmen rather than on the abstract principles of constitutional democracy (*Selection 1*). Between

1946 and 1948, Venezuela had a brief taste of civilian rule under the left reformist party Acción Democrática, but the military intervened once again. Constitutional democracy did not return until 1958, when a popular uprising led to the overthrow of the repressive regime of Marcos Pérez Jiménez.

Credit for the establishment of a workable constitutional democracy in a country that had never experienced it must go to Rómulo Betancourt, founder of Acción Democrática, who was elected president in 1958. Betancourt recognized that the economic development resulting from the new oil industry could encourage the growth of democracy only if the oil revenues were used in a rational manner for purposes of social and economic reform (*Selection 2*). Although his administration was subjected to pressures from the military on the right and Castroite guerrillas on the left, Betancourt was able to use the oil revenues to finance an extensive welfare program. In 1960, he secured the adoption of an agrarian reform law, which emphasized the social function of property, i.e., the need to use agriculture productively, and gave a considerable role to Acción Democrática–sponsored peasant syndicates in its execution (*Selection 3*). The Venezuelan land reform is evaluated in *Selection 4*.

In 1964, Betancourt turned over power to his successor, Raúl Leoni, also from Acción Democrática, after elections that the Castroites and Communists attempted to disrupt. By this time, Acción Democrática had lost its Marxist left wing, although it continued to use a class analysis of Venezuelan society in its ideological appeals. Although the party recognized the need for peasant and worker support—and, indeed, much of its electoral strength was based on AD-influenced labor and peasant unions—it also attempted to enlist the support of the middle class and of the "productive bourgeoisie" (*Selection 5*). The Venezuelan Christian Democratic Party (COPEI) appealed to the same groups, and in 1968, when Acción Democrática split, on personal more than ideological grounds, the Christian Democratic candidate, Rafael Caldera, won the presidency by a narrow margin.

Because of its importance as a showcase of successful democratic reform under the Alliance for Progress (see *Selection 6*), and because of the large American investment in the oil industry there, Venezuela has been a particular target of Cuban subversion. Castro's support of Venezuelan guerrillas was the occasion for Cuba's exclusion from the Organization of American States, in 1964 (see pp. 95 ff.). The Communist Party of Venezuela at first supported the guerrilla effort, and as a result was declared illegal in 1962, although Betancourt had earlier recognized the Party's right to function (see *Selection 2*, p. 232). Following the failure of their attempt to disrupt the 1963 elections, and the defeat of most of the guerrilla effort, the Venezuelan Communists decided to return to electoral politics. This decision, which prompted Fidel Castro's fierce attack of March, 1967 (see pp. 101 ff.), was defended by Jesús Faria, Secretary General of the Venezuelan Communist Party, at a meeting of Communist parties in Prague, in July, 1967 (*Selection* 7). The Party participated in the 1969 elections under another name, and subsequently was legalized by the Caldera government. The domestication of the Communist left, combined with the acceptance of democratic norms by the military, seems to indicate that constitutional democracy has at last succeeded in becoming established in Venezuela.

1. DEMOCRATIC CAESARISM

LAUREANO VALLENILLA LANZ

If, from that time [1830]* on, the bases for economic development were not created to repair the horrible effects of war and
prepare the country for European immigration, as Bolívar had
planned, the fault lay not with the Caudillo [General Antonio
Páez], who always gave power to those whom he considered to be
intellectually superior. Rather, it was due to the lack of a true
culture and of a practical and historical sense, which was characteristic of the period, as well as to the belief, which unfortunately
still persists today in intellectual circles in nearly all [Latin
American] countries, that the solution to social, economic, and
political problems consists in the application of abstract principles
that most of the semiliterate leaders knew about from fragmen-
tary readings of the encyclopedists and French Jacobins. All of
them, conservatives and liberals, were imbued with an exotic and
intransigent radicalism; they proposed to solve our problems with
the free ballot, freedom of the press, and, above all, a limited
term for the president, not considering that the power of General
Páez in the republic, like that of the regional caudillos, could not
be transferred because it was personal. It was not derived from
political doctrines or constitutional precepts, for its roots were
in the most profound political feelings of our people, and especially those of the plainsmen, whose influence developed in the
crucible of the revolution.

Like the German barbarian in the Roman Empire, the Venezuelan plainsman introduced a feeling that was unknown in
colonial society. The plainsman, like the nomad at all times and
places, is characterized by [in the words of Andrés Bello] "love of
his independence, joy in his impulses, freedom in the midst
of a changing world, happiness in activity without labor, a love
for the unknown and the dangerous; these were the dominant
feelings and the moral needs that impelled those human beings.
But, in spite of the admixture of brutality, materialism, and
stupid egoism, the love of independence is a noble moral feeling,
the power of which stems from the human intellect. It is the

* The date of Venezuela's secession from Gran Colombia.—ED.

Translated by the editor from Laureano Vallenilla Lanz, *Cesarismo Demo-
crático* (Caracas, 1919).

pleasure of being a man, the experience of the development of personality and free will." In the absence of the collectivist and gregarious influences created by Roman law and by Catholicism, which were never influential in our plains and whose institutions choke the individual, calling (especially in the case of the Church) for sacrifice and personal renunciation in the name of humanity, the individualism that emerged from the ruins of colonial society brought with it a new element of government, unknown among us until then, as it had been unknown in the Old World before the fall of the Roman Empire. It does not exist in those Latin American countries that have neither plains nor horses, whose evolution has taken place in a pure colonial mold, with weak governments, overbearing clericalism, and the predominance of the old oligarchies. That [new] element was military domination, the supremacy of the strongest, the wisest, the most vigorous, the most courageous, the tie established among individuals, among warriors, that without destroying individual freedom or the characteristic equality of the pastoral tribes . . . established a hierarchical subordination out of which grew, as in the Middle Ages in Europe, our caudillo feudalism. From this time on, our organic constitution and political morality were based on the relationship of man to man, the social tie between individuals, personal loyalty rather than collective obligation based on the general principles of society. Its final result was the recognition of a supreme leader as representative and defender of national unity. "General, you are the nation!" the separatists told Páez in 1830.* . . .

By prescribing the panacea of a written constitution, ideologues throughout [Latin] America have gone against our nature. By considering whatever does not fit the abstract dogmas of the Jacobin theoreticians as treasonable, they have prevented us from adjusting our written precepts to the realities of government and have established a constant and fatal contradiction between law and fact, between the theories taught in our universities and the realities of public life, between the foreign forms and the practical modes of our daily political laws—in short, between the written and the real constitution.

In Venezuela, as in all Hispanic America, history proves that the Law of Bolívar [rule by caudillos], adapted to different environments, is the only one that could have had a positive effect on political stability, social and economic development, and the consolidation of national sentiment—if the theorists had not opposed it with anarchic principles that have legitimized the

* The separatists were those who favored Venezuela's secession from Gran Colombia.—ED.

ambitions of some and the disorganized impulses of others, favoring revolution and perpetuating both anarchy and tyranny. . . .

Roberto Michels, the great professor of the University of Turin, has said that the essential quality of democracy is that, under its aegis, each person carries in his bag a marshal's cane. Referring to Venezuela, the Colombian writer Ricardo Becerra parodied this statement when he said that since the wars of independence, the magistrate's cane has been in the pack of every soldier.

The real quality of Venezuelan democracy since independence has been the predominance of one individual, who derives his origin and legitimacy from the collective will: the will of the popular majority, tacitly or explicitly expressed. Our egalitarian instincts, our individuality—still undisciplined, adventurous, free, and heroic—have made it impossible for a caste, class, or oligarchy of any kind to gain control. It is well known that the Catholic Church, limited to a purely spiritual mission and without influence in political life, is subject to the power of the president, who exercises greater power in this respect than did the Spanish king in colonial times.

A democratic Caesar . . . is always the representative and regulator of popular sovereignty. He is the personification of democracy, the nation in one man. In him two supposedly opposite concepts are synthesized, democracy and autocracy. In other words: Democratic Caesarism, equality under one leader, individual power emanating from the people over a collectivity of equals.

2. VENEZUELA AND ACCIÓN DEMOCRÁTICA

RÓMULO BETANCOURT

I. DEMOCRACY IN VENEZUELA

Independence, which freed us politically from Spain, was frustrated as a movement of social emancipation. Bolívar was in fact expelled from Venezuela by the oligarchy, which did not want an economic and social change. Bolívar had been the first

---

Excerpts from Rómulo Betancourt, *Trayectoria Democrática de una Revolución* (Caracas: Imprenta Nacional, 1948); translated by the editor.

to suggest the question of agrarian reform in Venezuela. In 1830, in place of a division of the land, pieces of paper and military goods were distributed. This enriched certain speculating business-men and some of the military leaders. . . .

Because of the great role that we played in the war of inde-pendence, because of the fact that the Liberator [Bolívar] was born in Venezuela, there has always been a warlike sentiment in the national subconscious and, together with this, permanent dis-content among the people that they cannot enjoy the most ele-mentary advantages of material and spiritual life. The popular masses of Venezuela have always been ready to follow the first military leader who launches a demagogic proclamation. This explains our constant civil wars and also why Venezuela has been a land of successful military leaders.

Little by little, the economic and social realities have changed. The discovery of oil—despite the very slight benefit the country received during the dictatorship of Gómez—permitted the state to construct highways. Although it was hardly the intention of the dictator, these highways, with all their imperfections, contributed to bringing Venezuelans together and establishing links among them. They basically undermined one of the negative factors in our history, the interregional rivalries and struggles among the states, which were based on the lack of contact and mutual acquaintance among the various regions of a country like ours, with a population that numbers less than 4 million inhabitants and is dispersed throughout an immense geographical area of 625,000 square miles.

The evolution in military technique obliged the dictatorship to create a military school. Since modern arms cannot be handled by illiterates, it was necessary to have education. But culture is the most vigorous enemy of autocratic governments. This military school created by the dictatorship was dominated by the spirit of that young, technically minded officialdom of our country, which, together with the people, made possible the revolution of October 18, 1945.

Simultaneous with the creation of the petroleum industry, the dissatisfied and class-conscious proletariat of that industry ap-peared in various regions of the country. Beginning in 1936, this alert and vigilant proletariat was one of the most resistant and solid bulwarks of the democratic movement of the country. In 1937, the popular candidates received 96 per cent of the votes in the municipal elections, despite official repression and the lack of liberty. Our country has demonstrated its capacity for democracy, and each time that there have been elections, not-withstanding the skepticism that the fear of fraud created, the electorate has responded by casting its votes in the voting booths. All this demonstrates that the pessimistic sociologists are wrong. Venezuela, like Colombia, Brazil, Chile, Cuba, and all the other countries of Latin America, is perfectly capable of organizing itself in an economic, political, and social order. We are a people who can be governed democratically and legally. We are resolved to follow our own course, to make our own history. We do not wish to adopt a contemplative attitude with regard to the past, burning incense before the portraits of our liberators and behaving like descendants unworthy of them. We are a people who are accomplishing something that will be the pride of the new America.

II. POSITION AND DOCTRINE OF ACCIÓN DEMOCRÁTICA

Democratic Planning

The additional income that Venezuela can obtain from its petroleum and its iron ore must be distributed in an honest and rational fashion, but even with the greatest administrative honesty, if there is no system of priority of public investments, if the country is not convinced that there are basic problems the solution of which is indispensable, we would not be responding to the challenge that is presented to all Venezuelans—the challenge of being a country that is paradoxically among the most wealthy in Latin America and the most burdened with problems and calamities. The investment of public income cannot be carried out, in our opinion, without a system of planning, without a coherent plan. Indeed, there are two forms of planning—the authoritarian form, which is carried out in Russia, for example, by compulsory methods, and democratic planning, such as is taking place in India under Nehru and in Puerto Rico under Muñoz Marín. . . .

Democratic planning means the orientation of public investments in accord with a strict system of priorities and the creation of an atmosphere favorable to private activities that are productive of wealth. It does not mean a police state imposing on every business what must be produced and how much should be produced but a system for the rational application of fiscal re-

---

Excerpts from Rómulo Betancourt, *Posición y Doctrina* (Caracas: Edición Cordillera, 1959); translated by the editor.

sources and the orientation of private capital in directions useful
for the whole community. . . .

AGRARIAN REFORM

It is also necessary to carry out agrarian reform in Venezuela.
This is a thorny question, but we must discuss it with direct
frankness. Agrarian reform and the modification of the system
of landholding and development is necessary in Venezuela for
reasons of economic development and for social harmony. There
is dangerous social discontent in Venezuela. Profession George
Hill, who directs the faculty of sociology at the Central University of Venezuela, wrote thirteen years ago about the average
peasant in our country. Now, coming back here, he has said
publicly that he encountered in rural areas exactly the same problems he had seen more than a decade ago: lack of land, of schools,
and of sanitation for the peasants. In addition, today there is the
difference that the vast, impoverished peasant masses compare
their own backwardness and misery with the economic development of the city. . . .

Agrarian reform is possible, and we Venezuelans concerned
about the national future will carry it out by normal means, without violent conflict, through the application of reasonable laws.
There is no question of expropriating the farmer or the plantation
owner who cultivates his own land, since in this country, where
there is a tendency to invest in urban development, whoever
goes to the country to work the land ought to be actively encouraged. When the necessity arises to expropriate a certain piece
of land, the logical course is to pay its owner partly in cash and
partly in agrarian bonds issued by a financially solvent state such
as Venezuela. There is no need to resort to demagogy in order
to proceed in accordance with the differences of the various
regions into which we are divided geographically and even culturally. In some places, we will have to establish a system of
small landholding. In other areas, we will establish systems of
cooperative production similar to those that were called "agrarian
communities" in 1947.* And in still other areas, there will be a
system of industrialized agricultural enterprises. But in every case,
we must confront in a serious and responsible fashion the
dramatic problem of Venezuela—that of the thousands of men
without land and the thousands of acres of land without men.
Any responsible government in Venezuela must confront this

* The agricultural cooperatives set up by the first Acción Democrática
government of 1946–48.—ED.

problem, and I am sure, because I am a rational optimist with regard to the level of maturity of this country, that this agrarian reform can be realized normally, as it was realized in Japan after the war under the government of a person who can hardly be called a revolutionary, General Douglas MacArthur. . . .

REGULATION OF THE OIL INDUSTRY

What, then, can we do about the problem of the oil industry? There are two possible attitudes: one is that of the demagogue, who says that the "bloodsuckers of Wall Street" and the "vultures of international finance capital" have a stranglehold on the country; the other is the serious attitude of a responsible nationalist, who believes that a government that has the support of the country because it has been chosen in free elections, and which acts on the basis of the reports of a National Petroleum Commission, on which all political parties, economic sectors, and technical groups are represented, can suggest to the oil industry a change in the present situation.

Because I am not a demagogue, I have said more than once that this suggestion would have positive results. In 1945, when I had the responsibility of presiding over the destinies of the republic, our government initiated new negotiations with the oil companies. We decreed the payment of a special tax on profits in the years 1944–45, because we believed that those profits had been excessive. In that form, the treasury obtained a supplementary income of 5 million bolivars.* We established a fifty-fifty participation between the companies and the nation. For the first time, the Venezuelan state utilized the part of the oil that belonged to it as a royalty, as a matter of exchange, thus rectifying the absurd conception, which had been accepted without question by previous administrations, that the government of our country could not receive commercial benefits from oil because the oil did not belong to it but to the companies.

Finally, the companies made contracts for the first time with the trade unions, and in three years this permitted an increase of nearly 200 per cent in the income of the workers' sector, as well as increases in salaries and social assistance, with evident favorable effects throughout the whole national economy—especially in the sectors of Zulia and the eastern states which produce petroleum, because the increased capacity for consumption of these areas evidently raised their purchasing power.

I have said that these negotiations can be carried out in the quiet manner of a commercial transaction, because it is not a

* Approximately $1 million.—ED.

question of making oil into an explosive political issue but one
of acting like the proprietors of wealth who negotiate in business-
like fashion with those who wish to develop and exploit this
wealth. I do not have the least doubt that a government elected
by the people, representative, responsible, and made up of trained
personnel with information regarding administrative problems,
can secure a favorable readjustment in Venezuela concerning its
principal and almost sole industry for the stabilization of the
whole country. . . .

The Principles of Acción Democrática

We [Acción Democrática] are an organization that is democratic in philosophy, and, as a consequence of this, we affirm cate-
gorically that sovereignty resides in the people and that the people
are the sole legitimate source of power. Only through the electoral
process can the nation be governed legitimately.

We are a revolutionary organization—revolutionary in the sense
that the word has in the contemporary political lexicon. That is
to say, our organization is fundamentally interested in carrying
out a structural change in the state and in Venezuelan society,
but without resorting to violence—carrying out that change
through normal and peaceful means of legal regulation. We do
not conceive of democracy as simply a formal cover for an unjust
social order. Hence, together with the guarantee of the exercise
of civil liberties to all Venezuelans, we propose the redistribution
of national income (which is very high in this country because of
oil receipts) in a form that will make the economic misery of the
majority of the people and social injustice disappear from the
Venezuelan scene. Liberty, yes, but, together with it and com-
plementing and stabililizing it, land and credits for the dispossessed peasant, the vigorous development of national industry
(both that of manufacturing and that of agriculture and husbandry), and the radical termination of all administrative luxury
expenses, to be replaced by expenditure on the basic problems of
the nation—manufacturing that is really Venezuelan; education;
sanitation; worker; peasant, and middle-class housing; highways
and other communications; public services; and irrigation.

We are a nationalist and anti-imperialist party. We are nationalist because we think Venezuela should defend and strengthen
its national character in face of the risks to its particular way of
life that threaten a small nation in a world in dispute among
great powers. But our nationalism is neither backward nor chauvinistic. We believe that Venezuela cannot aspire to be an island
outside the international community and, above all, outside the

Latin American community. The mandate of history and the demands of today force the people of Latin America to move quickly toward forms of continental understanding and integration.

We are anti-imperialist because our party strongly rejects the idea that Venezuela should be the satellite of any other country. We labor for dignity on the international plane, and respect only those multilateral pacts that are consented to freely. We do not admit the idea that foreign investors can treat a country as a colony. The natural riches of Venezuela should be exploited, preferably with Venezuelan resources and techniques, for the full profit of the country. The importation of foreign capital into areas where it is needed ought to be allowed only if it comes by legal negotiation. We must reject definitively the conception held by sectors of international capitalism that when they invest in our country, they can consider it a zone of occupation.

We are primarily a party of the people. Workers, peasants, and members of the middle class form the wide base of our activists. The organized front of the exploited classes which comprise Acción Democrática coincides in its basic lines with the advance of other social classes. The industry, agriculture, and husbandry of our nation cannot help deriving benefits from the policy, put forward by Acción Democrática, of increasing the now subhuman level of income of the immense majority of Venezuelans.

We are a civilian party in the sense that we assign the function of directing and orienting public life to political parties formed of militants recruited in the streets and not in the barracks. But we have not been and are not anti-military. We have always maintained—and we have confirmed this in government action—that Venezuela needs armed forces that are appropriate, sufficient, well organized and well equipped, that enjoy the respect of the nation and are free of political influence. . . . We support the legitimate right of the Communist Party to function in Venezuela as a legal organization.* When we are in power, we respect that right. We believe that "witch-hunts" in the twentieth century are contrary to the very essence of the democratic form of government, and everyone who supports an idea or purveys a doctrine has a perfectly legitimate right in a democracy to organize politically in favor of that idea and doctrine. But Acción Democrática—yesterday, today, or tomorrow—has not had, does not now have, nor will it ever have any ideological sympathy with the Communist Party. The Communist Party is organized in support

* Because of its involvement in terrorist attacks, the Venezuelan Communist Party was suspended in 1962 and not permitted to participate in the 1963 elections.—Ed.

of an international doctrine, and the doctrine of Acción Democrática has been forged to deal with a national reality. It is a
doctrine with a definite, categoric, and irrevocably Venezuelan
national character.

3. THE AGRARIAN REFORM LAW OF 1960

(EXCERPTS)

Article 1. The objective of the present law is the transformation
of the country's agrarian structure and the incorporation of its
rural population into the economic, social, and political development of the nation, through the replacement of the latifundia
system by a just system of property, land tenure, and use, based
on the equitable distribution of the land, an adequate organization
of credit, and integrated assistance to rural producers, so that land
may constitute, for the one who works it, the basis of his economic
stability, the foundation of his progressive social well-being, and
a guarantee of his liberty and dignity.

Article 2. With respect to the above goals, this law: (a) guarantees and regulates the right of private ownership of the land according to the principle of the social function that it must fulfill
and the other regulations established by the Constitution and by
law; (b) guarantees the right of all qualified individuals and groups
that lack land, or possess it in insufficient quantities, to be given
land that is economically workable, preferably in areas in which
they work or live or, when circumstances make it advisable, in
areas duly selected within the limits and norms of this law;
(c) guarantees the right of peasants to remain on the land that
they are cultivating within the terms and provisions of this law;
(d) guarantees and acknowledges to the Indian population that is
organized into communities or extended families, without impairment of the right that they have as Venezuelans in accord with
previous paragraphs, the right to enjoy the land, forests, and water
that they occupy or that belong to them in the places in which
they habitually dwell, without prejudicing their incorporation into
the national life according to this or other laws; (e) favors and
protects in a special manner the development of small and medium
rural properties, and of agricultural cooperatives, in a way that
will enable them to become stable and efficient.

Translated by the editor from *Ley de Reforma Agraria* (Caracas, 1967).

To this effect, the right to small family–sized property is established in accord with the norms of free distribution established by this law. . . .

Article 9. Persons with the right to ask for distribution of land may report the existence of persons who are not fulfilling their social function.

This report shall be made to the respective delegation, and this delegation, within thirty days, shall open an investigation and inform the person who has been reported.

While the report is being processed, those lands shall remain subject to acquisition or expropriation, in accord with this law. . . .

Article 19. With respect to the goals of agrarian reform, private ownership of land fulfills its social function when it conforms to all the following essential elements: (a) efficient exploitation of the land and its appreciable utilization in such a way that the factors of production are efficiently applied to it in accordance with the zone in which it is found and its own characteristics; (b) that the work, personal direction, and financial care of the agricultural enterprise are carried out by the owner of the land, save in cases of possible indirect exploitation with sufficient cause; (c) the fulfillment of the provisions for the conservation of natural resources; (d) observance of the legal rulings that regulate salaried labor, other rural labor relations, and agricultural contracts in the conditions that this law defines; (e) the registration of rural landholding in the National Survey Office of Lands and Waters, in accord with the pertinent legal regulations.

Article 20. In particular, the existence and maintenance of idle or uncultivated estates, especially in regions of economic development, shall be considered contrary to the principle of the social function of property and incompatible with the welfare and economic development of the nation. Likewise, indirect systems of exploitation of the land, as practiced through renters, sharecroppers, middlemen, tenants, or occupants, shall be considered contrary to the principle of the social function of the land.

The state shall discriminate against lands that are idle or uncultivated by imposing on them progressive tax burdens, as established by the respective laws, without prejudice to their expropriation in the cases provided by this law. . . .

Article 26. The rural landholdings that fulfill their social function as defined in Article 19 are not expropriable, save in cases expressly established by this law.

Article 27. The expropriation procedure shall be utilized when vacant land at or near the place where grants are to be made is nonexistent, insufficient, or inappropriate . . . and the National

Agrarian Institute has been unable by other means to acquire land that can be exploited economically. The expropriation of land that is not fulfilling its social function shall take place in the following order:

1. Uncultivated lands, beginning with those of largest area, those worked indirectly through renters, sharecroppers, colonizers, or occupants, and those not worked during the five years previous to the initiation of the expropriation procedure.

2. Land intended to be subdivided among private individuals, if that subdivision has not taken place, it being understood that the National Agrarian Institute, when it seeks expropriation, shall guarantee the rights of those who have already received land.

3. Agricultural land used for pasturing of cattle on an extensive basis. Other lands shall also be expropriated when the possibilities listed above are no longer available and there is no alternative method of resolving a serious agricultural problem. . . .

Article 29. Exempt from expropriation are lands and farms no larger in area than 150 hectares of first-class land, or its equivalent in land of lesser quality, as established by the regulations. . . .

Article 61. The granting of plots shall be made with property titles, free of charge or with a corresponding debt in the conditions and with the limitations that this law establishes. . . .

Article 63. The plots that are distributed free of charge shall be of a size that this law or the regulations establish as the minimum necessary to satisfy the needs of the beneficiary and his family, which they can work without the need of permanent help by wage workers. . . .

Article 64. The beneficiaries of free plots may later request to buy additional land, if it does not exceed the legal limit. . . .

Article 66. The annual payment due shall be equal to the result obtained by dividing the price of the plot by the number of years fixed for payment, which may not be less than twenty nor more than thirty. These payments shall begin at the time fixed by the National Agrarian Institute in accordance with the nature of the crops, but not before the third year after the reception of provisional title by the grantee. In no case may the National Agrarian Institute require that the annual installments be larger than 5 per cent of the annual gross sales of the products of the plot. . . .

Article 172. For the purpose of contributing to the financing of the agrarian reform in the terms of the present law, the establishment of a public debt is authorized which shall be called the Agrarian Debt, charged to the National Agrarian Institute and guaranteed by the nation.

Article 173. In conformity with the preceding article, the Director of the Institute is authorized to issue Agrarian Debt Bonds. . . .

Article 174. The bonds to which the preceding article refers shall be of three classes:

1. Class A bonds, for a period of twenty years from the date of issue, with an annual interest rate of 3 per cent. . . . The bonds in this class must be accepted obligatorily and shall be used to pay for the expropriation of farms that are uncultivated or worked by others.

2. Class B bonds, for a period of fifteen years from the date of issue, with an annual rate of interest of 4 per cent. These bonds must be accepted obligatorily and shall be used to pay for expropriable farms not included in the preceding section and for those acquired by negotiation or peaceful settlement between the Institute and the property-owners. . . .

3. Class C bonds, for a period of ten years from the date of issue, with an annual rate of interest that shall be fixed in accordance with market conditions and shall be exempt from income tax. These bonds shall be placed on the market by the Central Bank. They shall be used for the financing of other investments by the Agrarian Reform and for the payment for farms that are still fulfilling their social function.

4. AN EVALUATION OF THE AGRARIAN REFORM IN VENEZUELA

DOREEN WARRINER

The [agrarian reform law of 1960] lays down that distribution shall begin with publicly owned land, of which there are about one million hectares, mostly poor land, but also including some properties on good land, grabbed by former dictators from their owners. In the expropriation of privately owned properties, priority is to be given to land which is uncultivated, or badly farmed, or used for extensive cattle grazing. The maximum areas which can be retained are fixed at 150 hectares of first-class land, 300

Excerpts from Doreen Warriner, *Land Reform in Principle and Practice* (Oxford: Clarendon Press, 1969), pp. 354–57; reprinted by permission of the publisher.

hectares of second-class land, and 2,000 and 5,000 hectares respectively of first- and second-class grazing land. In relation to
the objective of "replacing the latifundia system," these limits
seem high; but they have little significance, as estates are sold
as a whole.

However, these provisions are not at present of much practical
importance, since there is no need to use compulsion. An estate
may be taken over by an invasion, and IAN [National Agrarian
Institute] then proceeds to negotiate its purchase if it is private
property. The law lays down the procedure by which local syndicates can petition the Institute for the expropriation and division
of an estate; it also lays down the procedure for property valuation
and the payment of compensation to landowners. Dr. Olivares,
Secretary-General of IAN, said in an interview that "the aim is
to reach agreement as to the purchase price on a friendly basis."
When the proprietor refuses negotiations, or when the title to
the property is in dispute, the matter is referred to a special
tribunal. The chief concern of the Institute is to settle up with
the landowners. It is an intermediary between them and the
government, just as the [Venezuelan Peasant] Federation [FCV]
is the intermediary between the government and the rural workers. Since funds are available, agreement is easily reached; estates
are purchased at their market value. Thus the initiative still rests
with the syndicates, which continue to put forward petitions to
the FCV for land redistribution, or for services in connection
with it, in the same way as they formerly petitioned for social
services. The extent to which petitions can be granted depends
on whether the funds available are sufficient to undertake purchase. Under these conditions the estates purchased are likely to
be those which landowners wish to sell. . . .

SCOPE OF REDISTRIBUTION

As to the number of families which have received land, there
is some doubt as to the meaning of the published figures. An
official report on results to the end of 1965 gives the total number
of families as 114,398. However, of this total a large proportion
(possibly as much as half) have abandoned their holdings altogether, or have taken up other work while continuing to draw
income from their holding; small absentee ownership seems to
be a quite prevalent state of affairs. Assuming that this figure is
correct, insofar as land has been distributed to this number, and
that the number of landless families amounted to 200,000 before
the reform, then Betancourt's promise to give land to half the
landless has been fulfilled, though evidently not to their satisfac-

tion. Even so, Venezuela has done more than most Latin American countries.

Whether the recipients of land were all former wage-paid workers on the estates, or whether they also include the squatters, could not be ascertained. On some settlements visited the squatters had not received land, while on others the former paid laborers, being unable to work the holdings allotted to them, had reverted to the *conuco* * practice of cultivating subsistence patches in the jungle.

As to land area distributed, the 1965 official figures give a total of 2.7 million hectares, in *campesino* settlements, of which 1.4 million had been purchased from private owners, and 1.3 million had formerly been public domain, so that average area per family amounts to about 25 hectares, which would be an adequate holding, if the land were cultivable. But the figures do not distinguish between cultivable and other land; and observation showed that the area in cultivation amounted to a small proportion of the area of the divided estates, so that the cultivable areas actually distributed per family were quite small.

Up to mid-1965 the total cost of the reform amounted to 511 million bolivars.† Of this total, 60 per cent had been used for the purchase of land (at market values), livestock, and farm equipment for the former estates, and the remainder used for new investment. Obviously the amount of new investment per family could not be large, after deduction of the cost of the land; it is in fact extremely small.

It is commonly asserted, by people who know, that the landowners themselves encourage syndicates to invade their estates, or to petition for purchase and division, in order to dispose of their property at a good price. . . . Of course there is nothing wrong in buying out landowners at good prices, or settling people at high cost, though it is unusual, because few countries can afford to spend so much. But it seems that the landowners have gained more than the *campesinos*. To a far greater extent even than in the other three Latin American countries visited, the landowners are shifting their interests into urban building and speculation in urban land values; so that it must often be convenient to sell a derelict estate, and with the proceeds build a skyscraper apartment block in Caracas.

* Under the *conuco* system a tenant farmer is given a small plot of the owner's land for subsistence farming.—ED.
† Approximately $110 million.—ED.

5. A CLASS ANALYSIS OF VENEZUELAN SOCIETY

ACCIÓN DEMOCRÁTICA

Venezuelan society may be divided into the following principal social classes: the capitalist class or bourgeoisie, the middle classes, and the working classes (workers, low-income employees, and peasants). However, the first two classes are not by nature homogeneous, and it is therefore necessary to examine their dynamic social role and the attitudes that they adopt toward the democratic transformation of Venezuelan society.

The Capitalist Class

The capitalist class, or bourgeoisie, may be generally divided into two large groups: one that devotes itself exclusively to parasitic or sterile activities, that does not cooperate in increasing the reserve of goods or in promoting national independence; and another whose activities move it, directly or indirectly, to the production of goods and services useful to the nation as a whole. The first of these groups occupies a reactionary and anti-national position, while the position of the second coincides with many of the interests of the common people. However, it is well to mention that these two sectors of the bourgeoisie are not always clearly differentiated at the personal level, as there exist persons and enterprises that are dedicated simultaneously to productive and to parasitic activities, enabling them to play a progressive part in one field and a reactionary one in another. Without doubt, one of these activities always tends to predominate, although it is both possible and necessary [for Acción Democrática] to adopt a varied and flexible political position with regard to the bourgeoisie as a whole.

Reactionary Forces

In Venezuela, there are a number of social groups that tend to adopt attitudes contrary to the development of democracy, to the

Translated by the editor from *Tesis Política, XIV Convención Nacional* (Caracas, 1965).

redistribution of income, and to national economic independence. The following elements may be included in this group of reactionary and conservative forces:

1. *The remnants of semifeudal latifundism.* Although the penetration of capitalism into the country and the progress of agrarian reform have tended in recent years to weaken the latifundism of the traditional landlord, there still exists a group of landholders that is tied to the rural land tenure patterns of the past and fights all social progress in the country. At the present time, these latifundists do not constitute an oligarchy, and in many cases they find themselves under pressure from mortgage capital, the impact of legal democratic reforms, and the actions of the peasants through their class organizations. The latifundists are a precapitalistic social class destined to disappear. Their reactionary mentality is a reflection of their anachronistic situation in a society on the road to development.

2. *The nonproductive capitalist sector.* The reactionary and nonproductive sector of the bourgeoisie invests primarily in commercial activities not linked to economic development and in credit activities oriented not toward the promotion of production but toward the exploitation of the productive entrepreneur, the renter, and the tenant. Capitalists of a nonproductive type constitute, at the highest level, the real Venezuelan oligarchy, holding immense riches in their hands and exercising a reactionary influence in the economic, political, and social areas. This group is opposed to economic and political nationalization, combats agrarian reform and planned industrialization, and yearns for the regimes of force that were its best representatives and defenders. For this reason, popular and democratic forces, through legislative, fiscal, and administrative measures, must make this reactionary sector disappear, diverting now parasitic capital to the production of goods and services.

Professionals and technicians in the service of the capitalistic nonproductive oligarchy and of economic imperialism, although they do not form a group, are sometimes identified with the antinational interests of the exploiters of our natural resources because they are interested only in raising their own incomes, having no social awareness or public vocation.

The Productive Bourgeoisie

The productive bourgeoisie is the sector of the capitalist class that controls and directs the industrial, cattle-raising, commercial, financial, and service enterprises that are oriented toward production, the creation of jobs, and the erection of an independent national economic infrastructure.

This sector of the bourgeoisie agrees on some points with the aspirations of the popular classes: It is opposed to the intervention of foreign capital in the national economy and favors industrialization, agrarian reform, and those methods of social betterment that tend to reinforce the position of Venezuelan consumers and to create an internal market for national products. Politically, it favors representative democracy, which permits its ideas to be heard and allows it to influence public opinion. No doubt, as has been mentioned before, there are cases in which the same men and groups invest capital in both productive and parasitic enterprises, which tends to dilute their progressive character. Also, at certain points the attitude of the productive bourgeoisie may coincide with the conservative positions of the nonproductive bourgeoisie or with the representatives of imperialism. Although the productive bourgeoisie favors independent economic development, it is not disposed to allow the common people effective control of the life of the nation. It wishes rather to reserve for itself the key fruits of wealth. In the initial phase of democratic development, when the help of the state was essential to break the domination of imperialism's usurious capital, the productive bourgeoisie accepted the necessity of public regulation of economic activities. But from the moment that the position of national industry was secure against the traditionally dominant forces, internally and externally, this sector began to demand a diminished role for the state and to voice Manchesterian watchwords in domestic matters (while at the same time calling for increasing protection against foreign competition). From the moment that the productive bourgeoisie penetrated the countryside, transforming semifeudal estates into agricultural ventures of a capitalistic type, it tried to turn the agrarian reform, which was initiated to aid the peasant, to the benefit of the rural entrepreneur. For this reason, the sociopolitical role of the productive bourgeoisie has two faces: progressive when it tries to combat imperialism's usurious and semifeudal hegemony, and conservative when it seeks to consolidate positions already acquired and to combat the classic demands of workers or the regulatory initiatives of the democratic state (although there are certain sectors that are receptive to the interests of the common people). In Venezuela, a developing country, the productive bourgeoisie is allied for tactical reasons with the common people in the fight for economic development but disagrees with them on the questions of income distribution and control of the production process.

THE MIDDLE CLASSES

By "middle classes" we mean a group of heterogeneous sectors, located socially between the bourgeoisie and the working classes and capable of collaborating, economically and politically, with one or the other of the two main groups. For this reason, the middle classes do not have the structure and class consciousness that would give them unity and common attitudes, since their greater social mobility enables them to adopt the attitudes of one class or the other.

Within the middle classes are the small proprietors and entrepreneurs; craftsmen and independent farmers; owners of small and medium-sized businesses; certain professionals, technicians, and employees; and others.

Because of the economic and technical development of the country, the number of professionals and technicians graduating from universities and technical schools is rapidly increasing. In many cases, they become part of the middle sectors of the population. In Venezuela, as in the majority of the developing nations, the university-trained professionals constitute one of the most dynamic elements of the society. From them are recruited the majority of the leaders of the different political groupings.

The upper-level employees, who occupy positions as managers in the private sector, are generally oriented toward the ideas and aspirations of the bourgeoisie and do not form part of the popular revolutionary forces. On the other hand, there is an important sector of upper and middle level civil servants that feels closely identified with the interests of its more modest colleagues and with the working classes in general.

The small property owners, exploited through all Venezuelan history by usury capital and oppressed by dictatorial regimes, are basically democratic in their thinking and act as allies of the working classes in the fight for political liberty, national economic independence, and a more equitable distribution of income.

The middle classes contain a democratic majority, a conservative minority, and other elements that are fluctuating or undecided. The middle layers of modest circumstances, who are closer to the working classes in living conditions and attitudes, and the professionals and intellectuals, who are sympathetic to the popular interests, constitute the democratic sector.

The democratic middle class is part of the organic alliance of the exploited or popular classes that forms the Acción Democrática party and contributes decisively to the realization of the Venezuelan revolution.

THE WORKING CLASSES

The Peasant

In the countryside, various groups, with differences in behavior and working conditions, exist together—peasants who are involved in relations of a patriarchal character, in which the remnants of latifundism survive; those who are enjoying the benefits of agrarian reform in the agrarian settlements and are acquiring income, technology, and education that are raising their standard of living; the small and intermediate independent farmers, toward whom the peasants feel both personal friendship and class hostility; and the salaried workers of the sugar mills and capitalist cattle-raising enterprises, who are not peasants but members of the working class.

As long as the agrarian reform has not been completed, the peasants still constitute the most oppressed and needy social class in the country and one of the principal sources of revolutionary energies. In spite of the agrarian policy pursued by the Acción Democrática government, a part of the peasant population, even in 1964, leads a borderline existence.

Since its founding, Acción Democrática has been the party of the dispossessed peasants, who constitute a substantial part of its militants in the countryside. The party has promised the peasants to carry out a revolutionary agrarian reform in such a way that its benefits can be fully enjoyed by the present generation.

It is evident that the peasants are strongly in favor of social revolution in alliance with the working class, and they will continue this way as long as a positive policy in the countryside helps prevent the rise of individualism and develops cooperative forms of production, consumption, and service. In this way, class consciousness is reinforced and the greater solidarity of all workers is established.

The Working Class

The working class, or proletariat, constitutes the most disciplined and militant nucleus of the laboring classes and the alliance of exploited classes organized in Acción Democrática. It is composed of the workers who directly manage the instruments of production in the capitalistic enterprises in the city and the countryside. The importance of the working class increases progressively with the industrial development of the country. It is reinforced by the addition of revolutionary employees and intellectuals, by the rural workers who have left the peasant class, and by the dispossessed elements that the rural exodus brings to the industrial centers to join its ranks.

Their living and working conditions, and the revolutionary action of the party, have infused the members of the working class with a sense of class solidarity and social responsibility. The proletariat seeks its salvation not in individualistic solutions but by placing the entire national economy under the democratic control of the people. The conditions for their triumph are the improvement of trade-union organization and a constant rise in the level of education and political consciousness, with the help of democratic revolutionary intellectuals.

In the Venezuelan democratic revolution, the working class plays and will continue to play a role in the vanguard.

Acción Democrática, Organic Alliance of the Exploited Classes

Within Acción Democrática, the workers (peasants, laborers, and employees with low incomes) and the democratic middle class (small property owners, higher civil servants, professionals, technicians, and intellectuals with a progressive attitude) form an organic alliance that determines the course of party action through the workings of the party's internal democracy.

The party adopts an open and objective attitude with respect to the productive bourgeoisie and demonstrates many points in which it agrees with it in democratic and nationalistic objectives, the attainment of which requires a tactical alliance between the progressive entrepreneurs and the popular classes. At the same time, the party maintains its right to oppose any effort to turn the national revolution to the exclusive benefit of privileged groups.

With respect to the reactionary forces (latifundism, imperialistic capital, and parasitic or usurious capital, as well as their agents), Acción Democrática adopts a position of opposition in the name of the popular classes, alone or together with the productive bourgeoisie. The conflict is not with the individuals who belong to the forces of reaction but with these forces as negative factors in national life. Acción Democrática, as a party in the service of Venezuela, battles to eradicate imperialism and the remnants of latifundism and to achieve a full political, economic, and social democracy. . . .

As a revolutionary party, Acción Democrática reaffirms its unequivocal intention to carry out the economic and social transformation of Venezuela, to lead the people in a responsible fashion to take charge of their own destiny, to acquire the qualifications to secure their rights, and to assume the responsibilities inherent in their participation in public life.

We do not advocate violence to bring about these changes. Violence erupts when a nation, exasperated at finding the roads to frank and free action in defense of its rights closed, adopts a destructive course that leads to results which many times retard or frustrate the process of the liberation of the masses.

Through the exercise of democratic freedoms, defended, supported, and realized by Acción Democrática, the people have clarified the objectives of their fight. They have chosen their own leaders, behind whom they march with confidence toward the achievement of their demands. In Acción Democrática, the people have always found a clear doctrine of salvation and a definite and loyal guide to this goal. For this reason, they have made the party the instrument for the realization of the national revolution and of the great economic and social changes that can eradicate the conditions which produce the violence to which the dominant classes resort in order to impede the birth of regimes founded on justice and equality.

The application of the principles of social democracy is indispensable for the full realization of the human personality. We consider liberty as the condition and goal of the profound social transformation that will eliminate all types of servitude: of man to man, of group to group, of nation to nation.

The enemies of democracy do not cease to deny the validity of liberty for people and classes deprived of even the minimum necessities of life. But if it is true that the exercise of democratic liberties is meaningless under an economic system that denies the majority an equitable participation in the social wealth, it is no less true that these liberties constitute a crucial instrument of the people in their struggle to change a social system based on inequality and privilege. The experience of this century with totalitarianism offers sufficient proof that without liberty there can be no social justice, and that when the people cannot participate directly in the great decisions that affect their interests, those decisions remain in the hands of minorities, who enslave them under the pretext of ensuring their welfare.

The system of liberties supported and established through the effort of the party goes beyond the traditional guarantees proclaimed by the French Revolution of 1789. For [Acción Democrática], freedom signifies equality of opportunity for all, and this implies that property does not confer its benefits on a few while the majority of the population remains in conditions of bare subsistence. Property must function for society and for the collective benefit of the entire community. Equality of opportunity means that culture and education are available to all and that work is not an oppressive burden for the many. Work must, rather, be converted into a protected activity so that the wage does not represent a payment for merchandise but the participation of the worker in the returns of social employment, sufficient for the full satisfaction of his needs.

6. U.S. AID OPERATIONS IN VENEZUELA

THE AGENCY FOR INTERNATIONAL DEVELOPMENT

The AID program seeks to help Venezuela build its democracy upon a sound economic and social base while achieving developmental progress.

Based on a careful 1961 Alliance for Progress study, AID assistance from the beginning has been directed at major socioeconomic problems where Venezuela lacked resources to act with required urgency. The early loan program addressed housing and agrarian reform problems; the technical assistance program complemented the loan program, and also chose key targets in human resources development. Because of Venezuela's impressive economic performance, its abundance of natural resources and financial strength, AID has carefully designed a highly selective technical assistance program intended to be catalytic in its effect. This U.S. technical assistance program has always been of a special nature not only with regard to content but also administration. The most is obtained from a slender budget by: concentration in five well-defined projects, frequent use of highly qualified and specialized short-term consultants rather than resident employees, cooperation with other private and public national and international developmental entities and, above all, by Venezuela's close participation and financial support in all programs (especially evident in training programs by which 1,392 participants have been sent to the United States or third countries since 1962) The full-time American staff averages twenty-two program technicians and five administrative personnel.

U.S. assistance efforts have been enhanced by Venezuela's positive self-help posture; in particular by: (1) Venezuela's choice of a democratic government as the proper environment for Ven-

Published by the Program Office, United States Agency for International Development, U.S. Embassy, Caracas, 1967.

ezuela's progress; (21) Venezuelan determination to plan and carry out basic reforms including agrarian reform; and (3) formulation of a competent Central Planning and Coordination Office (CORDIPLAN).

By means of a technical assistance program averaging less than $1.5 million annually and development loans of prior years (Fiscal Year 1962 and Fiscal Year 1963) totalling $55 million, AID/Venezuela seeks to serve both U.S. and Venezuelan interests as advantageously as possible.

ACTIVITIES

Human Resources Development: To help Venezuela develop human resources necessary to carry out its development plan: AID program to reach 100,000 persons per year. There is a clear consensus of expert opinion—both Venezuelan and foreign—that the nation's most serious developmental problems are socioeconomic in nature; most concern human resources. Princeton's manpower expert Dr. Frederick Harbison has termed human resources development in Venezuela as the most critical of some forty developing countries that he had visited. Most experts agree that the most serious obstacle to reaching developmental plan objectives is a general lack of skilled manpower—technicians, skilled workers, managers. Concurrently, the nation has a serious unemployment problem with about 10 per cent of the work force without jobs.

In technical training and education, the two major AID efforts are: (1) with INCE,* the vocational and technical training entity, to carry out extensive programs in trade training (60,154 persons were trained in 1964, 76,890 in 1965, 92,476 in 1966, and an estimated 102,440 will receive training in 1967); important aspects include setting up a large scale program to reach unemployed youth (about 80 per cent of the unemployed are under twenty-four); and introduction of new techniques such as Latin America's first correspondence course in trade training; (2) with the Ministry of Education, helping with re-structuring the entire secondary education system as a basic change indispensable for economic and social development; this with the assistance of Wisconsin University, which provides consultants and a concentrated participant training program reaching 150 secondary educators and administrators.

Technical assistance is being supplied the Ministry of Labor in establishing an effective national employment service. The American Institute of Free Labor Development under an AID

* The National Institute of Educational Cooperation.—ED.

contract has since 1965 trained Venezuelan workers for democratic trade-union leadership and in the administration of worker
cooperatives. AID is also providing free modern textbooks, references and teaching materials to public school students and helping to establish University Textbook Rental and Reference
Libraries.

Training assistance is being provided Venezuelan police personnel to improve the capabilities of twenty-three local agencies
in maintaining law and order and to preserve internal security
as important requisites for orderly development, and to foster
the proper climate for democratic political stability and growth.

AID has supported the improvement of the Venezuelan civil
service through technical assistance in public administration intended to promote the growth of democratic institutions. Over
400 persons from selected Venezuelan agencies have received
training in budgeting, organization and methods, personnel management, and procurement. Reorganizations of the tax audit system
and tax administration have received technical assistance. Major
efforts have been with the Ministry of Finance in administrative,
budget, and tax reform and in local government through the
Foundation for Community Development and Municipal Improvement. Especially interesting features are: (1) a continuing,
solidly based relationship between New York State and Venezuelan budget and planning entities which has already proved
beneficial and promises even greater successes not only in budget
operations but in such varied but important fields as national
development planning and regional planning for public works
and national resource utilization; (2) a local government training
program in collaboration with the Creole Foundation, the Venezuelan Foundation for Community Development, and the University of Southern California.

*Rural Improvement: Help create and strengthen rural institu-
tions which will increase farm income and in general make rural
Venezuela a positive factor in national development.* The Rural
Development Activity is scheduled to terminate September 30,
1967. AID assistance in agrarian reform in recent years has been
confined chiefly to supervised agricultural credit. One major
obstacle to land reform success is the lack of credit for small
farmers. In 1962, the Agriculture and Livestock Bank (BAP)
began a supervised credit program financed by a $10 million AID
loan and its own matching funds. To build a permanent institution, AID assisted with training over 200 administrators and field
supervisors; BAP now operates this program in seventeen states
and as of July 31, 1967, had approved 8,593 loans to small farmers

totalling about $34,093,469. With the BAP administrative structure almost complete, this program is well underway and is benefiting small farmers.

AID cooperated with the Peasant Federation helping to organize twenty "capacitation" schools (one in each state) for adult *campesino* farm training and helped to set up a system of farmer marketing and purchasing cooperatives. Also Venezuela's first rural electric cooperatives are being established with the assistance of the National Rural Electric Cooperative Association. With this cooperative movement as a base, [the state of] Tennessee is working on a Partners of the Alliance relationship with Venezeula involving a broad range of activities. Other activities included high level technical assistance for the Ministry of Agriculture in the areas of Ministry and BAP reorganization, plant quarantine, extension, forestry, soil testing, and the integral development of land and water resources.

Housing and Urban Renewal: Primary goals include assisting Venezuela in the creation and improvement of public and private institutions in housing, urban renewal and related areas, and to increase the participation of the private housing sector in the mass market. AID's $5 million worker housing loan involving 2,810 units to the privately financed Mendoza Foundation was fully disbursed by December, 1963. The Savings and Loan System, recipient of a $10 million loan in Fiscal Year 1962, has grown in twenty-two chartered associations with 41,795 savers having deposits of Bs 140,227,000 ($31.2 million) and 5,879 loans amounting to Bs 316,362,000 ($70.3 million) as of April 30, 1967.

The Foundation for Community Development and Municipal Improvement began slum clearance activities in 1963 financed by Venezuelan government funds and supplemented by a matching $30 million AID loan now fully disbursed. As of June 30, 1967, 10,798 units were under construction or had been completed. Other Foundation activities involve urban and community development including training municipal administrators, technicians, and planners.

In the private sector AID is actively encouraging the promotion of an internal mortgage system and secondary mortgage system.

Population and Demography Program: To assist and support Venezuelan public and private agencies in action and training programs in population and well-being. AID will provide financial aid to the Venezuelan Family Planning Association, to the Maternity Hospital Concepción Palacios, and to the Centro Venezolano de Población y Familia (CEVEPOF). Assistance mainly has been limited to research and training.

OTHER ACTIVITIES

Food for Peace. The P. L. 480 Title III Program was begun in 1962 to help alleviate most urgent human needs. Catholic Relief Services administers this program in cooperation with the Venezuelan CARITAS organization; focus is on depressed areas of major unemployment and in the interior rather than the Caracas urban areas; family feeding and school lunch programs presently reach 220,000 persons of whom 68 per cent are children. From the program's beginning in Fiscal Year 1962 through 1966, food supplies with a value of about $22 million had been distributed through this voluntary agency program. The government has been increasing its school feeding program and it is planned to phase out the Food for Peace program by Fiscal Year 1970.

Programming for Private Enterprise. The Investment Guarantee program is the most significant of AID services in support of private enterprise in Venezuela's development. The Investment Guarantee program began with an exchange of letters between the respective governments in November, 1962. AID/Washington through July 31, 1967, has issued 110 specific risk guarantees to 37 U.S. firms for a total insured value of $97,200,892; sixty applications are pending. Under the Housing Investment Guarantee program, four guarantees representing an investment of $48,749,-096 have been approved.

AID/Washington Regional Projects. Besides occasional visits from contract consultants in various fields of regional interest, AID/Washington has programmed and financed projects in Venezuela from regional funds in the fields of labor union leadership training, establishment of settlement houses, savings and loan cooperatives, and agriculture.

7. A DEFENSE OF THE VENEZUELAN COMMUNIST PARTY

JESÚS FARIA

It is not true that the Communist Party has given up any form of the struggle, including armed conflict. Eighty to ninety per cent of those who were engaged in guerrilla warfare in Venezuela

Excerpts from a speech delivered in Prague in July, 1967; translated by the editor from *Confidencial* (Caracas), No. 42 (June-September, 1967).

were Communists. The government and the opposition both know this; everyone does. The number of dead, and the political affiliation of those dead confirm it, as does the number of those jailed and persecuted. The roll call in any prison in Venezuela will reveal that more than 80 per cent of the inmates are members of the Communist Party, or of the Venezuelan Communist Youth. This fact, no doubt, weakened our forces and put us on the defensive. That is to say, we could not win the war. But that does not mean that we have betrayed our people, and it does not mean that we have abandoned any form of struggle. On the contrary, here, without any pressure and independent of any outside pressure, the Venezuelan Communist Party has not lied to the people or to its friends abroad, and it has no reason to lie. And if we resolve to adopt a particular political line, we are not afraid to defend it to anyone, because we are certain that we have chosen a path that we can prove corresponds, if not totally, at least in great measure, to the aspirations of our people.

When the Party took up arms in 1962, a revolutionary situation already existed, and the people would have resorted to arms in any case, with or without us. We took up arms and placed ourselves at the head of our people. If there is some decline in our forces today—forces that have been so bestially decimated by repression and by the military superiority of the enemy—that does not mean that we, today, yesterday, or ever, have rejected any form of struggle. We are convinced that it is not in the form of struggle that the error lies, but in the timing of its use. Our failure was not due to our method of battle but only to the fact that the moment was ill chosen. The situation was adverse for our group; nor was it the first time that a party has been defeated by superior forces—infinitely superior forces, in the case of Venezuela.

It is thus clear that our Party has not eliminated its guerrillas or handed over its arms, nor has it betrayed or renounced the past. On the contrary, let it be said here firmly that it was right to take up arms.

However, in the past, the Party had the following attitude toward elections: In 1963, we resolved to boycott the elections and we failed, and we were thus unable to boycott them again. The elections took place, and because we did not participate in the electoral process, we were accused of having suffered an electoral defeat. Now we realize, from courageous self-criticism, that we must participate in the elections and that, if we do not take part, our enemies will benefit from our position. We reached the conclusion that, without any illusions on our part and without trying to create the illusion in the mass of people that we are going to triumph through the electoral method, we still must participate in this process in which millions of Venezuelans take part. Obviously, the participation of the Communist Party in a mass process, if that participation is carried out correctly, following a revolutionary Marxist-Leninist line, cannot and will not damage us. Elections are events that take place in our country every five years, and in our country, as distinct from others, they are not yet discredited. On the contrary, millions of Venezuelans consider elections to be a popular victory of the masses because in Venezuela the electoral process is a recent phenomenon, historically speaking. In Venezuela, for a century, power was always disputed by force of arms. The one who was most powerful governed and continued to govern until power slipped from his hands. When a more powerful coalition was formed, he was overthrown by force of arms and there was a change of government.

Recently, electoral processes have been achieved that the people consider, rightly or wrongly, to be a victory for them, and we must participate. [We must do so] not to spread the illusion that we are now going to liberate the people, that the social and economic problems of the masses will be resolved, but to denounce the demagogy of the government and the bourgeois parties, and to provide an example: to counterpose the proletarian, revolutionary line of the Communists and affirm the necessity of voting against candidates who will be elected only to betray their demagogic programs. It is a task that Communist parties perform in almost all the capitalist countries, and we can do it well in our country. We have proved historically that we can do it; we can and must continue to do it. . . .

We aspire to form a broad patriotic front capable of defeating the present government. The watchword is this: Neither the continuance of Acción Democrática and its gorillas nor the triumph of the Christian Democrats, the other relatively large force in the Venezuelan electoral system.

Is the victory of such a front possible or is it not? Certainly, it is possible. In the elections of 1963, the governing party received 32 per cent of the votes. Obviously, that party was opposed by enormous segments of the Venezuelan people. The Christian Democratic party received 20 to 22 per cent of the votes. Thus, the practical possibilities of the Christian Democrats taking power are nonexistent.* On the other hand, however, there does exist the possibility of a group of opposition parties—parties of the bourgeoisie that oppose the present regime, together with the legal

* Due to a split in the Acción Democrática party, the Christian Democratic candidate, Rafael Caldera, narrowly won the presidential election of December, 1968.—ED.

and illegal forces of the left—forming a broad front capable of defeating the official sectors and clerical groups. Admittedly this would not be easy but extremely difficult, because the imperialists would try by every means to prevent the bourgeois parties from uniting with the legal and illegal forces of the left. They have immense means of diplomatic, military, and economic pressure to utilize. But, in addition to a just cause and the desire that the gentlemen who oppose the government have for power, we have the effective contribution of our electoral force, which would whet the appetite of the leaders of other parties and might incline them, at the crucial moment, to enter this broad front and permit us to elect a president, although he would certainly not be a man of the left.

Then some of our friends ask us: Why are we going to take a man of that type? Nothing would change, because in time he would become one of the imperialists, if he were not already. This danger no doubt exists, but the displacement of the present government and of its party would create such a great convulsion in our country that confusion would result, and this very convulsion might be the trampoline from which we could easily leap to a higher stage in the development of the revolution. We are not confident that the candidate coming from these forces would soon ally himself with the Communists, or that he would pursue a program of national liberation, but we propose a program for change, a change in favor of the independence and sovereignty of our country and the solution of some of the most urgent problems of the working masses. It would be a change that would be possible within the context of Venezuelan reality, a reality involving tremendous pressures from military forces outside and within Venezuela. . . .

We have not built a party to fight other parties. It pains us, it pains us terribly, that there are governments that call themselves Communist and yet use the fact that we are crippled to try to destroy the Party. This is an evil thing, and the people of Venezuela repudiate it. And we, who are true Communists, despite the fact that we do not have the glory others do, will never lower the banner of solidarity with Cuba, with Vietnam, with Colombia, and with all our brothers the world over. We will never do it because we cannot confuse the irresponsible acts of people who scorn the international solidarity of revolutionaries that is so useful and so necessary—we cannot confuse those acts with our international duty of solidarity with all the peoples who fight imperialism. This we will never do. . . .

For our part, we will never attack any democratic or revolutionary personality, regardless of our opposition to what his group does or claims to do. However, we are, of course, a Party made up of men with blood in our veins and, as such, just as we confront the bitter enemies of our cause, the imperialists, we know that we must respond with stature and dignity to those of the supposed left who think that they can destroy our work and can tell us what we must do. We do not accept orders from anybody. We accept advice, we accept criticism, but we do not accept being told who are our leaders and who should be removed in the leadership. This we will never accept, because we feel it is wrong. And never will one of us suggest such things to any other party or group, because it prejudices the good relations between parties.

VIII. *Colombia: Elite Democracy in Transformation*

Unlike Venezuela, Colombia has known constitutional democracy throughout much of its history. National politics, however, has been dominated by a few families and by the two traditional parties, the Liberals and the Conservatives. So intense was the politicization of even rural areas that when the rules of the democratic game began to break down in the late 1940's, especially after the assassination of the charismatic Liberal leader Jorge Eliecer Gaitán, in 1948, large-scale violence broke out in the countryside between traditionally Liberal and Conservative areas. Before *la violencia* was ended in the 1960's, it is estimated that between 100,000 and 200,000 people had been killed.

In 1953, in the face of the civilian politicians' incapacity to deal with the violence, and following a period of increasing politicization of what had been a largely apolitical army, a military coup took place under the leadership of General Gustavo Rojas Pinilla. The military government proved to be repressive and inept, and the civilians came back to power under an agreement for a National Front worked out between the Liberals and the Conservatives and approved in a constitutional plebiscite in December, 1957 (*Selection 1*). The parties agreed to share power for a period of twelve years, with equal representation of each party in all government bodies. Unless otherwise specified by Congress, all legislation was to be adopted by a two-thirds majority. The two parties later agreed to extend the terms of the arrangement until 1974, with the presidency alternating between the two parties, thus giving each party two terms in office (*Selection 2*).

In practice, the National Front arrangement often made it very difficult for the executive to get reform measures through Congress. Within each of the two parties, a minority group developed that was opposed to the agreement: the *Laureanistas* in the Conservatives and, until 1968, the Movimiento Revolucionario Liberal in the Liberals; each group ran candidates under the party label and received a share of seats proportional to its vote. The issue was further complicated in 1966, when supporters of former dictator Rojas Pinilla formed a group that also presented candidates under the labels of the two parties. Yet the Colombian modified democratic system survived, and in 1961 the Congress was able to adopt an agrarian reform law that established an Institute of Agrarian Reform (INCORA), limited property rights in areas of public irrigation projects, and provided for expropriation, with partial payment in bonds, of land not used productively (*Selection 3*).

Yet to much of the voting public, the National Front seemed a device to keep political control in the hands of the traditional elite. One of the most vocal critics of Colombian politics was Camilo Torres Restrepo, the chaplain at the National University and a member of one of Colombia's oldest families. In 1965, Torres engaged in a public polemic with his superior, the Cardinal of Bogotá, over the question of the Church's acquiescence in the existing order. He secured his release from his religious vows and subsequently joined the Castroite guerrilla National Liberation Army (ELN), which, he said, had the same goals as his religiously based United Front. A short time later, Torres was killed in an encounter between the guerrillas and the army (see *Selection 4*). Torres' name has been adopted by Catholic leftists in many parts of the continent who feel that revolution is the only solution to Latin America's problems.

The two traditional parties and the National Front have been criticized not only for their monopoly of political power but also for the weakness of their organization, the conservatism of their leadership, and their lack of clear ideological programs (*Selection 5*). The Liberal Party, anticipating the termination of the National Front arrangement, has attempted to develop a more detailed program. It has committed itself to promoting "intermediate groups" between the individual and the state (an idea influenced by the Promoción Popular program in Chile) and has proposed replacing the proportional representation system by single-member district elections, like those in the French Fifth Republic (*Selection 6*).

Both the Liberals and the Conservatives are beginning to prepare for a gradual transition to competitive politics as the National Front is "dismantled" along lines proposed by President Carlos Lleras Restrepo, a Liberal who took office in 1966. As outlined by Minister of the Interior Misael Pastrana Borrero, a leading candidate for the nomination to fill the 1970–74 Conservative presidency, the *Desmonte* ("Dismantling") calls for the introduction of competitive elections for departmental (state) and local offices in 1970, balanced by an extension of equal representation in the public administration until 1978 (*Selection 7*).

In this as in other fields, the Lleras Restrepo government has exercised vigorous leadership, and recent figures indicate that Colombia has succeeded in overcoming its earlier economic difficulties. Colombia also seems to have solved the problem of rural violence and partisanship, although a small number of Castroite guerrillas remain in the mountains. Political apathy, however, reflected in the large abstention rate in recent elections, is increasing, and many problems remain, among them the underlying structural imbalances in the system of landholding, inadequate education, and a continuing high birth rate. But although Colombia is not the "showplace" that was hoped for in the early years of the Alliance for Progress (see *Selection 8*), it has made substantial progress toward the restoration of political democracy and the promotion of economic development.

1. THE PLEBISCITE OF DECEMBER 1, 1957

(EXCERPTS)

Article 1. Women shall have the same political rights as men. . . .

Article 2. In the popular elections that are held to elect public bodies, up to 1968 inclusive,* the posts corresponding to each electoral district shall be allotted, half-and-half, to the traditional parties, the Conservatives and the Liberals. If there are two or more lists for the same party, and there are more than two posts assigned to that party, the electoral quotient system shall be applied in allotting them, taking into account, however, only the votes cast for the lists of that party. In the elections held during the period referred to in this article, an even number of members shall be elected to public bodies in all electoral districts. To obtain this result, the constitutional rules establishing the number of members of such bodies shall be observed, but another post shall be added whenever the number is odd. No department with more than one million inhabitants may have fewer than six senators or fewer than twelve representatives.

Article 3. In the public bodies referred to in the foregoing article, the majority for all legal purposes shall be two-thirds of the votes; however, the Congress, by means of a law approved by two-thirds of the members of each house, may stipulate, for periods of not more than two years, the subjects with respect to which approval by an absolute majority will be sufficient. . . .

Article 4. Cabinet ministers shall be freely appointed and removed by the President of the Republic, who shall, however, be obligated to see that the political parties are represented in the ministries in the same proportion as they are represented in the legislative houses.

Since the purpose of this constitutional reform is to ensure that the two political parties, the Conservatives and the Liberals, placed on an equal footing within the framework of a broad and permanent agreement, have joint responsibility for the government and that this is exercised in the name of the two parties, the appointment of officials and employees who are not civil servants shall be made in such a way that the political composition

* In 1959, the provisions of Article 2 were extended to 1974. (See *Selection 2.*)—ED.

Excerpts from the *Constitution of the Republic of Colombia* (Washington, D.C.: Organization of American States, 1962).

of the Congress will be reflected evenly in the several spheres of the executive branch of the government.

The foregoing shall not hinder members of the armed forces from being appointed to fill positions in the public administration. . . .

Article 5. The President of the Republic, the governors, the mayors, and, in general, all officials having the power to appoint and remove administrative employees may exercise this power only within the standards set by Congress for the establishment and regulation of conditions for entering the public service, for meritorious and seniority promotions, and for pensions, retirement, and dismissal. . . .

Article 11. Beginning January 1, 1958, the national government shall allocate for public education not less than 10 per cent of its general budget of expenditures.

2. LEGISLATIVE ACT NO. 1 OF 1959

(EXCERPTS)

Article 1. In the three constitutional terms between August 7, 1962, and August 7, 1974, the office of President of the Republic shall be held, alternately, by citizens who belong to the two traditional parties, the Conservatives and the Liberals, in such a manner that the President who is elected for either of the aforesaid terms shall belong to a party different from that of his immediate predecessor. Therefore, to start the system of alternation referred to in this article, the office of President of the Republic in the constitutional period between August 7, 1962, and August 7, 1966, shall be held by a citizen who belongs to the Conservative Party.

Any election of the President of the Republic that is held in contravention of the provisions of this article shall be invalid. . . .

Article 6. Article 2 of the Constitutional Reform approved by the Plebiscite of December 1, of the year one thousand nine hundred fifty-seven (1957), shall govern until the year one thousand nine hundred seventy-four (1974) inclusive.

In the bodies elected in accordance with this article, the rule of Article 3 of the aforesaid Constitutional Reform approved by plebiscite shall be applied.

Reprinted from *The Constitution of the Republic of Colombia* (Washington, D.C.: The Organization of American States, 1962).

3. THE LAW OF AGRARIAN SOCIAL REFORM OF 1961

(EXCERPTS)

CHAPTER I: OBJECTIVES OF THE LAW

Article 1. Inspired by the principle of the common good and the necessity of extending to ever increasing sectors of the Colombian rural population the exercise of the natural right to property and harmonizing its use with the social interest, this law has the following objectives:

First. To reform the agrarian social structure by means of appropriate procedures, to eliminate and prevent the inequitable concentration of rural property or its anti-economic division, to establish adequate operating units in the *minifundio* zones and to grant lands to those who do not have them, with preference to those who work the lands directly and incorporate their own personal labor therein.

Second. To stimulate the adequate economic exploitation of uncultivated or deficiently utilized lands, in accordance with programs that are aimed at their orderly distribution and rational utilization.

Third. To increase the over-all volume of agricultural and livestock production in harmony with the development of the other sectors of the economy; to increase productivity by application of appropriate technical methods; and ensure that the lands are used in the manner best adapted to their location and characteristics.

Fourth. To create conditions under which small renters and sharecroppers will enjoy better guarantees, and under which they as well as salaried farmhands will have better access to land ownership.

Fifth. To raise the standard of living of the rural population as a consequence of the measures already indicated, and also by the coordination and development of services related to technical assistance, agricultural credit, housing, the organization of markets, social health and security, storing and conservation of products, and the development of cooperatives.

Selections from the translation made by the Land Tenure Center, University of Wisconsin, Madison, Wisc.

Sixth. To ensure the conservation, defense, improvement, and adequate utilization of natural resources.

The purposes enumerated in this article shall serve as a guide for the regulation, interpretation, and execution of the present law.

Chapter II: Colombian Institute of Agrarian Reform

Article 2. The Colombian Institute of Agrarian Reform (INCORA) is created as a public establishment, i.e., as an entity endowed with administrative autonomy and its own property.

The Institute shall carry out the functions dictated by the present law, shall have indefinite duration, and its headquarters shall be in Bogotá. . . .

Article 5. The government shall name a special commission composed of four members, of equal bipartisan political composition, in order to prepare the statutes, which, once approved by the government, shall control the activities of the Colombian Institute of Agrarian Reform. The powers and obligations of its different agencies may be changed at any time by the Board of Directors, with the approval of the government. . . .

Article 8. The Colombian Institute of Agrarian Reform shall be administered by a Board of Directors, a General Manager, and other officers determined by the statutes.

The Board of Directors shall be of equal bipartisan political composition and shall consist of the following members:

The Minister of Agriculture as Chairman.

The Minister of Public Works.

One representative each of the Agrarian Credit Bank, the National Institute of Supplies, the Agustín Codazzi Geographic Institute, the agricultural cooperatives, the Colombian Agricultural Society, and the Colombian Cattlemen's Confederation, chosen by the President of the Republic from bipartisan lists to be presented by the respective organizations.

One representative of the Catholic Social Action organizations, designated by the Archbishop Primate of Colombia, and a further representative of the rural workers, chosen by the President of the Republic from lists made up in a manner to be determined by the government.

One member of the General Staff of the Armed Forces, designated by the President of the Republic, whose presence on the Board shall not be taken into consideration for the application of party parity.

Two senators and two representatives elected by the respective chambers, observing the rule of party parity. These four members of the national Congress shall be chosen in such a way that the different regions of the country shall be represented by them. . . .

CHAPTER V: NATIONAL AGRARIAN FUND

Article 14. The National Agrarian Fund consists of:

1. The sums that are voted to it in the national budget. An annual amount of not less than 100 million pesos * shall be appropriated which the government must include in its budget bill, and without which the bill shall not be accepted by the budget committee of the House of Representatives. . . .

3. The agrarian bonds that the government may issue and deliver to the Fund for the accomplishment of the present law. . . .

CHAPTER VII: TERMINATION OF PROPRIETORSHIP OF UNCULTIVATED LANDS

Article 22. Every proprietor of an area greater than 2,000 hectares shall present to the Institute, together with the respective certificate extended by the Register of Public Documents and a copy of the registered title that establishes right of proprietorship over said land, a detailed description of said land, in which shall be included also all the data and explanation that the Institute requires in respect to the location and the manner in which it is worked. The same obligations are required of proprietors owning land of smaller area but which formed part of areas of the size stated above on September 1, 1960, and from those who, without having title, have material possession of such areas. . . .

Article 24. In the administrative proceedings that take place before the Institute and in the review by the Supreme Court mentioned in the previous articles, the burden of proving economic exploitation of the property or of a part thereof falls upon the proprietor or proprietors, and they alone must prove that they have economically exploited the land in accordance with the following test schedule:

1. The fact that the property, or a determined area thereof, has been exploited with agricultural crops, must be demonstrated by an ocular inspection in which the experts shall clearly indicate the state of the land, specifying whether the original spontaneous vegetation has been felled and cleared, and which crops exist at that instant, or whether there are evident signs that the respective land has been submitted previously to regular agricultural exploitation. . . .

* In 1961, the equivalent of about $12 million; in 1970, about one-half that amount.—ED.

Article 26. Farming by squatters with no recognized relation to the proprietor shall not be taken into consideration for the purpose of demonstrating economic exploitation of a property. When the resolution on termination of private ownership is confirmed, the Institute may award to the squatters the portions corresponding to each according to the norms in effect for the public domain on the date of their establishment. . . .

CHAPTER VIII: PUBLIC LANDS

Article 29. From the date of entry into force of the present law, with the exceptions contemplated therein, no grants of public lands may be made except to individuals and in a size not exceeding 450 hectares. . . .

Article 36. Married males who have reached eighteen years of age may obtain grants of public land or of family-farm units in colonizations or parcelizations and, consequently, contract all inherent obligations, without the necessity of judicial authorization. . . .

CHAPTER IX: COLONIZATION

Article 43. The Colombian Institute of Agrarian Reform shall carry out colonization of public lands that it reserves for this purpose according to the terms of this law.

Such colonizations shall be preceded by as complete a study as possible of climatic conditions, soil, water, topography, and accessibility, with the object of establishing that they are suitable for economic exploitation and to indicate the orientation that such exploitation should take. . . .

Article 48. Family-farm units shall be assigned to workers with the obligation to put at least half of the plot into use within the following five years, and by means of a written contract in which the following conditions must be included:

a. That the definitive ownership title shall only be given when the assignee proves to the Institute's satisfaction that he has fulfilled the economic-use obligation described in the previous clause.

b. That, without the Institute's permission, the assigned land or the improvements made thereon cannot be transferred before the ownership title has been given, and that the transfer can only be made to persons indicated in Paragraph 3 of Article 45 or to cooperatives of agricultural workers.

c. That the assignee is under obligation to submit to the rules that this law sets out for family-farm units.

Cooperatives of agricultural workers that obtain assignments of land in the directed colonization zones shall also be subject to the same rules, insofar as possible. . . .

Chapter X: Family-Farm Units

Article 50. The Institute shall preferably try to constitute family-farm units in its colonization work, as well as in the lands divided for parceling and in consolidations of small holdings.

By "family-farm units" is understood those that meet the following conditions:

a. That, depending on the nature of the zone, soil, water, location, topography, and possible type of production, the area of land is sufficient, when exploited in a reasonably efficient manner, to provide a normal family with an adequate income for its maintenance, for paying off debts incurred in the buying or conditioning of the land, as the case may be, and for a progressive improvement in housing, farm equipment, and general living standard.

b. That to be utilized with reasonable efficiency, the said area normally does not require more than the work of the owner and his family. It is understood, however, that this latter rule is not inconsistent with employment of extra labor at times for certain farm work, if the type of use so requires, nor with the mutual help that neighbors may render for specific jobs. . . .

Article 55. Except in the cases dealt with in Article 58 of the present law, the granting of lands by the Institute shall be made utilizing, in the first place, the public lands that are easily accessible to the rural population of the respective region and that offer, also, all the necessary conditions for the establishment of colonization as indicated in Article 43 ff.

If it appears necessary to acquire privately owned lands for grants, the procedure used shall be according to the following order or priority:

1. Uncultivated lands which do not fall under the rules for termination of private proprietorship.

2. Lands inadequately used.

3. Those properties which, in their total extension or major part thereof, are exploited by means of renters or sharecroppers, when, in the latter case, the proprietor does not exercise the direction of the exploitation and is not charged with part of the costs or operations thereof under the share contract. Those lands shall be excepted which are the property of minors and disabled persons.

4. Adequately used lands not falling under the preceding pro-

vision, the proprietors of which are disposed to sell them voluntarily under the conditions established in this law. . . .

Article 57. In endeavoring to acquire privately owned lands, the Institute shall be subject to the following rules:

First. Priority shall be given to those zones where land congestion is notable or where total or partial unemployment exists among a large part of the farm population, and to those other areas where active erosion exists, where labor relations are unjust, or visibly low standards of living of the rural population occur in relation to other parts of the country. . . .

Article 58. Adequately used lands may be expropriated only if a *minifundio* area has to be enlarged with adjacent or nearby properties in order to permit the consolidation of small holdings; in order to assist small renters and sharecroppers to acquire or enlarge the holdings that they have been working or their establishment on other lands of the same region when the latter seems to be more appropriate; if the acquisition is necessary to establish small owners, renters, or sharecroppers of the neighborhood who are occupying lands that have to be retired from use; in the case of Section 3 of Article 55; or to facilitate water installations, drainage, and transportation in rural zones.

Any proprietor affected, nevertheless, shall have the right to exclude from expropriation an area of 100 hectares. The same right shall apply to owners of inadequately used lands that the Institute may resolve to expropriate for the purposes cited in this article. . . .

Article 59. Except for the cases to which the previous article refers, the owner of inadequately used lands shall retain the right, if subjected to expropriation, to have an area up to 200 hectares excluded therefrom, of which not more than 100 hectares may be lands suitable for crops. . . .

Article 62. The lands that the Institute might acquire by voluntary purchase or expropriation shall be paid for as follows:

1. Uncultivated lands, by Class B agrarian bonds, which are ordered to be issued by this law.

2. Inadequately used lands, 20 per cent of the price in cash, but not exceeding 100,000 pesos, shall be paid on the date of the operation. The remainder shall be paid in eight successive annual installments of equal value, the first of which shall be due one year after the same date.

The same payment procedure shall apply to lands exploited by small renters or sharecroppers, when the proprietor does not participate in the exploitation by directing it and participating in the cost of operation thereof, and the lands referred to by Section 3 of Article 55.

3. Those lands not contemplated by the previous sections, 20 per cent of the price in cash, but not exceeding 300,000 pesos, shall be paid on the date of the operation. The balance shall be paid in five successive annual installments of equal value, the first of which shall be due one year after the same date. . . .

The Institute shall pay interest at a rate of 4 per cent annually on the balance due in the case of Section 2 and at a rate of 6 per cent in the case of Section 3 of this article. These interest payments shall be made in six-month periods. . . .

Article 75. Agrarian bonds shall have the following characteristics:

Class A. 7 per cent interest per annum. Amortization period of fifteen years.

Class B. 2 per cent interest per annum. Amortization period of twenty-five years. . . .

CHAPTER XIV: SUBDIVISION OF LAND

Article 80. As a general rule, the properties that the Institute acquires by purchase or expropriation may only be used for the following purposes, except as the Board of Directors of the Institute, with the favorable vote of the Minister of Agriculture, and after due consideration of the special circumstances existing in a piece of property, issue a specific regulation:

a. to establish family-farm units and cooperative-use units;

b. to consolidate small holdings;

c. to establish the necessary public services for the respective areas, as well as demonstration or experimental farms, agricultural farm machinery stations, schools, agricultural industries, storage, premises for agricultural cooperatives, rural-action units, and communal pastures;

d. to enlarge municipal urban areas. . . .

Article 81. The family-farm units to be formed in parcelation areas may be sold only to poor people or to those of very small means, and they shall be subject in their entirety to the terms of Articles 50 and 54 of the present law. . . .

Article 83. The interest rate to be charged the parcelee shall be 4 per cent per year. During the first two years only half of this rate shall be charged.

The buyers shall pay the cost of the parcel and the corresponding interest over a fifteen-year term, by the cumulative amortization system. But the amount of the principal shall not begin to be collected until the third year. . . .

Chapter XVI: Minifundios and Consolidation of Small Holdings

Article 87. Except for the cases indicated later, rural properties with an area equal to or less than three hectares shall be considered for all legal purposes as a unit that does not permit further material division.

No act of division shall be made on areas that results in the establishment of properties with an area less than that mentioned.

Consequently, acts or contracts that violate the prohibition established in the preceding clause are null and void. . . .

Article 105. The Commander-in-Chief of the Armed Forces shall take appropriate measures, insofar as circumstances permit, to provide instruction to those in compulsory military service on farm-machinery operation and other types of farm-production work.

Said Commander shall enter into an agreement with the Institute on: (a) the manner by which personnel of the armed forces are to lend their help in execution of agrarian reform; (b) the allotment of family-farm units to members of said forces who wish to return to farm work at the end of their tour of duty and lack sufficient land of their own; (c) the organization of colonization projects specifically for honorably discharged armed forces personnel.

4. CAMILO TORRES, THE CHURCH, AND REVOLUTION

I. PASTORAL LETTER OF LUIS CARDINAL CONCHA, ARCHBISHOP OF BOGOTÁ (AUGUST 15, 1965)

The ancients considered the two-edged sword one of the most deadly weapons. In these days we could compare certain words to a two-edged sword, because of the variety of meanings to which they lend themselves. One of those words is the word

Excerpts from Germán Guzmán, *Camilo Torres*, trans. John D. Ring (New York: Sheed and Ward, 1969), pp. 135–38, 239–42, and 249; © 1969 by Sheed and Ward; reprinted by permission of the publisher.

revolution. The Spanish dictionary defines it: "violent change of the nation's political institutions." And this is the sense which spontaneously comes to mind when one hears or reads the word revolution. Sometimes in pronouncing or writing it we intend to give it another meaning, omitting anything whch might explain that we do not want to speak of "violent change," which causes confusion in the spirit of our hearers or readers. Other times we add another explanatory word saying, for example, *peaceful revolution,* or something similar. But would it not be better to dispense with the word *revolution* when we want to understand an evolution, a change which is justifiable, peaceful, and lawful. . . .

Those among us who promote revolution judge that it is necessary to begin with "the seizure of power." But to make an attempt against a legitimate government is condemned by natural law, and if the mandate of the natural law would seem doubtful to some, that of the Sacred Scripture promulgated by the Church would show, as the Supreme Pontiffs have constantly taught, that it is illicit when it means disobedience, rebellion, or the overthrow of civil power legally constituted.

St. Paul, with words which leave no room for doubt, wrote in his Epistle to the Romans: "You must all obey the governing authorities. Since all government comes from God, the civil authorities were appointed by God, and so anyone who resists authority is rebelling against God's decision, and such an act is bound to be punished" (Rom. 13:1-2). And it is interesting to note the fact that St. Paul wrote when the tyranny of the pagan emperors was manifest and presaged days of tremendous trial for the Christians. Nine years after writing the Epistle to the Romans the head of St. Paul fell under the sword of the executioner.

The teachings of St. Peter with respect to duties to legitimate authority do not differ from those of St. Paul and, if you will, are even more strict than those of the Apostle to the Gentiles.

But what is of extraordinary significance in this matter is that during all the time that the Roman emperors governed the Roman Empire, the Christians who were the victims of atrocities and bloody persecutions never attempted rebellion against the tyrannical imperial authority. On the contrary they always obeyed it and respected it in everything which was not against the Law of God. St. Cyprian declared in the presence of the judge who had the power to condemn him to death that the Christians prayed for the welfare of the Emperors.

It is undeniable that every nation must have changes in its institutions, in accord with the circumstances of the times. But it is equally undeniable that, under penalty of falling into chaos and anarchy, these changes must be carried out in a regular legal way and never in a violent way. Certainly there are many evils which must be remedied here as elsewhere, and it is undeniable that every effort must be made to remedy them. The use of violence for this purpose would only bring greater evils and would not correct the existing ones.

Those who proclaim revolution seduce the multitudes with illusory promises. They promise them an ideal world in which they will be free of all those evils which weigh on them, a true paradise on earth. The final result is infinitely far from what was promised. In changing a legal regime which has its defects like every human system, and yet within which they could make their voice heard, they finally come under the domination of an absolute master or a tyrannical oligarchy which suppresses their just requests and now vain complaints.

II. CAMILO TORRES RESTREPO: A LETTER TO THE COLOMBIAN PEOPLE

January, 1966, From the mountains

Colombians:
For many years the poor in our country have waited for the call to battle in order to launch the final attack against the oligarchy.

Whenever the desperation of the people reached the extreme, the ruling class always found some way to trick the people, to distract them, to appease them with new formulas which always amount to the same thing: suffering for the people and good living for the privileged class.

When the people asked for a leader and found him in Jorge Eliecer Gaitán,* the oligarchy killed him. When the people asked for peace, the oligarchy spread violence in the country. When the people could no longer put up with violence and organized the guerrillas to seize power, the oligarchy invented the military coup to trick the guerrillas so that they would be betrayed. When the people asked for democracy, they were again tricked with a plebiscite and a National Front which imposed on them a dictatorship of the oligarchy.

Now the people no longer believe. The people do not believe in elections. The people know that legal avenues are exhausted and that only the way of force is left. The people are desperate and determined to gamble their lives so that the next generation of Colombians will not be slaves. So that the children of those who now wish to give their lives may have education, houses,

---

* Popular leader of the Liberal Party, assassinated in 1948.—ED.

food, clothing and, above all, dignity. So that future Colombians can have their own country, independent of North American power.

Every sincere revolutionary must recognize the way of force as the only one that remains. Nevertheless, the people await leaders who, by their example and their presence, will give the call to battle.

I want to tell the Colombian people that this is the moment; that I have not betrayed them; that I have passed through the plazas of the towns and cities campaigning for the unity and organization of the people for the seizure of power; that I have asked that we dedicate ourselves to these objectives even though it may mean our death.

Now everything is prepared. The oligarchy wants to organize another electoral farce with candidates who resign and then accept, with bipartisan committees, with movements of renovation based on ideas and persons who not only are old but who have betrayed the people. What more can we expect, Colombians?

I have involved myself in the armed battle. From the mountains I will continue the fight with arms in hand until power is conquered for the people. I have joined the Army of National Liberation because I have found in it the same ideals as in the United Front. I have found both the desire for and the fulfillment of a unity which has a peasant base, without religious differences or traditional parties . . . without any desire to battle the revolutionary elements of any other sector, movement, or party . . . without caudillos. It is searching for a way to free the people from the exploitation of the oligarchy and from imperialism. It will not put down its arms as long as power is not totally in the hands of the people. In its objectives it accepts the Platform of the United Front.*

All of us Colombian patriots must place ourselves at the service of the war. Little by little experienced guerrilla leaders will arise in all the corners of the country. In the meanwhile we must be alert. We must collect arms and munitions, seek guerrilla training, talk with the more experienced, bring together clothes, food, provisions and drugs in order to prepare ourselves for a prolonged fight.

Let us carry out small actions against the enemy; in this way we will assure victory. Let us prove to them what revolutionaries are. Let us throw out the traitors. Let us not fail to act, but let us not be impatient. In a prolonged war all will have to act at some time. What is important is that the revolution finds us ready at that precise moment. It is not necessary for everyone to do

* Camilo Torres' program, issued in the spring of 1965.—Ed.

everything. We must divide the work. The militants of the United Front must be the vanguard of initiative and action. Let us have patience in the hope and confidence of final victory.

The battle of the people must become a national battle. We have already begun, but the journey is long. Colombians, let us not fail to respond to the call of the people and of the revolution. Militants of the United Front, let us make our objectives a reality.

For the unity of the people! Until death!

For the organization of the people! Until death!

For the seizure of power for the people! Until death!

Until death because we have decided to persevere to the end.

Until victory because once a people gives itself completely it always obtains victory.

Until final victory for the objectives of the Army of National Liberation!

Not one step back! Freedom or death!

III. THE DEATH OF CAMILO TORRES

Military Communiqué No. 007:

The Commandant of the Fifth Brigade reports to the citizenry the following: Because of the ambush which an armed group of about 25 men produced Tuesday, February 15th, against a patrol of this unit in the place called Patio Cemento of the district of El Carmen, municipality of San Vicente de Chucurí, we have the results which were given to the public. Five men who were shot down by the patrol have been identified where possible, even though their identification has not been definitive:

(1) Camilo Torres Restrepo. . . .

Among the arms recovered by the troops who participated in the action there was found the M-1 .30 caliber rifle which was carried by one of the soldiers who died at the hands of the bandits in the assault on Simacota, January 7, 1965. This rifle, with the number 5,188,554, was found in the hands of someone later identified as Camilo Torres Restrepo. It has been technically proven that it had been fired moments before its capture.

The bodies of the persons enumerated in this list were buried in a place located within the general area where the armed encounter, to which reference has been made, occurred.

> Colonel Alvaro Valencia Tovar
> Commandant of the Fifth Brigade

Bucaramanga, February 17, 1966

5. WHAT ARE THE TRADITIONAL POLITICAL PARTIES?

EDUARDO SANTA

Both parties [Liberals and Conservatives] have been traditional, not only in the sense of their permanence but also in their structure and dynamics. This traditionalism is manifested in the following phenomena:

1. *In the popular base.* It is readily apparent that individuals in Colombia are Liberals or Conservatives by tradition, generally following the party affiliation of their father or mother, just as they adopt their names.

2. *In the leadership.* Two traditionalist phenomena operate in the formation and mechanics of the leadership. The first of these is the presence within the governing groups in the parties, throughout our political history, of what are referred to as "natural leaders," that is to say, hereditary chieftains. The son of a great leader, of a great caudillo, generally emerges in national politics aided by the prestige of his father and reflecting the very qualities of his parent.

The second traditionalist phenomenon is that of caudillism. It has existed from the beginning of our country until our own times. It seems that our organized groups have had an extraordinary inability to move except at the command of the powerful personalities who have given Colombian politics such a remarkably personalist character.

3. *In their organization.* The traditional political parties are traditionalist in this sense, too. From the first stages of their development until today, the parties have had weak organizations. A Colombian student has said, with reference to our traditional political parties, that they are a cloud of dust. In truth, the traditional political parties have never been organized on a sound basis. . . . In a sense, the parties exist at the time of elections and seem to die in the ensuing periods. Or, better said, they exist only for elections. It is their only reason for existence. We now come back to the idea of the "dust cloud," of men who vote more

Translated by the editor from *DC Avanzada* (Bogotá), No. 14 (July, 1968).

against their partisan adversaries than in favor of their own party. In this sense, the vote is typically an act of negation, an expression of resentment developed in the public mind: One votes against the opposing party or a candidate of that party.

4. *As for their programs,* our traditional parties have been equally traditionalist. We have carefully reviewed the history of these parties, and we have found that for an entire century they have copied each other's programs. . . . Our two traditional parties —Liberal and Conservative—originated from the party that secured our independence. This thesis was brilliantly propounded by Mariano Ospina Rodríguez in an article published around 1850. If this is correct, one must not forget that this distinguished patrician was one of the principal actors in the original formation of political parties and was also one of the framers of the first Conservative Party platform in 1849. Thus, the traditional parties have a common origin, the same foundation of liberalism derived from Montesquieu and the encyclopedists. It is enough to examine and compare the programs of our parties to find in their contents a common origin. Their programs are almost identical. Perhaps the initial programs of the Conservative Party were more liberal. Of such liberal political bent were the Conservatives of that era that they proposed to name their party "Liberal-Conservative."

The indifference not only of some sectors of youth but also of a good portion of the people to the party struggle is a typical manifestation of disillusion with the traditional parties, of skepticism toward them, of a lack of political ideals, of a lack of concern for problems of the nation. . . . Those disoriented young people, enclosed in their unconscious egoism, removed from political life, without faith or goals, will have to be shaken up soon and given some motivation, so that they may definitely cooperate in finding the fatherland that they have not received from their elders.

6. THE DECLARATION OF TISQUESUSA
(JULY 11–13, 1968)

THE LIBERAL PARTY

To be able to fulfill its duties to the Colombian nation in light of the principles that we have enunciated, Liberalism must become, in the first place, the party of political development. This is conceived as the construction of a mechanism that will open the way to a participatory democracy, where not only will the people be able to obtain simple goods and services, but social power will be distributed, expressed, and exercised by each person and each community.

The problem of development is above all a problem of political organization. Only through the construction of coherent forms and systems of co-participation of the citizenry in the decision-making process is it possible to consider the remedies for the social, economic, and cultural problems that affect the present or threaten the future of a social group. This is true not merely because informal and formal political organizations are the only way to reach and direct the general interests of the society, but also because the structures of power inexorably condition the forms and results of all other types of development.

The question of finding appropriate formulas for the generation, distribution, and utilization of power is of crucial importance in any type of society, but it acquires greater seriousness and urgency in a society whose explicit goal is the development of democracy. Where democracy is the ideal, it is not possible to direct the energy of the community toward a goal if the mechanics of its organs of co-participation, communication, and delegation of responsibility have not been previously defined. The essential problem—how to promote and express the will of society—must be solved first. If this basic necessity has not been satisfied, it will be possible to draw up inventories of social problems and even to offer partial solutions to some of them, but over the long run it will be impossible to achieve the progressive and coherent elimination of these problems, because the collective energies of the people will not be utilized in the task.

These obvious considerations, valid for any society, seem to have been dangerously forgotten in Colombia, especially by Liberals who, if they are serious in wanting to become the party of development, must become capable of generating, guiding, and utilizing the social energy of Colombians to overcome the crushing conditions of backwardness that plague us.

For complex historical and social reasons, Colombian political groups, and the forms of government that they have developed, have only to a limited degree been able to make possible the exercise of effective political power by the citizens and the communities, or to distribute the social decision-making power in such a way as to be both popularly based and yet effective at the

Translated by the editor from *Encuentro Liberal* (Bogotá), No. 58 (August 3, 1968).

leadership level as an emerging force for change and development of a permanent and progressive sort.

Decision-making power has come to be exercised by a minority, whose inability to channel the desires of the people and the social force of the populace in the direction of an urgent transformation is not so much the result of their small numbers as of the fact that they do not respond to constant and systematic pressures exerted by the primary organizations of society on all the centers of decision, for the purpose of changing what is inconvenient, outmoded, or unjust.

All this produces a type of society composed mainly of millions of politically marginal people, whose only theoretical possibility of achieving personal or social betterment consists in the nearly mechanical ritual of voting in popular elections for candidates who are periodically presented to or imposed upon them. Such phenomena as the absurd violence that lashed the country a few years ago, the notorious tendency to obtain social goods and services by the exercise of anarchical pressure outside the framework of established institutions, the growing and alarming apathy toward elections, are evident symptoms that the political energy of the nation is being sold short or wasted, simply because the great mass of politically marginal people do not feel that the electoral process is a means of emancipation but rather an instrument of minority domination, a domination exercised without any popular base. Under these conditions, when there do not exist normal organisms for the expression of the popular will that could contribute their dynamism to the modification of the prevalent socioeconomic conditions, it is utopian to speak of social change. The social efficacy of a democratic community depends on power being fully achieved, effectively divided, and responsibly exercised by the majority of the population. It cannot and should not be expected that, through simple technological or economic change, a "modernizing," "progressive" minority will arise that, without motivation or legitimate political pressures, either can or will want to exercise and ably direct the national power toward a permanent solution of the nation's problems.

However, political action by the population cannot be exercised, nor can its multiplying dynamic emerge, merely by supporting or rejecting decisions made at the national level, as occurs today in our centralized party organizations and in the institutions of Colombian government. It is necessary to give serious attention to the "intermediate organisms" between the individual and the centralized state, all those spontaneous associations that permit the individual to make use of his own decision-making power in the framework of societies smaller than the nation but larger and more efficient than his own isolated person, or simple groupings of unorganized persons.

The municipalities, geographic and socioeconomic regions, professional and labor organizations, and spontaneous civic associations are all generators of power, and only in and through them can the will of society express itself and develop its dynamic in a responsible and meaningful way. It is through these intermediate organisms that the desire for participation at the most concrete and important level is identified and made effective. And it is only there that a social democracy can be developed that can give basis and force to the simple rhetorical democracy that the laws or the will of minority groups draw up or impose.

Although it is evident that in a democratic society only parties can serve as coordinators and catalysts of the will of society at the national level, and although it is certain that the success of the fight against anarchy depends on their solidity and organization, these parties are merely theoretical and transitory electoral organizations if they do not represent and organize the elementary force of the "generators of power," that is, the intermediate organizations.

The Liberal Party must modernize both itself and the national government, conceiving this fundamental change as a total policy of integration of the people. This implies fundamentally:

Giving organized expression to the transitory groupings that voters form today, within which simple demagogic and emotional demands, or pressures exercised by minorities, impede and frustrate the exercise of decision-making power by the great marginal majority of the nation.

Incorporating into the life of the party the various social segments that make up the nation and, in particular, the popular sectors that today feel isolated from the centers of political decision-making and from the reasons for which they are made. . . .

Specifically, the Liberal Party must promote the following in the search for the modernization of the party and the establishment of an authentic democracy of social participation, within which the parties may fulfill their function as effective proponents of national development:

1. To incorporate into its organization the private popular groups (labor unions, community action organizations, consumer associations, youth organizations, women's organizations, associations of producers) and, in general, all the vital forces of the country. For this, two initiatives must be taken: (a) in the immediate future, within the present structure of the party, to ask

departmental and municipal directorates to stimulate the formation of representative organizations that will give political expression to the various segments, sectors, and groups that these forces represent, so that they may be represented in the assemblies and decision-making organisms of the party; and (b) to name a commission to prepare a basic statute of the Liberal Party for these purposes and to establish the rules relating to the institutionalization of these groups, so that they may fulfill their proper function in the exercise of modern democracy. The commission's conclusions are to be presented to the national convention of the Liberal Party.

2. In order to guarantee the effective participation of all citizens in the exercise of suffrage, to alter the party-list system of election, replacing it with single-member district elections, with the purpose of making the candidates present their programs and qualifications directly to the public, so that they will be elected with full knowledge of those who vote for them. Equally, to put the citizen identity card on a national basis, so as to free the elector from the existing legal requirement of previous registration in the place where he happens to reside at the time of election.

3. To adopt legal rules that will rationalize the political process and the direct participation of organized popular groups in party activities, as an efficient way for the people to give legitimate expression to their desires in the face of the pressures of powerful economic and financial groups. . . .

7. THE SIGNIFICANCE OF THE SECOND CONSTITUTIONAL REFORM

MISAEL PASTRANA BORRERO

THE ORIGIN OF THE NATIONAL FRONT

It is worth while to recall the content of the [National Front] agreement—this interim period, this parenthesis—which was achieved in a form that does credit to our democracy, so that we might bury our hatreds, re-establish the roots of our republican-

---

Translated by the editor from *Sentido y Alcance de la Segunda Reforma constitucional* (Bogotá, 1968).

ism, and put the nation on a progressive course at a different pace. Above all, it was a highly temporary arrangement, as is stated in all the documents by which it was established. Liberal and Conservative leaders alike were in agreement that they did not want to establish a distorted democracy on a permanent basis. Far from their minds, also, was an agreement that would give the two parties a permanent right to represent public opinion on an exclusive basis, because they did not wish to limit the expressions of conscience within narrow confines that could asphyxiate it. They sought a transitional system that would enable the country to shoulder its responsibilities with confidence and to treat the ills that afflicted it, so as to put the country on a surer course. It was a highly provisional system, agreed upon initially for twelve years, later extended to sixteen, that, among other things, did not in the beginning include alternation [of the presidency] but merely parity [of the two parties] in the three branches of government. Alternation came later, as a result of the decision by the Conservatives to give up their right to the first presidency when the candidacy of [Guillermo León] Valencia became impossible and Dr. Lleras Camargo was chosen [president]. . . .

What does the "dismantling" [of the National Front] involve? Does it mean, as our adversaries say, abandoning a defenseless party [the Conservatives] to the unconstrained desires of the Liberals?

In the first place, as I have just stated, according to the [1957] plebiscite, parity of representation in all the representative bodies was to end in 1970, but in 1959 the original period was extended to sixteen years, which means that it will expire in 1974. The alternation of the presidency of the republic will also terminate in that year, since it was precisely the purpose of those who made the bipartisan agreements that the provisional regime should end at that time. We now see, from the perspective gained with the passage of several years, that this was a dangerous mistake, because suddenly to remove all the restraints of the agreement could open the door to a return to the senseless politics of confrontation of absolute power.

The Participation of New Parties in the 1970 Elections

Thus, parity was agreed upon for all public bodies until 1974; now, by means of new agreements, we would like to advance the date of free democratic elections for the [departmental] assemblies and [municipal] councils so that other currents of opinion may participate, as was the case in the [1966] electoral campaign that culminated in the election of President Lleras [Restrepo].* We want to know the real strength of these new groups, in order to see whether they are light breezes or violent hurricanes and to measure whether these political currents, which today are prohibited by the Constitution from running, have grown in strength or lack the necessary vigor.

THE DEPARTMENTAL ASSEMBLIES AND MUNICIPAL COUNCILS

Furthermore, we will not elect [municipal] councillors and [departmental] assemblymen on the same basis as we do today [1968]. I have said several times that the constitutional reforms of the government form an organic whole that cannot be analyzed in its parts, as some groups of the opposition do who choose to attack one line or one paragraph of one article. One must judge the reforms as a whole, in their philosophical and institutional conceptions. Thus, in 1970, some assemblies and councils will be elected, but they will not be the tumultuous and politicized organs of today, which always oppose the regional or municipal [executive] rather than fulfill their function as joint administrators of the public welfare. What we are trying to do is to establish smaller regional and local administrative organs—with not more than twenty and normally from six to twelve members. The initiative for appropriations will be transferred to the governors and mayors, so as to avoid the dispersion of resources and wasteful expenditures. The legislative bodies will be able to name their representatives in the decentralized departmental and municipal institutions, but their directors will be freely appointed and removed by the executive. Thus, we are trying to modify the vicious habits that have made the assemblies and councils archaic institutions.

PARITY IN CONGRESS

Parity in the Chamber [of Deputies] and in the Senate will continue until 1974. But in an article appearing in *El Siglo*, I was surprised to find the assertion that parity in Congress would extend until 1978, an assertion that contradicts the agreements on the period of their operation and that also goes against the document sent by the [1957] Governing Junta to the Joint Representative Committee, which said that the plebiscite "introduced

* In the 1966 congressional elections, other parties were permitted to run candidates under the Liberal and Conservative labels. Only the National Popular Alliance (ANAPO), the group supporting ex-dictator Gustavo Rojas Pinilla, won enough votes to elect members to Congress.—ED.

a system of balance between the two political forces in the fundamental institutions of the Republic for twelve years". . . .

Thus, nothing is being "dismantled" as far as parity in Congress is concerned, since it will be maintained until 1974, the term specified in the provisional system adopted in the plebiscite and later modified in 1959.

THE EXTENSION OF PARITY IN THE EXECUTIVE

Far from "dismantling" the parity system in the executive branch, we are extending it until 1978 in the whole of the administration, precisely because we want to avoid an abrupt change that would throw the country into convulsions, torn by sectarianism in the dispute over who would hold power. A harmonious transition, by stages, will allow us to change over without difficulty from the present provisional regime to a permanent system that will prevent total hegemony and avoid absurd confrontations. And I say that, in the agreements contained in the reform under discussion, we are *increasing* parity in the executive, because according to the constitutional rules of the plebiscite, the executive is supposed to reflect the composition of the Congress, and, as indicated above, we would already have ended parity in the representative bodies. Nevertheless, the cabinet, the governors, the mayors, and all spheres of administration will continue to operate on the basis of parity until 1978. We support this extension in the conviction that it will promote national harmony.

For this reason, I believe that the representatives will agree that rather than carrying out a capricious "dismantling," we have amplified certain clauses in the plebiscite and that the part that will be terminated in the near future is what was agreed upon from the beginning.

8. COLOMBIA: A CASE HISTORY OF U.S. AID

SENATE FOREIGN RELATIONS COMMITTEE REPORT

The U.S. foreign assistance program in Colombia has achieved a basic political objective, but it has fallen far short of the economic and social goals of the Charter of Punta del Este.*

From the first program loan in April, 1962, a primary objective

* The Charter that established the Alliance for Progress, in August, 1961.
—ED.

has been political stability and maintenance of Colombia's democratic political institutions through support of the succession of National Front governments. This has been accomplished.

On the other hand, between 1961 and 1967, per capita gross national product increased only from $276 to $295 a year, an annual average rate of 1.2 per cent, compared to the Punta del Este goal of 2.5 per cent. The peso has depreciated from 8.50 to the dollar in 1961 to 16.45 to the dollar in August, 1968. The deficit in Colombia's balance of trade decreased from $142.6 million in 1961 to $64.5 million in 1967, but this improvement was more apparent than real, resulting from severe import controls imposed in early 1967 after a deficit of $290.2 million in 1966. An agrarian reform program, one of the earliest under the Alliance for Progress, was enacted in 1961, but through 1967 it had provided land titles to only 54,000 out of approximately 400,000 to 500,000 landless families, whose numbers, furthermore, are increasing by 10 per cent a year. Although the agrarian reform has received some U.S. assistance, the major emphasis of U.S. aid policy to agriculture has been directed to increasing production for export. These efforts have achieved some success, but until recently they concentrated on providing credits and other assistance for large commercial farmers at the expense of rural social progress. The education policies of both the Colombian Government and the United States have vacillated from an emphasis on primary education to an emphasis on universities, with the result that little progress has been made in either. The literacy rate has remained relatively constant, but the absolute numbers of functional illiterates have increased from approximately 5 million to more than 6 million. Taxes have been increased, but not until 1967 were serious efforts made to improve collection. Colombia has barely begun to tackle the problems of more equitable income distribution, and the country's social structure remains essentially unchanged, with close to two-thirds of the population not participating in the economic and political decision making process.

Thus, any evaluation of the aid program in Colombia must be subjective and will depend on the weight the evaluator assigns to the maintenance of political stability in a democratic framework. One of the factors which must be taken into account is the imponderable of what would have happened to Colombian politics if there had been no aid program or if different, or more rigorous, conditions had been attached to aid. At the time the various

Excerpts from *Colombia—A Case History of U.S. Aid*, prepared by the staff of the Senate Committee on Foreign Relations (Washington, D.C.: U.S. Government Printing Office, 1969), pp. 3–5.

program loans were signed and their successive tranches [install-ments] released, officials of both the Colombian and United States governments, as well as many independent observers, thought there was no acceptable alternative. In retrospect, this proposition seems less certain. Disbursement of program loans was chronically slow and was suspended more than once for periods of several months without bringing dire results. . . .

Further, it appears that although the aid program achieved some short-term successes with respect to economic stabilization and in influencing the Colombian Government's fiscal and monetary policies, the support which U.S. assistance provided at least con-tributed to making it possible for successive Colombian Govern-ments, especially that of President Valencia [1962–66], to post-pone making more basic reforms in such fields as public adminis-tration, taxation, local government, education, and agriculture.

One of the difficulties which the United States encountered in trying to help Colombia resulted from a combination of two factors. First, the United States discovered that its influence was severely limited with respect to moving Colombia towards eco-nomic and social reform, especially in terms of the application of U.S. methods to institutional change. The lack of Colombian absorptive capacity in this area proved to be greater than had been anticipated. This was a measure of the cultural gap. Second, despite these difficulties, and at the same time, the United States wanted to establish a visible economic presence in Latin America in the early years of the Alliance in order to prove the sincerity of its intentions. This led initially to an emphasis on impact project loans. But the lack of well-prepared projects led in turn to reliance on program loans to deal with macro-economic problems.

The aid program in Colombia has bought time for Colombian political institutions to work out the changes which almost every-body in a position of responsibility in either country agrees must come. But Colombians have used this time at their leisure. The question which this study raises but cannot answer is: Would they have moved more expeditiously if they had had less time, or would the pressures have been so great that the whole structure of the country would have collapsed into anarchy or dictatorship?

The record, studied with the benefit of hindsight, indicates the former.

IX. *Chile: Multiparty Politics and Democratic Reform*

In a continent characterized by frequent changes of government, Chile has a tradition of stability and constitutional democracy going back to the country's foundation in the early nineteenth century. Its present Constitution, adopted in 1925, retained elements of the 1833 Constitution, under which the country had been governed until that time, but considerably strengthened the powers of the president (*Selection 1*).

In 1964, Eduardo Frei, the candidate of the Christian Democratic Party, was elected president and promised a "revolution in liberty" that would transform the political, social, and economic life of Chile by democratic means. Frei promised an extensive agrarian reform and instituted a Promoción Popular program aimed at incorporating the inhabitants of the *callampas,* the squatter settlements around Chile's large cities, into the national political life through organization and education. (See *Selection 2* for an evaluation of the program.) Frei also sought to acquire a partial interest in the American-owned copper industry, Chile's chief source of export income, so as to ensure that it would be operated for the benefit of the nation (*Selection 3*). In 1967, under the Chileanization program, the government acquired 51 per cent control of the Kennecott Copper Company mines and 25 per cent of one Anaconda mine; in 1969, Anaconda agreed to the purchase of 51 per cent of its two major mines not included in the 1967 program, with provisions for gradual purchase of complete control during the 1970's.

Frei's agrarian reform law, which required a constitutional amendment, met strong opposition in the Chilean Senate, half of which had been elected in 1961, before the Christian Democratic sweep of 1964–65. Early in 1967, however, the Constitution was amended to permit payment for expropriated agricultural property in bonds and to emphasize the social obligations of property holders (Art. 10., Sec. 10). In July of the same year, the agrarian reform law was adopted. Probably the strongest agrarian reform ever effected by democratic procedures, it provided for a landholding limit of 80 hectares (about 200 acres) of prime land (in special cases, the limit could be raised to 320 hectares); compensation was to be in the form of bonds, only partially readjustable for inflation, and there was provision for a transition period of three to five years of government-assisted cooperative settlements before land was divided into family units (*Selection 4*). The law was criticized by Jorge Rogers, a former leader of the Christian Democratic Party and a prominent agricultural economist, who called it unworkable in some of its provisions, paternalistic in its attitude to the peasants, and more Marxist than Christian Democratic in its encouragement of collectivist forms of rural organization (*Selection 5*).

The Rogers attack blamed these features of the agrarian reform on the left wing of the Christian Democratic Party. The differences between the supporters of the Frei administration and the "rebel" faction, which felt the government was not moving quickly enough against the capitalist system, became increasingly pronounced and finally led to an open break in May, 1969. At that time, the rebel faction formed a new Movement of United Popular Action (MAPU), aimed at developing a common front with the Communist and Socialist parties in the 1970 presidential elections. The ideological differences between the two groups are evident in their conflicting interpretations of the new "communitarian" society that the Christian Democrats claim to be constructing. For MAPU leaders Julio Silva Solar and Jacques Chonchol, communitarianism means a socialist society in which all productive goods are owned in common by the workers (*Selection 6*). In the view of William Thayer, Frei's former Minister of Labor, communitarianism does not mean the abolition of capitalism but its restructuring, so as to give workers more participation and organized power. The abolition of private ownership of the means of production, Thayer believes, could lead to the replacement of private exploitation with exploitation by the state (*Selection 7*).

The Chilean effort has received considerable attention as an alternative to Cuban-style violent revolution. The United States has given the Frei administration substantial support within the Alliance for Progress—on a per capita basis, one of the largest programs in Latin America (*Selection 8*). Castro, for his part, has been especially critical of Frei, arguing that the Chilean capitalists will not voluntarily surrender power to the workers and peasants and that Frei's "bloodless revolution" is in fact a fraud (*Selection 9*). Castro has predicted that armed revolution will eventually be necessary in Chile, but he recognizes that because of its democratic system this is unlikely in the immediate future. The same ambivalence characterizes the Chilean Socialist

Party, which in theory is committed to revolution but in practice is deeply involved in the democratic constitutional system. (The Socialists' perennial candidate for the presidency, Salvador Allende, was president of the Chilean Senate from 1967 until 1969.) The Socialists are joined with the Communists in an electoral alliance, the Front of Popular Action (FRAP), but until 1970 they refused to cooperate with the centrist parties (see *Selection 10*). In January, 1970, they accepted Radical Party backing of their presidential candidate, Salvador Allende. The Chilean political system continues to express great ideological diversity, with five major parties and many splinter groups competing for electoral support.

The Frei government has run into economic difficulties, and continuing high taxes and inflation caused it to lose some of its middle-class support to the right-wing National Party in the 1969 congressional elections (see *Selection 11*). Yet the Frei administration was able to cite a solid record of accomplishments during its first four years in power (*Selection 12*). The reforms achieved so far, carried out with a scrupulous regard for constitutional procedures, compare favorably with those effected by Marxist and military regimes elsewhere and indicate that the democratic model retains considerable vitality in Latin America.

1. THE CONSTITUTION OF CHILE (1925)

(EXCERPTS)

CHAPTER I: THE STATE, GOVERNMENT, AND SOVEREIGNTY

Article 1. The State of Chile is unitary. Its government is republican and a representative democracy. . . .

Article 4. No magistrate, person, or assembly of persons, not even under the pretext of extraordinary circumstances, is empowered to assume any authority or rights other than those that have been expressly conferred upon them by the laws. Every act in contravention of this article is void.

CHAPTER II: NATIONALITY AND CITIZENSHIP

Article 7. Chileans who have attained twenty-one years of age, who are able to read and write, and who are inscribed in the electoral registers are citizens with the right of suffrage. . . .*

In popular elections voting shall always be by secret ballot. . . .

CHAPTER III: CONSTITUTIONAL GUARANTEES

Article 10. The Constitution guarantees to all the inhabitants of the republic:

1. Equality before the law. In Chile, there is no privileged class. In Chile, there are no slaves, and anyone who sets foot upon its territory becomes free. Chileans may not engage in the slave traffic. A foreigner who does so may not live in Chile or be naturalized therein.

2. Practice of all beliefs, liberty of conscience, and the free exercise of all religions not contrary to morality, good usage, and public order. Therefore, the respective religious bodies have the right to erect and maintain houses of worship and accessory property under the conditions of security and hygiene as fixed by the laws and regulations. . . . Churches and associated property intended for the service of religion shall be exempt from taxes.

3. Freedom to express, without prior censorship, opinions, orally or in writing, through the medium of the press or in any

---

* After the 1970 presidential elections, the literacy requirement will be abolished and the voting age lowered to eighteen.—ED.

Excerpts from the *Constitución política de la República de Chile* (Santiago, Chile, 1967); translated by the editor.

other form, without prejudice to liability for offenses and abuses that may be committed in the exercise of this liberty in the manner and in cases determined by law.

4. The right of assembly without prior license and without arms. In plazas, streets, and other places of public use, assemblies shall be governed by the general police regulations.

5. The right of association without prior license and in conformity with the law.

6. The right of presenting petitions to duly constituted authority upon any matter of public or private interest, without any limitation other than that of using respectful and suitable language.

7. Freedom of teaching. Public education is preferentially an affair of the State. Primary education is obligatory. . . .

10.* The right of property in its various aspects. The law shall regulate the method of acquiring, using, enjoying, and disposing of property as well as the limitations and obligations that will ensure its social function and accessibility to all. The social function of property is that which is required for the general interests of the state, public utility and health, better use of resources and productive energies in the service of the community, and the improvement of the conditions of community life of the inhabitants.

When the interest of the national community requires it, the law may reserve for the state exclusive control of natural resources, productive property, and other things which are declared of primary importance for the economic, social, or cultural life of the country. It will likewise encourage the convenient distribution of property and the establishment of family-sized property units.

No one may be deprived of his property except by virtue of a general or special law which authorizes its expropriation by reason of public utility or social interest as defined by the legislator. The owner shall always have the right to indemnification, the amount and conditions of payment of which shall be determined equitably, taking into consideration the interests of the community and of those whose property has been expropriated. The law shall regulate the indemnification, the court which will hear appeals on the amount (in any case the court shall decide in conformity with the law), the way in which that obligation will be fulfilled, and the opportunities and manner in which the expropriating agency will take material possession of what has been expropriated.

When rural agricultural land is involved, the indemnification shall be equivalent to the tax assessment plus the value of the improvements not included in that assessment. It shall be paid

* As amended in 1967.—Ed.

with one part in cash and the remainder in installments for a period which shall not exceed thirty years, in the form and under the conditions which the law shall determine.

The law may reserve as property of the nation for public use all waters in national territory and expropriate those which are privately owned for incorporation into said property. In this case the owners of the expropriated waters shall continue to use them as concession-holders with the right of use and shall have a right to indemnification only when, by reason of the total or partial cancellation of that right, they are effectively deprived of sufficient water to satisfy through rational usage the same needs they satisfied before that cancellation.

Small rural property that is worked by its owner and the dwelling that he inhabits may not be expropriated without prior payment of indemnification.

11. Exclusive property in every discovery or production, for such time as the law may concede. If the law requires its expropriation, the author or inventor shall be given suitable indemnification.

12. Inviolability of the home. The house of any person living in Chilean territory can be forcibly entered only for a special purpose determined by law and by virtue of an order from the competent authority.

13. Inviolability of epistolary and telegraphic correspondence. Public papers or effects shall not be opened, intercepted, or examined, except in cases expressly designated by law.

14. Protection of labor, industry, and the works of social security, especially with reference to sanitary dwellings and economic conditions of living, so as to give to each inhabitant a minimum of well-being adequate for the satisfaction of his personal needs and those of his family. The law shall regulate this operation. . . .

CHAPTER IV: THE NATIONAL CONGRESS

Article 24. The national Congress is composed of two branches: the Chamber of Deputies and the Senate.

Article 25. In elections of deputies and senators a method shall be used that, in practice, will result in giving an effective proportionality in representation to opinions and to political parties. . . .

The Chamber of Deputies

Article 37. The Chamber of Deputies is composed of members elected by the departments, or by groups of adjoining departments within each province, as the law may provide, by direct vote and in the manner determined by the electoral law.

One deputy shall be elected for each 30,000 inhabitants and for a fraction of not fewer than 15,000.

Article 38. The entire Chamber of Deputies shall be renewed every four years. . . .

The Senate

Article 40. The Senate is composed of members elected by direct ballot for the ten provincial groups,* as fixed by law, with regard to the characteristics and interests of the several regions of the territory of the Republic. Each group is entitled to elect five senators.

Article 41. A part of the Senate shall be elected every four years in the manner determined by law. Each senator shall remain eight years in office. . . .

Powers of Congress

Article 43. Exclusive powers of Congress are:

1. To approve or disapprove the annual statement of disbursement of funds intended for the expenses of the public administration, which the government must present.

2. To give its consent for the President of the Republic to leave the national territory.

3. To declare, when the President of the Republic tenders his resignation from office, whether or not the causes upon which he bases it do in fact disable him from holding the office, and in consequence whether to accept or to refuse the resignation.

4. To declare, when there may be occasion for doubt, whether the disability that debars the President from the exercise of his functions is of such a nature that a new election should be held.

5. To approve or disapprove treaties that, before their ratification, the President of the Republic presents to it.

All of the above resolutions shall be subject in Congress to the same procedure as a law. . . .

Article 44. Only by virtue of a law is it possible: . . .

4. To approve each year the estimate of receipts and in the same law to fix the expenditures of the public administration. . . . The Congress may not vote any new expenditure without creating or indicating at the same time the sources of the funds to pay for said expenditure. . . .

Enactment of the Laws

Article 45. Laws may be originated in the Chamber of Deputies

* As amended in 1968.—Ed.

or in the Senate, in a message sent by the President of the Republic, or on motion of any of their members. Such motions may not be signed by more than ten deputies nor by more than five senators. . . .

Supplementary financial measures or the general budgetary law may only be introduced by the President of the Republic.

The President shall also have exclusive power to initiate legislation involving the political or administrative division of the country, the creation of new public services or temporary positions, and the granting or increase of salaries and gratuities of the personnel of the civil service and the nationalized and semi-independent corporations. The national Congress may only accept, reduce, or reject the services, positions, emoluments, or increases which are proposed. This clause shall not apply to the national Congress itself or to the services that are dependent on it. . . .

Laws respecting taxation of any nature whatever, on the budgets of the public administration and on recruiting, may originate only in the Chamber of Deputies.

Laws respecting amnesty and general pardons may originate only in the Senate.

Article 46. The President of the Republic may declare urgency of dispatch for a bill, and in such a case the respective chamber must pass upon the matter within thirty days.

The declaration of urgency may be repeated in all constitutional steps of procedure on the bill.

Article 47. A bill rejected in the chamber of origin may not be reintroduced except after one year.

Article 48. A bill approved in the chamber of origin shall pass immediately to the other chamber for discussion.

Article 49. A bill rejected in its totality by the revisory chamber shall return to that of its origin where it shall be considered again, and if it is approved therein by two-thirds of the members present, it shall pass for a second time to the chamber that rejected it. It shall be understood that the latter disapproves it if two-thirds of the members present so agree.

Article 50. A bill that is added to or amended by the revisory chamber shall return to that of its origin, and in the latter it shall be understood that, with the vote of the majority of the members present, the additions or amendments are approved.

But if the additions or amendments are disapproved, the bill shall return a second time to the revisory chamber, where, if the additions or amendments are again approved by a majority of two-thirds of the members present, the bill shall return to the other chamber. It shall be understood that the latter disapproves the additions or amendments if two-thirds of the members present so agree.

Article 51. When, because of the insistence of either chamber, agreement between the two chambers on fundamental points of the bill is not reached, or when one substantially changes the bill of the other, mixed committees of an equal number of deputies and senators shall be designated in order to suggest a form and method of resolving the difficulties.

Article 52. A bill approved by both chambers shall be submitted to the President of the Republic, who, if he also approves, shall cause it to be promulgated as law.

Article 53. If the President of the Republic disapproves the bill, he shall return it to the chamber of origin with suitable suggestions within thirty days.

Article 54. If the two chambers approve the suggestions, the bill shall have the force of law and be returned to the President to be promulgated.

If the two chambers reject all or any of the suggestions and insist, by two-thirds of the members present, on all or part of the bill as approved by them, it shall be returned to the President to be promulgated.

Article 55. If the President of the Republic should not return the bill within thirty days counting from the date of its submission, it shall be understood that he approves it and shall promulgate it as law. If Congress should close its sessions before the expiration of the thirty-day period for returning the bill, the President shall return it within the first ten days of the following ordinary or extraordinary legislative session. . . .

CHAPTER V: THE PRESIDENT OF THE REPUBLIC

Article 60. A citizen with the title of President of the Republic of Chile administers the State and is the supreme head of the nation.

Article 61. In order to be chosen President of the Republic it is necessary to have been born in the territory of Chile, to be at least thirty years of age, and to possess the necessary qualifications for being a member of the Chamber of Deputies.

Article 62. The President of the Republic shall remain in the exercise of his office for the term of six years, and cannot be re-elected for the ensuing term.

Article 63. The President shall be elected by a direct vote of the citizens of all the Republic having the right of suffrage, sixty days before the day on which the term of the incumbent should expire, and in the manner determined by law. . . .

Article 64. The two branches of Congress, convened in public session, fifty days subsequent to the voting, a majority of the total membership being present and under the direction of the President of the Senate, shall take into consideration the general scrutiny made by the [Electoral] Qualification Court and shall proceed to proclaim as President of the Republic the citizen who has obtained more than one-half of the votes validly cast.

If the scrutiny does not show this majority, the joint session of Congress shall elect one of the two citizens who have received the highest number of votes; but if two or more citizens have received a tie in the voting, the election shall be carried out between them. . . .

Article 67. The President may not leave the territory of the republic during the time of his incumbency without the consent of Congress.

Article 68. The President shall vacate office on the same day that completes the six years for which the exercise of his powers lasts, and the newly elected President shall succeed him. . . .

CHAPTER VI: THE ELECTORAL QUALIFICATION COURT

Article 79. A special court, to be called the Qualification Court, shall have cognizance of the election returns for President of the Republic, deputies, and senators. . . .

CHAPTER X: AMENDMENT OF THE CONSTITUTION

Article 108. The amendment of constitutional provisions shall be submitted to the same procedure as a bill, saving the exceptions hereinafter indicated.

The proposed amendment must be approved in each chamber by a majority of the deputies or senators then in office.

The two chambers, in public joint session, with the attendance of a majority of their total membership, sixty days after the approval of a proposed amendment indicated in the preceding paragraph, shall take the proposal into consideration and proceed to vote thereon without further debate.

The proposal as approved in joint session shall pass to the President of the Republic.

If on the day appointed a majority of the total membership does not meet together, the session shall be held on the following day with such deputies and senators as may attend.

Article 109. The proposal may be examined by the President of the Republic only for the purpose of suggesting modifications or corrections in the amendments agreed on by the joint session.

If the modifications that the President of the Republic may suggest are approved by both chambers, the proposal will be returned to the President for promulgation.

If the two chambers reject all or any of the suggestions of the President of the Republic and insist, by two-thirds of the membership present, on all or part of the proposal approved by them, it shall be returned to the President for promulgation or, if he deems it advisable, in order that he may consult the nation within a period of thirty days by means of a plebiscite on the points in disagreement. A proposal approved by plebiscite shall be promulgated as a constitutional amendment. . . .

2. THE POLITICAL INTEGRATION OF LOWER-CLASS URBAN SETTLEMENTS IN CHILE AND PERU

DANIEL GOLDRICH, RAYMOND B. PRATT, AND C. R. SCHULLER

1. Squatter invasions are the consequence of urbanization and population growth without public or private provision for dwellings for the massive metropolitan lower classes. Reinforcing the effect of immigration and population factors are such "normal" urbanization phenomena as clearance of traditional lower-class dwellings in order to build streets, high-rise commercial establishments, and luxury apartments, and the continuous process of dilapidation of the remaining traditional lower-class quarters. As crowding and rent-squeezing of the poor increase, the only outlet for hundreds of thousands is seizure of unused lands or rental of tiny, makeshift quarters in clandestine settlements run as commercial enterprises.

The prevailing image of these settlements (and also of government housing projects) among middle- and upper-class people and local and foreign social scientists is that of the slum. It is an image of apathy, misery, filth, crime, delinquency, prostitution, and family disintegration. It is also commonplace to view these areas as breeding-grounds for political instability and extremism. Their inhabitants are considered the lowest social stratum, mainly recruited from the torrent of emigrants from rural and provincial

Reprinted from *Studies in Comparative International Development*, III, No. 1 (1967–68), pp. 4–5, 9–11, 16–18; by permission.

areas.[1] The settlements are treated as virtually invariant, and are indiscriminately labeled as *barriadas, favelas, callampas,* etc., which are the local equivalents of slums.

Actually, squatter settlements represent a wide range of conditions. The pioneering work of such people as John Turner,[2] principally in Lima, and Guillermo Rosenblüth [3] in Santiago introduces some typologies of settlement which differentiate vastly variant syndromes of human conditions. For example, Turner has distinguished two types of squatter settlements, the bridgehead and the consolidation. The bridgehead houses, the poorest of the city's lower class, are located near the urban center sources of employment. Here, crowding is extremely high and conditions generally very poor. These areas are declining in living standards and can be considered real slums. The consolidation, on the other hand, represents an attempt by the more organized and effective (but not, generally, the wealthier) segments of the lower class to attain economic and psychological independence. They seek better dwelling conditions—meaning primarily proprietorship and space, within their economic limits—and these motivations find outlet only in the organized invasion of peripheral, unoccupied land. These settlements thus represent considerable investment and continuously improving living standards. The residents consider them to be permanent, incipient communities, or "towns in formation." (Another type discussed by Turner is the mixed settlement, comprising combinations of the above sets of characteristics, but these will not be considered here.) Three of the four research communities are of the latter, permanent type. The fourth is also permanent, but is one of the new Chilean government settlements. Despite its obvious differences from the others in its relations with government—the receipt of dwellings and substantial urban services from the government, and not just post-

---

[1] See, for example, José Matos Mar, "The *Barriadas* of Lima: An Example of Integration into Urban Life," in P. Hauser (ed.), *Urbanization in Latin America* (New York: International Documents Service, 1961), p. 171; James L. Payne, *Labor and Politics in Peru* (New Haven, Conn.: Yale University Press, 1965), p. 15; and Tad Szulc, *The Winds of Revolution* (New York: Praeger Publishers, 1965), pp. 49–54.

[2] John Turner's work is so far available in "Three Lectures on Housing in Peru," presented at the Athens Center of Ekistics, November 1964 (mimeo); and in the special number edited by Turner, "Dwelling Resources in South America," *Architectural Design* (London), VIII (August, 1963), *passim.*

[3] Rosenblüth's work is available in *Problemas socioeconómicos de la marginalidad y la integración urbana; el caso de "las poblaciones callampas" en el Gran Santiago* (Santiago: Universidad de Chile, Escuela de Economía, 1963).

hoc title to seized lands—as a public housing project composed partly of invaders, it shares the depreciated status of the other settlements and the condition of being a community in formation. Politically these areas are a virtually unknown quantity.

These towns in formation represent some important experiences and characteristics with respect to the whole complex of development. While it is useful to keep in mind the questionable romanticism of "community development" mythology, this should not preclude recognition of what these towns in formation demonstrate. If the preindustrial mode of lower-class orientation is resignation before an immutable world, the invaders represent a significant departure, having successfully manipulated an important part of their environment. They have shown initiative and future orientation (the capacity to waive immediate gratification in pursuit of long-range goals). Many have persevered in the face of a hostile state, including armed attack on the provisional encampments. One of the more elusive capacities in the underdeveloped world is the capacity for organization, but many of these communities were carefully planned, and their successful establishment reflects a rather high level of organization regarding land allotment, provision for basic services, representation before the public and the state, etc. The capacity for organization seems not to derive from any mystical ancestral communalism,[4] but to be a creative response on the part of a highly selected, self-recruited set of people to an environment otherwise foreclosing opportunity. Theirs has been a major achievement, for independence in dwelling and land is the major way to economic and psychic security for the lower class,[5] when industrialization lags far behind urbanization and population growth, and ways out of national poverty remain unknown even to highly educated planners and intellectuals. In the face of their reputation for social disorganization, these settlers reveal remarkably little of it; crime, promiscuity, broken homes occur infrequently, particularly in comparison with the bridgehead settlements and traditional city

[4] Matos Mar cites traditional communalism as operative in the *barriadas, op. cit.*, p. 176. Richard N. Adams presents a contrasting analysis in "The Community in Latin America: A Changing Myth," *The Centennial Review,* VI (Summer, 1962), 409–34, as does Richard W. Patch, "How Communal Are the Communities?," American Universities Field Staff Report (Lima, June, 1959).

[5] See Turner, *op. cit.*, and Richard Morse, "Recent Research on Latin American Urbanization," *Latin American Research Review,* I (Fall, 1965), 35–74. In a study of Lima industrial workers, it was found that ownership of a house was *the* major objective. See Guillermo Briones and Jose Mejia Valera, *El obrero industrial* (Lima: Universidad de San Marcos, Instituto de Investigaciones Sociológicas, 1964), p. 71.

slums. Though born as illegal invasions, these communities display a prevailing orientation toward law and order.[6] . . .

2. Promoción Popular and Cooperación Popular.* Perhaps the major organization to perform national integrative functions in societies seeking to shake off poverty is the mass political party. Such organizations have occurred infrequently in Latin America, and there are very few cases of parties that have focussed directly in program or ideology on problems of urbanization and the condition of the settler. (Though little has been done about agrarian reform, it is much more common for "reform" parties to symbolize the *peasant* as the forgotten.) Our data show that, despite the very substantial differences between the Chilean and Peruvian party systems, political parties are evaluated as less personally helpful than the president, government officials, the municipality, and the local association in every case among the four settlements. Thus, in neither country does it appear that mass parties have yet developed with reference to the new urban settlements. . . .

3. Costs of political demand-making: sanctions and depoliticalization. Perhaps the most surprising aspect of recent Latin American politics to academic observers is, given its poverty and general deprivation, the relatively continuous apoliticalization or low politicalization of the urban lower class. Elsewhere we have tried to account for this phenomenon, citing the complex structure of the subculture of poverty, the restricted conception of time and space, the perceived immutability of the environment, the nature of lower-class occupations, the nonpolitical supports available, the effects of extreme deprivation, and vulnerability to sanctions.[7]

One might expect a higher level of politicalization among the permanent squatter settlements and housing projects because (1) the residents have had to anticipate dealing with the government before entry; (2) the invasion preparations involve sophisticated planning with regard to mobilizing political support and

---

[6] See Charles Abrams, *Man's Struggle for Shelter in an Urbanizing World* (Cambridge, Mass.: M.I.T. Press, 1964), chap. ii, "Squatting and Squatters," p. 23. Abrams fears that squatting will promote disrespect for law and government. This does not appear to be a major problem in the Lima or Santiago cases, however.

* The titles of the official programs of aid to lower-class settlements in Chile and Peru, respectively.—ED.

[7] D. Goldrich, "Toward the Comparative Study of Politicization in Latin America," in Dwight B. Heath and Richard N. Adams (eds.), *Contemporary Cultures and Societies of Latin America* (New York: Random House, 1965), pp. 361–78; and *Sons of the Establishment: Elite Youth in Panama and Costa Rica* (Chicago: Rand McNally, 1966), chap. i.

immobilizing agencies of governmental repression; (3) invasion itself is an illegal—and therefore governmentally relevant—act; and
(4) the residents have thus been faced with the problem of
acquiring urban services.[8]

An opposing factor, however, is the lower class' particularly high
vulnerability to sanctions in preindustrial and transitional contexts. Actual repression or the threat of it may under such conditions be sufficient to discourage any behavior that might an-
tagonize the establishment. The tangible gain through land
seizure, in the face of the desperate need to find permanent,
independent, economical housing, may represent the extreme
case where potentially costly political action is resorted to by
lower-class people. If this were so, the level of politicalization
might be low, even in the permanent settlements, and the political
orientations and behavior associated with the invasion planning
and occurrence (or even the application to the Housing Agency)
might have been exceptional.

How might such people be considered highly vulnerable to
sanctions? First, their level of occupational skill is low, the labor
market is glutted (unemployment and underemployment are
severe in Latin America), and they have little countervailing
power because of restrictions on or underdevelopment of unions.
Second, the distance between social classes, particularly between
middle and lower classes, is so great that general social support
for lower-class people in trouble with the government tends to be
low. Awareness of this may also serve to deter political risk-
taking on the part of those at the bottom. Third, the bureaucracy
tends to be staffed with middle-class people, frequently uncon-
cerned with service to the public, and skilled in the dispensation
of subtle humiliations to "inferiors" seeking administrative adjustments. One such form of discouragement is to relegate them
to endless waiting. Finally, a different kind of sanction is police
harassment of "troublemakers" from the lower class. Although
such activity is not directed only at lower-class representatives,
they are probably the most deprived in this respect in all societies. . . .

4. The actual patterns of legitimacy orientation are quite distinct. . . . The greatest differences are between the Chilean respondents and the residents of the two Lima *barriadas*. The
Santiago set respond much more positively than their Lima
counterparts to the system as a whole. They evaluate the President, the municipality, government officials, and a political party

[8] See Turner, *op. cit.*, and William Mangin, "Mental Health and Migra-
tion to Cities: A Peruvian Case," in Heath and Adams (eds.), *op. cit.*, also
his article in *Architectural Design*.

as being much more helpful than do the Peruvians. Many more of them report affiliation with a major political party (indicating at least provisional acceptance of the parliamentary system). Many more of them than the Lima residents evaluate the government's method of selecting people for public housing as fair. A much higher proportion of them endorse the proposition that people must make sacrifices to help the country develop (potentially a highly significant indicator of the elite's capacity for mobilizing the citizens to implement development policy). Finally, the Peruvians are considerably more disposed to condone violence as a means of settling political questions and to accept social disorder as a consequence of desired social change, which seem probable indicators of dissatisfaction with present political arrangements. Clearly, the Santiago respondents give much more support to and feel they derive much more support from the political system than do the Lima respondents.

3. THE CHILEANIZATION OF COPPER LAW (1967)

(EXCERPTS)

Article 13. When the President of the Republic grants a foreign company or group of foreign companies, in the categories of large or intermediate-scale copper mining, one or more of the benefits, tax exemptions, or rights permitted in Decree Law No. 258 of 1960 and in the dispositions that modify and enlarge it, the President shall, in the respective investment decree, require the company or group of companies to invest a part of their net profits in Chile.

Article 14. The [National] Copper Corporation is hereby legally recognized with headquarters in the city of Santiago under the supervision of the Central Bank of Chile. Its finances shall be controlled by the Superintendency of Banks, and it shall have the same powers as the other entities subject to control by the Superintendency. It shall have at its disposition the resources allotted it by this law and all goods of any type that it acquires in the development of, or as a consequence of, the carrying out of its duties.

Translated by the editor from *Código de Minería* (Santiago, 1967).

Relations between the Copper Corporation and the government shall be handled by the Minister of Mines . . . .

Article 15. The functions [of the Copper Corporation] shall be the following:

1. To participate in international trading in copper and its by-products, in the regulation of copper prices, in the maintenance or expansion of copper markets, and in the improvement of copper distribution and the prevention or counteraction of any act that would tend to control or restrict it.

2. To encourage the maximum possible purchase of goods and services within Chile by the copper-producing companies.

In purchasing, including that for expansion or new installations, preference shall be given to Chilean products.

3. To regulate the purchases of goods and services that the copper-producing companies make abroad, to the end that these be limited to indispensable items and that they be made under conditions as favorable as possible; the Copper Corporation may cooperate for these purposes with whatever national or foreign persons or groups it finds most suitable. . . .

8. To promote the production of copper and its by-products. The Corporation, for these duties, may, with prior authorization of the President of the Republic, form, participate in, or organize mining companies, in particular those of a mixed [public and private investment] character. . . .

Article 18. If, due to the condition of the international market, the copper companies feel obligated to reduce their production, the reduction of these companies' activities in Chile may not be proportionally greater than the reduction made by these companies, their branches, and associated companies in their operations outside Chile. . . .

Article 21. . . . There shall be an Executive Commitee composed of the Minister of Mines, or his Subsecretary in the Minister's absence, the Executive Vice-President of the Copper Corporation, two directors representing the President of the Republic, and one director representing the Central Bank. . . .

This Executive Committee shall have exclusive power: . . .

4. To apply administrative sanctions to the companies, after a hearing, without prejudice to appropriate penal action, for failure to observe this law or the agreements, resolutions, or regulations approved by the Board of Directors and the decisions of the Executive Committee, especially in the following cases:

a. Violations of authorized export and import operations or general contract conditions approved by the Copper Corporation. . . .

d. Obstruction or denial of free access to their offices and operations by authorized employees of the Corporation charged with reviewing materials related to the execution of the functions and faculties of the Corporation, and

e. Unjustifiable delay in the fulfillment of the obligation to transfer, within the time limits fixed by the Corporation, the quotas of copper and its by-products reserved by the Corporation for the Chilean manufacturing industry, either for internal consumption or for export, and the quotas that are due to authorized entities.

The sanction will consist of a fine of up to an amount equal to fifty basic annual salaries in the department of Santiago. . . .

These sanctions shall be applicable to companies that operate in Chile, even if they result from acts of the companies' representatives or agents abroad. . . .

Article 55. Mixed mining companies shall be understood to mean incorporated companies in which the [National] Copper Corporation, the [National] Corporation for the Promotion of Production [CORFO], the National Mining Company, or the National Electric Company acquires, or on the date of the registration of the company has an agreement to acquire, at least 25 per cent of the company's public capital. The principal purpose of these companies shall be one or more of the following: exploration, extraction, exploitation, production, mine development, or trading of minerals, concentrates, precipitates, and bars of copper or of nonferrous metals and the products and by-products obtained from them. . . .

4. THE AGRARIAN REFORM LAW OF 1967

(EXCERPTS)

PRELIMINARY TITLE

Article 1. The following definitions are established for the effect of the present law. . . .

h. *Family agricultural unit:* The area of land, given the quality of the soil, location, topography, climate, exploitation possibilities, and other characteristics, in particular soil-use ca-

---

Excerpts from Law No. 16,640, published in *Diario Oficial* (Santiago), July 28, 1967; translated by the editor.

pacity, that, when personally exploited by the producer, permits a family group to live and to prosper through its rational use. . . .

r. *Communitarian property:* that which belongs in common to all those who work it personally, or to a cooperative formed by them which constitutes a human and economic community. Each member contributes with his personal effort to the common work and participates in the income obtained, according to the nature and contribution of the work he performs. . . .

TITLE I: LAND AFFECTED BY THE AGRARIAN REFORM

Chapter I: Rural Property Subject to Expropriation

Article 2. In order that agricultural property may fulfill its social function, rural properties are hereby declared to be of public utility, and the total or partial expropriation of those found in any of the situations specified in Articles 3 and 4–13, inclusive, of the present law is hereby authorized.

Article 3. Individually owned rural properties, whatever their location in the national territory or the type of land, are subject to expropriation when, singly or together, they encompass an area that exceeds 80 basic irrigated hectares, calculated according to the conversion table established in Article 172. . . .

Article 4. Rural properties that are found to be abandoned and those that are poorly exploited are subject to expropriation.

However, as regards rural properties that, prior to November 4, 1964, had an area that did not exceed 80 basic irrigated hectares, expropriation due to poor exploitation shall take place only after three years from the date of publication of the present law. . . .

Article 6. Except for exceptions expressly established in the present law, rural properties whose proprietors or co-proprietors are corporations in public or private law are subject to expropriation. Exempt, however, are all those that belong to peasant and agrarian-reform cooperatives that fulfill the requirements established in the regulations. . . .

Article 10. Rural properties whose acquisition is necessary to carry out the agrarian reform program, and which have been offered for transfer by their owner to the [Agrarian Reform] Corporation, are subject to expropriation.

Article 11. Rural properties that constitute *minifundios* are subject to expropriation for the sole purpose of regrouping them and assigning them in any one of the manners indicated in Article 67. The ex-proprietors who demonstrate the greatest capacity for agricultural work shall have priority as assignees. . . .

Article 13. Rural properties located inside an area in which the state is carrying out or will carry out works of irrigation or improvement of the same, and which are declared irrigation areas, are subject to expropriation. . . .

Chapter II: Rights of Reserve and Acquisition of Land in Relation to Expropriation

Article 16. Any exclusive owner of a rural property expropriated for the reasons stipulated in Article 3 shall be entitled to keep under his domain an area of not more than 80 basic irrigated hectares. In computing basic irrigated hectares, any other land owned by the said owner shall be included. If the owner has more than five children, who work with him or whom he maintains, the maximum area mentioned above shall be increased by ten basic irrigated hectares for each child over that number, but with the limitation that the total of the reserved land may not exceed one hundred basic irrigated hectares. Owners shall be entitled to exercise the right of reserve only over land that is not rented or given out in any manner for operation by third parties. Owners of abandoned or poorly exploited rural property shall not have the right to reserve land. . . .

Chapter III: Exceptions to Expropriability

Article 20. An owner expropriated of one or more holdings, under the provisions of Article 3 or Article 6, shall be entitled to request expropriation exemption for the rural properties regarding which he is complying with the requisites of Article 21. In the event that the owner is an individual, he must be working the land directly; in the event that the owner is a corporation, it shall be entitled to this right only if its primary activities are in agriculture or cattle-raising, and as long as the property in question is not rented or in any way operated by a third party or by sharecroppers.

The area of land that shall enjoy expropriation exemption as stipulated in this article shall not be more than 320 basic irrigated hectares . . . .

Article 21. In order that an owner may have recourse to the exemption system established in the preceding article, he must fulfill all the requirements indicated below on all rural properties for which he is seeking an exemption:

1. At least 95 per cent of the usable irrigated area of rural property in question must be devoted to annual or permanent crops or artificial pastures. With regard to dry land, at least 80 per cent of the usable land must be devoted to annual or permanent crops or to improved natural or artificial pastures.

2. The rural property in question must be operating at a higher level of productivity than that prevailing on lands of similar possibilities in the region. . . .

3. Soils and other renewable natural resources must be maintained in good condition. . . .

4. Workers employed on the rural property must have a partnership share according to the provisions of Article 189.*

5. As provided in the preceding section, employees and workers must be paid salaries, remunerations, and partnership shares for an annual total of not less than twice the minimum peasant wage and the basic wage of scale B of the corresponding department with regard to working days and months worked. To fulfill these provisions, fringe benefits shall be computed only for an amount of not more than 25 per cent of the total amount of salaries and remunerations paid. Salaries and partnership shares paid to workers must be calculated separately from salaries and partnership shares paid to employees. . . .

6. All legal provisions regarding peasant housing, education, and sanitation must be complied with, and the owner must not have received a judicial sentence nor have been sanctioned by administrative regulations for a serious violation of social or labor legislation during the two years prior to the expropriation decree. Infractions committed in the following matters shall be considered serious: (a) rights of union organization, including procedures regarding legal rights of organized labor; (b) benefits in money or kind to which the workers are entitled; (c) procedures for termination of labor contracts; (d) procedures for freedom in collective bargaining; (e) procedures for prevention of accidents, hygiene, and, labor security; and (f) procedures for social security and family allowances.

The burden of proof in the requirements to which this article refers shall fall on the owner. . . .

Title II: The Expropriation Agreement, Its Effects and Indemnification

Chapter IV: Indemnification

Article 42. Indemnification of the owner of the expropriated property shall be equivalent to the appraised value in force for the land tax, plus the value of improvements not included in the above-mentioned appraisal. Such improvements shall be appraised by the Agrarian Reform Corporation, based on the value they have at the time of the expropriation decree.

---

* Article 189 authorizes the president to fix a percentage of the profits to be shared with the workers.—Ed.

Appeals may be filed with the Provincial Agrarian Court against the appraisals made by the Agrarian Reform Corporation, in conformity with the preceding clause, within a period of thirty days from the date of notification of the decision of the Board of the Corporation approving the appraisal.

Article 43. Expropriation indemnification shall be paid partly in cash, with the balance in agrarian reform bonds, as established by this law and according to procedures laid down in the following articles. Such bonds shall be accepted at their face value.

The value of necessary and useful improvements added to the property after November 4, 1964, shall be paid for in cash. . . .

Article 45. With regard to expropriations performed in conformity with the provisions of Articles 3, 6, 10, and 12, the indemnification shall be paid 10 per cent in cash, with the balance in agrarian reform bonds, type A. However, if the expropriated property was abandoned, only 1 per cent shall be paid in cash, and, if it was poorly exploited, only 5 per cent, and the balance in both cases shall be paid with agrarian reform bonds, type C. . . .

Article 47. With regard to expropriations carried out in conformity with Article 13, and without affecting the provisions of the following Articles, indemnification shall be paid 10 per cent in cash, with the balance in agrarian reform bonds, type A.

However, if the property was abandoned, only 1 per cent shall be paid in cash, and, if it was poorly exploited, 5 per cent, and the balance shall be paid in agrarian reform bonds, type C. . . .

Article 50. With regard to expropriations carried out in conformity with Article 11, the owner shall have the right to receive the corresponding indemnification in cash, as long as he, or his spouse, or one of his direct descendants has been personally working the rural property expropriated since a date prior to that of the expropriation decree. A joint owner shall have a similar right when he or his spouse or one of his direct descendants has personally worked all or a portion of the property.

If the owner does not come within the scope of any of the cases mentioned in the preceding clause, the indemnification shall be paid 10 per cent in cash, with the balance in five equal annual installments. Seventy per cent of each annual installment shall be readjusted on the date of payment according to the variation in the consumer price index as determined by the Bureau of Statistics and Census, between the calendar month prior to the expropriation decree and the month prior to the due date of each installment. Each installment shall receive interest of 3 per cent per year, which shall be calculated on the amount of the installment plus 50 per cent of the readjustment. . . .

Title IV: Destination and Distribution of the Land

Chapter I: General Provisions

Article 66. When a rural property has been expropriated and the Agrarian Reform Corporation has taken possession of same, the Corporation shall proceed to establish a peasant settlement [*asentamiento*].

An *asentamiento* is the initial transitory stage in the social and economic organization of the peasantry, in which land expropriated by the Agrarian Reform Corporation is operated in the intermediate period between the physical taking possession of the land and the time that the land is allotted to the peasants according to Article 67 of this law.

Its primary basic objectives are those indicated below:

1. The efficient exploitation of the land in the *asentamiento*, improving production through assistance lent or contributed by the Agrarian Reform Corporation;

2. The training and qualification of the members of the *asentamiento* so that they may be able, when the *asentamiento* period terminates, to assume the responsibilities of owners and agricultural entrepreneurs;

3. The orientation and promotion of community development, encouraging the preparation, establishment, and strengthening of cooperatives and basic organizations;

4. The promotion of capital investment by members of the *asentamiento*, so that increases in income may be used primarily for this purpose;

5. The building of a minimum infrastructure necessary for the development of the family and community life of the members of the *asentamiento* and of future assignees, as well as the necessary infrastructure for the normal present and future exploitation of the land.

The President of the Republic shall determine the standards according to which agrarian reform agricultural associations, constituted by the Corporation and the peasants, shall be regulated during the period of the *asentamiento*, for the operation of the property acquired by the Corporation.

Article 67. The land acquired by the Agrarian Reform Corporation shall be divided into family agricultural units according to Section *h* of Article 1, and shall be assigned to the peasants in individual ownership.

However, when the Board of the Agrarian Reform Corporation considers that this type of assignment is not possible for technical reasons, due to the nature of the agricultural activity, as may be the case with land exclusively suited to forestry, grazing, fruit orchards, vineyards, or other types of land that, due to their natural condition, are not suitable for division without a deterioration of the soil or of its economic management possibilities, such land may be assigned in exclusive ownership to peasant cooperatives or to agrarian reform cooperatives, or in joint ownership to peasants, peasant cooperatives, or agrarian reform cooperatives. . . . The Board may also assign land in any of the ways indicated in this clause when the peasants selected as assignees so request by mutual agreement.

The assignments mentioned in the preceding clauses must be made within a period of three years from the date on which the Corporation took physical possession of the land. However, in special cases, the President of the Republic, through an executive order, may extend this period for up to two more years. . . .

Chapter II: Assignment of Land to Peasants

Article 71. The essential requirements that beneficiaries of land must fulfill are those indicated below: (a) to be a Chilean citizen; foreigners, however, may be beneficiaries if the Board of the Agrarian Reform Corporation so determines by a vote of at least two-thirds of the members present, including the vote of the Minister of Agriculture; (b) to be a peasant; (c) to be more than eighteen years of age; (d) to have an aptitude for agricultural activities; (e) not to own land, or to own land of an area smaller than that of a family agricultural unit; and (f) to be married or to support a family as head of the family. However, those who do not meet such qualifications may be beneficiaries if the Board of the Agrarian Reform Corporation so determines by a vote of at least two-thirds of the members present.

Article 72. For the selection of assignees, the following shall be reasons for priority: (a) to have worked permanently on the rural property to be assigned for at least three of the last four years prior to the date of the expropriation decree, or the date on which the property was acquired by the Agrarian Reform Corporation; (b) to have been an occupant, without violence or concealment, of the land to be assigned on the date of the expropriation decree and to have worked it personally for at least five consecutive years. . . .

Article 75. A beneficiary shall be subject, in any case, to the obligations indicated here below: (a) to pay the price of the assigned property; (b) to work personally the land that has been assigned; (c) to have his residence at a locality compatible with the personal operation of the land assigned; and (d) to belong to an agrarian reform cooperative, when the [Agrarian Reform] Corporation at the moment of carrying out the assignment has established an obligation to belong to it, for the period that it determines.

Article 76. In the ownership title deed, the following prohibitions, among others, shall be included. It is prohibited: (a) to sell land assigned in exclusive ownership or rights over land assigned in joint ownership, except when the Agrarian Reform Corporation gives the corresponding authorization to peasants who fulfill the requirements mentioned in Article 71, as approved by the corresponding cooperative; (b) to divide the assigned land; the Agrarian Reform Corporation may authorize such division only in the cases indicated in Article 80; (c) to rent the land or give it in any way for exploitation to third parties or to sharecroppers, without the official sanction of the Agrarian Reform Corporation and the respective cooperative; (d) to encumber the land in any way without previous official permission by the Board of the Agrarian Reform Corporation; (e) to operate the land in any way that may damage its fertility and the conservation of soils, to abandon the land, or to allow it to be covered with brush or exposed to diseases that may hinder its good exploitation or damage neighboring land; and (f) to engage in the commerce or sale of alcoholic beverages. . . .

Chapter IV: Payment for Lands Assigned or Transferred by the Agrarian Reform Corporation

Article 88. The price of land and payment terms shall be determined in the deed of assignment.

Payment shall be made partly in cash, with the balance in equal annual installments for a period that may not exceed thirty years.

Article 89. Each installment of the balance shall be subject to an interest payment of 3 per cent per year from the date on which the assignment deed is registered, which shall be paid together with the respective installments. However, the first three installments shall not be subject to interest payments. In the case of delay in payment, the interest shall be 6 per cent per year.

Seventy per cent of the value of each installment shall be readjusted in proportion to the variation of the consumer price index, as determined by the Bureau of Statistics and Census, between the calendar month prior to that in which the assignment was made and the calendar month prior to that in which the payment is made. Interest shall be calculated on the amount of the installment plus 50 per cent of the readjustment. . . .

TITLE VI: AGRARIAN REFORM BONDS

Article 131. The President of the Republic is hereby authorized
to issue state bonds, to be known as agrarian reform bonds, for up
to the amount of 1 billion escudos,* which shall be applied to the
payment of the balance of the indemnification for expropriations
carried out by the Agrarian Reform Corporation in accordance
with the provisions of this law.

Article 132. Agrarian reform bonds shall be divided into types
A, B, and C and shall be amortized in twenty-five, five, and thirty
equal annual installments, respectively. These bonds shall be expressed in national currency. . . .

* Approximately $120 million, in 1967.—ED.

5. THE WRONG WAY TO AGRARIAN REFORM

JORGE ROGERS

The [Christian Democratic] bill for agrarian reform presented to
Congress last November is a bad project in pursuit of a good idea
that is urgently needed in this country. . . . The bill contains two
basic and fundamental errors, one legal and administrative, the
other economic and technical. Both have developed out of the
same conception. The wording of the law reverses the legal
aphorism that "good faith is assumed, bad faith must be proven."
The bill assumes that property-owners who possess more than the
basic 80 hectares, with readjustments for local conditions, are
inefficient, and it declares them subject to expropriation. It
obliges the efficient producer to obtain a declaration of non-
expropriability in order to continue with his efficient operation.
The requirement that the state concern itself excessively with approving the conduct of the increasing number of efficient producers will compromise and obstruct the useful task of taking
action against the negligent and inefficient producer.

No attention has been paid to the fact that a reform intended
for simultaneous application on a national scale cannot at the
same time allow for the exercise of legal rights with regard to the

Translated by the editor from Jorge Rogers, *Dos Caminos para la Reforma
Agraria* (Santiago: Editorial Orbe, 1966); by permission.

extension and excess of a legal maximum, the type and amount of a reserved property right, and the scale of indemnification in different cases, because of the time and personnel required to review all these circumstances in legal proceedings.

For the action to be massive and simultaneous, it can only be a de facto proceeding, limited to recognizing what has already taken place. If legal rights have been established that can be exercised to block the expropriation, the expropriation can be selective, progressive, and regional only if it conforms to legal provisions. It is completely illusory, and demonstrates a lack of knowledge of judicial proceedings, to believe that one can act at the same time with regard to all landholdings that exceed a legal size, without setting up a system of area priorities, based on the financial and, above all, human resources required for the execution of such an ambitious plan. If the reform is massive, it cannot at the same time be legal. If it is legal and juridical, with guaranteed rights, it cannot be general and instantaneous. . . .

It is an illusion to believe that the forms of collectivized property, forced cooperatives, co-ownership and special association of CORA [the Agrarian Reform Corporation] with the beneficiaries, and other forms different from private property holding will be only provisional and supplementary. The reasons given for creating them, and the fear that the property will return to its original form, will continue, and they will become permanent and indefinite in duration, as we know from experience in similar cases. . . .

. . . [The] plan put forward under the banner of Christian Democracy proposes institutional changes that are more like those of the opposite doctrine [Marxism]: the creation of forms of collectivized property that will become permanent, in spite of the provisional character in which they are described; the perpetuation of an agricultural proletariat that is dependent on the state, instead of the establishment of an independent middle class in the countryside; and the stimulation of typical class opposition within each agricultural enterprise—all these results and methods are characteristic of the Marxist ideology rather than of the doctrines of Social Christianity. To insist on this method is to abandon the banner under which two generations of Christian Democrats have struggled: "Overcome the right and the left." It is to replace it with a new party slogan, "Overcome the socialists by pretending to be more socialist than the socialists." . . .

6. DEVELOPMENT WITHOUT CAPITALISM: TOWARD A COMMUNITARIAN WORLD

JULIO SILVA SOLAR AND JACQUES CHONCHOL

Communitarianism promotes a social structure founded on the principle that land and productive goods (industrial, financial, and commercial capital) should belong to the workers. This significantly supersedes the fundamental conflict of the capitalistic system—the class struggle—in which the antagonism between a small class of owners of capital and the masses who lack any property other than their labor, which they must put at the service of capital in exchange for wages, generates a whole series of obstacles to economic development and social justice.

This conflict can only be resolved by a social order of a communitarian character, in which capital and labor are not separated but united in the same persons.

The dynamism of a communitarian society is based not on the desire for gain or on the power of a handful of capitalists or would-be capitalists but on the collective will of all the people, who become owners of the economy and organize their advance as a community without class differences.

An economy organized on a communitarian basis is in a position to multiply the energies of society in a manner that capitalism cannot even conceive of. It can achieve a much more rapid economic development, with a humanity and justice unknown to the present regime. The communitarian economy is a prerequisite if men are to integrate themselves in a truly fraternal community. The communitarian idea is, therefore, an idea of human liberation.

By putting an end to the exploitation of some men by others, of one class by another that claims to be superior, it creates the necessary bases for the elimination from the earth of every form of oppression, segregation, and servitude among men, and every form of abuse or subjection exercised against peoples, races, or classes considered as inferiors. Only in a community of free and equal men, born in a society that has succeeded in eliminating the social differences that divide men and dehumanize their rela-

---

Translated by the editor from *Desarrollo sin Capitalismo: Hacia un Mundo comunitario* (Caracas: Nuevo Orden, 1964); by permission.

tionships, will they be able to realize in our time the great Christian ideals of peace, justice, brotherhood, and love.

The communitarian society does not allow persons or social classes to live by exploiting the labor of others. It operates by the principle enunciated by Saint Paul: "He who does not wish to work will not eat." The productivity of money and capital, which showers profits on owners in a capitalist society, will reveal its true nature as the productivity of labor, once capital comes under the control of all the workers. The product of labor will always pass into the hands of the capitalists as profit, as long as the workers do not have the capital goods in their control.

The communitarian society is a society of workers which fulfills the biblical teaching that the purpose of material goods is to serve all men, that material goods are objects with a social purpose. Differences in income, which will have to continue as long as education does not give equal qualifications to all, will be based solely on labor. Private ownership of goods of a private character (which under capitalism exists only for the rich) will be extended to all.

The social services, above all education and health, which serve the whole community, will take precedence over individual luxury goods in the employment of the economic resources of the new society. Comfort presupposes the previous satisfaction of the necessities for the entire population.

The revolutionary process is an objective process; it is not arbitrary, and it cannot be directed haphazardly. This objective process, whatever varieties it may have, involves modern society in a transition from capitalism to socialism. We refer to the structures, or bases, of society, not to the political or ideological context, which allows a rather wider and more flexible scope.

The communitarian ideal describes this social change. But what is communitarianism? Is it a form of neocapitalism? Is it a form of socialism? Is it a third position? We believe that it is a form of socialism, a communitarian socialism. Why? Because socialism is a system in which productive goods of a social character belong to the community. That is its basis. That is also the basis of the communitarian ideal. Both cases involve a society of workers who possess the means of production in common.

Communitarian socialism differentiates itself from state socialism in its assertion that the role of the state is subsidiary to the self-management of the workers. That is, the state does what the workers, by themselves, cannot yet do. It would be utopian not to recognize that, in the beginning, the state will expand its scope. But as soon as the new state functions are organized, they should be assumed by the organizations of the people.

At the outset, the action of the state, closely linked to the mass of the people, will be very important in bringing about the new social discipline, organizing the running of the enterprises and the economy by the workers, and planning the whole process of production, distribution, and development. But it is the people who will really create and determine the new system. Thus it is that the workers must play a direct part in the development of the permanent forms that the communitarian structure will acquire in the city and in the countryside—without converting the state machinery into an all-absorbing and unresponsive power.

7. COMMUNITARIANISM AND CHRISTIAN DEMOCRACY

WILLIAM THAYER

The question of communitarianism, particularly in relation to the ownership of productive enterprises, is viewed with a certain ambivalence or confusion by several sectors of Christian Democracy.

Jacques Chonchol and Julio Silva have tried to defend a communitarian socialism, the details of which are specified in several works, most notably in *Development Without Capitalism: Toward a Communitarian World.* . . .

For Chonchol and Silva, communitarianism is characterized by the abolition of private ownership of capital goods and of the means of production. They define it as a variety of socialism, "because socialism is a system in which productive goods of a social character belong to the community. That is its basis. That is also the basis of the communitarian ideal. Both cases involve a society of workers who possess the means of production in common."

More recently, the report of the so-called Political-Technical Commission of the Christian Democratic Party, presided over by Jacques Chonchol and including, among others, Julio Silva, returned to the question of communitarianism in relation to state enterprises: [the report] calls for the "self-management of [state] enterprises by the workers in those enterprises, with the state

Translated by the editor from *Trabajo, Empresa y Revolución* (Santiago: Editorial Zig Zag, 1968), by permission.

maintaining ownership and certain basic forms of control." These assertions seriously worry us, because with regard to the state enterprises, which usually involve aspects that are essential to the economy of the country (ENAP [National Petroleum Company], the State Bank, ENDESA [Chilean National Electric Company], ENAMI [National Mining Company], the railroads, etc.), we believe that it would be highly unfortunate and improper if self-management were demanded by the workers. Logically, self-management would mean the democratization of power within these enterprises, the election of management by the community of workers in each one, in businesses or services whose essential importance to the state requires that they be run by a direct representative of the state. [This representative] should operate with more or less autonomy with respect to the central government and be assisted by a consultative and informational advisory council, made up of workers, consumers, and technicians, whose opinion would influence the action and decision of the direct representative of national authority.

We must be realistic: What circumstances or previous experience could assure us that the democratic will of the small community that comprises, for example, the workers of the National Petroleum Company (ENAP) will express the interests of the state and of the entire community better than the public authority elected specifically to govern the nation in accordance with the general interest of all? I am completely in favor of experiments with communitarian enterprises, such as production co-operatives or others in which the workers organize, elect their managers, and obtain the cooperation of capital in the form of loans and not of grants, in order that we may have the full experience of a worker community governing an enterprise. But this should be done in businesses that operate in the private sector, that are not reserved for the state by reason of their strategic importance. In the case of the latter, it has to be the decision of the state that fixes their policy, establishes their goals, and governs and orients them, with the advice and information of the representatives of the consumers, workers, and technicians.

We believe that one of the most valuable historical achievements of the Christian Democrats has been the stand it has taken for the community of free men: the national community, made up of lesser communities, seeking to obtain the desired objectives of the universal community. But community is above all a way of life, a relationship between persons, a result of the personal and social character of man, which is based on his essential equality, his fraternal, loving, and educative destiny—which generates, because of this fraternity and this community of ideals, common forms of property. We do not believe in the reverse. We do not believe that a community of men has to be produced by property in common, because we do not believe that the spiritual is produced from the material. We do not believe that in the beginning is matter, but that in the beginning is the spirit. For this reason, we can easily see how goods can be held in common in religious communities, where there first exists a spiritual community. For this reason, we believe that to the extent that individualism is replaced in social life by a sense of national solidarity, all forms, uses, applications, and systems of individual property will be superseded by social forms of property. And when I say social forms of property, I mean forms in which both the personal and the social sentiments of man are respected.

We do not believe in the Marxist dogma that private ownership of the means of production necessarily means the exploitation of man by his fellow man. Historically, private ownership of the means of production created a sinister form of exploitation of man. It developed at a stage in which the role of the state was minimized—in accordance with the liberalism that was derived from the individualistic philosophy that predominated in the world after the triumph of the French Revolution—and it resulted in the atomization of the workers. It is evident that, in the framework of the liberal state, economic individualism, the lack of trade-union organization, the glorification of mechanization and industrialism, the organization of owners or representatives of capital, led to the uncontrollable power of the capitalists and the exploitation of man by his fellow man through private control of the means of production.

But it is not private control of the means of production that causes exploitation. It is the weakness of one sector vis-à-vis another in private activity, which is the result of inaction by the state, of predominant individualism, of the power of some and the weakness of others. There are too many examples in history of state exploitation of man for us to insist on the abolition of private ownership of the means of production as a condition for the abolition of the exploitation of man by his fellow man. We have said this many times. Slavery was created so that the state could make use of those whom it had defeated. The pharaohs, the absolutist governments, many modern dictatorships—all show how far the exploitation of man by his fellow man can go in systems in which the state has full control over the means of production. In order to end one man's exploitation of another, there must be a popular government capable of overseeing the organization of the national community, and the smaller communities within it, which will permit each man to realize himself personally and socially in the local family, working, or functional communities so that, through them, there will arise not only the elective democracy that we have had in Chile but a genuine participatory democracy. This we consider the purest, most valuable tradition of Christian Democracy. . . .

There are not two ways to development in the government of President Frei and the Christian Democrats. There is only one way, which is not capitalist but humanist; but that does not mean paralyzing, discouraging, or restricting investment or the activities of capitalist enterprises, which the majority are today, but their direction in accordance with the planning and development of human, labor, and community elements in a manner that will gradually become less "capitalistic" and more "communitarian." One cannot view the enterprise as a static and unchangeable entity. The enterprise is a "resultant"; it is the product of a system; it is a unit of production that serves the oligarchy, minorities, a single class, or the bourgeoisie when the orientation of economic life leads that way. However, it will serve the people and the community if these are the goals of the prevailing economy. Businesses are capitalist precisely because their human, worker, or communitarian possibilities have not been realized, because, through the course of several centuries, they have not taken account of the dignity of man, the significance of work, the importance of human relations, and the value of popular participation.

In order to reach these goals, the following are necessary: (a) a popular government elected to achieve them; (b) the construction of social power through the organization, training, and participation of the people in carrying out the tasks of the elected government; (c) an essential change in the structure of economic power, not by the destruction of what exists but by the creation of what has not existed up to this moment. This is the incorporation into economic life of the mass of the people, with their buying power, their capacity to save and to invest, their value as a productive force, and their massive political power in a democratic governmental structure.

8. THE UNITED STATES ASSISTANCE PROGRAM TO CHILE

AGENCY FOR INTERNATIONAL DEVELOPMENT

Since 1945, the U.S. Government has provided more than $1.46 billion to Chile in various forms of economic and technical assistance. More than $936 million of this amount have been provided since the announcement of the Alliance for Progress by President Kennedy in March, 1961. The administration of U.S. assistance programs is the responsibility of the Agency for International Development (AID) of the Department of State. . . . Other public agencies and institutions participating in this U.S. assistance effort include the U.S. Treasury, Export-Import Bank, Peace Corps, Food for Peace, and the Social Progress Trust Fund of the Inter-American Development Bank. Many private foundations, universities, and voluntary relief organizations have contributed and are continuing to provide substantial additional assistance. . . .

U.S. assistance through the Agency for International Development to Chile is principally provided through four specific techniques: (1) general program loans; (2) specific project and sector loans; (3) technical assistance grants; and (4) PL 480 food sale and donation programs. U.S. assistance is provided to support Chilean developmental activities and self-help efforts in undertaking reforms and increasing investment for economic development. This assistance is specifically planned to support over-all U.S. assistance program goals, which are indicated below.

I. U.S. assistance seeks to support the development of an effective Chilean government capability to formulate and implement a set of economic policies and programs designed to obtain stabilization, reform, and development. This is supported by the following AID projects.

A. *Program Loans*

	(1)	(2)	(3)	(4)
Date of agreement:	1/31/63	4/3/64	1/5/65	2/15/66
Amount:	$35 million	$55 million	$80 million	$80 million

Reprinted from the publication of the United States Agency for International Development (Santiago, Chile, September, 1967).

Terms of repayment: Loans (1) and (2): forty years including ten years grace period, ¾ per cent interest. Loans (3) and (4): forty years including ten years grace period, 1 per cent interest during grace period, 2½ per cent thereafter.

Description: The main purpose of AID program loans is to assist Chile to implement its economic development programs through dollar financing for imports essential for those programs. The escudo proceeds of these loans, generated by the sale of loan dollars to private importers, support projects in Chilean government's capital investment budget such as construction of housing, highways, educational facilities, ports, agricultural installations, irrigation, industrial and agricultural credit programs.

B. Public Law 480, Titles I and IV Sales

Chile has purchased some $119 million of U.S. surplus food under Titles I and IV of Public Law 480, legislation adopted by the U.S. Congress in 1954 which established the basis for U.S. concessional food sales and food assistance programs called the Food for Peace Program. Most of the proceeds of the sales for escudos under Title I have been set aside for Chilean government programs contributing to economic development, especially for low cost housing, farm-to-market roads, and agricultural marketing facilities. A minor portion of these proceeds are used for credits to U.S. associated industries and for financing U.S. Government expenses in Chile. All escudo proceeds of the long-term dollar credit sales under Title IV are being used by the Chilean government for public sector investment.

C. Tax Modernization Program

Started: 1962
Scheduled to end: 1970
Estimated total cost: $2,451,000

Description: U.S. technicians are advising on the reorganization and administrative improvement of the Chilean Internal Revenue Service and the tax collection functions of the Ministry of Justice. In addition, tax policy assistance (research, analysis, and training) is being provided to the Chilean Internal Revenue Service under an AID financed contract with Harvard University's International Tax Program. The objective is to develop those tax policies and administrative capabilities which will help to generate the substantially increased revenue needed to finance national development policy and foster economic growth within a framework of equitable distribution of the tax burden.

D. Customs Administration

Started: 1963
Scheduled to end: 1968
Estimated total cost: $353,000

Description: This activity is designed to expand customs revenue collections through improved administration of the Customs Service. Other targets include reduction in the transaction and handling time of incoming merchandise, reduction in damage and loss, the production of accurate trade and financial statistics, reduction in contraband, and improved manpower utilization within the Customs Service.

E. Feasibility and Sectoral Studies Loan

Date of agreement: March 15, 1965
Amount: $3 million
Terms of repayment: 40 years including 10 years grace period, ¾ per cent interest.

Description: This loan finances engineering and economic studies for both public and private sector projects. In the public sector, funds are being used for general economic studies as well as for feasibility studies of projects with high development priority. In the private sector, funds are being used for project feasibility studies. The Chilean Development Corporation (CORFO) has responsibility for reviewing private sector applications, while the Chilean Budget Office reviews public sector project applications. A similar second loan has been signed in 1967.

II. The U.S. also supports Chilean efforts to effect a fundamental transformation of Chilean agriculture based on land tenure reform, expanded production, more efficient marketing systems, and improved social conditions in the rural areas. The following projects are directed toward this end.

A. Agricultural Development

Started: 1965
Scheduled to end: 1970
Estimated total cost: $1.156 million

Description: This activity is designed to assist the Chilean government in establishing policies, programs, and the institutional base needed to attain its Development Plan goal targets for agriculture by 1971. To foster structural changes in the agricultural sector permitting more efficient production practices, the following will be emphasized:

1. Improving the marketing system to increase returns to farmers through assistance in grading and standards, marketing

organizations, market information and reporting, and storage, transportation and processing facilities.

2. Adopting price policies that will provide incentives for increased production.

3. Increasing production, especially in export items such as fruits and melons.

B. Fertilizer Import Loan

Date of agreement:	January 11, 1966
Amount:	$3 million
Terms of repayment:	40 years including 10 years grace period, 1 per cent interest during grace period, 2½ per cent thereafter.

Description: This loan is financing the importation of approximately 44,000 tons of triple superphosphate fertilizer for use in the 1965–66 and 1966–67 agricultural seasons. The fertilizer is sold by the Empresa de Comercio Agrícola (ECA) to agricultural cooperatives for resale on credit terms to cooperative members. This loan supports Chilean efforts to expand agricultural production through increased use of fertilizers.

C. Cooperative Development Bank Loan

Date of agreement:	August 28, 1965
Amount:	$3.65 million
Terms of repayment:	25 years including 10 years grace period, 1 per cent interest during grace period, 2½ per cent interest thereafter; or the government can assume the loan obligation at its option with terms of 40 years including 10 years grace period, 1 per cent interest during grace period, 2½ per cent interest thereafter.

Description: This loan to the newly created Instituto de Financiamiento Cooperativo (IFICOOP) provides seed capital for the initial financing of a cooperative development bank to provide credit facilities, technical, and managerial services to Chilean cooperatives.

D. Rural Electric Cooperatives Loan

Date of agreement:	March 5, 1965
Amount:	$3.3 million
Terms of repayment:	40 years including 10 years grace period at ¾ per cent interest.

Description: These loan funds are utilized by CORFO to further development of fourteen rural electric cooperatives by financing projects which will bring electricity to 5,481 new rural consumers. The Chilean National Electric Company (ENDESA) is responsible for technical supervision of the project. A revolving fund, financed by loan repayments, is being created for further expansion of these cooperatives.

III. The U.S. supports the attainment of a basic modernization and expansion of Chilean educational systems so that they may serve increasingly as effective instruments for social mobility and the manpower essential for economic growth. The following projects support the attainment of this goal.

A. *Education Modernization*

To start:	1968
Scheduled to end:	1970
Estimated total cost:	$815,000

Description: U.S. advisors under this technical assistance project will be directing their efforts toward the further development of Chilean leadership in (1) educational administration, (2) quality improvement, (3) vocational education, (4) guidance, testing, and evaluation. These priority areas are not covered under existing U.S. or other assistance programs. This technical assistance will be provided to the Chilean Government through an AID financed contract with a U.S. university.

B. *Education Sector Loan*

Date of agreement:	September 14, 1967
Amount:	$10 million
Terms of repayment:	40 years with 10 years grace period at 1 per cent interest during grace period, 2½ per cent thereafter.

Description: This loan provides $10 million to improve educational facilities and instructional materials and techniques at the primary as well as vocational and secondary level. Construction of facilities in low income areas as well as pilot regional centers for middle level education are stressed under the loan.

C. *Industrial Training*

Started:	1958
Scheduled to end:	1968
Estimated total cost:	$1.053 million

Description: Under an AID contract with the University of Pittsburgh, assistance is being given to the Federico Santa María Technical University to improve and expand its graduate level programs in electrical, chemical, and mechanical engineering. The project includes curriculum and staff development through the introduction of the latest teaching and research methods. University of Pittsburgh staff are teaching at Santa María and Santa María students and faculty are receiving advanced training in the United States.

D. Training for Development

Started: 1964
Scheduled to end: Continuing
Estimated total cost: $921,000

Description: Graduate level training in the United States is provided for selected university graduates to prepare them for positions in universities, public agencies, and other institutions concerned with Chile's development effort.

IV. U.S. assistance is designed to support a substantial expansion of industrial production through a liberalization of economic policies, improved resource allocation, and institutional reforms affecting industry. The following projects are directed toward this goal.

A. Private Sector Imports Loan

Date of agreement: June 2, 1966
Amount: $10 million
Terms of repayment: 1 per cent interest during 10 years grace period and 2½ per cent interest thereafter.

Description: This loan to the Central Bank provides financing for imports from the U.S. of essential capital goods for the private sector on medium credit terms of from three to eight years at 8 per cent interest. Loans are made by the Central Bank and are channelled through the regular commercial banking systems.

B. Savings and Loan Bank Loans

Date of agreement: June 14, 1961
Amount: $5 million
Terms of repayment: 25 years including 10 years grace period, 4 per cent interest.

Date of agreement: March 18, 1964
Amount: $8.7 million
Terms of repayment: 30 years including 5 years grace period; 4 per cent interest; or the government can assume the loan obligation at its option with terms of 40 years including 10 years grace period, ¾ per cent interest.

Description: These loans, together with two $5 million Inter-American Development Bank Social Progress Trust Fund loans for housing cooperatives, a $5 million AID grant, and a $1,310,000 loan under Public Law 480, Title I, have stimulated home construction throughout Chile and have made possible a rapid expansion of the savings and loan system established in 1961. Created with U.S. technical and capital assistance, the Chilean savings and loan system has been especially effective in attracting local savings and is one of the most successful savings and loan systems in Latin America. . . .

. . .

B. *Food for Peace*

From July, 1966, through June, 1967, some 1,795,000 persons representing slightly less than 24 per cent of the total population of Chile received some food donated under the Food for Peace program. Of this, 1,200,000 were children receiving school lunches of which the U.S. contributed the total meal. Another 140,000 pre-school children and pregnant mothers were assisted, principally with rations of U.S. non-fat dry milk. Some 122,000 individuals received food at authorized institutions including summer camps. The remaining recipients were primarily in the family-feeding category (396,000) consisting of hardship cases in which the nominal breadwinner of the family was either unemployed, under-employed, or deceased.

The purposes of food donations are (1) to meet famine or other urgent or extraordinary relief requirements, (2) to combat malnutrition especially in children, and (3) to promote economic and community development especially through well-planned self-help projects. Voluntary agencies active in food distribution are preparing donation programs increasingly directed towards voluntary self-help accomplishment activities designated to alleviate the causes of the need for such assistance.

9. CHILE MUST HAVE A SOCIALIST REVOLUTION

FIDEL CASTRO

The imperialists wish to convert the so-called "Chilean experiment" into one rivaling that of Cuba. Sr. Eduardo Frei, the Christian Democratic president of Chile, and his party and its doctrine were presented to the people of Latin America as an example of what they called a "bloodless revolution." . . .

We talked with those [Chilean] deputies. And we explained to them that in order to carry out a revolution, it is necessary in the first place to confront imperialism; that in order to carry out a revolution—even if it is not a socialist revolution but a bourgeois-democratic revolution, a national revolution—they themselves had to confront imperialism, they themselves had to confront the oligarchy.

I told them, in addition, that I did not believe that, given the conditions in Chile, one could carry out a bourgeois revolution, but that if one wanted to make a revolution it would have to be a socialist revolution. Why? Because an underdeveloped country like Chile, burdened with debt, where large masses of the population exist under the worst conditions, necessarily had to strike at the interests of imperialism, of the oligarchy, of large industry, of the import and export business, and of banking, if it wished to accomplish something, to give something to the masses of peasants and workers of the country. And that, in addition, in order to wage a battle against the oligarchy and against imperialism, it was necessary to get the support of the peasants; and that the masses of workers and peasants would not support a bourgeois revolution because the workers and peasants were not willing to serve the interests of an exploiting class.

I told them that I did not judge the character of the Chilean revolution by whether or not it nationalized the copper industry, because nationalization would have occurred sooner or later; that what defined a revolution was really the determination to change the social structure to the benefit of the exploited classes; that the policy they followed with respect to copper did not determine whether or not there was a revolution, because there have been governments that have nationalized a foreign enterprise and have not made a revolution; that the time at which they nationalized copper was not decisive—but that the character of [the Chilean] revolution had to be judged by all its actions, by its policy in relation to each of the classes, by its determination to carry out a revolution to benefit the peasants and all those who were exploited.

They said that they were going to carry out an agrarian reform in which they were going to establish a limit of 80 hectares. And I told them: If you carry out a revolution of 80 hectares, you will have to fight against the oligarchy, and you will not be able to

Excerpts from a speech at the University of Havana, March 13, 1966; translated by the editor from *Política Internacional* (Havana), No. 13 (first trimester, 1966).

struggle against them without the support of the peasants and workers.

We recalled that our agrarian reform established a minimum of more than 300 hectares at the beginning, and everyone knows how the landowners resisted our agrarian reform—how they immediately began to conspire against us. And I asked them: If you pay compensation in cash to the landowners, what resources will you have left to help the peasants? With what resources will you raise the level of agricultural technology? . . .

The first great fallacy of those efforts is the belief that it is possible to reconcile the interests of imperialism and those of the nation, the interests of the oligarchs and those of the peasants, the interests of the bourgeoisie and those of the workers.

All this is very familiar. These problems have been discussed for more than a century. What has happened in reality? The workers are against the Christian Democratic government, and they are against the Christian Democratic government because they will never be willing to make sacrifices that benefit the bourgeoisie, that benefit the rich. . . .

FREI: BLOOD WITHOUT REVOLUTION

To tell the truth, I have always believed that Frei was a representative of the Chilean bourgeoisie. I have never believed that Frei would carry out any revolution. You will remember that we spoke of this at the time of the triumph of the Christian Democrats. But I thought that Frei was trying to establish a different kind of bourgeois government. I thought that Frei was at least an individual of bourgeois ideals, that he was at least a man of Christian ideals, not a revolutionary, but one who favored a bourgeois government of a different type from the bourgeois governments and oligarchs of the rest of the continent. . . .

We did not believe that Chile could carry out a revolution by peaceful means, but we also did not believe that armed struggle was the order of the day in Chile. We believe that while certain liberties, constitutional rights, and institutions exist in a country and when all other ways are not closed in a country—as happens in the immense majority of the countries of Latin America—armed struggle is not the order of the day.

Therefore, we have never believed that in the conditions in Chile in recent years guerrilla warfare could be considered as an appropriate tactic. We do believe that, in the long run, the class contradictions, the struggle of the people against imperialism, oligarchy, and the bourgeoisie, will lead, sooner or later, to armed struggle in Chile. . . .

Frei is a reactionary; Frei has demonstrated with this deed*
that he is not an individual with a strong hand but a coward who
abuses his power and sends his troops against the workers. Frei
has demonstrated that he is a liar; Frei has demonstrated that he
is a vulgar *político* who, in order to justify his bloody action,
tries to blame the Tricontinental Conference.† Frei has unmasked
himself; Frei is showing the people of Chile and the world the
kind of government he is going to put forward, that is to say,
not a revolution without blood, but a policy of blood without
revolution

Blood without revolution! That is the policy of Frei.

Blood without revolution! That is the government of Frei.

Blood without revolution! That is the policy of the Alliance
for Progress.

* This is a reference to the shooting of workers at the El Salvador mine,
in March, 1966.—ED.

† The First Solidarity Conference of the Peoples of Africa, Asia, and
Latin America, held in Havana in January, 1966.—ED.

10. THE SOCIALIST PARTY OF CHILE
AGAINST REFORMISM

DECLARATION OF THE EXECUTIVE COMMITTEE
OF THE SOCIALIST PARTY

It is sometimes said that our country is an oasis of "democracy"
and "legality," where in the final analysis the will of the citizens,
as expressed in elections, is decisive. It is asserted that for us to
view the problem of power in terms of force and not of votes is
a demonstration that we do not understand Chile, that we do not
interpret our country correctly or understand its special character
and historic evolution.

Nothing could be more false. Chilean socialism came into
existence precisely as a requirement of our history and our
national interests. We do not deny what we are. On the contrary, we aspire to develop our policy in close relationship with
the nature and specific characteristics of the country. It would
be useless to deny that Chile is distinctive in Latin America because of a long history of struggle and effort by our people to

Translated by the editor from the supplement to No. 46 of *Punto Final*
(Santiago), January 16, 1968.

establish a political system that is considerably more developed and mature than those of our sister republics. For this reason, Chile is also the place where the limits and contradictions of those political systems that are called democratic are most evident. The experience of today and of the past demonstrates that the democratic system will be maintained up to the moment at which the dominant classes begin to feel that their fundamental interests are threatened. When that occurs, they do not hesitate to break through the institutional structure that previously served them in order to defend their privileged situation by force. . . .

It has also been said of our policy that it is isolationist—as if the Socialist Party rejects any contact with other forces or supports only a type of ideological purism that prevents us from reaching an understanding with other sectors and from forging political alliances with related parties. Nothing could be further from the truth.

On the contrary, our general congress has expressly stated that all understandings and alliances with similar forces that will help us in our purpose of gaining power for socialism are just and necessary. However, it has also rejected any alliance that does not tend toward that objective, that makes more difficult the radicalization of the movement of the people, that hands over the predominant role to forces, parties, and ideologies of the bourgeoisie. Thus we could not accept an alliance with the government or with Christian Democracy, on the basis of superficial contradictions between it and the old oligarchy, because we well know that Christian Democracy is the new face of reaction and the present instrument through which imperialism attains its purposes in Chile. Likewise we cannot accept alliances with the Radical Party, for this would merely re-establish another version of the now discredited policy of conciliation and compromise, which has created the present crisis in Chile. We know that because of its social composition, its ideological history, its political habits, and the interests and aspirations of its leaders, as well as its links with imperialism, the Radical Party could not form an alliance with the revolutionary social and political forces.

We know that the reformist parties of the center can succeed in gaining the support of certain popular sectors for their political objectives. We recognize this fact, and we will try to convince these popular sectors through a vast campaign of ideological enlightenment to free themselves from the political tutelage of the bourgeois forces.

With this united and aggressive outlook, we call on all persons and forces that are authentically leftist in these parties to work for their progressive integration into a single anti-imperialist front, which will place the real interests of the people of Chile above the worn-out party structures and will establish a nucleus around which the workers can develop their political action of liberation, a nucleus that cannot be other than the FRAP [Front of Popular Action]. It is not by utilizing existing party organizations, which do not respond to the real problems, that we will arrive at a broad, audacious, and vigorous regrouping of the left. On the contrary, only by bypassing these traditional structures will it be possible for the workers to consolidate and forge a true instrument of struggle, apart from the distortions introduced by old and new centrist parties. . . . The Socialist Party does not reject the utilization of peaceful and legal methods, such as the struggle for just demands, ideological and mass activity, and political processes, but it considers that those methods alone will not lead to the conquest of power. They are complementary elements in a political action that seeks the final overthrow of reactionary internal forces and the destruction of every form of imperialist penetration.

In the application of its policy of the Workers' Front, the Socialist Party fights for the unity of the proletariat, peasants, and lower middle class, and the incorporation of sectors of students and progressive intellectuals in an unwavering political struggle for the establishment of socialism.

The overriding political mission and the social content of the Workers' Front line exclude all possibility of compromise with the bourgeoisie, which historically has shown that it is a docile ally and obsequious instrument of foreign imperialism. The alliance of the revolutionary left with elements of the bourgeoisie has led to a series of frustrations on the part of the exploited classes, postponing the hour of their final victory. Consequently, the alliances and compromises that the Socialist Party will establish can be justified only to the extent that they contribute to the realization of the strategic objectives already specified.

The Socialist Party values the importance and great political and social role exercised up to this time by the Front of Popular Action. For nearly eleven years, the FRAP, based on an understanding between the Socialist and Communist parties, has made important contributions to the service of the people of Chile, developing a greater consciousness on the part of considerable social sectors and making possible the establishment of a powerful popular movement that has decisive weight in national life. We realize that there are differences in the concepts of the two parties, but beyond these differences we reiterate our firm decision to strengthen the bonds between the Socialists and the Communists, so that the FRAP may better carry out its role as a unified political front of all anti-imperialist and liberating forces that struggle meaningfully for the socialist revolution. For the Socialists, the FRAP represents and will continue to represent the only real alternative in the conquest of power in Chile.

The evident failure of the policies of the Frei government, characterized by economic stagnation, dependence on American imperialism, accelerated inflation, increasing unemployment, the use of force to put down popular protests against its wage policy— all these have made the Chilean crisis more acute and demonstrated the sterility of reformist solutions, producing a grave national situation that official propaganda tries in vain to hide.

Parallel with the increasing intensity of the problems that unify larger and larger sections of the population in the struggle, we find that in the heart of the centrist parties, both the Radicals and the Christian Democrats, there is increasing concern on the part of sectors of the middle class, who demand of their leadership stronger policies for a real change and a definite anti-imperialist position. Combined with the sharp decline in the popular support that the Christian Democratic Party had at the outset of its mandate, we find a favorable movement toward the left, which every day involves more extensive sectors of the Chilean population. This, joined with the general sense of discontent, permits us to conclude that real bases are being created for a definitive and decisive change in the struggle for political power.

11. AFTER THE CONGRESSIONAL ELECTIONS OF MARCH, 1969

EDITORIAL IN EL MERCURIO

The results so far show a perceptible decline in the electoral strength of the Christian Democratic Party, although it remains the strongest political force. The National Party increased its vote significantly, coming in second in the voting and forming the second largest parliamentary group in the Chamber of Deputies, as well as gaining five seats in the Senate, after it had lost all its

* The National Party was formed by a fusion of the Liberal and Conservative parties in 1966.—ED.

Translated by the editor from *El Mercurio* (Santiago), March 9, 1969.

seats that were contested in the 1965 elections.* The Communists showed a moderate but solid advance. They remain as the third ranking party in number of votes and in seats in Congress. The Chilean Socialist Party achieved an appreciable advance after its division. The Radicals remained stationary, and the smaller parties disappeared.

The general tendency of the electorate was one of a search for defined and logical positions. Thus, the sector of the Christian Democrats that obtained a favorable endorsement from the public was made up of the candidates who frankly supported the government. The losses suffered by the rebels and the "third-position" party groups are attributable to their open or covert opposition to the government and their flirtation with Marxism.

An analogous situation seems to be the cause of the Radical paralysis. The main body of voters of that party did not support its attempt to form the "popular unity" sought and supported by the Communists. Voters who in past elections were counted among the active Radicals now give their support to the National Party or to the Marxist left, thus preferring a clear definition in one direction or the other.

The collapse of the dissident Socialist sector likewise indicates that the opinion of the Chilean left is concentrated in the Communist and Socialist parties, which present different party lines but which both represent political continuity and a clear ideological definition.

One should note also the greater importance of the personal factor in the Congress elected at this time. A few parties, in particular, presented candidates who will excel in future legislative debates.

The election shows the importance of the Chilean middle class, the sector that has suffered the most from the increase in taxes and the rise in the cost of living. The parties that socially should represent the middle class have not understood this in the last several years: the determination of the Radicals to unite with the Communists cannot assure the middle class of future well-being and security. Yet, if the Radicals have not taken advantage of the middle-class citizenry, which is decisive in a country with such a high degree of income redistribution as ours, the Christian Democrats thought they could ensure themselves of permanent control of power and elections by attending to the needs of the peasant sector and the marginal poor, without noticing the many signs that showed the need to consider the powerful middle-class element.

The government [Christian Democratic] propaganda itself was counterproductive with the middle groups of the nation. It seemed wasteful to modest employees in straitened circumstances, to established workers burdened with family needs, and to the vast number of young professionals and technicians oppressed by daily unavoidable expenses. Moreover, the defense of the government that was offered was not on the sophisticated mental and social plane of our middle class. Always thinking of the marginal groups, the government propaganda forgot that it had listeners and spectators with a keen critical sense, who were irritated by the arbitrary character of some of its assertions and concepts. . . .

12. THE ACCOMPLISHMENTS OF THE CHRISTIAN DEMOCRATIC GOVERNMENT

EDUARDO FREI

Economic Development

To carry out their functions, the institutions in the public sector incurred expenses in fiscal year 1968 which totalled 9.641 billion escudos. In 1964, the total expenditure in 1968 figures was 5.911 billion escudos, which means that in the course of the last five years public expenditure has increased by 63 per cent as a result of the support given by the government to programs of economic and social development. Among the reasons for the increase in current expenditures we may mention the improvement in the real remuneration of employees in the public services and the programs of social development, such as education and health, whose expenditures are largely computed in terms of current spending. The increase in capital expenditures over the past five years is explained by the government's basic purpose of expanding the productive capacity of the country. The sectors that received the majority of this effort were those of housing, education, agriculture, and industry. . . .

Mining

As a presidential candidate I proposed for the consideration of

Excerpts from the presidential message of May 21, 1969; translated by the editor from *Quinta Mensaje del Presidente de la República de Chile* (Santiago, 1969).

the country a program for the copper industry that consisted basically in the Chileanization of the productive enterprises, the development of an investment plan, and an increase in national production. I have maintained, and I will always maintain, that the duty of Chile is to defend its legitimate interests in the matter of basic resources, for no nation can progress by mortgaging its decision-making capacity in the most important areas of its economy. A proof of this is my proposal for the nationalization of the Chilean Electric Company, the creation of a National Nitrate Company, and the fact that the state has increased its share in the Pacific Steel Company from 33 per cent to 58 per cent.

The first step of the government in the area of copper policy was to carry out what had been proposed to the citizenry, and I can state with considerable pride that what we have accomplished has had a very favorable effect on the economy of the country. . . . Not only is the program being fulfilled in accordance with what had been planned, but all the projects are ahead of schedule, and some goals have already been fulfilled. Such is the case with the increase in our capacity for the refining of copper, which rose from 196,000 tons in 1964 to 578,000 tons in 1968. The building of an infrastructure is being carried out fully; a housing plan that will comprise 10,000 housing units has been put into effect; control organisms have been created that will effectively protect the interests of the state; the trade-union activities of the workers have been strengthened; a marketing policy has been adopted that has permitted Chile to sell its production at the best market prices; and all this has been accompanied by international cooperative action, the importance of which there is no need to emphasize.

Nevertheless, in the last few years the world price of copper has experienced a constant increase. At first it was thought that this was the result of a transitory situation which was a product principally of international events. Later we saw that this situation had become stabilized. This obliges the government of Chile to re-evaluate the share of the state in the profits of this vital activity in our country. This is to say that the state should share in the more favorable prices that are being obtained—and in the Chileanization of enterprises that was sought earlier but in some cases not achieved.

The determination of the government to obtain a greater share in the high prices for copper satisfies a just national goal and takes account of new factors that the copper market is indicating will be permanent. This determination will mean greater benefits for the country and will permit us to rely on new resources in the course of the coming years.

But this is not all. Together with this very important step, I consider it necessary that the copper companies that have not participated in the past in the Chileanization program now enter into it in order to ensure that this policy, which was proposed to the country and which it approved in granting me my office, is applied across the board without exception.* This is what the present circumstances in the development of our country de= mand. . . .

The facts have demonstrated the advantages of Chileanization. To operate the mines requires technological and human expertise and quantities of financial capital which the country does not possess at the moment but which it can rapidly acquire through the process of Chileanization that the government is carrying out and intends to complete. This will permit the production of copper to continue without disturbances and without deleterious consequences for the economy of the country, which depends so directly on the production of, and especially the income from, copper. It is also necessary to consider that northern Chile, a zone in an especially delicate economic situation, makes its living basically from this activity, which at present is guaranteed a vast expansion.

The system of Chileanization enjoys considerable prestige abroad and permits us to finance development plans without difficulty and in accordance with our capacities. This system permits the government of Chile to acquire a majority of shares of the copper mines, and whoever has a majority in any company in the world is able to run the industry in a short time. . . . The system avoids grave internal and external difficulties and permits the country to advance without creating the tensions and problems no one wishes to provoke, through a Chilean formula that will permit the country to arrive at full ownership.

I have the responsibility for the government of this country. For years I have studied this problem, and I believe that if we can obtain the full control of our basic resources in a rapid and progressive manner, no one would advise us to expose the country to unnecessary risks when we can arrive at the same goal in a way of our own choosing which has been defined and approved by the country.

Nevertheless, I cannot help but recognize that among the

---

* On June 26, 1969, President Frei announced that the Chilean government had agreed with the Anaconda Company for the purchase of 51 per cent of the stock of its two Chilean subsidiaries that had not participated in the earlier Chileanization program. The agreement also provided for the purchase of the remaining 49 per cent of the shares (i.e., nationalization with compensation) between 1972 and 1981, and granted Anaconda a three-year service and training contract.—ED.

leaders of the political parties represented in this Congress there is insistent talk of the need for nationalization of the enterprises that were not Chileanized in the past. Those that have already been established as mixed companies cannot be included, of course. I am afraid that I am justified in my fear that, given the acute political division that now exists prior to the coming presidential election, the necessary concrete and specific support will not be forthcoming except in words. Each party will try to maintain its own position and make this problem a new issue. In Chile, we have experience of verbal agreements on problems such as the struggle against inflation or the reform of social security, to cite only two examples, which did not bring about any specific agreement in practice. . . . In this situation I call upon the men, women, youth, and workers of Chile to support the government in its policy of responsible defense of our basic riches, with the understanding that we will leave nothing undone to assure the best use of our national patrimony for the benefit of the entire country. . . .

FARM PRODUCTION

Agriculture and cattle raising have advanced in these years [1964–68] by an annual average of 4.1 per cent, where previously the rate was 1.8 per cent. Had it not been for the drought, we would have had an increase of 6 per cent or more, according to the Planning Office.

Agrarian reform has been one of the principal tasks of the present government. Conscious of the imperative necessity of actively incorporating the peasantry in the economic, social, and political progress of the country, I have made special efforts and sacrifices to attain these goals. The urgency of carrying the agrarian reform forward led us to expropriate 650,560 hectares during 1968. This figure is the highest attained up to this date, twice that of 1967. This was done at a time when some professional falsifiers of the truth were saying that the agrarian reform was paralyzed. The land expropriated from 1965 until March 31, 1969, exceeds 2 million hectares. Up to December 31, 1968, 404 agrarian cooperative settlements (*asentamientos*) have been established, benefiting 14,594 families. In addition there are 4,265 associates affiliated with these same settlements, which gives a total of 18,859 direct beneficiaries of the agrarian reform. . . .

EDUCATION

In 1968, 2,204,000 students were enrolled in primary and secondary education, including both public and private schools. A comparison of this figure with that for 1964, which was 1,690,000, indicates an increase of more than 500,000 students, or an increase of more than 30 per cent. . . .

The total number of schools built in the period 1965–68 amounts to 2,639, so that from the time I took office Chile has built two schools per day. When I think of certain critics who speak for "the people" and attack the government, I answer them with two schools a day for the children of Chile. Their opposition and their words will pass without effect, but the schools and the children who are educated there will be a lasting testimonial. . . .

In 1968, the number of students enrolled in all the universities in the country reached 61,200 which, compared to an enrollment in 1964 of 35,280, means an increase of 73.4 per cent. To carry out this extraordinary expansion, the financial resources devoted to the universities have increased by 85 per cent in real value between 1964 and 1968. . . .

LABOR

The unemployment rate mentioned in the 1960 census was 6.5 per cent. The Statistical Office, with the collaboration of the University of Chile and the assistance of the International Labor Office, indicates that this rate fell to 5 per cent in January, 1967, and to 4.4 per cent in January, 1968, the last date for which information is available.

Under the present administration, we have continually increased the workers' share of the national income, which has now reached the highest level in the history of the country. In the last four years, there has been a real improvement of salaries and wages of 54 per cent, in relation to the period 1959–64. This improvement has been especially favorable in the agricultural sector, which was ignored in earlier years.

Special mention should be made of the agricultural syndicates, which as a result of the law adopted in April, 1967, have increased by 76 per cent over those of 1967. The percentage of workers in trade unions has increased from 10.3 per cent in 1964 to 17.4 per cent in 1968. . . .

HOUSING

During 1968, the number of houses financed by the public sector or projected by the private sector reached 50,200 in the entire country. The number of new dwellings registered in the last ʿour years comes to 175,000, which can be compared to 131,420 ʿor the period 1961–64. During 1968, we also distributed 35,000 urbanized housing sites,* in addition to 1,600 provisional

---

* Under the self-construction program of the Chilean government, a foundation, electricity, and water are supplied in a lower-class housing area and the resident completes the construction himself.—ED.

dwellings with partial water supply, to solve the problems of the eradication of marginal slum clusters. In 1968, there were 86,000 resolutions of housing problems, which have benefited about 500,000 citizens. In the period of the present administration we have solved the housing problem of 312,000 families, representing about 1.8 million inhabitants, at the same time that the population increased by about 830,000 persons. . . .

Interpretation of Development

I invite everyone to look at his own home and see how during these [four] years he has acquired either a house, a car, a television set, radio, refrigerator, washing machine, sewing machine, stove, or new clothes for his family. I know that no one is satisfied. This is inevitable. If someone gets a radio he wants a television set. If he buys a house he would like to furnish it better. If he has a bicycle he would like to have an automobile, and when each acquisition is paid for there is an economic strain. This happens to all of us, each at his own level. But how can people forget the lines that used to exist to take a bus or buy milk, the mushrooming slums, the houses without electricity, potable water, or plumbing, the lack of beds in the hospitals, the children without schools? . . .

Social Progress

In 1968, I saw one of my greatest and most fundamental goals realized: to give the people a juridical structure that would permit them to incorporate themselves effectively into the active life of the country. This is what is meant by the promulgation last August of the law legally recognizing Neighborhood Committees and other community organizations. . . . Through the coordination of the policies of governmental and nongovernmental institutions for social development, the program of Popular Promotion [Promoción Popular] has carried out its efforts to obtain material benefits for communities through the installation of potable water, plumbing, electricity, telephones, and the promotion of shows of popular art, artisanry, and small industry. The Chamber of Deputies has recently approved a bill that gives legal form to the Popular Promotion Council, a bill that was sent to the Congress in 1966. Popular Promotion, which is aimed at incorporating the popular sectors into the active life of the country, has been one of the fundamental points in my governmental program. . . . During 1968, Popular Promotion established 2,213 new basic units in addition to 20,000 neighborhood committees, mothers centers, cultural centers, cultural, youth, and sport centers with more than 130,000 members. . . . The agricultural workers, who previously lacked representation (in 1964, there were only twenty-four agricultural syndicates, grouping 1,658 workers), have now formed a wide syndical structure. Today, there are more than 500 agricultural syndicates and 3,500 farm committees with 190,000 peasants as members. . . .

INFLATION

The country has witnessed the efforts of my government to reduce inflation, which has been a factor in the economic life of the nation for nearly a hundred years. Nevertheless, this is perhaps the only basic point in my program that has not been fulfilled. In the economic history of this century, there have been various factors that have promoted the inflationary process. In some cases, there were problems with foreign trade; in other cases, the government budget, or agricultural production, or mismanagement of monetary and fiscal affairs; and always there has been the growing aspiration of both employers and workers to increase their participation in the national income in a way that was incompatible with the real resources of the economy.

As president, I have promoted all forms of organization of the people in order to assure to workers and to all the people the instruments which they need to make their voice heard, and to avoid a situation in which the few most powerful and better-paid receive the majority of the benefits. This is because I am convinced that a people who are not organized are a people without voice, without force, and without vitality. However, in a democratic system, organization should be used for progressive and not for destructive purposes. If the organization of the people means that efforts to contain inflation and at the same time accelerate development will be frustrated, I would have to say that there is no hope for democracy. This cannot be the case with the people of Chile. Often the superstructures of the professional and trade-union organizations, which do not reflect the true feelings of the members, try to use them for purposes that are opposed to the permanent interests of Chile. . . .

In 1964, I proposed that income be redistributed in favor of those who receive salaries by increasing salaries each year by 100 per cent of the increase in the cost of living, plus an addition for productivity—a rate that had rarely been achieved in Chile. During the first two years of my government, this rate was considerably exceeded. This had a serious effect on inflation, leading to figures which were out of keeping with the possibilities of the national economy, despite all my efforts to avoid it. In spite of the bills that I sent each year to the Congress, and my other political actions, I was not able to obtain the necessary powers to achieve stability for the benefit of the workers. In these efforts I received practically no help from the political parties or from the professional and trade-union organizations. Despite the fact that it was evident that in succeeding years these factors would lead to price increases, thus raising both the cost of private activities and the governmental budget, these wage increases took place. The inflation rate which, thanks to the application of a series of other anti-inflationary measures, decreased in 1965 and 1966, began to increase in 1967. In 1968 and 1969, despite my renewed efforts, inflation showed its virulence with still greater force; the effects of the drought are also being felt.

In the fight against inflation, some countries have sacrificed values that are very close to the hearts and minds of Chileans. This has occurred in a number of Latin American countries that have suffered a strong inflation in recent years. Among them, Chile remains alone in its lack of success in the fight against inflation, but I will continue to seek the support of Chileans in this struggle. The challenge is to demonstrate that we can achieve our objectives with the consent of the majority. If this does not exist, if we cannot count on the political backing and the solidarity and support of Chileans, we shall be demonstrating that our emphasis on liberty is purposeless. We shall be destroying democracy in Chile. . . .

CHILEAN DEMOCRACY

To construct a democratic society is to respond to the longing of modern man for participation and to create structures whereby he can carry this out effectively and systematically. The rationality that is required for the solution of present-day problems can be achieved in mass societies either by means of coercion, by dictatorship and totalitarianism, or by the conscious and free participation of all the social, economic, and political sectors in the establishment of the common goals of the nation. Chile has chosen the latter path. . . .

The broadening of the electoral base to include youth in the political process, the recognition of the role of unions in the micro- and macro-economic decisions, the new organization of the people into Neighborhood Committees, the creation of mechanisms for participation at various levels of decision of the state, agrarian reform, social promotion, the necessary reform of the constitution to eliminate vices incompatible with the very survival of democracy, which today requires unity and leadership and efficiency in execution—all these are steps toward real popular participation to preserve our liberty and to promote economic and social progress.

There is no doubt that the impressive democratic solidarity of Chile is due fundamentally to the increasing cultural maturity of our people, above and outside the ideologies that try to enclose it in a rigid dogmatism that paralyzes everything and encourages nothing for the advance of a people. But there is also no doubt that this is due in a fundamental way to the presence in the government and in the political party that supports it—Christian Democracy—of a determination to make economic and social progress compatible with unrestricted liberty; to make the struggle for justice in every plane of social life compatible with respect for the dignity of all persons, without distinction, who form our community; and, above all, to continue to open up broad access through which the people themselves can participate actively, consciously, and responsibly in the construction of their own destiny—and to do this without hatred, even when we feel the biting criticism of those who hate us. . . . And I say to the militants of my party throughout Chile that your task and your struggle have been noble and have represented the great aspirations of our people—that the painful and inevitable crises you have experienced will be overcome, that you will emerge better able to direct and serve your country, and that when your sufferings are past you will be proud of the noble and great enterprise that cheers your hearts and for which you have suffered and struggled.